Finding Our Place

FINDING OUR PLACE

100 Memorable Adoptees, Fostered Persons, and Orphanage Alumni

Nikki McCaslin,
with Richard Uhrlaub and Marilyn Grotzky

GREENWOOD

AN IMPRINT OF ABC-CLIO, LLC
Santa Barbara, California • Denver, Colorado • Oxford, England

Library of Congress Cataloging-in-Publication Data
McCaslin, Nikki.
  Finding our place : 100 memorable adoptees, fostered persons, and orphanage alumni / Nikki McCaslin, with Richard Uhrlaub and Marilyn Grotzky.
     p. cm.
  Includes bibliographical references and index.
  ISBN 978-0-313-34270-7 (alk. paper) — ISBN 978-0-313-34271-4 (ebook)
  1. Adoptees—Biography. 2. Foster children—Biography. 3. Orphans—Biography. I. Uhrlaub, Richard. II. Grotzky, Marilyn. III. Title.
  HV874.8.M43 2010
  362.73092'2—dc22   2009048640

ISBN: 978-0-313-34270-7
EISBN: 978-0-313-34271-4

13 12 11 10 1 2 3 4 5

Greenwood Press
An Imprint of ABC-CLIO, LLC

This book is also available on the World Wide Web as an eBook.
Visit www.abc-clio.com for details.

ABC-CLIO, LLC
130 Cremona Drive, P.O. Box 1911
Santa Barbara, California 93116-1911

This book is printed on acid-free paper ∞
Manufactured in the United States of America

For my kind mothers, Jean, Marian, and Marinell,
and dear daughters, Raquel and Sabryna. Always and forever.

CONTENTS

LIST OF ENTRIES

LIST OF ENTRIES
BY CHILDHOOD EXPERIENCE

LIST OF ENTRIES BY OCCUPATIONAL FIELDS

FOREWORD

This one-of-a-kind book reveals the often extraordinary lives of souls who, in popular culture, are also called adoptees, foster children, and orphanage alumni.

In the *curanderismo* of my Latino heritage, such souls are also called, "the twice-born." To be *nacido dos veces*, twice-born, means to come to earth with a heart that can love and coexist with paradox and duality—the very traits of artists, peacemakers, inventors, and visionaries.

The twice-born are believed to carry two ways of seeing—in the mundane sense, and in the more visionary sense. The twice-born carry at least two heritages, sometimes more. They often have two families (or more), and two given names, one overt and one hidden.

For all these reasons and more, as much as some layers of society might try to "normalize" the lives of children who have been separated from their natal parents by often highly-charged circumstances—as you will see in the following pages—the twice-born, when young, wander about learning who they are, just as all other souls do but often what they find to be true about themselves and about the worlds and families they bridge, what mettle they are called to develop despite all obstacles—and what they flower into—is anything but ordinary.

Those whose stories are within these pages—and the literally millions of adoptees, orphans, and fostered persons who stand with them—carry dual histories and the subsequent vitalities, gifts, and awarenesses that come from living in and across multiple tributaries.

The twice-born have often, in some significant way, as they have grown from infancy to adulthood, managed to cross many great divides and to have continued on, still spiritually alive and able. Their individual stories, both before and after their early watershed severances and subsequent graftings, are not just prequels or addenda, nor are they postscripts.

That someone sought a child, took a lone child in . . . often with longing, great love, and altruistic intent, is a part of a considerable number of life stories here. Many adoptees, orphans, and fostered children carry far greater and *full* life stories, centering often on the mythic journeys, similar to those of the heroes and heroines found in ancient legends.

In the oldest sagas, the child twice born must focus on and resolve myriad issues that are sad, happy, difficult, triumphant, horrifying, rich, cherishable—some, and often, all of the above.

In the mythic stories of heroes and heroines in ancient cultures, in holy books, and in folktales, the wandering, abandoned, or orphaned child is early on presented with harsh realities, difficulties of settled identity, and other challenges, these eerily similar to the life paths of many modern individuals who are adopted, orphaned, and fostered.

Notably the lone hero and heroine in myth most often remains, despite all to the contrary, dedicated in heart and capacity to love, regardless.

Also in the old stories, thence and often, the lone child is lost from one or more parent, and a subsequent immense change of realities descends. Thus in the child a striving to find some scant security—and in some cases, a rescue—of some ordinary or magical means might be offered.

But also, there will ultimately be a tempest, and a heartbreak, which, in some significant way, over time, create in the hero and heroine . . . a heart broken *open*—that heart of the hero and heroine remaining *open* ever after.

Thus, the hero and heroine will most often awaken to who is good, and will be able to see who only pretends to be so. They will often dodge death, take on incomparable tasks, and go on to contribute much to their world—not despite their struggles and early history, but in many ways, *because of the learning to be found in their struggles, and also in honor of those who carried them, protected them, and gave them life, and of those who helped shelter their lives after.*

Who might know better what it means to create family than one who has lost his or her own family—and then perhaps gained one? Who might know better what it takes to protect the tiny flame of the life force and to keep going? Who knows better how to weave together disparate people and ideas in life than the inquiring and thoughtful soul who has come from many heritages and crossed many boundaries not usually bridged by most?

Who knows better what it is to love . . . than those who were loved deeply, as well as those who were loved hardly at all?

As human beings, we learn the value of good things by experiencing them, but also— sometimes by not being granted them—and by either of these twists of fate, we often come to understand how vital loving ways are when speaking with any child, any heart . . . seeing through the child's eyes, the heart's eyes . . . remaining on the lookout for the child's unique talents, their unique talents—and overall encouraging and nurturing a child's spirit in full wild insight and mercy . . . so that the child's soul remains fully alive, joyfully curious, and ever inventive . . . instead of secretly fearful, feigning disinterest in the broadness and depth of this miraculous life, and walking deadened through life, disinterested.

Oddly enough, many orphans, adoptees, and foster children, many times caught in a maelstrom at the beginning of their lives, are the very ones capable of nonetheless carrying within themselves treasure that grows over the decades: that is, calming influences that derive from learning to live peaceably and with love in two worlds, in, across, and around two odd, unusual, bizarre and often loveable families, two coursing heart lines . . . making sense of both and of all worlds in their own unique ways, even despite traumas, being torn, even with others' mal-intentions surrounding, even when matters of personality, motives, and eccentricities remain mysterious.

The twice-born often become expert in striving to bridge much even when or if other actors involved are closed, or do not try—or are afraid to, or insist on coveting too much, or are inexperienced at showing forms of expansive love. Nonetheless, a mature and thoughtful adoptee, fostered child, orphaned person—often continues to keep to his or her unique consciousness with calm, bright heart—and, by example, is sometimes able to inoculate others with the same.

Our greater world has more than enough machines and cars and pencils and wars. What is needed more than ever is what the twice-born have great potential to bring forward: peaceful relationship among disparate persons and cultures . . . created by those able to understand and bridge differences, those able to sense and aright imbalances and wrongs; those who set the bar not in self-interest and unnecessary protectionism, but out of love for whatever and whomever are loveable and have the capacity to learn to love as well.

It is not survival of the physically fittest nor of the most financially flush that ought to set the bar for our world, but rather survival of the truest hearts, the most insightful minds, the most bridging spirits.

In my clinical and personal experience, regardless of foibles and imperfections, the twice-born often demonstrate what is exactly most needed, for they often innately carry the seeds of special insights about the profound elasticity of true love.

The twice-born tend to love many and love overall . . . tending to add people in, especially people of peace . . . rather than subtracting people. At work, at home, and in community life, they often become masters of the "and/and" philosophy, rather than limiting themselves and others to a deadly narrow life of either/or.

Adoptees, orphans, fostered children, are often in their own ways visionary gamblers; they bet with fullest heart, demanding that winners, in some way, do not "take all," but rather make their best efforts to "see all, hold all, bridge all."

· · · · · · · ·

Below are laid out certain issues many adoptees, foster children, and orphanage alumni continue to be challenged by, and in their own ways, continue to come to terms with. These are, in the main, human rights issues, and it is our hope that progress will continue to be made.

EQUAL RIGHTS FOR ALL HUMAN BEINGS
INCLUDING ADOPTEES, ORPHANS, AND FOSTERED PERSONS

There remain ongoing issues regarding adoptees, foster children, and orphaned children, those who are still young, and those who are adults. As you can see in this work, the stories of those who carry gifts for humanity and family—also often face challenges similar to the twelve tasks of Hercules . . . requiring them to step up and slay monsters of various kinds, to protect the unprotected, and to also fight for and gather resources, mastery, power, survivorship, and self-sovereignty . . . not only over their own stories and lives, but also toward unconditional liberty to enjoy all rights legally accorded others.

Full accord is not yet a fait accompli. Equal rights for all include: freely inquiring and knowing, if one so chooses, in detail and depth, one's own original name, having full control and sight of all legal papers and facts pertaining to one's life and one's family milieu from conception onward, getting full information about emotional, spiritual, and cultural heritages—and issues—in one's natal family.

Further, to equally know one's own blood family members, as well as to freely inquire and know one's own familial medical and legal information from back then, as well as in the present, and to have access to updates of this critical information for life.

So, ongoing, and from all sides of adoption, fostering, and lone child status, adults of conscience and of consciousness move powerfully to speak for reversing what has, for more than two hundred years, been too often a reckless and unconscionable erasure of vulnerable families' true stories, and how these affect the lone child's best interests—not only as children, but as adolescents, and when they are grown to adulthood, when they enter middle age, and when they proceed into elderhood.

In our time, there can no longer be depersonalized stances taken about adoptees, orphans, and foster children by those who want to decide which souls are worthy of full rights, and which are not. Today, as ever, this 'minority' of the twice-born still must press to be given all rights accorded others, including the right to knowledge of all kinds, and life-giving family contact if desired, and reunification without government interference, without "we know better Big Brotherism."

As in most heroic myths, while the heroes and heroines are striving for goodness and blessing, there are also some present who attempt to redefine and squelch free expression and humane treatment . . . in order to preserve a personal or hidden self-interest. So too, in our day and age, there is much work yet to be done legislatively and publicly . . . to gently educate whenever possible, to powerfully counteract whenever necessary, those who have no clear oversight and who thereby prevaricate and position themselves to deny the twice-born equal rights.

Yet, we can be heartened, for each day more and more persons who carry strong considerations for social justice and for the greater purpose of equal rights for souls in these matters worldwide, outnumber those who want to rule by personal greed, or by other self interests only. The old human rights–denying ideology which was used to subvert and to socially engineer families . . . no longer goes unopposed.

Today there are literally legions of educated hearts and educated legal minds with full sight on the issues. They are stalwart about standing up to, and speaking out for, and they will continue . . . until all souls, regardless of circumstances of birth, life journey, and parentage, are granted equal access, equal knowledge, equal freedom of information, equal freedom to communicate, and all other equal rights under the law.

HEALTH: INFORMATION CRITICAL TO LIFE, LIBERTY, AND PURSUIT OF HAPPINESS OF ADOPTEES, FOSTERED CHILDREN, PERSONS RAISED IN ORPHANAGES

If it can be said that all lives follow a heroic storyline, then each person on earth will have at least one, if not many, deep losses and demands from the soul that must be met, righted, overturned, or mastered during one's lifetime.

One matter of heroic proportions still at issue today for the once "lone children"— as in times past, is that literally millions of living adoptees, foster children, persons raised in orphanages, when and if they have managed to wrangle information about their natal families and lives, continue to have that critical information held away from them in legal records sealed "to protect the adopted, orphaned, foster child," no matter that they are now thirty, forty, fifty, sixty, seventy, eighty years old.

And too often, those most concerned with the twice-born's quality of actual physical life—the once lone-child, his or her adoptive parents, foster parents, or caregivers—have been given falsified, grotesquely redacted, woefully incomplete information about the child's holy origins, and most especially, about the child's inherited medical background, including pleasant or unpleasant facts that will be critical to watch over for strong psychological life and bodily health in the twice-born.

Health, a chance to have it . . . and keep it, strengthen it . . . cannot be well accomplished when heritage records carry bald-faced lies and deathly omissions, or are recklessly kept and then destroyed as though they were grocery receipts instead of life stories of heroes and heroines. Strong health in the once "lone child" is lessened when medical facts go unasked for, when the facts known are purposely suppressed, altered, or changed to make circumstances look either better, or worse, in order to please one party or another.

In agencies of many kinds, there remains the issue of more than superficial faithfulness to the concept of "in the best interests of the child," fully. Not just parts and pieces of the child. The full child, which includes critical facts about health issues, medical heritage, blood relatives, actual circumstances of birth, siblings, and extended family.

We know certain disorders occur with "adolescent onset" for instance. Some have middle age onset, and some can be counted on, almost like clockwork, to appear in old age. Yet many disorders progress with nary an outer clue beforehand, other than those disorders being hereditary. With even a bit more information, many "sudden" genetic disorders could have been side-tracked, mediated, or eliminated altogether . . . had the child and family been able to anticipate the potentiality of onset of ill health.

Many agencies, then, and today, collected no data in depth, nor made any effort to keep current what shreds of data they had. Physicians who oversaw the health of children in times past, and many today, were not trained to see such gaps in genetic knowledge as a health crisis meriting close watchfulness over decades, rather than just waiting for a serious genetic disease or disorder to suddenly develop full force . . . in either case weakening and devastating the innocent.

In this way, without adequate information, without being able to give a full generational medical history to doctors and hospitals throughout all of one's lifetime, the adopted, fostered, orphaned child or adult is disempowered, unable to anticipate and take initiatives to strengthen and preserve health and life. This egregious blocking of an individual's access to seek information fully grossly interferes with caring for and "seeing ahead" for the precious health and lives of oneself, and, as importantly, of one's own children, and the dearest health and lives of one's own grandchildren and great-grandchildren.

The *Declaration of Independence* states, "life, liberty, and the pursuit of happiness," but the part of the sentence that is sometimes forgotten says there preexists in our world a so essential set of human rights that they are *self evident* to us all.

Being at deepest knowledge and best peace regarding the extended natal family's health history, knowing clearly what to look out for that may impinge or harm self and future generations of one's bloodlines . . . is a strong tenet of calm, vigor, and happiness.

I'd just gently add that I am a witness to this, from agencies passing no medical information about my natal families or my early hospitalizations as infant and toddler. The serious genetic health issues handed down in my own mestizo, bicultural, and biracial natal family turned out to be profound. That my foundling caretakers, foster parents, and adopted family were uninformed—meant being roundhoused by severe hereditary bodily illness, and being misdiagnosed over and over as other serious genetic health issues took deep hold in adolescence and adulthood—life-threateningly so. Hereditary illnesses also adversely affected my children and grandchildren. We had no way to anticipate with early mediation.

Too often, those in a rush "to place" a child, to fulfill needs, also forget the subsequent financial devastations caused to grown adult or family from not being able to anticipate such severe health issues, thereby diagnosing and mediating them late. This matter is not rare among adoptees, orphans, and foster children. Inadequate health information is sadly common to many former "lone children."

Yet now, together, many agencies, world health organizations, and individuals, are rising to work toward the humane insistence that all orphaned children, foster children, and adoptees must be given timely, ongoing medical information about their kith and kin—from the time of birth—and for as long as they live. That there must be open and unencumbered means to pursue such knowledge by the former lone child. That there not be allowed any ideology or law made, or be allowed to stand, that bars anyone from pursuing or knowing fully what there is to know about his or her own health predictors from all bloodlines.

Though none of us can know the future health picture of our lives, and even though some have not been taught or have not yet learned to take good care of their one precious, wild body . . . it is merciful to give a fighting chance to adoptees, orphaned children, and foster children to be as healthy as they can be, to not cripple them or their precious offspring, by commission or omission . . . to grant full knowledge to them about the strengths and fragilities in their health heritages.

More conscious minds and hearts are beginning to insist that just like any other constitutional right guaranteed to all other individuals, a person who has been adopted, orphaned or raised as a foster child, must be treated with full parity . . . which in essence means being treated with full humanity, with mercy for the sanctity of all life, our lives included, not just the lives of the majority.

CHILDREN AND FAMILIES WHO ARE CURRENTLY UNPROTECTED

Wherever in the world there is no one to act with vigilance 24/7 with regard to unprotected children, there is profound danger of children being exploited, carried off through various illicit means. Children stolen, forced away from their kin, uprooted, and transported elsewhere without clear and truthful consent . . . also occurs whenever oversight is only "pretended" or without carefully preserving and telling the family's and child's . . . story truthfully and in full.

The perils to severing children from their natal families increases greatly during a killing war; wherever thugs force military conscription of children; when a child appears to have lost a parent through death or disease; during a famine in which rogue governments and close-in "helpers" purposely withhold resources in order to open an "adoption trade" to richer nations. Any child is vulnerable to being severed from family during natural disasters, after which predators swoop down to force unprotected orphans and 'refugee children' separated from their parents . . . into sex and workhouse slavery, and into "adoption rings" for money—with "adoption fees" amounting to $10,000 and far more per child.

Wherever there is rampant disease, naïveté of "the system" on the part of the child and parents; wherever there is law that depersonalizes children and their families; wherever there is heartbreaking poverty; wherever there is arrogance by those posturing rather than truly helping by getting down in the dirt with the people and unifying rather than breaking families; wherever there are opportunities to make money by covert theft of children; whenever there are present human predators of any kind—even those with clean clothes and smiling faces . . . anywhere there is lack of regard for the real souls of real children . . . and their families and their culture . . . it becomes as easy as passing a hot knife through butter to carry the children off, to cut them from their familial roots, to in some sense "disappear" their true history, their heritage, and all the broken hearts left behind.

There is also, worldwide, the ongoing issue of forcing good and decent fathers and mothers to surrender their children by starving the parents of knowledge about where to gain the essential resources to keep their families intact. Wherever in the world there are impoverished parents, especially unprotected mothers and children—there are also people who say they are "helpers."

But they are not: They are harvesters. They solicit the poor . . . but then give only cursory props, and/or withhold needed ongoing food, shelter, and education from those who come for help. The poor and naïve parents are offered no options for their child's survival other than surrendering their child.

To what ends will parents go in order to save their children, and not themselves, when deprived of resources? I suggest we know the answer from loving mothers and fathers in World War II. As they were pushed into cattle cars bound for the death camps, they dangled their little children out through the window bars to anyone on any train platform who would take them. They were saying the parents final prayer: "My heart will die and I die with it, but my child must live."

Too, we see in our own time that efforts are made to frighten and disempower parents until they will say they know they are "not as good as," and "cannot provide as much as" someone else. Afterward, the person or agency claims the child was "abandoned," "left by his or her mother," and that this surrender was "all agreed to by the entire family."

And now it is said, the child can be adopted by persons from domestic and foreign nations. The corrupting of the parent(s) by others more educated or wily, forcing any parent to imagine his or her child having a television or a bedroom as being more important than root maternal and paternal love is a breathtaking denouement and breaking of the parent.

Across the world, still, the true stories of the children and their parents are erased then, and it is not unusual that an adoptee later senses issues lodged within his or her own unconscious—regarding odd longings, concerns with severance, grafting, truth-telling, and other matters revolving around his or her own natural emotive life, . . . and/or else the person may carry "a dead zone" about his or her own suppressed story-line that was covered over with falsehoods from others.

Are there harmful parents in this world? Children who ought to be rescued? Indeed there are. And blessed are those who help, shelter tenderly, and love widely and deeply. But exploiters cannot be allowed.

In this century, UNICEF has decreed worldwide that it is a violation of human rights to willfully or illegally separate children from their families of origin in order to create a money-making business of warehousing or adopting children into other families under false pretenses.

Thus, many of us hope it will remain in this awakening world, that the harvesting of children, purchasing them from the abjectly poor, demeaning the impoverished, the young, and the uneducated until they surrender their children, stealing children off the street or from the marketplace, or in any way disempowering or shaming the vulnerable and loving natal parents whilst depriving them of needed resources to remain together as family, has been, is now, and shall ever be wrong.

And what shall ever be right? What shall ever be right in this world are all those concerned with the true welfare of children and families of many kinds, families of all and every kind that carry loving intent . . . for every real and down to earth family has its travails, its exasperations, its struggles. Yet there exists inextinguishably in those who love, a purity that shines like a fire in darkness, despite all else to the contrary.

May those who carry such fire within these pages ever shine. May those who stand outside these pages and who carry such fire of love in and for the world anywhere, any place, and for any soul . . . be blessed and protected over and over again.

ABOUT THE AUTHOR, AND THE LIFE JOURNEYS OF ADOPTEES,
ORPHANAGE ALUMNI, AND FOSTERED PERSONS IN THIS WORK

· · · · · · · ·

The author of this book, Nikki McCaslin, is a woman of great and tender sensitivity. When I first met her, I learned she was an adoptee. Divorced, she had a busy academic and personal life. She spoke to me of her great longing to adopt children. Just as she was seeking her future children, they were also wending their ways toward her arms. She has two lovely daughters who are also blood sisters. In addition to all the usual ups and downs of raising children, and some of the special areas critical to children and parents who adopt each other later in life, you can see that the children have completed her very great heart, and she, theirs.

I'd given keynotes and talks at many conventions and meetings of adoptive parents and adoptees. During one conference Nikki attended, she noted how inspired and hopeful a young Latina girl, Stephanie, became after reading about my life as an adoptee. My story was carried in a book called, *¡Latinas!*, a compilation of the two-steps-forward, one-step-back, boisterous, difficult, and often fulfilling achievements of many Latina women. Nikki says she received the idea to compile this book from seeing the epiphany that came to this shy, young girl by reading about someone who was "like herself."

Nikki McCaslin is one of the first, if not the first, adopted person to create an adoptee/ fostered/ alumni biographical compendium, highlighting famous persons such as Marilyn Monroe and Dr. Betty Shabazz, and lesser-known but as accomplished persons as well. This book offers the profiles of 100 adopted, fostered, and orphaned persons who overcame hardships, challenges, and exiles posed in their childhoods, . . . but who went on to make positive contributions nonetheless.

I sense that, if you are reading this book, perhaps you too are rooting for those who had so little at the beginning to "make it" in some way that matters to them, and often, to others as well. Me too. Those herein who have disabilities that directly played a significant part in their successes, their unfoldings of meaning in life, touched my heart deeply.

Examples are medal olympians Scott Hamilton and Dan O'Brien, and circus star Gunther Gebel-Williams. Hamilton took up skating as therapy for a type of paralysis. Immersion in sports helped O'Brien focus intensely and take charge of his ADHD. Gebel-Williams said that after his parents abandoned him at the circus, he had a hard time trusting human beings, but grew to love and bond with the animals there.

Nikki and I both find it true from our listening to other adoptees, and to those who were once foster children, and to those raised by other than their natal parents in orphanages and by extended family . . . that many say their early challenges have made them more insightful parents, more tolerant, open, and compassionate toward others.

In my clinical work, too, I see that, as in ancient mythos, people who have experienced a great travail when young are very similar to an old psychological metaphor that still holds true: from bloodshed the winged horse Pegasus was born.

For many authors and artists too, their often unusual childhood situations are sometimes profoundly connected to their mature art, to both its contents and processes. One can understand more about their works when these early events and influences are understood.

Nikki is a careful and inquiring craftswoman and scholar. She has discovered poignant commentary from the individuals herein and has quoted them in the main entry sections. She looked for the heart of their situations; how they learned they were adopted, and/or separated from their family of origin; how they were taken up into shelter, and sometimes with their adopted family, how they envisioned their relationships with natal and adoptive family members, what lessons were learned, whether they sought their natal families, and from their own points of view, how did all these matters reflect on their work and successes in life. You will see that each is to his or her own. There is no rote outcome.

She tells me that Betty Jean Lifton once said that adopted people should be called *the Adoptu*, as a form of tribal reference, a kind of cognate, for instance, like "the Bantu." This makes me smile, for there is often an instant tribal-like bond between those who have had unusual familial experiences early in life. We often sense we immediately "know" each other, and often with great affinity.

A case can be made that our common experiences are what makes adoptees, the orphaned, the fostered, the lone children . . . a unique community, a full culture of our own. It is true there are many heartfelt, beautiful, challenging, and successful adoptions, fosterings, and caregivings of children. And sometimes the twice-born find their deepest affiliations belonging to one family or the other. Sometimes they belong to both. And, sometimes too, people do not fit into either or any childhood family, natal or adopted.

Thus, I sometimes tell a little literary story I made up to tell to some of my patients, whether they are adopted or not—for the issue of *belonging*, as you already know, is a universal and *normal* question and reason for questing at various times in life. I call my little story "The Mistaken Zygote Theory." (A zygote is a fertilized human ovum.)

So, for those who have not found the family they longed for, I say:

> Well, see, maybe it was this way with you. One night, the zygote fairy was flying through the sky with a basket full of little zygotes. She was looking for women who had just made love. And, oh how lively and excited the zygotes were to think of being born on earth. But then you, a particularly feisty zygote, were jumping up and down in excitement so hard, that you accidentally fell over the side of the basket and were transplanted into the womb of a woman who was . . . well, let's just say you were meant for a different mother a few miles further down the road. Now, you know that person or that couple down the road whom you always loved and wished were your parents? Well, they may have really been meant to be . . .

This small parcel of lightheartedness is offered to say something of gravity: that we, whether blood born or not, all find, re-find, affirm, and reaffirm our "real" families as we grow and develop, not just to adulthood—but as we become *seres humanos*, true human beings.

And regardless of one's bonding by blood, by law, by whatever means if there has been love, it does not matter in any direction where anything or anyone began or where it all ends up. Wherever there is true and steady love, there is family.

This reality—where there is true and steady love, there is family—is especially poignant among those who have had solid dual-family experiences of calm instead of contempt or furors. But this reality is also found among those who have been rejected by a natal parent, or rejected within their adoptive families, or by their "placements," or during a difficult search and reunion process. Because, regardless of woundings and wonders, these good souls often seek, meet, and find deep companionship, laughter, authentic sense of kith and kin with others who hold the premise of love and more love. They make family of fellow travelers, those they find on the road of life anywhere, any time.

Interestingly, the "mistaken zygote" often bonds with persons from the adopted/fostered, and orphanage alumni community. In fact, many who find kindred spirits thusly, often find profound similarities in personality and, oddly, sometimes even physical resemblances. These deep affinities among souls of similar caring and/or similar early circumstances can hardly be rationally explained, except that the twice-born often recognize one another.

We also know that many souls reach out to become mother, father, brother, sister, child to one another, in turns, regardless of origin. The relationships thusly formed take on the genius of family, that is, genuine feeling and loyalties that often last a lifetime. Many who have found each other in this way remark that they seem to have somehow always felt "born to each other."

In these ways and many more, we continue to find that, for the twice-born, there are many ways of belonging, many ways of being family, many ways of contributing—and that these are not bound by bloodlines, but by soul-lines, through and through.

In this spirit, may the life stories in this book assure, inspire, encourage, and validate all souls, especially those who have traveled so far, carrying and protecting the flame of their one precious candle . . . so as to thrive in this world, but also to help light the way for others yet to come.

Clarissa Pinkola Estés, Ph.D., Psychoanalyst
Rocky Mountains

PREFACE

This work is a compilation of biographies about persons who were adopted, fostered, or who lived in orphanages as children. I sought, for the main entries, examples who distinguished themselves in a positive way. The scope is international and is not limited by time period.

The main entries contain the subject's major achievements, a brief vita, and then focus on the person's childhood experiences. I especially selected individuals who talked or wrote about their childhood experiences and tried to include some of their commentary. I was able to conduct personal interviews for some of the entries and used autobiographies and published letters or interviews for others. I was especially interested in whether and how people perceived that their backgrounds affected their careers and successes. Personal details were gathered from publicly available resources or were given during the interviews. Additional individuals who met the criteria are listed in Appendix A. Below are the specific criteria for inclusion in the main entry section of this work.

Adopted Persons or Adoptees: I selected persons who were relinquished, abandoned, or orphaned by both biological parents before the age of eighteen and who have had their family status changed by some legal form of adoption. The last name of the child was usually changed to the adoptive parent's name and the child regarded the adopter(s) as his parent(s) and vice versa. I chose **Erik Erikson** as a single representation of step-parent adoptions, where a child is retained by a biological parent and adopted by a step-parent. I selected Erikson because his adoption was such a major theme in his life and work, and he also was given fictitious birth information. I have listed additional well-known persons adopted by a step-parent in Appendix B. I have not included adopted children of famous parents unless they have distinguished themselves in their own right.

Fostered persons: These are children who were raised by caregivers other than their parents for a significant amount of time before the age of eighteen but who were not legally adopted. These include children with formal legal guardians and also those who were simply sent away to be raised by persons other than their parents. I am including children who were "put out to nurse," as it was called, even with financial provisions from a parent, as this was at one time the routine way of dealing with illegitimate or inconvenient children.

I am including with fostered persons a few individuals who were raised by relatives other than a parent. Children in kinship care can sometimes be affected in precisely the same ways as those who were adopted or fostered. I have included only a few such individuals, such as **John Lennon** and **Maya Angelou**, either because they were very articulate about their childhood experiences and how they affected them, or because they were representative of a particular time in adoption history. A list of additional persons raised by members of their extended family is found in Appendix B.

Orphanage Alumni: Persons who lived in an orphanage for any length of time as a child are included. Orphanages had various names and at times were part of more general institutions for the poor. I include workhouses and almshouses, hospices (the earlier definition was not associated with the terminally ill), and foundling hospitals as "orphanages." Included are children who were permanent residents, those who were adopted from an orphanage, and those who later returned to their families of origin. I did not include children sent away by their families to live at boarding schools, or children who were institutionalized for disabilities or behavior problems, unless they also met the main criteria.

Orphans: I designate as "orphans" persons who were under the age of eighteen when both biological parents died. They will be included in the main entry sections, even if they were adopted or raised by extended family members.

Illegitimacy: Illegitimacy is very closely associated with my topic and has always been the main cause for the relinquishment and abandonment of children. The majority of my population was born to parents who were not married to each other at the time. Persons so born were often profoundly stigmatized, and I will therefore mention it in main entries when appropriate. The stigma lifted for the most part in the United States because of the "sexual revolution" and the influences of the feminist and civil rights movements of the second half of the twentieth century. Today, over one third of American babies are born every year to unmarried parents and illegitimacy will not be considered a relevant factor in persons born after 1960.

I am including two examples of individuals who were raised by their biological fathers, **John James Audubon** and **Leon Battista Alberti**. I selected Audubon because of a racial element: specifically, Jean Jacques Audubon, Audubon's father, had five children out of wedlock with Mulatto and Creole women. He raised and legally adopted only his two light-skinned children, while abandoning his three darker daughters. I selected Alberti because his uncles used the boy's illegitimacy as grounds to steal his inheritance. A further list of notable persons who were born out of wedlock before 1960 but who were kept and raised by one or both first parents is given in Appendix B.

Foundling: I designate as a "foundling" a child who was exposed (the practice of leaving an infant to die in an uninhabited area) or illegally abandoned.

Fictitious Birth Information: This heading is for persons who were not told the truth about their family relationships or were forced to lie about them. This designation also includes "Late Discovery Adoptees," who are persons who were adults when they learned they were adopted.

Socially Isolated Children: This is the designation for a "feral" or "wild child." These are children who grow up with little or no social contact.

Indentured or Sold: I am including persons who were indentured, as that was an important historic form of foster care. Indenture differs from apprenticeship in that the family is paid for the child's labor and the child is bound by contract to work a given length of time, while apprenticeship has more of an educational aim for the child. I also included one example of a notable person who was sold as a child, **Sacagawea**.

ACKNOWLEDGMENTS

Many thanks for the support and assistance of editors Kaitlin Ciarmiello, Anne Thompson, Henry Rasof, and project manager Lisa Connery. I am very grateful for your skillful help and patience with a first-time writer.

I would also like to thank contributing authors Richard Uhrlaub and Marilyn Grotzky. Rich provided entries for Tim Green, Florence Fisher, Alexander Hamilton, Boris Karloff, Marilyn Monroe, Michael Reagan, and Orson Welles. In addition to providing unflagging encouragement and technical assistance, Marilyn wrote entries for Charlotte Ayanna, Sarah Bernhardt, Charlie Chaplin, Alexandra Danilova, Toby Dawson, Alexandre Dumas *fils*, Erik Erikson, Lawrence Ferlinghetti, Sheilah Graham, Faith Hill, Steven Jobs, Queen Liliʻuokalani, Nelson Mandela, Ana Mendieta, James Michener, Annie Oakley, Victoria Rowell, Buffy Sainte-Marie, Betty Shabazz, and Barbara Stanwyck.

I am most grateful to those persons who allowed me personal interviews and wish to thank them for their candor and generosity: Clarissa Pinkola Estés, who inspired this book, Stan Brakhage and his widow, Marilyn Brakhage, Fran Coleman, Carol Flax, Ron Grosswiler, Betty Jean Lifton, Jim Lucero, Damsel Plum, Sarah Saffian, Joe Soll, William Troxler, and Pekitta Tynes.

INTRODUCTION

The Greek word *orphanos* (ορφανός) means "deprived of parents," and its derivative *orphan* most often refers to a child or young person whose parents have both died. Wars, natural disasters, famine, and sickness have created vast waves of orphans throughout history. In addition, children have been separated from their original parents because of illegitimacy, poverty, cultural practice, or gender. Some have run away themselves, and others have been stolen. It is a human problem undiminished by time: in our world today, a child becomes an orphan every fourteen seconds according to a recent CNN report (Jolie 20).

The circumstances and solutions for what one author suggests we call "unaccompanied children" (Panter-Brick 2) are diverse, and the terminology related to such children is emotionally charged, controversial, and in the process of needed reform (see "Correct Adoption Terminology" Askeland 139). Even the idea of what constitutes "a child" is frequently challenged by scholars, who uncover considerable differences historically and among cultures. An early Anglo-Saxon, for example, was considered an adult at age ten, while the age of majority was twenty-five for a male in Byzantium and Rome. For the purposes of this book, I have used definitions from the United Nations' "Convention on the Rights of the Child" (November 20, 1989), which says that "a child means every human being below the age of eighteen years" (Article 1) and a child, "by reason of his physical and mental immaturity, needs special safeguards and care" (Preamble).

The personal and private nature inherent in adoption and child services has made scholarship on these topics difficult. John Boswell, in his excellent history of child abandonment, spoke of the "struggle to uncover evidence deliberately obscured by those with something to hide" (21). We do know, however, at least a few of the practices and laws that had an important impact on adopted and fostered children through the ages.

Adoption and Fosterage in the Ancient World

Mesopotamia, Babylon, and Sumer

One of the earliest adoption contracts still in existence is from Mesopotamia and is dated from between 3000 to 2350 BCE. The contract states:

> Yahatti-Il is the son of Hillalum and of Alittum. He shall share their good times and their bad times. If Hillalum his father and Alittum his mother say to Yahatti-Il their son 'You are not our son,' they shall forfeit house and property. If Yahatti-Il says to Hillalum his father

and Alittum his mother 'You are not my father. You are not my mother,' they shall shave him and sell him for silver. Even if Hillalum and Alittum have many sons, Yahatti-Il is the heir, and shall receive two shares from the estate of Hillalum his father; his younger brothers shall take shares brother like brother (Postgate Text 5:2).

The famous code of Hammurabi, the ancient Babylonian king who reigned from around 1795 to 1750 BCE, contains nine laws on adopted children (§§ 185–193), and some of its provisions and penalties are of current interest. A childless wife could offer her husband her maidservant or a concubine as a surrogate, and the wife would be considered the legal mother of any offspring from the union. A couple could also adopt a child in order to obtain an heir or for labor. An artisan's adopted child who was not taught a craft could legally return to the house of his biological father. If the adoptive father did not satisfactorily compensate the biological family for the loss of their child, the family of origin could reclaim the child. A courtesan's child, or any other child "against whom no one could lay claim" was said to have been "taken from the waters upon which it had been cast adrift" (Cook 134), and if "one of these [adopted children] should say to the father or mother that brought him up, 'thou art not my father, thou art not my mother,' the tongue, the offending member, is cut out, and if he has found out his father's house and has hated. . . . the parents who have adopted him, and goes to his father's house, his eye is torn out" (§§ 192–93). Finally, the code specifies that an adopted son may inherit one-third of a son's share of the household goods, but only blood offspring can inherit the parents' estate (fields, house, and gardens).

One of the earliest known personal accounts by an adoptee is that of **Sargon I,** who lived around 2334 to 2279 BCE in ancient Sumer and became a great king. He was the illegitimate child of a priestess and an unknown father. Like the later Moses (thought to have been born during the reign of Seti I, around 1291–1278), and Rome's mythic twin founders, Romulus and Remus, Sargon was a baby in a basket who was pulled from the river by his adopter. One scholar, whose theories are discussed further in Sargon's entry, believes that these legends could possibly reflect an early adoption ritual (Lewis 55).

Greece

In ancient Athens, a legitimate child who became fatherless or orphaned would be raised by an adult brother or paternal grandfather. If neither of these were available, one or more guardians could be appointed by another family member or by a royal official called an *archon,* whose job included overseeing the estates and dowries of orphans. Although they often were, guardians did not have to be family members, as was the case with **Aristotle,** whose guardian married his sister. Athenian fathers were expected to formally acknowledge their legitimate offspring at naming ceremonies (*dekatē*) held ten days after birth; otherwise the children were considered bastards and deprived of citizenship (MacDowell 91). Illegitimate children, even those living in the same household with their parents, had outsider status. Athenians practiced adoption primarily as a means to provide themselves with heirs, and they adopted adults and children of both genders. In sixth-century Athens, a man could adopt an heir after death through his will, although any legitimate child of his could not become disinherited by the adoption.

Rome

Roman law had two forms of adoption, *adoptio* and *adrogatio.* In *adoptio,* a child was sold to an adopter by the male head of family, the *paterfamilias.* To become legally released from his biological family, a male child had to be sold three times to the adopter and each time freed under the rule of the Twelve Tables. After the third sale, the boy was legally free for adoption. A female child had to be sold once before adoption. Roman law also allowed illegitimate children to become legitimized if their parents subsequently married.

Adrogatio was the adoption of a chosen adult for the purposes of inheritance. In this form, the adopter had to be over sixty years of age, unless special provisions were made, and the *adrogatio* ceremony was performed during legislation. *Adrogatio* changed the family and social status of the adoptee. Cicero and the emperor Augustus were both adopted in this manner.

By the time of Diocletian's reign (AD 284–305), laws were in place which forbade parents from selling their freeborn children to pay for debts, although the practice did continue (Boswell 68). But under Constantine, the first Christian emperor, Rome's legal protections for freeborn children were reversed and all children could be sold. Sold children could legally be prostituted or put to any labor at any age (Boswell 75), as the following law created by Constantine in AD 331 states:

> Anyone who picks up and nourishes at his own expense a little boy or girl cast out of the home of its father or lord with the latter's knowledge and consent may retain the child in the position for which he intended it when he took it in—that is, as child or slave, as he prefers. Nor may those who willingly and knowingly cast out of their home newborn slaves or children bring any action to recover them (Boswell 71).

Anonymous Child Abandonment, Foundling Hospitals, and Baby Farms

It is thought to have been a fairly common practice to abandon infants in the ancient world as an alternative to outright infanticide, which was also a common practice. Boswell estimates that twenty to forty percent of urban newborns were abandoned in early Rome (135). Babies were often left in public areas for people to find, especially at temples and on their grounds. One historian describes third-millennium BCE temple records that document the purchase of children:

> More poignant are a few sale documents in which the high-priest of the temple buys children, significantly for no specified price: this seems to be a case of the temple taking on extra mouths to feed when their families were unable to support them, and reflects a long-standing tradition whereby the temples gathered under their wing the rejects and misfits of society—orphans, illegitimate children, and perhaps the freaks hinted at above (Zettler 126–27).

Some infants were abandoned with marks or tokens, so that they later might be identified. **Jean d'Alembert** (1717–1783), for example, was a proverbial foundling, left one winter's night in a wooden box on a church step, and yet his birthparents were later able to identify and contact him. Other foundlings, such as **Kaspar Hauser** (circa 1812–1829) and **Pekitta Tynes** (circa 1962–), have backgrounds that are complete mysteries.

In 1198, Pope Innocent III established the first European foundling hospital in Florence, Italy, called the *Ospedale degli Innocenti*. Foundling hospitals were established to provide a safe place where a baby could be left in secret, sometimes in a receiving bassinet or in a "baby hatch."

The foundling system spread throughout Southern Europe, from Italy to Spain, Portugal and France, by the seventeenth century. In countries with large Protestant populations, especially England, Germany, and the United States, services for illegitimate children were very controversial, as further discussed in the next section, and these countries did not establish foundling hospitals until the late eighteenth century or the nineteenth century.

Prior to the invention of baby bottles and infant formula in the 1850s and 60s, foundling hospitals unsuccessfully experimented with other ways to feed their charges (Kertzer 43) and most commonly sent the infants to wet nurses. Wet nurses for foundlings were usually society's poorest married or widowed women, whose own babies had recently died. Undernourished, ill, and breast-feeding numerous infants in often squalid conditions, these women were nicknamed "angel-makers" (Panter-Brick 15).

In England, foundlings were placed in what were then called "baby farms." As discussed in the "Report to the Select Committee on the Protection of Infant Life," partially cited below, the mortality rate for baby farms was extremely high—60 to 93 percent, as compared to a 35 percent rate among the urban working class rate and an 11 percent infant mortality among the "well-to-do" (Rose 7).

In Victorian England, unwed mothers were practically forced to give up their babies, who were then sent to baby-farming houses where they were fed "a mixture of laudanum, lime, corn flour, water, milk, and washing powder. . . with rare exceptions they all of them die in a very short time" (Adamec xvii).

Governments and other authorities envisioned plans to use foundlings in a variety of ways. A drawing by artist William Hogarth, called *The Foundlings,* portrays children at the London Foundling Hospital holding tools that signify the occupations they were expected to enter—the boys to be farmers, soldiers, and sailors, and the girls to be domestic servants and weavers.

The London Foundling Hospital was established in 1739 by a retired ship captain, Thomas Coram, and became England's first children's charity and its first public art gallery. It is still associated with several of its famous benefactors, especially Hogarth, who inspired other artists, such as Rysbrack, Gainsborough, and Reynolds, to contribute works to the collection. The composer George Frideric Handel, who became one of the governors of the London Foundling, donated a pipe organ. His numerous other gifts to the charity included the original score of the *Messiah,* which he performed there every year until his death in 1759. He also gave other concerts in support of the orphanage.

Sometimes talented foundlings and orphans were gathered into children's choirs and bands or were boarded and trained through special provisions in music conservatories. Others were relocated to populate colonies overseas or agricultural areas, or they were designated for special military and citizen corps:

> These projects had one thing in common: they viewed foundlings as a stock of children at society's disposal. The state could redistribute the mass of children without families according to its needs. The justification for this was that foundlings were, of course, a charge on public finances, and it was felt that the state, having spent money on their upbringing, was entitled to exercise authority over them. In this way, preoccupations with the future of foundlings were bound up with the need to render a previous investment profitable. . . In reality, however, the lives of foundlings were quite different from the projects conceived on their behalf by politicians and theorists. The small proportion of foundlings surviving to adolescence and adulthood sufficed in itself to defeat such schemes (Panter-Brick 29).

Anonymous abandonment is still in existence today, although it is a fairly uncommon practice in the United States. Forty eight states and many countries have passed "safe haven" laws that permit the anonymous abandonment of infants at hospitals and fire and police stations.

Illegitimacy and the Workhouse

A very large percentage of all foundlings, adoptees, and fostered children were born to unmarried parents and have been affected by the attached stigma. The word "bastard" is still, to this day, one of the English language's harshest invectives. Jenny Teichman explains in her study that the stigma dates back probably as far as the concept of marriage:

> The word "bastard" is a term of abuse, almost a swear word. The word is used insultingly and metaphorically much more often than it is used literally. This can only be explained by reference to beliefs once widely held about illegitimate people. Such beliefs are presumably as old as the institution of marriage itself. Be that as it may, hostile feelings about bastards and the belief that they are generally very bad people find expression in very ancient archetypes (Teichman 126).

Although nearly every culture and age had sanctions and prejudices against illegitimate children and their parents, the Bible is probably one of the strongest influences on the development of the Western European stigma. Biblical references to bastards clearly differentiated them from orphans. Orphans enjoyed the special protection of God: "You shall not afflict any widow or orphan. If you do afflict them, and they cry out to me, I will surely hear their cry; and my wrath will burn, and I will kill you with the sword, and your wives shall become widows and your children fatherless" (Exod. 23:22).

Illegitimates, however, and even their subsequent offspring, were outcast: "No bastard shall enter the assembly of the Lord; even to the tenth generation none of his descendants shall enter the assembly of the Lord" (Deut. 23:2). Sexual violation in the Old Testament sometimes symbolized sin in general, as the following admonition to the "offspring of the adulterer and the harlot" illustrates: "Are you not children of transgression, the offspring of deceit, you who burn with lust among the oaks, under every green tree; slaying the children in the valleys, under the clefts of the rocks?" (Isa. 57:3). Like the literary "bastard villain" stereotype, biblical bastards carried automatic associations with other sins or crimes, such as lying, sorcery, rape, and murder. Indeed, the word "sinister" itself, which originally simply meant "left," evolved into its modern meaning of "evil, ominous, and threatening" through association with the *bend sinister*—the heraldic device denoting an illegitimate knight.

Biblical censure of illegitimates was especially regarded by the Puritans and formed the philosophical basis of the harsh English and American laws affecting these children. Lawmakers were both concerned with the affront to public morality an illegitimate child would represent and its potential cost to the community. The English Poor Law Act of 1576 is an example of such prejudice:

> Firste, concerning Bastards begotten and borne out of lawful Matrimony (an Offence againste Gods lawe and Mans Lawe) the said Bastards being now lefte to bee kepte at the chardge of the Parishe and in defrauding of the Reliefe of the impotente and aged true Poore of the same Parishe, and to the evill Example and Encouradgement of lewde Lyef: It ys ordeyned and enacted. . . (Kadushin 414).

The widespread idea of homeless children or destitute mothers and their children defrauding public funds is illustrated by Dickens in *Oliver Twist* when he sarcastically calls the young parish boys "juvenile offenders against the poor-laws" (48).

The English Poor Law Act of 1601 created an early social welfare system. Women at that time were still publicly disgraced and sometimes whipped or imprisoned for giving birth to an illegitimate child, but the authorities began to require whomever they named as the child's father, or "affiliated the child upon," to be responsible for its support and education. If fortunate, a deserted mother and child could live at their own home and obtain public funds, called "outdoor relief"—the precursor to Aid to Families with Dependent Children. The less fortunate mothers would be forced to abandon their children in what was termed "indoor relief"—the Almshouse, Poorhouse, or Workhouse. As these institutions usually provided the only resource for any and all social pathologies, illegitimate children would be housed together with the insane, aged poor, disabled, and ill.

Thomas Malthus, the population economist, heavily influenced the authors of the English Poor Law of 1834 when he argued that "bastardy could be checked by shifting the responsibility on to the mother, and denying her the support of the Poor Law" (Rose 27). The theory didn't work in practice, as between 40,000 to 44,000 illegitimate babies continued to be born each year in Britain from the time of the law until the rate lowered slightly after 1890.

The 1834 changes in the English Poor law resulted in perhaps the harshest of all environments for the illegitimate child. This specific law was the target of Dickens's criticism when he wrote *Oliver Twist* in 1837. Unwed mothers were no longer able to obtain or even ask for any support from their children's fathers or "outdoor relief," and all funds for "indoor relief" assistance were cut to the very bone. Orphan asylums would often only admit bereaved children from respectable married families, as it was the prevailing belief that bastard children were tainted morally and mentally and were destined to become criminals or "born to be hung," as a board member remarked about Oliver Twist (58). The famous explorer **Henry Morton Stanley** was a representative child of the English workhouse during this period.

Orphanages

In England and the United States, illegitimate children were often not accepted into the charitable institutions and programs providing for "legitimate" orphans until the early twentieth century, after which time they became the majority of the institutional population. After they began to be admitted, local communities were known to categorically censure orphanage residents and want them separated from their own children: "there was a felt need for institutions where the abandoned and the orphaned could be housed together. (Was this, one wonders, where the stigma attached to the one began to be transferred to the other?)" (Simpson 136). Some children were admitted to orphanages temporarily during difficult times in their families, as was the case with **Ben Nighthorse Campbell**, and were later retrieved when the crisis was over. Orphanages were established and administered through the state or through religious and other private charities.

Orphanages could sometimes resemble prisons in their environments and terminology. According to two alumni of the Colorado State Children's Home (Lucero and Grosswiler), the resemblance of the boys' overalls to prison uniforms in the photo shown here was not coincidental: the overalls had been made in the state prison with the same fabric and in the same style used for convicts.

Cook Bessie Robertson and toddlers from the Carla Swan Department, Colorado State Children's Home, 1953. [Courtesy of Jim Lucero, fourth child from the left]

This prison-like language shifted dramatically around the 1960s to a collegiate lexicon. Children who formerly had been called "inmates" on official reports began to be called "alumni," "matrons" became "houseparents," "wards" (with sometimes up to forty beds) became "dormitories" (often four, or even two, beds to a room). "Departments" became "cottages," and the "installations" became known as "campuses." "Lock-up," a sometimes several-day solitary confinement especially used for children who ran away, disappeared as a punishment around the same time.

This humanizing of language reflected the lifting of the illegitimacy stigma brought about by such broad social movements as feminism and the "sexual revolution." Both have done much to soften the moral taint of illegitimacy by causing society's ideas about marriage to change. As the definitions and boundaries of relationships expanded and altered, having children outside of those bounds became (largely) acceptable, and in due course the stigma lifted for mothers and their children. Women's changes in work roles, earnings, and education also began to make it possible for single mothers to keep and provide for their offspring. According to the 2009 *U. S. Statistical Abstract,* there were 1,527,000 live births to unmarried women in 2005 (table 84). These births represent well over a third of the total 4,138,000 live births in the United States for that year (table 79).

Foster Care and Kinship Care

During certain historical periods, it was a fairly common practice for parents to make arrangements for their children to live a significant part of their childhoods outside the home. Being "sent out to nurse" was especially the norm for an illegitimate child, but even children of married parents (**Balzac** and **Casanova** are examples of such children) could spend their childhoods in fosterage for various reasons. Orphanages and foundling hospitals also placed out some of their charges to foster homes. Some children lived briefly with many families, as was the case with **Marilyn Monroe** and **Art Buchwald**. These multiple placements were often very hard on the children.

Sometimes parents were able to choose persons as foster or adoptive parents who could advance their children's education or social standing. In some cultures, adoption and fosterage were used as means of establishing ties and creating political alliances, in much the same manner as royal marriages in the Middle Ages. Hawaii's **Queen Lili'uokalani** and South Africa's **Nelson Mandela** are two individuals who experienced such practices.

American orphanages were disbanded in the early 1970s when the federally-sponsored foster care system took over. Some of the former facilities changed their missions and began to serve troubled youth populations. These became known as "residential treatment centers" and "group homes." Sometimes hospitals keep "boarder babies" after their delivery from HIV+, drug-addicted, incarcerated, or ill mothers until a foster home can be found for them.

When family members other than a child's parents become its care-givers, the practice is known as "kincare" or "kinship care." Orphaned children, such as **Ingrid Bergman** and **Boris Karloff**, often have loving grandparents, aunts, uncles, or siblings who take them in. Other children, like the fictional Harry Potter, are less welcome and even suffer abuse by extended family members. In many cases, the child's parents are living; for example **John Lennon** was raised by an aunt after his parents divorced. In some cultures, it is traditional for children to be raised by grandparents or other family members instead of the parents.

American Adoption

The Orphan Trains were a unique part of American adoption history. They began in 1853 as part of the New York Children's Aid Society's "placing out" program. This society was founded by Charles Loring Brace, a Methodist minister. A large Catholic children's institution, the New York Foundling Hospital, soon also began participating in the Orphan Trains. Homeless children were sent from New York by train to rural areas across the United States in the hopes of finding adoptive homes. If selected, the children were under indenture or contract until the age of 18, but were also available for formal adoption. Much of our language of adoption comes out of the Orphan Train experience. "Placement" or "putting someone up for adoption," which came from the practice of putting the waiting children up onto platforms or stages at each stop for selection, are examples. At least 200,000 Orphan Train children were placed before the program ended in 1929. The program was very controversial, even in its own time. Some of the children found happy homes, as was the case with Alaskan Governor **John Green Brady**, but others were simply taken for labor. Many of the children were mistreated and ran away.

Beginning in the 1930's, states began to make laws that required adopted persons' birth and adoption records to be sealed and "amended" birth certificates to be issued, in the belief that they would protect the children from the stigma of illegitimacy. This practice prohibited adoptees from learning their own original identities or those of their birthparents. As a result, many involved in adoptions go through difficult, usually expensive and often unsuccessful searches for information or relatives.

The closed records system also allowed adoptive parents to conceal a child's adoptive status if they wished. Persons who discover their adoption status as adults are known as "late-discovery adoptees"; examples include **Dave Thomas** and **James Michener**.

In some cases, an illegitimate child is secretly kept within its biological family but is presented as the child of a family member other than the actual parent. **Jack Nicholson** and Eric Clapton, for example, both discovered when older that their "sisters" were in truth their mothers.

American adoptions today tend to be more open, with the members of the "adoption triad" (birthparents, adoptive parents, and adoptee) having information and/or contact with each other. Interracial and intercultural adoption is common, but controversial, as is adoption by gay parents and single parents. The majority of American children available for adoption today have parents whose rights were terminated due to drugs, alcohol, abuse, or neglect. The Internet has become a valuable tool used to facilitate and promote adoptions, help searchers locate missing relatives, and create community among people with common goals and experiences. Reproductive technology and choices have also had an impact, especially on the availability of infants for adoption. In addition, the first generation of "donor offspring" or "donor-conceived persons" has reached adulthood and they are searching, like many adopted persons, for anonymous parents and lost siblings. For a more detailed look at American adoption history and trends, Lori Askeland's excellent study, *Children and Youth in Adoption, Orphanages and Foster Care: A Historical Handbook and Guide* (Greenwood Press 2006) is recommended. Her work covers the Colonial to modern periods and also examines some Native American and African American adoption issues.

Child Abuse in Adoption

Although child abuse is considered rare[1] in adoption, there have been some very high-profile cases. One that attracted prolonged national attention is that of Lisa Steinberg. Six-year-old Lisawas beaten to death in her Greenwich Village home by her adoptive father, Joel Steinberg, in 1987. Charges were also brought against her adoptive mother, Hedda Nussbaum, but were later dropped. According to trial testimony (573 N.Y.S.2d 965), Joel Steinberg inflicted Lisa's head injury and then left the apartment while the unconscious child and Nussbaum remained home. When he returned several hours later, Steinberg and Nussbaum smoked cocaine until around 4:00 A.M., while Lisa lay unassisted on the bathroom floor more than twelve hours. Paramedics were called after Lisa stopped breathing, around 6:00 A.M. She was taken to the hospital, where she later died. Nussbaum, whom Steinberg also battered, did not get help for the child because she thought it would be considered a sign of disloyalty to Steinberg. She has subsequently authored a book and accepts speaking engagements about surviving domestic abuse. Lisa and Mitchell, a younger adopted brother, were brought into the home by Steinberg, an attorney, but neither child had ever been legally adopted. A judge returned Mitchell to his biological mother's custody in 1987. Steinberg was released from prison in 2004.

The highest fatality rate among adopted children occurs with Russian adoptees, which has prompted Russian officials to threaten a moratorium on their U.S. adoptions. Russia is the second most popular country for international adoptions following China.

---

[1]The *Encyclopedia of Adoption* says that abuse occurs in about 1% of adoptive families (Adamec 6).

According to an article in the *Washington Post* (3/2/2006, B05), fourteen children adopted from Russian orphanages have been killed by their American adoptive parents over the past twenty years. They include 2½-year-old Nina Victoria Hilt, beaten to death in North Carolina; 6-year-old Alex Pavlis, beaten to death in Illinois in 2003 for wetting his pants; 2-year-old David Polreis, Jr., beaten to death with a wooden spoon in Greeley, Colorado, 1996; 6-year-old Viktor Matthey, beaten with an aluminum bat and locked in an unheated pump room, where he died from hypothermia in Vermont, 1998; and 3-year-old Liam Thompson, scalded in 140-degree bath water by his adoptive father. His second- and third-degree burns were left untreated for several days by his adoptive mother, an LPN, and he died in 2003 in Columbus, Ohio. The others are Logan Higginbotham, age 3 (Vermont, 1998), Luke Evans, age 1½ (Indiana, 2001), Jacob Lindorff, age 5 (New Jersey, 2001), Zachary Higier, age 2 (Massachusetts, 2002), Maria Bennett, age 2 (Ohio, 2002), Jessica Hagmann, age 2 (Virginia, 2003), and Dennis Merryman, age 8 (Maryland, 2005).

One Russian adoptee, Masha Allen, was delivered to an undetected pedophile by her agency. Allen was adopted at age five by Matthew Mancuso, a divorced, Pittsburg engineer, who for five years raped Masha and used her to make child pornography. Mancuso starved Masha to delay her physical development in order to make her appear younger in the pornography he created. She weighed 52 pounds and wore a size 6x at the time of her rescue. She testified before the House Energy and Commerce Committee on May 3, 2006. Her testimony, entitled "Sexual Exploitation of Children over the Internet," persuaded congress to pass "Masha's Law" which went into effect July 27, 2007. "Masha's Law," part of the Adam Walsh Child Protection Act, sponsored by Senator John Kerry, "triples the penalty for downloading perverted images of children and allows young people 18 years and over to sue those who download pornographic images taken of them when they were children" (http://kerry.senate.gov/mass/family.cfm, retrieved 10/30/2007). Masha, now Masha Allen, was adopted by Faith Allen, a former Georgia foster child, in 2004. Mancuso was sentenced to thirty-five years in prison.

Defenses put forth in homicide cases involving adopted children often claim that the children cause their own injuries during tantrums or die as a consequence of reactive attachment disorders. Some children have even suffered abuse as a result of adults trying to protect or cure them from such disorders: Sharen and Michael Gravell of Ohio were convicted in 2007 of four felonies and seven misdemeanors for keeping their eleven adopted, special needs children in cages at night "for the safety of the children" (*State v. Gravelle* 2008 Ohio 4031).

In another case, Candace Newmaker, a ten-year-old adopted Colorado girl, died during "rebirthing" therapy designed to cure an attachment problem and help her bond with her adoptive mother. Candace was smothered to death during "rebirthing" treatment for her bonding problems in Golden, Colorado, in 2000. She was made to lie in a fetal position, and then was told to fight her way out of a simulated "womb" of a tightly wrapped flannel blanket topped with pillows, at which point she would be "born" to her adoptive mother. Two therapists and two assistants pushed against the "womb" to simulate labor contractions, producing a combined weight of approximately 700 pounds pressing against the 70-pound child. Throughout the procedure, which was taped, the child repeatedly tells the adults that she cannot breathe and is going to die. Candace remained in the "womb" over seventy minutes before the team realized that she had indeed smothered to death. The "rebirthing team," headed by unlicensed Evergreen therapists Connell Watkins and Julie Ponder, received sixteen-year sentences. Colorado passed "Candace's Law" in 2001, which forbids the use of "rebirthing" and other restrictive holding therapies to treat attachment disorders.

This book presents commentary from one hundred adults who experienced firsthand the various circumstances described in this brief history. Many were children who prevailed over tremendous misfortune and some have been left with scars, invisible and literal. All of the people selected for these profiles, however, went on to distinguish themselves and contribute positive gifts to the world.

I myself am an adoptee and the adoptive mother of two daughters. For us, many of these people have become role models. However, I believe that anyone can be inspired by these stories of resiliency and and courage.

Works Cited

Adamec, Christine A. *The Encyclopedia of Adoption.* 2nd Ed. New York: Facts on File, 2000.

Askeland, Lori. *Children and Youth in Adoption, Orphanages and Foster Care: A Historical Handbook and Guide.* Westport, CT: Greenwood Press, 2006.

Cook, Stanley A. *The Laws of Moses and the Code of Hammurabi.* London: Adam and Charles Black, 1903.

Dickens, Charles. *Oliver Twist.* London: Penguin, 1985.

Grosswiler, Ron. Colorado State Children's Home resident 1939–1957. Personal interviews, October–December 1996.

Holt, Marilyn Irvin. *The Orphan Trains: Placing Out in America.* Lincoln, NE: University of Nebraska Press, 1992.

Jolie, Angelina. "Angelina Jolie: Her Mission and Motherhood." *Anderson Cooper 360 Degrees.* CNN, New York, June 20, 2006. Lexis-Nexis Transcript, June 26, 2006.

Kadushin, Alfred. *Child Welfare Services.* 3rd Ed. New York: MacMillan, 1980.

Kertzer, David I. "The Lives of Foundlings in Nineteenth-Century Italy." *Abandoned Children.* Ed. Catherine Panter-Brick and Malcolm T. Smith. Cambridge, UK: Cambridge University Press, 2000. 41–56.

Lewis, Brian. *The Sargon Legend: A Study of the Akkadian Text and the Tale of the Hero Who Was Exposed at Birth.* Cambridge, MA: American Schools of Oriental Research, 1980.

Low, Donald. "Nurseries of Crime." *Thieves' Kitchen: The Regency Underworld.* London: J. M. Dent & Sons, 1982. 63–81.

Lucero, Jim. Colorado State Home resident 1950–1964, Personal interviews, August–December 1996.

MacDowell, Douglas M. *The Law in Classical Athens.* Ithaca, NY: Cornell UP, 1978.

Panter-Brick, Catherine. "Nobody's Children? A Reconsideration of Child Abandonment." *Abandoned Children.* Ed. Catherine Panter-Brick and Malcolm T. Smith. Cambridge, UK: Cambridge University Press, 2000. 1–26.

Postgate, J. N. *Early Mesopotamia: Society and Economy at the Dawn of History.* London: Routledge, 1992. *eHRAF*, Document No. 10. July 3, 2006.

Rose, Lionel. *The Massacre of the Innocents: Infanticide in Britain 1800–1939.* London: Routledge & Kegan Paul, 1986.

Simpson, Eileen B. *Orphans: Real and Imaginary.* New York: Penguin, 1990.

Teichman, Jenny. *Illegitimacy: An Examination of Bastardy.* Ithaca, NY: Cornell University Press, 1982.

Zettler, Richard L. *The Ur III Temple of Inanna at Nippur: The Operation and Organization of Urban Religious Institutions in Mesopotamia in the Late Third Millennium B. C.* Berlin: Dietrich Reimer Verlag, 1992. *eHRAF*, Document No. 10. July 3, 2006.

A

ALBEE, EDWARD (1928–)

Playwright
Adoptee

Career, Major Awards, and Achievements

Edward Albee has won the Pulitzer Prize for Literature three times: in 1967 for *A Delicate Balance*, in 1975 for *Seascape*, and in 1994 for *Three Tall Women*, his autobiographical play about the death of his adoptive mother. He has won countless national and international awards for his works, which include *Zoo Story* (1959), *The Death of Bessie Smith* (1961), *The American Dream* (1961)—a play about a family who adopt and then destroy a "bumble of joy"—and *Who's Afraid of Virginia Woolf?* (1963). Albee was inducted into Theater Hall of Fame in 1985 and received Kennedy Center Honors in 1996.

Family of Origin

Edward Franklin Albee III was adopted as an infant. He was born on March 12, 1928. One biographer says that Albee was born as Edward Harvey in Washington, D.C., to a woman named Louise Harvey and an unspecified father (Gussow 22). Another says that he was born in "somewhere in Virginia" and was "prohibited by law to discover either the identities of his natural parents or his actual place of birth" (MacNicholas 4). Albee was cared for at the Alice Chaplin Nursery at 444 West 22nd Street in Manhattan prior to his adoption placement. He has not searched for his birthparents, but he often thinks about them and about his genetic roots (Gussow 401). When Albee's friend and primary biographer, Mel Gussow, told him about a fantasy he had of the author and his birthmother being reunited at the Kennedy Center Honors, Albee seems to have enjoyed the idea: "If they had wanted to do it right, they could have this old, old lady come on stage in a spotlight. And then, 'Son, Son'; 'Mother, Mother,' That would have been lovely. I would have burst into tears" (Gussow 386).

Adoption

When he was eighteen days old, Edward was placed with Reed and Frances Albee through an adoption agency. The Albees were a wealthy couple, the heirs to a famous chain of vaudeville theaters. They brought the baby to their home in Westchester and

[AP Photo/Chad Rachman]

formally adopted him on February 1, 1929. Albee said later that the only reason they wanted a child was that his grandfather wanted an heir. "They bought me," he said. "They paid $133.30," explaining that sum was the cost for "professional services" (Gussow 22). At the age of six, Albee learned that he was adopted, but he pretended that he already knew.

Education and Significant Relationships

Miserable at home and school, Albee was thrown out of every private school his parents could get him into except one. Dr. Heely, a previous headmaster, overlooked Albee's "disastrous" school record and wrote a letter of reference that got him into Choate, a prestigious school that was later known as "the school that educated Albee." Heely's letter discussed Albee's intelligence, his promise, and his relationship with his mother:

> Ed is an adopted child and, very confidentially, he dislikes his mother with a cordial and eloquent dislike which I consider entirely justified. . . . She is a selfish, dominating person, whereas Ed is a sensitive, perceptive and intelligent boy. He feels he is not really loved and the psychological hurdle which has been built up in front of him was simply insurmountable. I can think of no other boy who, I believe, has been so fully the victim of an unsympathetic home background or who had exhibited so fully the psychological effect of feeling that he is not wanted (Gussow 53).

After Choate, Albee briefly attended Trinity College, and, while a student there, he left home for good after a serious argument with his adoptive parents. Some sources speculated that Albee was forced to leave home because of his parents' inability to accept Albee's homosexuality, but that does not seem to have been the case. Albee says that he never discussed his sexuality with his family—nor did he ever later discuss with them his thirty-five-year relationship with artist Jonathan Thomas, who died of cancer in 2005. Thomas was a Canadian artist and sculptor whom Albee had met in 1971 at a lecture that Albee gave at the University of Toronto, where Thomas was a student.

Albee and his parents especially disagreed about his plans to become a writer. Much later, Albee tried to reconcile with his mother during the years just before her death in 1989. After her death, it became clear that she had never forgiven him, even to the point of writing him out of her will:

> Was I thrown out or did I leave? . . . I didn't feel that I was left any alternative. And it had nothing to do with homosexuality. That's another fiction. That was never discussed between us. She could never bring herself to discuss the subject, and my father didn't talk about anything. I was aware of my own sexual nature and that I would never be able to function according to their standards. I'm sure that in the background that helped me in my decision to take off. It was clear to me: I was not what they bargained for, what they thought they had bought (Gussow 71).

In 1997, Albee wrote *The Play About the Baby*. His primary biographer thought it "seemed apparent that it derived from his lifelong obsession with the meaning of parenting . . . One impetus for writing the play may have been his own curiosity about his birth and adoption" (Gussow 390). Adoption is clearly an ongoing and important key to Albee's work, although he himself disapproves of "biographical correspondences" to his writings (Wasserman 14). One critic noted that Albee's "sense of being a lost and lonely human on an isolated planet, an adopted child with no idea of his real parents—may account for his lack of a consistent temperament and style" (Brustein 30). Gussow felt that Albee's adoption was "one of the most important factors in his life" (22). His alienation, loss, and the difficult relationships he experienced within his adoptive family are clearly connecting themes in his prize-winning work.

Works Cited

Albee, Edward. *Three Tall Women*. New York: Dutton, 1995.

Bottoms, Stephen. *The Cambridge Companion to Edward Albee*. Cambridge, UK: Cambridge University Press, 2005.

Brustein, Robert. "A Question of Identity." *New Republic* 221 (1999): 29–31.

Gussow, Mel. *Edward Albee: A Singular Journey*. New York: Simon & Schuster, 1999.

MacNicholas, John. "Edward Albee." *Twentieth-Century American Dramatists. Dictionary of Literary Biography* 7 (1981): 4.

Wasserman, Julian N. *Edward Albee: An Interview and Essays*. Houston, TX: Syracuse University Press, 1983.

ALBERTI, LEON BATTISTA (1404–1472)

Architect, Writer, Mathematician, Humanist, Artist, Scientist
Orphaned at age 16, deprived of inheritance

The term "Renaissance Man" might have been coined to describe Leon Battista Alberti. An ideal Renaissance man was skilled in all the arts and sciences; Alberti was an accomplished scholar, author, architect, mathematician, scientist, inventor, poet, playwright, sculptor, artist, athlete, cleric, and humanist philosopher.

"Battista," as he referred to himself, was the younger of two illegitimate sons of Lorenzo Alberti, a member of a powerful wool merchant family the ruling Albizzi factions had driven from their native Florence. Battista's mother, a widow from Bologna, gave birth to her younger son on February 18, 1404, in Padua. The boy's father eventually married a Florentine woman and settled in Venice, taking his sons, Carlo and Battista, with him. Battista Alberti was a bright and eager scholar, and his father gave him the best possible classical education, boarding him at Barzizza's Gymnasium in Padua. Some of his Gymnasium classmates went on to become the leading humanists and educators of the Renaissance. In 1421, during Alberti's first year at the University of Bologna, his father died, and the boys' care was taken over by their uncle, Ricciardo. When Ricciardo also died several months later, his remaining uncles, Adovardo and Lionardo, broke the promises made to the dying father to love, care for, and educate his sons (Alberti 40). The remaining Alberti family shunned the two brothers and used their illegitimacy to steal the inheritance left by Lorenzo's will. Alberti bitterly recorded his uncle Adovardo's promises to his father in the book *Della Famiglia*: "If I did not consider them as my very own children, Lionardo, I should not be a good relative or a true friend. In fact, you would consider me merciless, false, and of vile character, and I should be scorned and reproached for it. Who could feel no pity for orphans? Who could do anything but always remember the father of these orphans and the last words with which, at the point of death, this dear friend and relative recommended his dearest possessions, his children, to us?" (Watkins 52).

Impoverished and sick from grief and overwork, Alberti persevered with his studies in law and literature. He turned to mathematics first as a recreation for his nerves and later as a vital interest.

In 1426 the ban on the Albertis was lifted and the family returned to Florence. Battista Alberti became a religious cleric, the secretary of Cardinal Albergati, the Bishop of Bologna, with whom he travelled to France, Germany, and the Low Countries. Eventually he became a secretary in the papal chancery, after Pope Eugenius IV first issued two bulls annulling, in his case, the church's prohibition against illegitimate children receiving holy orders. Once his livelihood in the church was established, Alberti devoted him-

[Courtesy of the Library of Congress]

self to his writings, architecture, art, and inventions. His architecture includes the church of St. Francis of Assisi in Rimini, the Rucellai palace in Florence, and the church of Saint Andrea in Mantua. His writings include the dialogues on the family mentioned above, his *Ten Books on Architecture* (a treatise on the aesthetics of architecture), writings on lives of saints, poems, satirical plays, and essays on horsemanship, music, painting, and sculpture. His inventions include an early camera obscura. His knowledge of combined mathematics and art established the first Renaissance canon of proportions (Gadol 7).

The memory of his own youthful privations was clearly present when Alberti died in Rome in 1472. In his will, he designated money for the purchase of a house in Bologna "to be used as a college or place of study endowed with its own income, goods and property, where one or two members of the Alberti family wanting to study canon or civil law, or any other subject, could live free of expense. In the event of there being no heirs of the Alberti family, their places were to be taken by two or more poor students in the form of scholarships, but the house and its endowment were not to be transferred on any account" (Borsi 17). He also asked to be buried next to his father in Padua. Neither wish was honored, as it turned out; the house and endowment were transferred, and Alberti's remains were lost. His distinguished reputation, however, does survive: "I live and hover upon the lips of the learned" (Borsi 18).

Works Cited

Alberti, Leon Battista. *The Albertis of Florence: Leon Battista Alberti's* Della Famiglia. Guido A. Guarino, trans. Lewisburg: Bucknell University Press, 1971.

Borsi, Franco. *Leon Battista Alberti.* New York: Harper & Row, 1977.

Gadol, Joan. *Leon Battista Alberti: Universal Man of the Early Renaissance.* Chicago: University of Chicago Press, 1969.

Watkins, Renée Neu. *The Family in Renaissance Florence: A Translation by Renée Neu Watkins of* I Libri Della Famiglia *by Leon Battista Alberti.* Columbia, SC: University of South Carolina Press, 1969.

D'ALEMBERT, JEAN (1717–1783)

Mathematician, Encyclopedist
Foundling, adoptee

Career, Major Awards, and Achievements

Jean Le Rond d'Alembert was an influential French mathematician. He is known for the mechanical principle called d'Alembert's Law. His work dealt with the resistance of fluids and the mathematical dynamics of the planets, and his discoveries were important to physics, astrophysics, and mathematics. D'Alembert was elected to the French Academy in 1754 and became its permanent secretary. His published works include *Traité de Dynamique* (1743), *Éléments de Philosophie* (1759), and *Éléments de Musique, Théorique et Pratique* (1779). He is best known for his collaboration with Diderot on *La Grande Encyclopédie*. Diderot envisioned a great work in which all knowledge would be condensed and made available to all people. His encyclopedia epitomized the Enlightenment, an era dedicated to universal education. D'Alembert wrote the controversial *Discours Préliminaire* (1751), which introduced the work, served as the encyclopedia's mathematics editor, and contributed numerous articles. Diderot's encyclopedia was full of "dangerous thoughts" (De Ford 200), and it attracted much criticism and suspicion from the Catholic Church, especially from the Jesuits. In one of his essays, "On the Association of Men of Letters with the Great," d'Alembert denounced patronage of artists and writers by aristocrats. True to his opinions, he himself declined repeated invitations of patronage from Frederick the Great of Prussia and Catherine the Great of Russia. He was recognized as a brilliant conversationalist, eulogist, and storyteller, and

D'ALEMBERT.

After the Painting, by Chardin.

[Clergue, Helen, *The Salon: A Study of French Society and Personalities in the Eighteenth Century*, 1907.]

was a welcomed regular at the best Paris *salons*, which were gatherings of intellectuals in the homes of fashionable hostesses. He was a born wit and mimic and "possessed an enthusiasm and naïveté which caused the Duchesse de Chaulnes to declare that he was 'only a child, who lived in eternal infancy'" (Hankins 15–16).

Family of Origin

On a winter night in 1717, police found the newborn d'Alembert abandoned in a wooden box on the steps of St. Jean-Le-Rond, a church in Paris. The child was baptized, named after the church where he had been found, and taken to a foster home in Picardy. D'Alembert was the illegitimate child of a famous salonnière and literary patroness, Claudine-Alexandrine Guérin, Madame de Tencin. He was no more than a few days old at the time of his exposure on the night of November 16, 1717. The aristocratic Madame de Tencin ignored her son until he became famous, then

> she sent for him and told him as a thrilling secret that he was her son. D'Alembert's reply was worthy of the upright, simple man he always was. "Madame," he said, "the glazier's wife is my real mother; you are nothing to me but a stepmother" (De Ford 192).

D'Alembert's father was a cavalry officer, the chevalier Louis-Camus Destouches.

Adoption

Destouches sought out his son* and took him to a Madame Rousseau, the wife of a glass installer. Jean always referred to and considered Madame Rousseau as his adoptive mother, although it is unknown if his was a formally legalized adoption. He himself later selected his last name, d'Alembert. Jean was very attached to his adoptive mother, a simple, good woman, and he remained at her home in his tiny garret room until he was "weaned," in his words, at the age of 48, when he went to live with the woman he loved.

Education and Significant Relationships

After his birthfather died in 1726, d'Alembert received an annuity of 1200 livres, which gave him a certain amount of financial independence. His birthfather might also have been responsible for his son's education, although the boy invariably outstripped his masters in mathematics and largely educated himself in his favorite field. He was admitted to the "Collège des Quatre Nations where he entered as *gentilhomme* largely through the influence of the Destouches family" (Hankins 18). In 1735, d'Alembert earned his baccalaureate, then studied law for two years and became a licensed advocate in 1738. He was only twenty-four when he entered the Academy of Sciences, "an honor which would scarcely come at twice twenty-four to a self-taught man with the added handicap of 'namelessness'" (De Ford 196).

D'Alembert fell in love with his friend, salonnière Julie de Lespinasse, who had tended him through a serious illness. She was the illegitimate daughter of the Comtesse d'Albon and fifteen years his junior. D'Alembert left his adoptive mother and moved in with her, but Julie loved other men. She reputedly died of a broken heart over her unrequited love for the Comte de Guibert. D'Alembert was said to have never emotionally recovered from her death in 1776: "His heart was buried with a woman who had never pretended to love him" (De Ford 212). On October 29, 1783, he died at the age of 67. His death and Diderot's the following year are said to mark the end of the Enlightenment's epoch of the *Philosophes*.

Works Cited

De Ford, Miriam Allen. *Love Children: A Book of Illustrious Illegitimates.* New York: Dial Press, 1931.
Hankins, Thomas. *Jean d'Alembert: Science and the Enlightenment.* Oxford: Clarendon Press, 1970.

---

*It is unclear whether Destouches and d'Alembert knew one another. Many sources say that Destouches secretly funded his son's care and education.

AMES, WILLIAM (1576–1633)

Theologian
Orphaned in childhood, fostered with relatives

William Ames was an English Puritan scholar, educator, and theologian, who was considered one of New England's spiritual fathers. His beliefs forced him out of a fellowship at Cambridge and into exile in Holland, where he became a primary spokesman for Calvinist thought. Between 1613 and 1618, Ames wrote four important works that defended Calvinism. At The Hague, Ames became a military chaplain for Sir Horace Vere, who commanded the English forces in the Low Countries. He also served as minister to the English inhabitants of The Hague from 1611 to 1619. In 1618, Ames became a theological advisor to the president of the tumultuous Synod of Dort, which was called to settle a religious and political controversy between Calvinism and Arminianism. The main controversy dealt with opposing views about determinism and free will. The Calvinists were victorious at the Synod and were soon free to remove Arminian curators from the Dutch universities and install their own faculty in their places. Ames was offered the Professorship of Theology at the University of Franeker in Friesland, where he moved with his family in 1622. One of the illustrious graduates of Franeker was Rene Descartes, who enrolled there in 1629. The eleven years Ames taught at Franeker gave him a wide reputation and time to write. His best known works are a compendium called *Medulla Theologiae* (1619), intended as a textbook; *De Conscientia* (1630); and the posthumous writings *Workes* (1643) and *Opera Omnia* (1658). Ames left his professorship at Franeker in 1632 to become a minister and teacher in Rotterdam, but his life there was tragically cut short. His writings were important texts for the American Puritans, and, although he never reached the new world, he influenced thought there: "'Our way of the church,' promised John Cotton, 'we received by the light of the Word from Mr. Parker, Mr. Baynes, and Dr. Ames'" (257–258).

Family of Origin

William Ames was born in Ipswich, Suffolk, in 1576 to William Ames, a merchant of Ipswich, and Joane Snelling Ames, also from a merchant family. When William and his sister Elizabeth were very young, both parents died. William was sent to his mother's brother, John Snelling, a clothier in Boxford. Elizabeth went to live with another uncle, Robert Snelling, who remembered her in his will as "my maide and kinswoman" (9) and left her £10. In 1612, Elizabeth married the rector of Wrentham, John Phillip. William grew up in an active religious environment, as his guardian was a Puritan, and Boxford, located in East Anglia, was an important center for Puritan nonconformists. Snelling provided well for his nephew, and his generosity made it possible for William to enter Christ's College at Cambridge around the age of seventeen. Ames finished his bachelor's degree in 1597/98 and his Master of Arts in 1601. He was elected a fellow in 1601 and, as the fellowship required, was ordained as a minister. He was a diligent student whose "candle was burning by night, when others were put out" (11). Ames continued as a fellow until 1610. Around that time King James I ordered conformity to Church of England doctrines and Puritan dissenters were actively dispersed. When Anglican Valentine Cary was made master of Christ's College in 1609, Ames and other Puritans soon resigned or were forced out. Marked as radicals and unable to earn a living in England, Ames and the others joined a group of English exiles in the Netherlands.

Ames married twice. His first wife, the daughter of a John Burgess, died young without leaving children. His second wife, Joane Fletcher, married Ames when she was about 30 years old, sometime around 1618. They had three children, two sons and a daughter. The family moved with Ames when he left his Professorship in Franeker to go to Rotterdam as a new minister. His new life was cut short when his house was inundated in a flood barely two months after his arrival in Rotterdam. Ames died from shock and exposure in the flood. He was buried November 14, 1633. After his death, his wife and children returned briefly to England and then emigrated to the American colonies.

Work Cited

Sprunger, Keith L. *The Learned Doctor William Ames: Dutch Backgrounds of English and American Puritanism.* Urbana: University of Illinois Press, 1972.

ANGELOU, MAYA née MARGUERITE ANN JOHNSON (1928–)

Author
Fostered with relatives from age 3

Career, Major Awards, and Achievements

Maya Angelou is a prominent and popular African American author, poet, speaker, and actress. She appeared in Jean Genet's plays *The Blacks* (1961) and *Medea* (1966), won a Tony Award nomination for *Look Away* (1972) and an Emmy Award nomination for her role as Nyo Boto, Kunta Kinte's grandmother, in Alex Haley's *Roots* (1977). She has appeared in the television movie *There Are No Children Here* (1993) and the film *How to Make an American Quilt* (1995). Her plays and screenplays include *The Least of These* (1966), *Getting Up Stayed on My Mind* (1967), *Georgia, Georgia* (1972), *Ajax* (1974), *And Still I Rise* (1978), *Sister, Sister* (the film, 1982), and *On a Southern Journey* (1983). Angelou's best known works are her multiple volume autobiography: *I Know Why the Caged Bird Sings* (1970), *Gather Together in My Name* (1974), *Singin' and Swingin' and Gettin' Merry Like Christmas* (1976), *The Heart of a Woman* (1981), *All God's Children Need Traveling Shoes* (1986), and *A Song Flung up to Heaven* (2002).

She has also written, produced, and directed numerous plays, screenplays, and educational documentaries. Her poetry collections include *Just Give Me a Cool Drink of Water 'Fore I Diiie* (1971), *Oh Pray My Wings Are Gonna Fit Me Well* (1975), *And Still I Rise* (1978), *Shaker, Why Don't You Sing* (1983), and *Now Sheba Sings the Song* (1987). Angelou was active in the civil rights movement and worked for Martin Luther King, Jr. She also served on President Ford's American Revolution Bicentennial Council and President Carter's National Commission on the Observance of International Women's Year. She was named Woman of the Year in Communications (*Ladies Home Journal*, 1983) and won an Eagle Award for her documentary *Afro-Americans in the Arts* (1977). She has received three Grammy Awards for Best Spoken Word (1994 for *On the Pulse of Morning*, 1996 for *Phenomenal Woman*, and 2003 for *A Song Flung up to Heaven*).

She was invited to read her poetry at President Clinton's inauguration (1993), the Million Man March in Washington, D.C. (1995), and the fiftieth anniversary of the United Nations (1995). She holds honorary degrees from over fifty colleges and universities. In 1981, she received a lifetime endowed appointment at Wake Forest University

[Courtesy of the National Archives]

as the Reynolds Professor of American Studies. Angelou was named one of the one hundred best writers of the twentieth century by *Writer's Digest* in 1999. In 2006, she received the Quill Award, a literary award sponsored by Reed Business Information and NBC, for her poem *Amazing Peace*, which she read at the White House during the 2005 lighting of the national Christmas tree.

Family of Origin and Kinship Care

Angelou was born Marguerite Ann Johnson on April 4, 1928, in St. Louis, Missouri. Her parents, Vivian (Baxter) Johnson and Bailey Johnson, a doorman, divorced when Maya was three years old. They sent Angelou and her four-year-old brother, Bailey, Jr., from their home in Long Beach, California, to live with their paternal grandmother, "Momma Henderson," a religiously devout storekeeper, in Stamps, Arkansas. Angelou was closest to her bright, good-natured brother, Bailey. It was Bailey who gave his sister the name Maya, a shorter version of "Mya Sister" (Angelou 68). Uncle Willie, Momma Henderson's disabled son, also lived with the family and helped run the store.

The children grew up in this small, racist, segregated southern community. Angelou wrote of how upset they became one year when they received unexpected Christmas gifts from their forgotten parents: "The gifts opened the door to questions that neither of us wanted to ask. Why did they send us away? And what did we do wrong? So wrong? Why, at three and four, did we have tags put on our arms to be sent by train alone from Long Beach, California, to Stamps, Arkansas, with only the porter to look after us?" (Angelou 53).

During her childhood, Angelou had only two visits with her father, Bailey, Sr., and she writes of them both as being very traumatic. On the first visit, he took the children to St. Louis to visit their mother and their mother's boyfriend, Mr. Freeman. Freeman began to sexually abuse the eight-year-old Maya, but in her innocence she interpreted the abuse as fatherly affection: "[He] held me so softly that I wished he wouldn't ever let me go. I felt at home. From the way he was holding me I knew he'd never let me go or let anything bad ever happen to me. This was probably my real father and we had found each other at last" (Angelou 73). Eventually, he forcibly raped the little girl and was brought to trial. Shortly after his conviction, Freeman was found dead, presumably dropped or kicked to death. Angelou, who had to testify in court, did not reveal the earlier abuse and says she felt responsible. She refused to speak to anyone except her brother Bailey for five years following Freeman's death.

This self-imposed silence created in her an extraordinary listening ability, an important skill for a poet. Her mother, upset and frustrated by her daughter's silence, returned her to her grandmother. Mrs. Bertha Flowers, a neighbor in Stamps, finally coaxed the child into speaking again by introducing her to the world's great literature. Angelou once told an interviewer: "[There] isn't one day since I was raped that I haven't thought about it. . . . I have gotten beyond hate and fear, but there is something beyond that" (Bloom 5). On the second visit with her father, when Angelou was a teenager, she ran away after she was attacked and injured by her father's girlfriend.

Education and Significant Relationships

At the age of twelve, Angelou graduated from Lafayette County Training School in Stamps at the top of her class. Soon afterwards, she and her brother moved to San Francisco to live with their remarried mother, who was now a professional gambler. She graduated from Mission High School in 1944, at the age of sixteen. A one-time sexual encounter with a neighbor boy she does not name left Angelou pregnant with her only child, Guy Johnson. She soon moved out of her mother's home and took various jobs to care for her new son. She worked as a waitress, nightclub dancer, and even an amateur "madam" for two lesbian prostitutes:

At eighteen I had managed in a few tense years to become a snob at all levels, racial, cultural, and intellectual. I was a madam and thought myself morally superior to the whores. I was a waitress and believed myself cleverer than the customers I served. I was a lonely unmarried mother and held myself to be freer than the married women I met (Smith 12).

When she was around twenty-two, she married a white ex-sailor, Tosh Angelos, whose family name she retained. They divorced within three years and Angelou resumed her career as a dancer. She studied dance with Martha Graham, Pearl Primus, and Ann Halprin. She also studied drama and began writing. Her acting career began as a member of a touring cast of *Porgy and Bess*, but she felt guilty about leaving her nine-year-old son and soon returned. She had an unformalized marriage with Vusumzi Make, a black South African freedom fighter, and lived with him in Africa. She stayed in Africa for a time after her separation from Make in order to nurse her son, who had suffered a nearly fatal automobile accident there. Guy Johnson has gone on to become an author and poet in his own right. His debut work, *Standing at the Scratch Line*, was published in 1998. From 1973 to 1981 Angelou was married to Paul du Feu, a French author and cartoonist.

Works Cited

Angelou, Maya. *I Know Why the Caged Bird Sings*. New York: Bantam Books, 1997.

Bloom, Lynn Z. "Maya Angelou." *Afro-American Writers After 1955: Dramatists and Prose Writers. Dictionary of Literary Biography* 38 (1985).

Renuard, Lindsey. "Maya Angelou." *The Greenwood Encyclopedia of African American Literature 1*. Eds. Hans Ostrom and J. David Macey, Jr. Westport, CT: Greenwood Press, 2005. 36–38.

ARISTOTLE (384–322 BCE)

Greek Philosopher, Scientist, Educator
Orphaned when a boy, adopted or fostered by the executor of his father's will

Career, Major Awards, and Achievements

Aristotle is one of the most important and influential thinkers of all times. His ideas were especially prominent in the works of early medieval and Renaissance thinkers, such as St. Thomas Aquinas and Francis Bacon. The range of Aristotle's work is remarkable, including profound contributions to biology, meteorology, literature, political science, psychology, aesthetics, logic, philosophy, and physics. The *Organon*, which comprises six treatises, is considered one of his most important works. It examines various means for discovering what is true and forms the foundation for the scientific method. His *Metaphysica,* a collection of fourteen books of philosophy and physics, examines the nature of existence. His *Parva Naturalia* is a series on biology, zoology, and psychology. Aristotle's ideas for the ideal city-state are presented in an eight-volume work called *Politics*. He wrote two series on ethics, the ten-volume *Nicomachean Ethics*, named after his son, and the seven-volume *Eudemian Ethics*, named after, or compiled by, a favorite student, Eudemus. Both works present Aristotle's belief that ethics and morality are important branches of political science. He also wrote three books on the art of persuasion and

[Corel]

public speaking, called *Rhetoric*, and his *Poetics* is the earliest surviving study of literary criticism. Aristotle was also renowned as a brilliant natural scientist and educator.

Family of Origin

Aristotle was born during or slightly after July 384 BCE in Stagirus, an Ionian colony in Macedonia (Chroust 73–74). His mother, Phaestis, was a woman from Chalcis. His father, Nicomachus, was descended from the famous Homeric physician, Asclepius. According to Galen, all Asclepiad sons were trained in the arts of dissection and medicine (Ross 1), and Aristotle possibly also received such training under his father. He supposedly spent much of his boyhood at Pella, where his father was court physician and a close personal friend of the Macedonian king, Amyntas II. Both of Aristotle's parents died while he was still a boy. He had two siblings: a sister, Arimneste, who married his adoptive or foster father, and a brother, Arimnestus, probably younger, who died without issue.

Adoption

Following his parents' death, Aristotle became the ward, and possibly the adopted son, of Proxenus of Atarneus, who also became his sister's second husband. Arimneste, who must have been older than Aristotle, was a widow with one daughter, Hero, when she married Proxenus. They had one son, Nicanor. Proxenus, who was the executor or "mandatory" of Nicomachus' estate, may also have been a relative:

> When Nicomachus was about to die, he made a will in which he stipulated that Proxenus should take care of Phaestis—provided she was still alive at the time—and of the children (Arimneste, Aristotle, and Arimnestus), as well as of the whole estate. He also provided that Arimneste, who apparently had lost her first husband (Demotimus or Callisthenes), should be given in marriage to Proxenus. (It is presumed here that at the time of Nicomachus' death Arimneste was still fairly young.) Proxenus was to take care of the three children and of all matters that concerned them, including the estate (also an indication that he might have been a remote relative, for under Greek law only an agnatic relative was charged with such duties), as if he were their father and (older) brother (Chroust 78–79).

Aristotle was apparently fond of Proxenus and Arimneste, since he honored them in several ways. Most notably, after their deaths he legally adopted their son, Nicanor, and he also commissioned a memorial for his sister/mother:

> In his last will and testament, Aristotle also provides that the executors "shall see to it that the image. . . of Nicanor's mother [Arimneste], executed by Gryllion, shall be set up." By this generous gesture the testator gracefully remembers not only his departed sister, but apparently also honors his former "foster mother" to whom he must have been greatly attached. Moreover, in his last will Aristotle makes some very magnanimous provisions for Nicanor, the son of Proxenus and Arimneste, thus commemorating also his "foster parents" (Chroust 79).

Education, Marriage, and Children

Proxenus, who was thought to have been a friend of Plato, took his seventeen-year-old ward to Athens in 367 BCE and entered him into Plato's academy. Aristotle remained there for twenty years, first as a student, and later as a teacher. He left the academy around 347 BCE during a period of tension between Athens and his native Macedonia and traveled to a princedom in Asia Minor ruled by a Platonist named Hermias. There he married the prince's niece and adopted daughter, Pythias, with whom he had a daughter by the same name. His last will and testament states "that when Pythias, the daughter of Aristotle, 'shall be grown up, she shall be given in marriage to Nicanor [Aristotle's nephew and adopted son]'" (Chroust 79–80). After his wife's death, Aristotle took a Stagirian mistress named Herpyllis, who bore him a son, Nicomachus, named after Aristotle's father. Because of a clause in his will, it is believed that Aristotle either legally adopted or legitimized his son in some way:

"As to my estate and my son [Nicomachus] there is no need for me to make a special will and testament." . . . From this unusual clause it seems to follow that at one time Aristotle had adopted Nicomachus, or had formally declared him legitimate (Chroust 82).

In 343 BCE, Aristotle moved near Pella where he became the teacher of his most famous pupil, Alexander the Great. In 335 BCE, he returned to Athens where he founded the Peripatetic School, also known as the Lyceum, where he taught, sponsored research, and established a library. When Alexander the Great died in 323 BCE, Athenians began to persecute Macedonians and Aristotle fled to Chalcis, the homeland of his mother, where he died the following year. He had just passed his sixty-second birthday at the time of his death.

Works Cited

Chroust, Anton-Hermann. *Aristotle: New Light on His Life and on Some of His Lost Works.* Vol. I. South Bend, IN: University of Notre Dame, 1973.
Ross, Sir David. *Aristotle.* London: Routledge, 1995.

AUDUBON, JOHN J. (1785–1851)

Painter and Naturalist
Adoptee

Career, Major Awards, and Achievements

John James Audubon was a well-known American naturalist and artist who once resolved to paint all the birds of North America "in the size of nature and to report their life histories" (Ford vii). His major work, the *Birds of North America*, contains 453 hand-colored plates and 1,065 life-sized figures representing 489 species. Although his artwork was criticized as being too photographic and his narratives were considered too emotional and careless to suit a scientific community, Audubon is considered a great early natural historian, and his unique artwork is widely known and loved. His former home in New York, Audubon Park, is now a wildlife preserve.

Family of Origin

Audubon was born "Jean Rabin, créole de Saint-Domingue." He was the illegitimate son of Lieutenant de Vaisseau Jean Jacques Audubon, a French naval officer and merchant. His mother, a chambermaid known as Jeanne Rabin, met his father on a voyage to the Caribbean when she was twenty-five. At Les Cayes, Jeanne left her employer and moved in with Audubon and his mulatto mistress, Sanitte. Sanitte managed Audubon's estate during his absence from Les Cayes and was the mother of his four daughters, John Audubon's half-sisters: Marie-Madeleine, born in 1776, a second daughter born in 1777, Rose Bonnitte, born 1786 and Louise Françoise-Josephine, born around 1789. Although he had five children, Audubon legally adopted only the two with light skins, John and Rose, after bringing them with him to France. Audubon also had a legal wife in France, Ann Moynet, the daughter of a wine merchant friend, whom he had married when he was twenty-eight. At the time of their marriage, Ann was a childless widow and fourteen years her husband's senior. Jean Audubon seems to have divided his time between his households in France and the Caribbean.

[Courtesy of the Library of Congress]

Jeanne Rabin became ill soon after she gave birth to Audubon's only son on April 26, 1785. She died on November 11, 1785, from breast infection and island fevers. When slave rebellions broke out in Les Cayes, Audubon sold everything except his warehouse and returned to France with his son, officially listed as "Le Mr. Maison Neuve (young Mr. Newhouse), son of Mr. Audubon." A year later he went back for Rose, Sanitte's only light-skinned child. Audubon registered her as the natural daughter of himself and the "orphan daughter of Demoiselle Rabin, white" (Streshinsky 13).

Adoption

Audubon and Ann decided to legally adopt Jean and Rose, in order that the children could inherit their property. In March 1794, they began adoption proceedings, changing Jean's name to Fougére (Fern) and Rose's name to Muguet (Lily of the Valley).

Audubon was mostly away at sea and Ann brought the children up: "My mother, an extraordinarily beautiful woman, died shortly after my birth in Saint Dominguez on April 26, 1785. I was removed to France when only three years old and received by that best of women, Ann Moynet Audubon, my foster mother, and raised and cherished to the utmost of her means." (Ford 3–4).

Audubon first learned his love of nature from his father, though it was his adoptive mother who allowed him the abundant leisure in which his interests fully developed:

My father was mostly absent on duty, so that my mother let me do much as I pleased. Instead of applying closely to my studies I preferred to go with my friends in search of birds' nests, or to fish and shoot. I usually made for the field, my little basket filled with good eatables for lunch at school, but to burst with nests, eggs, lichens, flowers, and even pebbles from the shore of some rivulet by the time I came home at evening. On my father's first return from long duty at sea he complimented me on my various collections. But when he inquired as to what else I had been doing, I, like a culprit, hung my head (Ford 5–6).

Audubon's father responded by sending his son off as a naval cabin boy. He did not do well at sea, and after several miserable years he was allowed to return to his adoptive mother. She "was devotedly attached to me, completely spoiled me, hid my faults, boasted to everyone of my youthful merits, and—worst of all—said frequently in my presence that I was the handsomest boy in all France" (Ford 5).

Jean became worried that his teenage son would be conscripted into Napoleon's army. Following a baptism ceremony to please his mother, he sent the young man to Mill Grove, his property in Pennsylvania, with forged papers listing him as John James Audubon, born in the Louisiana Territory: "my father, anxious as he was that I should [not] be enrolled in Napoleon's army as a Frenchman, found it necessary to send me back to my own beloved country, the United States of America. And I came with intense and indescribable pleasure" (Audubon 9).

Marriage and Children

In 1808, Audubon married Lucy Bakewell, the daughter of a neighboring family in Mill Grove. Lucy had great faith in her husband's genius, and she stuck by him through severe failures, the worst being a complete bankruptcy and imprisonment for debt in 1819. She worked for twelve years as a governess and supported the entire family with her salary. The Audubons had two sons, John Woodhouse and Victor, both of whom became assistants to their father. In the year of their father's death, they completed and published Audubon's second work, *The Viviparous Quadrupeds of North America*. John Woodhouse Audubon produced some of the paintings, as his father's mind and eyesight had begun to fail as early as 1847 from what his biographers believe were either a series of small strokes or Alzheimer's disease. Audubon died on January 27, 1851, at the age of sixty-five.

Works Cited

Audubon, John James. *Selected Journals and Other Writings*. New York: Penguin, 1996.
Ford, Alice, Ed. *Audubon, By Himself*. Garden City, NY: The Natural History Press, 1969.
Gabler-Hover, Janet. *Dreaming Black/Writing White: The Hagar Myth in American Cultural History*. Lexington, KY: University of Kentucky Press, 2000.
Rhodes, Richard. *John James Audubon: The Making of an American*. New York: Knopf, 2004.
Streshinsky, Shirley. *Audubon: Life and Art in the American Wilderness*. New York: Villard Books, 1993.

AYANNA, CHARLOTTE LOPEZ (1976–)

Actress, Miss Teen USA 1993
Fostered, adoptee

Career, Major Awards and Achievements

Under her birth name, Charlotte Lopez, Charlotte Ayanna won the 1993 Miss Teen USA title. Her book *Lost in the System* describes winning the Miss Teen USA and Miss

Teen Vermont contests but focuses on her many years as a foster child. She dedicated the book "to all the kids in this country who are still lost in the system." She said,

> Maybe because I had been flipped around from one foster home to another when I was little, maybe because I never really felt secure, maybe because I felt so completely helpless to control anything that happened to me in the foster care system, I always loved the big talent shows, like Star Search and Miss Universe, where nobodies became somebodies and people who weren't famous went out and did the best they could and transformed their lives (Lopez 14).

Charlotte had always enjoyed performing and, after winning Miss Teen USA, she made guest appearances on *Weird Science* and *Entourage* and in the Ricky Martin music video *She's All I Ever Had*. By 2007, she had appeared in 14 movies, most notably *Jawbreaker* (1999), *The Rage: Carrie 2* (1999), *Dancing at the Blue Iguana* (2000), *Kate & Leopold* (2001) and *Love the Hard Way* (2001). In 2006 she starred as the sexy vampire in the horror-comedy *The Insatiable*.

Charlotte Lopez renamed herself Charlotte Ayanna after she discovered that Lopez was the name of her maternal grandfather who had abandoned his daughter. She says that *ayanna* is Cherokee for "blessed," and she chose it because she felt truly blessed in her life.

Family of Origin

Charlotte Ayanna was born Charlotte Lopez on September 25, 1976, in Puerto Rico. Her mother, Emma Lopez, had been born in Puerto Rico and raised in the Bronx. Emma attended high school and two years of college in Puerto Rico before returning to the United States, where she married Manuel Caraballo in 1967. Emma took their son, Duane, with her when she separated from Manuel in 1968. Unable to hold a job and showing signs of mental instability, she returned to Puerto Rico and became a welfare recipient. She believed that mysterious forces sent demons to rape her in 1975 and 1976, when Charlotte and her sister Diana were conceived (Lopez 18).

Foster Homes

Shortly after Charlotte was born, Emma put Duane and Charlotte in a temporary foster home. In 1977, Emma moved to Vermont with Duane and Charlotte, perhaps hoping to escape her demons. Social and Rehabilitation Services (SRS) intervened just prior to Diana's birth when they placed the older two children into another temporary foster home. Shortly afterward the family reunited and moved to an apartment in Manchester, Vermont. According to Charlotte, their apartment often lacked heat, electricity, furniture, and food. All three children were usually dirty and had disorders resulting from nutritional deficiencies. After Emma became violent and threatened other tenants, she was arrested, and two-year-old Charlotte, with her brother and sister, was sent to live with the Taylor family. Charlotte at first had a difficult time adjusting, but after a few weeks she decided that she wanted to stay forever.

Emma reclaimed her three children after a custody hearing, but once again they became malnourished, sick, filthy, and cold. Emma did not keep the children's appointments with doctors and speech therapists. Charlotte credits her brother for initiating a way out for the children—he attracted attention by getting into trouble. After "six long, scary months" with Emma, the children were returned to the Taylors and Emma left

Vermont. The Taylors decided to divorce and the children became separated: Duane stayed with Mr. Taylor and their son, and Charlotte and Diane were placed with another family, the Petersons, Charlotte's fourth foster home.

Charlotte loved the Petersons' trailer and felt loved by Mrs. Peterson and her mother, "Grammy," who often brought treats for the girls. She felt disliked by Mr. Peterson, who was, however, kind to Diana. When Mrs. Peterson became pregnant, the Petersons told SRS that the Lopez children would have to be placed elsewhere. "Grammy," who was divorced and had a large house and a good job, would have happily adopted the girls, but at that time there were rules against single parent adoptions.

Charlotte, now three, and Diana, a year younger, were placed with Cari and Bill Wensley. By now Charlotte badly wanted a permanent home. She repeatedly told Cari that she loved her and asked if the Wensleys would adopt her. At the same time she was afraid of everything and felt angry at everyone. She was weak from lack of exercise as a toddler, couldn't run well, and often fell. The Wensleys bought ladders for the girls to climb and gave Charlotte a tricycle. They tried to give the girls separate beds, as SRS rules required, but the girls were too insecure to sleep separately. Eventually they were given bunk beds, which they loved. They gained strength and their energy increased. Charlotte recalls learning to enjoy herself, noticing the new feeling and loving it (Lopez 31).

A new caseworker, Catherine Cadieux, located Emma and arranged for a final custody hearing. This time testimony showed that Emma had had another child and abandoned it in the parking lot of a hospital where it was rescued by a passer-by. The baby was adopted shortly thereafter. In late 1981, Charlotte and Diana were cleared for adoption. SRS asked the Wensleys if they wanted to adopt Charlotte and Diana or if the girls should be placed elsewhere. The Wensleys were considering a subsidized adoption, but at that point Catherine Cadieux left the SRS and the subject of adoption was effectively dropped. Neighbors and friends assumed that the Wensleys had already adopted the girls, and the Wensleys, Charlotte says, probably felt that since they loved the children and continued to keep them under a long-term care agreement, adoption was only a formality with no real meaning. To the girls, however, it was a symbol of love, commitment, and security.

The Wensleys were a protective and a religiously fundamentalist family and Charlotte's youthful rebellion brought them to the point of an ultimatum. Charlotte, then aged 15, was told that if she wanted to remain in their house, she had to live by their rules, but she refused to agree. The Wensleys asked if she wanted to leave, and she said, "Yes." The next morning, February 11, 1991, Mrs. Wensley drove her to a group home run by Janet Henry, a woman with a talent for dealing with "wayward, desperate, lost, victimized, and screwed-up kids" (Lopez 93). Charlotte says, "I had suddenly been transformed from a girl with a home and a family to a rejected outcast, living on the public dole, in the next thing to a prison. . . . I felt so lost, so robbed of my dignity that I thought I would lose my mind. I threw myself into academic work just to think about something besides who might still love me in this world" (102–103).

Janet Henry was successful with children, Charlotte wrote, because she had "common sense, moral authority, and a sense of humor" (99). Henry herself had been a young runaway and had raised four biological children and close to two hundred foster children. The Wensleys had intended the move to Henry's group home to be a "short-term" thing, in order to teach Charlotte a lesson, and it broke their hearts when she made the decision not to return to them (Lopez 104). The Wensleys soon formally adopted Diana.

Charlotte attended Mount Anthony High School where she made new friends on the track team and enjoyed being on the team. She also began to adjust to and enjoy the other residents at Janet Henry's home: "They were like a course in the great wide world that I had never been allowed to take before. Can *you* imagine living with fifty-three different people from completely different backgrounds over two and a half years? I tell you, it's the best education you can get" (Lopez 111).

Janet Henry encouraged Charlotte to enter the Miss Teen Vermont contest and to raise the money for the contest by asking local people to sponsor her. Charlotte found asking people for money difficult, but she enjoyed thanking them for their support after she won. Janet expressed a wish to adopt Charlotte, but Charlotte felt that being an adopted daughter in a house full of foster children would cause too much tension.

Adoption

On July 12, 1993, Charlotte, 16, left Henry's group home in Dorset, Vermont, for her seventh foster home. Her new foster mother, Jill Charles, had recently married Al Scheps, who ran an Italian deli. Jill managed a professional summer theater, The Dorset Theatre Festival, and worked as a freelance writer. She had heard Charlotte, then Miss Teen Vermont, and her sister Diana sing at the annual Foster Parents Association's Christmas party.

One of the first things Charlotte and Jill did together was to prepare for the Miss Teen USA pageant. Charlotte and Jill found a store with dresses they liked, all marked down to very low prices. At home, Jill decided that Charlotte's main event gown might not be dressy enough and asked the theater's costume designer for advice. The designer came up with some "fabulous beaded trim" and Jill stayed up until 2 A.M. adding the trim to her new daughter's dress. The total price for the dress Charlotte wore when she was chosen Miss Teen USA was $37. Since Janet had been with Charlotte during the Miss Teen Vermont contest, Charlotte told Jill that she'd like Janet to accompany her to the Miss Teen USA pageant, and Jill agreed. Al and Jill formally adopted Charlotte on March 7, 1994, when she was seventeen years old. Jill Charles died of cancer in June 2001.

Charlotte, her sister Diana, and their brother Duane were reunited in 1993 and the three siblings continue to be in contact. Ayanna feels that it is very important that adopted and fostered persons maintain contact with their biological relatives:

> I tell you, the absence of a blood connection is like a hole in your soul. To be all nurture and no nature is to be like an artificial person. If I hadn't had Diana, I think I would have gone nuts. . . . And now that I've heard that Emma had at least three more children by other men and that those kids are out there somewhere—half-brothers and sisters to the three of us—it electrifies me with curiosity and longing (Lopez 181).

Works Cited

Arenofsky, Janice. "Adoption: Teens Talk about Their Experiences." *Current Health* 22 (March 1996): 23.

Lopez, Charlotte, with Susan Dworkin. *Lost in the System*. New York: Fireside, 1996.

Sanz, Cynthia. "Crowning Glory: Foster Kid Charlotte Lopez Wins Miss Teen USA—and a Family She Can at Last Call Her Own." *People Weekly* 40 (August 30, 1993): 110.

BACH, JOHANN SEBASTIAN (1685–1750)

Classical Musician and Composer, Organist, Pianist, Music Director
Orphaned at age 9, raised by brother

Career, Major Awards, and Achievements

Johann Sebastian Bach is regarded as one of the greatest composers of all time. He was the most acclaimed member of his large family of brilliant German musicians. At age fourteen, he joined the choir at St. Michael's Church in Lüneburg and was later made the church organist in Arnstadt. In 1708, Bach was given the appointment of court organist at the ducal chapel in Weimar and began there the most productive and brilliant period of his career. The perfection of his performances earned him a widespread and illustrious reputation from his many musical tours. After one such occasion in Cassel, a prince in attendance took a diamond ring from his hand and gave it to Bach in appreciation.

Prince Leopold of Anhalt at Cothen made Bach his Kapellmeister and director of chamber music in 1717. For the next six years, he arranged and directed performances of instrumental music, writing the *Brandenburg Concertos*, orchestral suites, concertos for solo instruments and orchestra, sonatas, suites and partitas for solo instruments, and the *Well-Tempered Clavier*, a collection of forty-eight preludes and fugues.

Bach was a simple man whose only explanation for his fabulous output and achievements was that he worked hard. Neither his contemporaries nor most of his successors realized the true extent of Bach's genius. In his lifetime, he was honored primarily for his virtuosity on the organ. When, almost eighty years after Bach's death, Mendelssohn played the *Passion According to St. Matthew* in concert for the first time since Bach's own day, its enormous appeal led to a revival of other Bach compositions and so the world came to realize the greatness of this extraordinary artist.

Family of Origin and Kincare

Johann Sebastian Bach, sometimes called Sebastian to distinguish him from the other Johanns in the family, was born on March 21, 1685, in Eisenach, Germany, to Johann Ambrosius Bach, a musician, and Maria Elisabeth (Lämmerhirt) Bach, the daughter of a town councilor. Sebastian was the youngest of eight children, three of

[Courtesy of the Library of Congress]

whom died in infancy. The Bach family had been producing remarkable musicians since the sixteenth century, including many members of Sebastian's immediate family:

> The congregation of St. George's was fortunate indeed to enjoy the Sunday music provided by the Bachs, with Johann Christoph producing magnificent sounds on the organ, Ambrosius performing in a masterly manner on a stringed instrument, and little Sebastian singing in a pure soprano voice, joined by other relatives who were all intensely musical. And fortunate were the Bach children who grew up in this atmosphere of deep-rooted and natural musicianship (Geiringer 6).

Maria Elisabeth died on May 3, 1694, when Sebastian was nine years old. Although their father remarried a few months before his death on February 20, 1695, the family broke up in 1694 and the Bach children went to live with various relatives. Sebastian and his brother Jakob, who was three years older, went to live with their eldest brother, Johann Christoph Bach. Fourteen years Sebastian's senior, Christoph did not grow up with his youngest brother. After receiving his initial music training from his father, Christoph left the family shortly after Sebastian's birth to study in Erfurt with the famous organist Johann Pachelbel. Christoph was a newlywed with a child on the way when his brothers moved in and the stipend he earned as organist and music instructor at Ohrdruf was meager. Jakob stayed only a year and then returned to Eisenach to apprentice with the musician who had succeeded his father.

Education and Significant Relationships

In 1690, while his parents still lived, Sebastian entered one of Eisenbach's German schools, and in 1692 he attended the Lateinschule where Martin Luther, also from Eisenbach, had once been a student. After their deaths, Christoph sent his brothers to the Lyceum, which offered an Enlightenment curriculum of literature and writing, religion, mathematics, singing, history, and the natural sciences. Sebastian was fourth in his class when he left Ohrdruf in 1700.

Christoph trained Sebastian in music, but the boy's precocity at times seems to have aroused his elder brother's envy. Bach's biographies illustrate this with a famous story in which Christoph forbade Sebastian access to a desired collection of music:

> The pieces which his elder brother put before him were quickly mastered and exhausted, as to their technical and theoretical difficulty; he demanded more difficult tasks and loftier flights. Still, pride of seniority made Johann Christoph withhold this collection from the boy, who every day could see the object of his longing lying within the wire lattice of a bookcase. At last he stole down at night, and succeeded in extracting the roll of music through the opening of the wires. He had no light, so the moon had to serve him while he made a copy of the precious treasure. By the end of six months the work was finished—a work which none but the most ardent votary of his art could ever have undertaken. But his brother soon discovered him with the hardly won copy, and was so hard-hearted as to take it away from him (Spitta 186).

In spite of this incident, Sebastian learned much from his brother and from watching a new organ being built at his brother's church. He left his brother's household to make room in the house for Johann Christoph's increasing family:

> That Sebastian was, on the whole, not treated too harshly in Ohrdruf is apparent from his subsequent attitude toward his relatives there. He dedicated one of his early clavier works

to Johann Christoph . . . and repaid his elder brother by giving two of the latter's sons musical training in his own house (Geiringer 8).

Fifteen-year-old Sebastian and a friend, Georg Erdmann, traveled to Lüneburg where they joined the Matins Choir at Saint Michael's Church. As members of the choir, the boys received room, board, a small wage, and free schooling at St. Michael's school. Sebastian completed his final year of school in 1702.

At age 22, Bach became organist of the St. Blasius Church in Muhlhausen. His small salary was augmented by an inheritance from his maternal uncle. This allowed him to marry a cousin, Maria Barbara Bach, on October 17, 1707. The couple had seven children, of which four survived.

Maria died in 1720, and a year later Bach married Anna Magdalena Wuelcken, the daughter of a court trumpeter and herself a talented musician. Bach had thirteen children from his second marriage, and his wife inspired many important pieces, including *The Little Clavier Book of Anna Magdalena Bach*, the *French Suites,* and the *English Suites* for clavier.

In May 1723, Bach took his last job as cantor of the Thomasschule in Leipzig. He underwent an unsuccessful operation for his poor eyesight and eventually became completely blind, yet he continued to work. He produced eighteen chorales and *The Art of the Fugue* during his time of blindness. Bach's sight mysteriously returned ten days prior to his death but a stroke followed and he died on July 28, 1750, at the age of 65. Bach was buried in an unmarked grave in the churchyard of St. John in Leipzig. His remains were later moved to a sarcophagus beneath the church.

Works Cited

Geiringer, Karl. *Johann Sebastian Bach: The Culmination of an Era*. New York: Oxford, 1966.
Sadie, Stanley, ed. "Johann Sebastian Bach," *The New Grove Dictionary of Music and Musicians*. Second Edition. Vol. 2. New York: Grove Dictionaries, 2001. 309–382.
Spitta, Philipp. *Johann Sebastian Bach: His Work and Influence on the Music of Germany, 1685–1750*. Vol. I. Trans. Clara Bell and J. A. Fuller-Maitland. London: Novello, 1951.

BAIUL, OKSANA (1977–)

Figure Skater, Olympic Gold Medal 1994
Father abandoned at age 2, mother and grandparents died by age 13, fostered by skating coach

Career, Major Awards, and Achievements

Oksana Baiul won the 1994 Olympic Gold medal at the age of sixteen. She had earlier won the Ukrainian National Competition (1992), taken the silver medal at the European figure-skating competition, and won the 1993 World Championship.

Family of Origin

Oksana Baiul was born on November 16, 1977, in Dnepropetrovsk, a Ukrainian town that manufactured nuclear missiles. Her father, Sergei, left the family when Baiul was two years old, and she did not see him again until they had a reunion in 2003, when she was 26 years old. Marina Baiul, her mother, who had once been a dancer, taught French at the local school. Baiul's grandparents also lived with the family. Marina hoped that

[AP Photo/Lee Jin-Man]

her daughter would also become a ballerina, but Baiul was considered too overweight to enter the ballet schools (Baiul 9). As a remedy, her grandfather gave her a pair of ice skates just before her fourth birthday in the hope that skating would help her lose weight. The child was a natural skater and began to train at the age of five with a notable coach, Stanislav Koritek. He entered her in her first local competition by age seven, and by the age of nine, she was successfully landing the difficult triple Lutz and other jumps.

Baiul was still very young when she began to experience a series of tragedies: "But when I was ten, my life began to change. My grandfather died unexpectedly. I missed him terribly, especially his funny stories and jokes. Now I came straight home from the rink alone" (Baiul 12). Less than a year later, her grandmother died, and finally, when Oksana was thirteen, she lost her mother to ovarian cancer. After the funeral, she "ran to the one place that still felt like home: the ice rink. It was nighttime when Coach Stanislav found me at the rink. He took me to his house to live with his wife and baby daughter" (Baiul 15). A short time later, Stanislav, the coach who had trained her for almost nine years, left suddenly for a new job in Toronto: "We waited and waited. But he didn't come back. We finally learned that he had a new job and a new life in Canada. He was never coming home" (Baiul 18). Baiul was so devastated that she threw away her skates and vowed to never skate again.

Foster Homes

The young girl lived briefly with her mother's boyfriend until Galina Zmievskaya, a renowned skating coach, agreed to take her as her student and ward. Coach Koritek had contacted Zmievskaya from Canada and tried to make suitable arrangements for his gifted former student to continue her training. Zmievskaya had trained Viktor Petrenko, who had won the 1992 Olympic gold medal and who had recently married her oldest daughter, Nina. In 1992, Zmievskaya took Baiul to Odessa to live with her and her 14-year old daughter, Galya, in her three-room apartment. Coach and student began the rigorous training that turned her into a world champion.

For the 1994 Olympics, Baiul skated a program from *Swan Lake*, her mother's favorite ballet. The day before the competition, she had a serious collision with another skater, Tanja Szewczenko of Germany, and suffered a painful back and leg injury. In spite of this, the sixteen-year-old won the gold medal, beating Nancy Kerrigan and Chen Lu. She says that she skated *Swan Lake* for her mother: "I touched the medal and closed my eyes. 'This is for you, Mama'" (Baiul 42).

Following the 1994 Olympics, Oksana, Victor, Nina, Galina, and Galya emigrated to the United States and settled in Simsbury, Connecticut. Oksana, suddenly a rich, famous, and somewhat unguided teenager, went through an aftermath of associated problems. After an extended break from her career and an alcohol recovery program in 1998, Baiul resumed figure skating when she joined the Smucker's *Stars on Ice* program in 2004. Baiul lives with her fiancé, Gene Sunik, who runs a sports clothing company.

Works Cited

Baiul, Oksana. *Oksana: My Own Story*. As told to Heather Alexander. New York: Random House, 1997.

Lambert, Pam. "From Russia with Love: Strengthened by Her Sobriety and Fiancé's Support, Skater Oksana Baiul Meets the Father She Never Knew." *People Weekly* 60 (November 24, 2003): 145.

BAKER, JOSEPHINE (1906–1975)

Dancer, Singer, Comedienne
Indentured at age 8, fostered

Career, Major Awards, and Achievements

Josephine Baker was an African American entertainer who became a legend in Paris during the Jazz Age. Baker began her career in New York in 1923 as a dancer in the musical comedies *Shuffle Along* and *Chocolate Dandies*. She appeared in the floor show at the Plantation Club before accepting a lead dancing part in 1925 in *La Revue Negre*, an

[Courtesy of the Library of Congress]

American jazz theater company located in Paris. Baker soon became the star attraction with her supple, energetic, and exotic performances. She abruptly left the *Revue* for a better paying job with the French *Folies Bergère*, prompting the first of several lawsuits which she would face during her lifetime. At the *Folies*, Baker began performing her best-remembered act, in which she danced nude except for a string of rubber bananas around her waist. She established her own nightclub, Chez Josephine, in 1926. From 1928 to 1930 she covered twenty-five countries on a World Tour. She added singing and verbal comedy to her acclaimed dance performance at the Casino de Paris in 1930. Disgusted with American racial discrimination, she became a French citizen in 1937. During a trip to the United States in 1951, she was honored as the NAACP's Most Outstanding Woman of the Year.

Family of Origin

Josephine Baker was born in Saint Louis, Missouri, on June 3, 1906. She was the first child of Carrie McDonald, an unmarried laundress, and an entertainer named Eddie Carson. Baker's sister, Margaret, relates the following: "What happened was this: Mama was swept off her feet by a handsome, olive-skinned boy—a 'spinach,' as we called Spaniards—with disastrous results. His family wouldn't hear of marriage to a black girl" (Baker 5).

Baker's mother was later "taken in" (Baker 5) by a man named Arthur, who promised to raise Josephine like his own. However, when Arthur's first child, Richard, was born, Josephine was sent away to live with her Grandmother and Aunt Elvara. Baker's mixed race also seemed to cause her problems early in life:

> One day while I was helping Mama with a load of wash, I asked, "Is it true that my father was a buckra? Am I really different from the others?" Mama pushed aside her work and pulled me onto her lap. "Listen carefully, Tumpy. You're just like Richard and Margaret and baby Willie May [Carrie and Arthur's third child] even though your skin is lighter. Daddy Arthur loves you like his own. So just ignore what people say" (Baker 8).

The family lived in extreme poverty and moved often to escape creditors, eventually ending up in "Boxcar Town," East St. Louis, Illinois. Baker remembers watching with her mother from behind bushes as most of the settlement burned down during a violent racial incident around 1917.

Indenture and Foster Family

When Baker was eight years old, the family sent her to work as a live-in domestic with a white family: "Mama had explained to me that we were very poor, that Daddy couldn't find work. As the oldest child, it was up to me to help out. A white woman was coming to take me away. I was to call her Mistress and do as she said. In return she would give me shoes and a coat" (Baker 3). "Mistress" used to remove Baker's clothes before beating her "to protect them from wear" (Baker 4), and once, when the dishwater was too hot and it cracked one of her plates, Josephine's first employer "became so angry that she plunged my hand into the steaming water" (4). Baker was treated at a hospital and then returned to her mother. "Mistress" was booked for maltreating a child.

Baker next went to a family that she liked, the Masons: "The day came when I thought my life had changed for good. Mama explained that a kind white lady with no children of her own wanted to take me in and raise me like a daughter. In return, I would help take care of her beautiful house, so different from our single room" (10). It was at the Masons' that Baker created a theater stage in the basement and began to perform for neighbor children. Mrs. Mason returned Baker to her mother after Mr. Mason made a sexual advance to the girl (Baker 11).

Baker left home for good at the age of thirteen with a traveling vaudeville troupe named the "Dixie Steppers." During the 1950s Baker would bring her mother and sister Margaret to live near her in France. Carrie died in 1959.

Military Service and Significant Relationships

During World War II, Baker worked for the French Resistance, transmitted underground intelligence for the Allied forces, entertained soldiers in North Africa, and helped refugees as a Red Cross volunteer. For her wartime service, Baker was awarded the Legion of Honor and Rosette of the Resistance decorations.

Baker was a fourteen-year-old waitress when she married her first husband, Willie Wells, but the couple soon divorced. She married William Howard Baker, whose name she retained, in 1920, Jean Lion in 1937, and Jo Bouillon in 1947. During her marriage to Bouillon, Baker bought a 300-acre medieval chateau she called "Les Milandes." She populated the restored chateau with animals of all kinds, hoping that it would become a tourist attraction. Between 1954 and 1962, Baker and her husband adopted their "rainbow tribe," ten sons and two daughters from different countries and ethnic backgrounds. They made sure that each child learned his or her own native language and culture, as well as the religious practices of his or her birth family. The Bouillon adoptees are: sons Akio (Korean), Luis (Colombian), Jari (Finnish), Jean-Claude (French), Janot (Japanese), Moses (Israeli), Brahim (Arab), Mara (Venezuelan Indian), Koffi (African), and Noël (French), and daughters Marianne (French) and Stellina (Moroccan). The marriage began to fail in 1960, but the couple remained together for a few more years, as Bouillon points out:

> And it was for their sake, since they bore my name, that Josephine and I refused to divorce. . . . Josephine was unique, and, like all exceptional beings, a difficult day-to-day companion, yet together we had realized her dream, which some called madness, proving that children of different colors, races and religions could live together as brothers, seed of a common species, man (Baker viii).

They divorced in 1962, and Jo Bouillon moved to Buenos Aires. Baker began to suffer from ill health and financial problems. The problems reached their peak in 1968 when she was forcibly evicted from Les Milandes for nonpayment of a $400,000 debt. Baker and the children went to live at a villa in Monte Carlo, through the assistance of Princess Grace of Monaco, who provided the down payment. She married her last husband, American artist Robert Brady, in 1973. Josephine Baker died of a stroke on April 14, 1975, in Monaco. She was sixty-five.

Works Cited

Baker, Josephine, and Jo Bouillon. *Josephine.* New York: Harper & Row, 1976.

Johns, Robert L. "Josephine Baker." *Epic Lives: One Hundred Black Women Who Made a Difference.* Jessie Carney Smith, ed. Detroit: Visible Ink, 1993. 15–22.

Wood, Ean. *The Josephine Baker Story.* London, Sanctuary Publishing, c2000.

BALZAC, HONORÉ DE (1799–1850)

Author
Fostered

Career, Major Awards, and Achievements

Balzac was an important and influential French novelist. His most famous work was the *Comédie Humaine*, a series of novels he wrote during the 1830s. Additional works include *Scènes de la vie privée* and another series of collected novels known as his *Studies of Manners*: *Le médicin de campagne, La Femme de Trente Ans, Eugénie Grandet, Le Père Goriot, Les Chouans, Le Lys dans la vallée, Illusions perdues, Cesar Birotteau, Une passion dans le désert, Le Curé de Village, Béatrix, Ursule Mirouet, Une ténébreuse affaire, Le Cousin Pons*, and *La Cousine Bette*. Balzac began writing in the Romantic era, but his work greatly influenced and helped define later literary styles. His realism, attention to naturalistic detail, and emphasis on how the way their environment affects his characters were especially influential. His work is valued for its imagination, powers of observation, and its profound scope. Balzac primarily lived away from his parents from birth until the age of ten.

Family of Origin

Honoré Balzac was the second son of a fifty-one-year-old law secretary of peasant origins, Bernard-Francois Balzac. His mother, Anne Charlotte Laure Sallambier, had been only eighteen years old when her father, a banker, arranged her marriage in 1797. The couple's first son, Louis-Daniel, was born on May 20, 1798, and died when he was twenty-three days old. Honoré was born exactly one year later, on May 20, 1799 in Tours, France. The baby was named after St. Honoré, the saint whose feast day had just been observed.

Foster Homes

Honoré was only a few hours old when his mother sent him "out to nurse" with a gendarme's wife, who raised poultry at Saint-Cyr-sur-Loire. Balzac lived with this family until he was four, at which time his parents sent him to a dismal monastic school in Vendome. "Who can say how much physical or moral harm was done me by my mother's coldness? Was I no more than the child of marital duty, my birth a matter of chance. . . ? Put out to nurse in the country, neglected by my family for three years, when I was brought home I counted for so little that people were sorry for me" (Maurois 24). Balzac's parents rarely visited him, and he felt deserted and unwanted all his life: "My Mother [sic] hated me even before I was born" (Robb 6).

Balzac had three younger siblings. His sister Laure was also sent to Honoré's wet-nurse at the time of her birth in 1800. Balzac maintained a close relationship with her during his life. Another sister, Laurence, was born in 1802, and later a half-brother, Henry, was born. Henry, the illegitimate child of his mother and her lover, Jean de Margonne, was much loved and pampered by their mother, in cruel contrast to the treatment given to Balzac and his sisters (Robb 18). In return, this trio, whom Balzac called the "bitter fruits of conjugal duty" (Maurois 41), were scornful of Henry.

Education and Significant Relationships

Balzac rejoined his family at age ten when they moved to Paris in 1814. He studied law at the Sorbonne, but wished to become a writer. His parents did not support this

[Courtesy of the Library of Congress]

decision, and the young author was forced to live an austere existence in a bare attic, supporting himself with jobs writing sensational and melodramatic pieces. Later, when his work became known, Balzac began to display a marked attraction to the aristocracy. He got into chronic financial problems by unsuccessfully trying to emulate their wealthy and luxurious lifestyle.

The enormous volume of work he wanted to produce caused him to rise at midnight and write without stopping, sometimes for sixteen hours or more at a time, drinking incessantly his strong, black coffee. Balzac's way of working was very hard on his health and probably caused his lung problems and weak heart. One biographer attributes Balzac's drive to his feelings of maternal loss: "There are bastards of the imagination, born in wedlock, who nevertheless feel themselves to be rejected by their parents, without knowing why. These more than others long for worldly triumphs, to compensate for their deep-rooted sense of loss" (Maurois 28). Balzac was romantically drawn to older, nurturing women, probably as mother substitutes. Laure de Berny, his first such love, was twenty-three years his senior.

Balzac was the father of several illegitimate children. He had a daughter, Marie-Caroline, with Maria Du Fresnay in 1834. The Contessa Visconti-Guidoboni (born Frances Sarah "Fanny" Lovell, in Wiltshire, England) gave birth to one of his illegitimate children in 1836. A married Polish noblewoman, the Baroness Evelina Hanska, gave birth to Balzac's daughter, a stillborn infant, in 1846. After her husband's death, Baroness Hanska promised to marry Balzac, but she put off the marriage for nine years. They married on March 14, 1850. Balzac became seriously ill only a few months after the marriage. He died August 18 of the same year, at the age of fifty-one. Literary giants Victor Hugo and Alexander Dumas were pallbearers at his funeral in Paris.

Works Cited

Maurois, Andre. *Prometheus: The Life of Balzac*. New York: Harper & Row, 1966.
Robb, Graham. *Balzac: A Biography*. New York: W. W. Norton, 1994.

BANKHEAD, TALLULAH (1902–1968)

Actress
Fostered by relatives

Tallulah Bankhead was a sultry, deep-voiced stage, radio, and motion picture star. She won two New York Drama Critics Circle awards for best acting of the year for her performances in Lillian Hellman's *The Little Foxes* (1939) and in Thornton Wilder's *The Skin of Our Teeth* (1942). Her other Broadway credits include *Foolish Notion* (1945), *When the Eagle Has Two Heads* (1947), and *Private Lives* (1948). Bankhead's performance in the motion picture *Lifeboat* (1944) won the New York Film Critics Award. In 1950, she entered her radio career as mistress of ceremonies on NBC's *Big Show*, a popular variety show broadcast in the United States and England. Her autobiography, *Tallulah*, became a best-seller soon after its publication in 1952.

Family of Origin

Tallulah Brockman Bankhead was born in Huntsville, Alabama, on January 31, 1902. She was the second daughter of William Brockman and Adeline Eugenia (Sledge)

[Courtesy of the Library of Congress]

Bankhead. Her mother, who had been famous for her beauty, died soon after Tallulah's birth:

> I never knew my mother. She survived my birth by but three weeks. Her death was brought about by complications arising from my birth, but I never had feelings of guilt, even when old enough to be aware of the association of the two events. From the start I was too pampered by Daddy, by Aunt Marie and Aunt Louise, by my grandmother and grandfather, to brood over the loss of a mother I could not remember. Until her death, Grandmother was Mama to me (Bankhead 27).

Bankhead's grandmother, also named Tallulah, was the wife of Alabama senator John Bankhead. Tallulah Bankhead remembered her stern grandmother pouring buckets of cold water over her in order to control frequent childhood tantrums (Gill 200). She was said to have been a difficult, histrionic child and a "show-off" (Carrier 2).

William Bankhead, Tallulah's father, was a long-time congressman and eventually U.S. Speaker of the House. Bankhead's biographers often discuss the effects on Tallulah of her father's absence, drinking, and his obvious favoritism toward his older daughter, Eugenia. The two sisters were very different in appearance and temperament, and they had a lifelong rivalry for affection and attention (Gill 16). Bankhead credits her father for encouraging her interest in the theater:

> I was all of five when Daddy took me to Birmingham to have my tonsils removed—the start of my mezzo-basso voice. As a reward for my courage under the knife, he took me to a vaudeville show. A woman single, to use a trade term, sang slightly risqué songs as she played the piano. A born mimic, I mastered her routine overnight. . . . [Daddy] was fascinated by my impersonation. Sometimes he'd come home a little high from vin du pays—bourbon, that is—wake me up, bring me downstairs, ask me to give my impression of the Birmingham lark. Then he'd roar with laughter. I reacted violently to applause, to recognition from my elders. (Bankhead 17)

Bankhead and her sister were educated at Fairmont and Mary Baldwin seminaries and in a variety of convents, including the Convent of the Visitation in Washington, D.C., the Convent of the Holy Cross in Virginia, and the Convent of the Sacred Heart in New York. Her formal education ended when she was 14. She obtained a small film role when she entered and won a picture contest in *Picture Play* magazine. She persuaded her father, who had once wanted to be an actor himself, to let her pursue a theatrical career in New York City. At the age of 15, Tallulah Bankhead moved with an aunt into the famous Algonquin Hotel and soon made her stage debut in the play *Squab Farm* (1918).

Bankhead eloped with John Emery on August 31, 1937. They divorced in 1941. She eventually earned her increasingly wild reputation. One biographer attributed the drugs, alcohol, and sex scandals to her earliest fears of abandonment:

> All the rest of her life, Tallulah was to suffer from the fear of being deserted, of being left alone by day or night, unguarded, unnursed, unloved. She wanted parties never to end and bridge games never to end and conversations never to end. She would turn friends into prisoners, locking their hats and coats in closets to keep them from saying good-bye. Like most of us, she feared the night more than the day, and her fear increased with age; predictably, her means of dealing with it grew more and more unbecoming as they grew more unsuccessful. Drink, drugs, sex; they were for her the means by which to outwit an intolerable prospect, and they did not suffice (Gill 19).

Bankhead had no biological children; however, she sponsored several children in an international foster parent program. She contributed $180 per month for the support of each foster child until he or she was removed from the program at age 17. She actually met only one of these children, a badly injured Greek war orphan named Barbara Nicholai, who came to the United States for plastic surgery on her face. However, she corresponded frequently with the children, who included twin boys from Spain, a Maltese boy, and several Chinese children. She rarely discussed this part of her life, "probably because it didn't fit in with her image" (Carrier 2). Bankhead lived with an assortment of unusual and pampered pets, including dogs, birds, monkeys, and a lion cub named Winston Churchill. Her chain-smoking and drinking finally led to the illness that took her life on December 12, 1968, at the age of 66.

Works Cited

Bankhead, Tallulah. *Tallulah: My Autobiography.* New York: Harper & Brothers, 1952.
Carrier, Jeffrey L. *Tallulah Bankhead: A Bio-Bibliography.* New York: Greenwood Press, 1991.
Gill, Brendan. *Tallulah.* New York: Holt, Rinehart & Winston, 1972.

BARTON, BENJAMIN SMITH (1766–1815)

Botanist, Zoologist, Physician, Educator
Orphaned at age 14, raised by family friends and relatives

Career, Major Awards, and Achievements

Dr. Benjamin Smith Barton was a distinguished physician and professor of natural history and botany at the University of Philadelphia. In 1803, he created *Elements of Botany,* the first botany textbook written by an American. Other works include a *Materia Medica of the United States* (1798–1804), *Memoir Concerning the Fascinating Faculty Which Has Been Ascribed to the Rattlesnake and Other American Serpents,* (1796), *New Views of the Origin of the Tribes and Nations of America* (1797), and *Fragments of the Natural History of Pennsylvania* (1799). Barton was an influential teacher whose notable students included botanists William Darlington, Charles Wilkins Short, William Baldwin, Thomas Horsfield, and Meriwether Lewis. He was one of the curators of the American Philosophical Society from 1790–1800, and served as vice-president from 1802–1815. Between 1797 and 1807, he assembled what was then the largest herbarium of native American plants.

Family of Origin

Benjamin Barton was born on February 10, 1766, in Lancaster, Pennsylvania. He was the son of an Episcopalian minister, Thomas Barton, and Esther Rittenhouse Barton, the sister of Dr. David Rittenhouse, a distinguished scientist who became the first director of the U.S. Mint. Barton's mother died when he was eight years old. His father left Pennsylvania to embark on a trip to Europe in 1778, but he fell ill and died in May of 1780, leaving his son an orphan at age fourteen. Thomas Barton had taken care to provide for the children and Benjamin and his older brother, William, were left financially secure.

Foster Home

Benjamin went to live in the country with family friends for the first two years after his father's death. He was not an athletic young man or fond of "active bodily pursuits" (Barton 5), and his health was poor most of his life. He was, however, an excellent scholar, and his interest and talents in natural sciences and botanical drawing began to flower during these rural years. In 1780, Benjamin was sent to an academy in York, Pennsylvania, where he studied under Dr. Andrews, who was the academy's provost and a former student of Benjamin's father.

[Courtesy of the Library of Congress]

Education and Significant Relationships

In 1782, Benjamin went to live in his elder brother's household while he began college studies in medicine. The boys' uncle, Dr. Rittenhouse, noticed his young nephew's uncommon abilities and allowed him to accompany him on his research travels:

I followed in his footsteps in the wilderness of this country, where he was the first to carry the telescope, and to mark the motions and positions of the planets. In the bosom of his family, I listened to his lessons, as an humble disciple of Socrates or Plato. Science mixed with virtue was ever inculcated from his lips. But to me Rittenhouse was more than a friend and preceptor. He was a father and supporter (9).

Barton left for the University of Edinburgh to study medicine after four years at the College of Philadelphia. There he became a member of the Royal Medical Society and won a Harveian prize. In 1789, he took his MD degree at the University of Göttingen in Germany. Barton returned to Pennsylvania, where he practiced medicine and taught at the University of Pennsylvania as a professor of natural history, botany, and chair of medicine.

Barton married Mary Pennington of Philadelphia in 1797. They had two children, Thomas and Hetty. Thomas became one of the first serious American Shakespeare collectors. Benjamin Barton died of tuberculosis on December 19, 1815, at the age of forty-nine.

Works Cited

Barton, William C., MD. *A Biographical Sketch, Read Pursuant to Appointment Before the Philadelphia Medical Society, at a Stated Meeting, on Saturday, 16 February 1810, of Their Late President Professor Barton.* American Culture Series 347.4.

BATES, DAISY (1914–1999)

Civil Rights Leader, Journalist
Adoptee

Career, Major Awards, and Achievements

Daisy Bates was a newspaper journalist who became an important civil rights leader. She is best known for her landmark fight for school integration in Little Rock, Arkansas. As president of the Arkansas NAACP, she organized and mentored the "Little Rock Nine," the nine African American students who enrolled in 1957 at the formerly all-white Central High School. Reacting to the climate of threats and violence, President Eisenhower sent federal troops to Little Rock to enforce the 1954 Supreme Court decision upholding school desegregation (*Brown vs. Board of Education*). The nine students completed the school term, but those involved suffered attacks, cross-burnings, and other acts of bigotry. The Bates home was bombed and received thousands of dollars worth of damage. The *Arkansas State Press*, a civil rights newspaper founded by Bates and her husband, was closed in 1959 because of economic reprisals. For her tireless work for civil rights, Bates became a symbol of hope and courage, as well as a target of racist hate.

In 1962 she wrote an autobiography called *The Long Shadow of Little Rock*, from which all quotations here are taken. It received the American Book Award in 1988. Bates received over 200 citations and awards in the course of her long life. She and the Little Rock Nine were awarded the 1958 Spingarn Medal for upholding the ideals of democracy. She was named "Woman of the Year" by the National Council of Negro Women and the St. Louis NAACP and won the Chicago Robert S. Abbott Award. She holds honorary doctorates from Lincoln University, University of Arkansas, and Washington

[Courtesy of the Library of Congress]

University. In 1985 she reestablished and operated the Arkansas State Press. In 1996, at age 81 and in a wheelchair, Bates carried the Olympic torch in Atlanta.

Family of Origin

In 1914, Bates was born Daisy Lee Gatson in Huttig, Arkansas, a small sawmill town. She was a happy child until a neighbor boy revealed a family secret during a quarrel shortly after her eighth birthday. He told her that her first mother had been killed by a white man:

> The next day, Bates' older cousin, Early B., revealed that when Daisy was a baby, her biological mother had been kidnapped, raped, and murdered by three white men. Later, Bates visited the mill pond where her mother's body had been found. She sat for a long time at the site and when she turned around, her adoptive father was there: "It's time to go home, darling." I turned and saw my daddy sitting beside me. He reached out in the darkness and took my hand. "How long have you known?" he asked. "A long time," I said. He lifted me tenderly in his arms and carried me home. The next morning I had a high temperature (13).

Adoption

Her adoptive parents, Orlee and Susie Smith, began to answer some of the child's many questions, such as what her first parents looked like, what happened to her mother, and why her father left. Her adoptive father wanted her to "understand that my mother wouldn't have died if it hadn't been for her race—as well as her beauty, her pride, her love for my father" (15).

Daisy Bates vowed to find her mother's killers, who were never charged with the crime: "Dolls, games, even my once-beloved fishing, held little interest for me after that. Young as I was, strange as it may seem, my life now had a secret goal—to find the men who had done this horrible thing to my mother"(15). She believed that she actually was able to identify one of them, a man she called "Drunken Pig," who slept outside the local commissary. Every day until he died the child came and stood in front of him and she believed that she tormented him with her "uncanny resemblance" (16) to her mother.

In Huttig, Bates experienced the "Old Southern System" of segregation and racism, and this, compounded with her anger over her mother's murder, caused her to hate white people. She found a way to constructively focus her anger during what she called her "rebirth" at the deathbed of her adoptive father, Orlee. He told her:

> "You're filled with hatred. Hate can destroy you, Daisy. Don't hate white people just because they're white. If you hate, make it count for something. . . . Hate the discrimination that eats away at the soul of every black man and woman." . . . As I walked along the street taking in the freshness of the early morning air, I knew that as surely as my father was dying, I was undergoing a rebirth. My father had passed on to me a priceless heritage—one that was to sustain me throughout the years to come (29–31).

Education, Military Service, and Significant Relationships

At age 15, Bates fell in love with a family friend, L.C. Bates, an insurance agent. L.C. had majored in journalism at Wilberforce University. They married in 1932 and moved to Little Rock, Arkansas, where Daisy attended college at Philander Smith and Shorter. Together they started the *Arkansas State Press*. Its purpose was to fight discrimination and publicize brutality.

Bates was the sole female pilot in the Arkansas Civil Air Patrol during World War II. When Daisy Bates died on November 4, 1999, at the age of 84, her body lay in state at the Arkansas State Capitol.

Works Cited

Bates, Daisy. *The Long Shadow of Little Rock.* New York: David McKay, 1962.

BERGMAN, INGRID (1915–1982)

Actress
Orphaned by age 10

Career, Major Awards, and Achievements

Ingrid Bergman was a Swedish-born actress known internationally for her talent and beauty. She starred in such memorable films as *Casablanca* (1942), *For Whom the Bell Tolls* (1943), *Gaslight* (1944), *Saratoga Trunk* (1945), *Spellbound* (1945), *The Bells of St. Mary's* (1945), *Notorious* (1946), *Under Capricorn* (1949), *Anastasia* (1956), and *Murder on the Orient Express* (1974). Her performances in *Gaslight* and *Anastasia* won Oscars for Best Actress, and she was chosen the Best Supporting Actress for *Murder on the Orient Express.* In 1957, she was awarded the New York Film Critics Award.

Family of Origin

Bergman was born in Stockholm, Sweden, on August 29, 1917. Her mother was Friedel Adler, a German woman from Hamburg. Her father, Justus Bergman, was a Swedish artist and a photographer. Her parents operated a camera shop in Stockholm, and the family lived in the apartment above the shop:

> Their worlds were so different. My father was a bohemian, an artist, very easygoing, and my mother was the complete bourgeois. But they were very happy together. My mother had three children. The first died at birth and the other a week after birth, and I arrived seven years after that. I don't remember my mother at all. My father filmed me sitting on her lap when I was one, and then again when I was two, and at three he photographed me putting flowers on her grave (Bergman 19–20).

Kinship Care

Bergman became fond of her Aunt Ellen, who came to take care of the little girl following Friedel's death: "So when my mother died, Aunt Ellen came to us. I was three years old and really loved her and I called her Mama. She was always a bit upset about this, especially in the shops where they knew her as *Miss* Bergman" (Bergman 20). Bergman was also especially close to her father. He wanted his daughter to become an opera singer, and it was he who encouraged her interest in the stage. Her father died when she was ten years old, after a long battle with stomach cancer. Six months later, her Aunt Ellen died suddenly in Bergman's arms, before help could arrive. The girl then went to live with her Aunt Hulda and Uncle Otto until the time of her marriage: "The death of my father was of course a shattering experience, and then, only six months later, Aunt Ellen died. . . . Coming so soon after my father's death six months earlier, it was a terrible

[AP Photo]

shock, and I think inside, I really took a long time to get over it. . . . Uncle Otto and Aunt Hulda did everything they could. They were a hard-working, middle-class Swedish family, and I started a new life in that house with my five cousins" (Bergman 25).

Education and Significant Relationships

Bergman attended a private school for girls in Stockholm until she was seventeen. She describes herself as lonely, shy, and self-conscious about her tallness. She had a pronounced love of acting and a natural gift for drama, but her family didn't approve of her career choice. Despite their resistance, she passed the difficult entrance examination to the School of the Royal Dramatic Theatre and began her studies there in 1933. While there, she attracted the attention of a Swedish film industry talent scout and thus began her film career. She was fluent in five languages and soon became a versatile international star. Early in her career, Bergman met her future husband, Petter Lindstrom, then a medical student in Stockholm. They were married in 1937 and their daughter Pia was born the following year.

Bergman had become impressed with the films of Italian director Roberto Rossellini, and she wrote to him in 1948, offering to make a film with him. He accepted her offer and in 1949 she arrived in Italy to begin work on *Stromboli* (1950). Bergman fell in love with Rossellini and gave birth to his son, Robertino, shortly before *Stromboli* was released. The romance created a scandal, and Bergman found herself ostracized by much of the American public. She obtained a heavily disputed divorce from Lindstrom in May 1950 and married Rossellini in Mexico, by proxy. The couple had twin daughters, Isabella and Ingrid Rossellini, in June 1952. The scandal slowly abated during the "sexual revolution" of the 1960s and 1970s, and Bergman's popularity returned. She won an Emmy award in 1982 for her performance as Golda Meir, though she was terminally ill with breast cancer throughout the filming. She died in London on her sixty-seventh birthday, August 29, 1982.

Works Cited

Bergman, Ingrid, and Alan Burgess. *Ingrid Bergman: My Story*. New York: Delacorte Press, 1980.

Chandler, Charlotte. *Ingrid: Ingrid Bergman, a Personal Biography*. New York: Simon & Schuster, c2007.

Steele, Joseph Henry. *Ingrid Bergman, an Intimate Portrait*. New York: D. McKay Co., 1959.

BERNHARDT, SARAH (1844–1923)

Actress and Artist
Illegitimate child, raised by a nurse and other guardians

Career, Major Awards, and Achievements

Sarah Bernhardt was the French tragedienne whose extraordinary talent and sixty-year career made her the most famous actress ever produced by the Western world.

During her mid-twenties, Bernhardt enjoyed a brilliant six years (1866–72) at Théâtre de l'Odéon, the second-ranked theater in Paris. Only the Comédie-Française was considered a more prestigious theatre. Early reviews of her work were unenthusiastic, but in

[Courtesy of the Library of Congress]

1868, playing the part of Anna Damby, the female lead in *Kean,* Alexandre Dumas *père's* play about the English Shakespearean actor **Edmund Kean**, she won the recognition that would soon make her one of the best known women in the world. The following year she played Zanetto, a male troubadour, in *La Passant*; this is considered her first major success.

During the Franco-Prussian War, she left the theater briefly (1870–72) to open a hospital with herself as head nurse. At the end of the war, she returned in triumph and was hired by the Comédie-Française for the role of Junie in *Britannicus*, the play that had first inspired her to become an actress. She became a phenomenon. If she starred in a production, it was an inevitable success. If the male lead was also a star of the first magnitude, critics and public alike were nearly hysterical with enthusiasm.

In 1879, she led the Comédie-Française to success in its first London engagement but then left the company after a disagreement. Returning to London, she formed a company of her own and traveled to Belgium and Denmark before making the first of several very successful tours of the United States in 1880. The company toured fifty-one cities, often performing the favorite of her American audiences, *La Dame aux Camélias* (*Camille*), written by **Alexandre Dumas, *fils***. She is said to have appeared nearly 3000 times in both *La Dame aux Camélias* and *Phèdre*. Her third favorite was the title role of Eugene Scribe's *Adrienne Lecouvreur*.

In 1886 the company toured Latin America and added *La Tosca*, by Sardou, to their list of successes. Sardou, who directed Bernhardt in this and others of his own plays, is given credit for changing her style, making it broader and more flamboyant, and staging productions that featured more elaborate and exotic sets and costumes.

In 1889 the 45-year-old Bernhardt portrayed a 19-year-old Joan of Arc with her usual great success. In 1900 she established her own theater, the Theatre Sarah Bernhardt, where she would perform until her death in 1923. In 1900 also, she played the part of Napoleon's young son in *L'Aiglon*. In 1914 "the Divine Sarah" was made a Chevalier of the Legion d'Honneur.

The amputation of a leg the following year, due to either illness or an old stage injury, did little to stop her. If she became less mobile, her voice never failed to enthrall a worldwide audience as she continued to tour, sometimes playing male roles, most famously that of Hamlet, and to perform in her own theater.

In addition to her brilliant acting career, Bernhardt had a less well-known but successful career as a sculptor, producing fifty known works, exhibiting at the Paris Salon from 1875 to 1886 (winning a silver medal in 1876) and at the 1990 Exposition Universelle in Paris, and having individual shows in London (1879) and New York (1880). She was an important patron of two major Art Nouveau artists, René Lalique and Alphonse Mucha, and a friend of Gustav Doré. Mucha was responsible for a number of the posters advertising Bernhardt's theatrical productions during the 1890s; reproductions of these striking posters enjoyed a vogue during the 1960s and 70s.

Her published writings include *My Double Life* (1907), *The Art of the Theatre* (1925), *The Memoirs of Sarah Bernhardt: Early Childhood through First American Tour*, and the novella *In the Clouds* (ed. Sandy Lesburg, 1977). She made eight motion pictures and two documentaries about her life.

Family of Origin

The exact details of Bernhardt's life are controversial and difficult to ascertain, as she notoriously changed and enhanced many events. Other details were lost, unknown, or deliberately obscured by others. Referring to her first volume of memoirs, one biographer wrote: "While [*My Double Life*] seems to present a woman of disarming frankness, a closer reading reveals the prototypical actress impersonating—and consummately— a character called Myself" (Gold 9).

Sarah Bernhardt was baptized at the convent at Grandchamps when she was eleven years old. According to her baptismal certificate of May 21, 1856, Sarah Bernhardt was born Sarah Rosine Marie Henriette Bernhardt.* Her mother was Julie Van Hard, a young, unmarried woman who had been born in Rotterdam, Holland, in 1823 to Dutch parents. Julie's mother, Lisa, was a dressmaker of Jewish ancestry and her father, Gustave, was a bookkeeper and a devout Catholic. Following Gustave's death, the three elder of the couple's six children, Julie, Rosine, and Henriette, left Holland. Julie, the third daughter, was fourteen when she and her sisters traveled to Germany and later, to Paris. Julie had been apprenticed as a milliner or dressmaker, but she was probably also working as a prostitute around the time of Sarah's birth. By 1850, she was a well-known courtesan, and her salon was frequented by an upper-class clientele, including Dumas *père*, Rossini, and the Duc de Morny, who bequeathed her a large fortune. Julie died in 1876.

Julie gave birth to twin girls in Le Havre, France, on April 22, 1843, but both babies died during their first two weeks of life. Sarah was the first of Julie's surviving three daughters, each fathered by a different man. Jeanne, Julie's second child, was born when Sarah was seven or eight. Règina, the third child, was born in 1854 and died at the age of twenty.

Edouard Bernhardt** is the name given as Sarah's father on her baptismal certificate, but the name was possibly a pseudonym used by her mother to conceal the child's illegitimacy. Many sources say that her father is unknown. Verneuil, an important biographer and close friend of Bernhardt, supports Sarah's claim that her father, Edouard Bernhardt, was a law student from Rue des Arcades, Havre, France, who recognized his daughter, gave her his name, and died in 1857 (29–30).

Guardianship

Sarah was born in Paris on October 23, 1844, and was immediately sent away to live with a peasant wet nurse near Quimperlé, Brittany, for her first four years. Though many babies sent "away to the country" perished there, young Sarah lived to return with her nurse to the Rue de Provence in Paris, though she was in fragile health and may have had tuberculosis. Until she was sent to boarding school around age seven, Sarah was cared for by her nurse, whose own baby was dead and who "loved in the way that poor people love—when she had the time" (Bernhardt 3) and by other guardians. The opening paragraphs of Bernhardt's first memoir, *My Double Life*, show a great deal of bitterness about her mother's neglect:

> My mother loved to travel. She would go from Spain to England, from London to Paris, from Paris to Berlin—from there to Christiania; then she would come home to kiss me and set off again for Holland, the country in which she was born. She would send my nurse clothes for her and cakes for me. She would write to one of my aunts, "Look after little Sarah, I'll be back in a month." A month later she would write to another sister, "Go and see the child at her nurse's, I'll be back in two weeks."
>
> My mother was nineteen, I was three. One of my aunts was seventeen, the other twenty. . . . My young aunts would promise to come and see me, but rarely kept their word (Bernhardt 3).

---

*Bernhardt's name has a number of variations, including Sara-Marie-Henriette Rosine Bernard; Henriette Rosine Bernard; Marie-Henriette Bernardt and Henriette-Rosine Bernard. She is sometimes given credit for adding the *h* to both Sarah and Bernhardt. Her mother's name also has several variations.

**Edouard's name has variations of Bernard and Bernardt. Gold and Fizdale note that Sarah's uncle, Edouard Ker-Bernhardt, had possibly been her father instead (11). The *Dictionnaire de Biographie Française* listed Sarah's parentage as "a Jewish courtesan, Julia Bernardt, and the naval officer, Paul Morel" (Aston 1)

Education and Significant Relationships

At the age of seven or eight, around the time of her sister's birth, Sarah was sent to a boarding school, Institution Fressard, and in 1853, at age nine, she entered an Augustine convent school called Grandchamps, near Versailles. Her first acting role was at the convent school, where she played the Queen of the Fairies in *Clothilde*. This was also her first experience with stage fright, which would stay with her for the rest of her long career.

Possibly because her health was precarious, Sarah became deeply interested in religion and death. From the time she was ten, she hoped to become a nun, and she persuaded her mother to buy her a casket, in which she sometimes slept. Later in life, she identified herself as an atheist. When Sarah was fifteen, she developed pleurisy and was brought home to her mother's salon to convalesce. Sarah completed her education with a private tutor, Mademoiselle de Brabender.

Bernhardt found her real vocation at fifteen, when she was taken to the Comédie-Française to see *Britannicus*, by Jean Racine. She became so caught up in the drama that she burst into incontrollable tears until she was consoled by Alexandre Dumas, *père*, one of the greatest of the nineteenth-century French playwrights. He is said to have declared that Sarah would be an actress. Other biographers say that the Duc de Morny, her mother's lover, made the decision. Most agree that he arranged an audition for Sarah at the Paris Conservatoire in 1859 and that she was immediately accepted through his influence:

> At the age of almost sixteen years she had never thought of acting. In order to take her off her mother's hands, who did not like her, one of the latter's lovers said one fine day: "Why not try and make an actress of her?" In order to get away from her mother, whose life as a kept woman shocked her, Sarah replied: "All right, let us try" (Verneuil 41).

The school was a stepping stone to the Comédie-Française, and after two years, she made her debut there as Iphigénie in *Iphigénie en Aulide*. She was given more roles but continued to make no particular impression on the public or the critics. Dismissed from the company for fighting with another actress, she found a position as an understudy in a small theater and then apparently gave up on acting as a career.

Her only child, Maurice Bernhardt, was born on December 22, 1864, the son of a Belgian nobleman with whom Sarah had had an affair. Sarah was twenty years old at the time of her son's birth.

Having rejected the stage, Bernhardt may have realized that it was what she truly wanted, and she became determined to do the work necessary. In *The Art of the Theatre*, written much later, she indicated that she had always considered the voice as the actor's most important asset in revealing character, and it was after her return to the theater that critics began praising her voice, calling it "golden," "silvery," or "flute-like." Sigmund Freud, who first saw Bernhardt in 1885, when he was a student in Paris, wrote of her "lovely, vibrant voice" (Gold 4). After her son was born, she took small roles until in 1866 she was hired by the Odéon, where, after two years of intense work with a company she found congenial, she entered theatrical history.

In 1882 she married Jacques Damala, a Greek actor. A separation or divorce followed, attributed to Damala's morphine addiction. Damala died in 1889. Bernhardt's marriage cost her her French citizenship, which was not restored until 1916. Throughout her career, her name was connected romantically to various men, often artists or actors.

During the late 1880s, it was rumored that she had an affair with the Prince of Wales (later King Edward VII).

Sarah Bernhardt died on March 26, 1923, of uremia. She was being cared for by her son. She is buried in the Père Lachaise Cemetery in Paris. Her star on the Hollywood Walk of Fame is located at 1751 Vine Street.

Works Cited

Aston, Elaine. *Sarah Bernhardt: A French Actress on the English Stage.* Oxford: Berg Publishers, 1989.

Bernhardt, Sarah. *My Double Life: The Memoirs of Sarah Bernhardt.* Albany, NY: The State University of New York Press, 1999.

Gold, Arthur, and Robert Fizdale. *The Divine Sarah: A Life of Sarah Bernhardt.* New York: Alfred A. Knopf, 1991.

Verneuil, Louis. *The Fabulous Life of Sarah Bernhardt.* Trans. Ernest Boyd. Westport, CT: Greenwood Press, 1942.

BLAKEY, ART (1919–1990)

Drummer, Band Leader
Fictitious birth story, kincare, runaway

Career, Major Awards, and Achievements

Art Blakey was one of the world's greatest drummers and was the pioneer of "hard bop," a style of bebop music that uses the drums as the leading instrument rather than a supporting one. Blakey headed the group known as the Jazz Messengers for thirty-four years. He recruited and mentored many new musicians and is credited with the discovery of such jazz greats as Wynton Marsalis, Freddie Hubbard, McCoy Tyner, Donald Byrd, and Keith Jarrett. Blakey was inducted into the *DownBeat* Hall of Fame in 1981. The Jazz Messengers won a Grammy Award for best instrumental performance by a jazz group in 1984 and their *Live at Sweet Basil* album won Japan's Gold Disc Award.

Art Blakey was born on October 11, 1919, in Pittsburgh, Pennsylvania. His mother, Marie Roddericker, had been abandoned by her husband on their wedding day:

> My father used to sneak out—because my mother was very pretty, and he used to sneak out and see her. She lived out in the country. So I happened along. They had a shotgun wedding, you see. They had this big church wedding, and they came out and got in the carriage. My mother was carrying me at that time, and he rode two blocks and got out of the carriage and went into the drugstore to get some cigars, and he went out the back door and went to Chicago. And after sitting out there for four or five hours—she was so stunned about it—she was very stunned, very hurt, and really they say she really didn't care [about anything after that]. She died of a broken heart. She just gave up and took about four or five months to die (Enstice 18–19).

According to Blakey, his paternal relatives would not accept the child because of their racial prejudice:

> You see I was sort of an orphan, and I was rejected by my father's parents. My mother died when I was six months old, and I was rejected by his parents. And they even had racial prejudice in my family—on my father's side was mulatto, and my mother, who was very, very

[AP Photo]

black. Her father—my grandfather—and my great-grandfather, who I knew were all descendants of Africa, were very black people. And the part of Africa where they come from was Guinea, West Africa (Miller 82).

Blakey was taken in by his mother's first cousin, Sarah Parran. He describes her as a hard-working woman with a strong sense of dignity and honor. Blakey and his foster mother both worked at the Jones and Laughlin steel mill. The young teen had the dangerous job of pouring melted steel into giant cauldrons. Blakey once remarked in a *DownBeat* interview (11/79) that he never had a childhood. "She let me stay there, and I always felt that guilt, and I always felt that I had to work. I would work and go to school" (18–19). Blakey also played music at night with other students at his junior high school. His foster mother had never told Blakey about his origins. When he was thirteen, Sarah's two children told him that Sarah was not his real mother. The news upset him so much that he ran away: "The news just tore me up.... When I found that out, I didn't say nothing. I just split" (*Current Biography* 1988).

Blakey married Clarice Stewart at the age of fourteen and became a father at fifteen. He learned to play drums in order to survive: "so that's how I started playing drums—I had to survive.... I was working day and night and goin' to school. 'Cause I wanted to support myself and I wanted to help the woman who raised me, so I left there. And I took the band, and I went out on the road, and we worked" (Enstice 20–21).

Blakey married four times. He has seven biological children and five adopted children. In 1947, Blakey made a trip to Africa to study philosophy. While there, he embraced the Islamic faith and took the new name Abdullah Ibn Buhaina. Blakey died in New York on October 16, 1990, from lung cancer. He was 71.

Works Cited

"Art Blakey." *Current Biography*. New York: H. W. Wilson, 1988.

Enstice, Wayne, and Paul Rubin. *Jazz Spoken Here: Conversation with Twenty-Two Musicians.* Baton Rouge: Louisiana State University Press, 1992.

Miller, Jim. "Surviving the Blues." *Newsweek* 98 (July 13, 1981): 82.

BRADY, JOHN GREEN (1848–1918)

Governor of Alaska 1897–1906, Missionary and Minister
Orphan train rider, adoptee

Career, Major Awards, and Achievements

President McKinley appointed John Green Brady as the territorial governor of Alaska in 1897. Theodore Roosevelt reappointed him to a second and third term, but Brady resigned as governor in 1906, following an inquiry into his relationship with the Reynolds-Alaska Development Company. He had originally gone to Alaska in 1878 as a minister with the Presbyterian Board of Home Mission to Alaska. Brady was best known for his charitable projects, the establishment of an industrial school for Alaskan natives in Sitka, and his active interest in developing the vast Alaskan territory.

Family of Origin

John Brady was born on Roosevelt Street in New York City on May 25, 1848, to Irish-American parents. His mother died when he was a toddler, leaving him with his alcoholic and brutal longshoreman father:

> When he was past seven the boy found the beatings in his home past endurance. He determined not to go back to this place of agony. It seemed simple enough to his childish brain. And it was no great feat, in fact. His father was sick of him. The boy struggled for some months. Between the meager sale of newspapers, and such sporadic generosities as passing old ladies and occasional drunks afforded, the boy managed to get through the summer; but winter found him ragged, penniless, and freezing. He couldn't carry the fight much further.
>
> One bad night a policeman wakened him, where he lay curled up in a doorway near the old Chatham Street Theatre. The boy denied having a home, and begged to be taken in. The

[Courtesy of the Library of Congress]

officer arrested him out of pure pity, put him into a warm cell for the night and saw that he had food. The next morning the boy went to [an orphanage on] Randall's Island and was later placed in the care of the Children's Aid Society. He was now eight years old (Children's Aid Society, 1919, 12).

Orphan Train and Adoption

In 1859, Brady went west with twenty-six other boys from Randall Island on an "orphan train," a program created by Charles Loring Brace, a Methodist minister. Homeless children traveled by trains across the United States in the hopes that they would find adoptive homes. Brady's lifelong friend, Andrew H. Burke, another Irish-American boy who rode the same train, was also adopted during the trip. He grew up to become governor of North Dakota in 1890.

Brady was adopted under the terms of the Children's Aid Society, Loring's charity, in Noblesville, Indiana, by Judge John Green, and took Green as his middle name. Judge Green described the children of that train as "'the most motley crew of youngsters I ever did see.' He took John Brady home because he considered him the 'homeliest, toughest, most unpromising boy in the lot,' and he had a desire to see what he could do for the boy" (Pearson). Although Brady was treated kindly and given a good education, he left Green's household while still an adolescent after a quarrel about his career choice (Children's Aid Society, 1919, 12). Green wanted Brady to follow his example and enter the law profession, but the boy was determined to become a minister.

Education

Brady went to a small college in the west and around 1870 passed the entrance examinations at Yale. After graduating from Yale four years later, he completed a degree at the Union Theological Seminary. Brady continued to support and correspond with the Children's Aid Society all of his life. They said of him: "To all this striking achievement, one detail of wonder needs to be added. John Green Brady never forgot his origin or those first benefactors who took him away from his brutalized father. He bore the marks of his childish beatings to his grave. But no less did he bear the marks of the kindnesses done him" (Children's Aid Society, 1919, 13–14).

Already ill with diabetes, Brady died from a stroke on December 17, 1918. He is buried in Sitka, Alaska.

Works Cited

Children's Aid Society. *Fifty-Eighth Annual Report.* New York: Children's Aid Society, 1910.
———. *Sixty Seventh Annual Report.* New York: Children's Aid Society, 1919.
Pearson, Michelle. "New Homes, New Lives: The Era of the Orphan Trains." *America's Past* (Web site). 24 June 2002. http://www.americaspast.com/article1007.html

BRAGG, WILLIAM HENRY (1862–1942)

Scientist, Nobel Prize for Physics, 1915
Fostered by relatives

Career, Major Awards, and Achievements

Sir William Henry Bragg invented the X-ray spectroscope and together with his eldest son, Sir W. Lawrence Bragg, founded the science of X-ray crystallography. The

[AP Photo]

spectroscope William Bragg built allowed scientists to use X-rays to explore the structures of various crystals. This pioneering discovery was an important foundation for such fields as molecular biology, materials science, and mineralogy. For their contributions to science, the Braggs jointly won the 1915 Nobel Prize for Physics.

Sir William Bragg was a professor of Physics at Adelaide University in Australia from 1886 to 1909 and then returned to England as the Cavendish professor at Leeds. In 1915, he became a Professor of Physics at London University. He held the post of Resident Professor and Director of the Royal Institution Laboratories from 1923 until his death in 1942. In addition to the Nobel Prize, Bragg's many awards included the Rumford Medal (1916) and the Copley Medal (1930) of the Royal Society. He was knighted in 1920 and received the Order of Merit in 1931. President of the Royal Society from 1935 to 1940, Bragg was also a member of the leading scientific academies of other countries. He held sixteen honorary doctorates from British and foreign universities.

Family of Origin

William Henry Bragg was born on his parents' farm near Wigton, Cumberland, on July 2, 1862. His father, Robert John Bragg, a retired merchant marine officer, was in London attending the International Exhibition of 1862 on the day his first child was born. William's mother, Mary (Wood) Bragg, was a vicar's daughter. The Braggs had two more sons, Jack and James, before Mary died in 1869, leaving her husband with three very young children:

> I do not remember my mother very well, as she died when I was barely seven. Just a few scenes remain. I think she must have been a sweet and kind woman. I remember how one day I was sitting on the kitchen table, and she was rolling pastry, and how I suddenly found I could whistle: and how we stared at one another for a quiet moment amazed and proud of the new accomplishment (5).

She had a "mathematical head" (14), which clearly lived on in her son and grandson.

William was only seven when his father sent him to live with his grandmother and two uncles, while his younger brothers remained with their father. Uncle William had been apprenticed to a chemist at age twelve, after his own father had been lost at sea. The extended family lived over a chemist shop owned and managed by Uncle William. Young William was raised with his cousin, Fanny Addison, and her brother, Willy: "When I was taken in 1869 to live at Harborough there were my two uncles, my grandmother [Bragg] and Fanny Addison [Aunt Mary's daughter]. I don't quite know how my Uncle managed to collar both Fanny and myself. I suppose our respective parents were talked to and forced to give us up" (17). Uncle William was "a fine character" and "rather domineering" (16) and Uncle James was "a dear kind man, very simple and earnest, repressed and overpowered by Uncle William" (17).

Education and Significant Relationships

When William was thirteen, his father sent him to King William's College, where he proved to be a gifted student: "In 1875 my father came to Harborough and demanded me. . . . I think he became alarmed lest he should lose me altogether" (19). In 1881, Bragg entered Trinity College, Cambridge, where he distinguished himself in mathematics. After graduation, Bragg left for Australia, where he was appointed professor of mathematics and physics at the University of Adelaide. William's brother Jack, whom their father thought "the cleverest of the family" (21), died suddenly in 1885, a few days before William embarked. William's father also passed away the same year, at the age of 55. The remaining brother, James, entered King William's College four years after William left.

Bragg met his bride, Gwendoline Todd, in Adelaide. She was the youngest child of Sir Charles Todd, Inspector of Telegraphs, Government Astrologer, and Postmaster in South Australia. William and Gwendoline married in 1889 and had three children. William Lawrence, the eldest son, inherited his father's interests and shared the Nobel Prize with his father. The second son, Robert, was killed at Gallipoli during World War I. Their youngest child, Gwendoline Mary (Bragg) Caroe, became her father's biographer. She characterized him as a kind and humble family man, who was "undemanding and self-effacing" and "too shy to make intimate friends" (172–73). Bragg died in London on March 12, 1942, after a brief illness.

Works Cited

Caroe, G. M. *William Henry Bragg 1862–1942: Man and Scientist.* Cambridge: Cambridge University Press, 1978.

BRAKHAGE, STAN (1933–2003)

Film Director, Author, Educator
Adoptee, fostered

Career, Major Awards, and Achievements

Stan Brakhage was an avant-garde American filmmaker, author, and educator. He is best known for his many experimental, poetic, visionary, and intensely personal films:

[Courtesy of Marilyn Brackhage, for the estate of Stan Brakhage]

I grew very quickly as a film artist once I got rid of drama as prime source of inspiration. I began to feel all history, all life, all that I would have as material with which to work would have to come from the inside of me out rather than as some form imposed from the outside in. I had the concept of everything radiating out of me, and that the more personal and egocentric I would become, the deeper I would reach and the more I could touch those universal concerns which would involve all man (*World Film Directors* 1987).

Brakhage received many independent filmmaker awards, including the Maya Deren Creative Film Foundation (1954), the Maya Deren Award for Independent Film and Video Artists (1986), the James Ryan Morris Award (1979), the Telluride Film Festival Medallion (1981), and the MacDowell Medal (1989). The Telluride Film Festival and the Denver International Film Festival each presented him with a Lifetime Achievement Award in 1998. The Museum of Modern Art featured four retrospectives of his work, in 1971, 1977, 1995, and 2001.

The following is a partial list of his more than 350 films:

Interim (1952)
Desistfilm (1954)
In the Way to Shadow Garden (1954)
In Between (1955)
Reflections on Black (1955)
The Wonder Ring (1955)
Flesh of Morning (1956)
Daybreak (1957)
Whiteye (1957)
Loving (1957)
Anticipation of the Night (1958)
Wedlock House: An Intercourse (1959)

Window Water Baby Moving (1959)
Cat's Cradle (1959)
Sirius Remembered (1959)
The Colorado Legend (1959)
The Ballad of the Colorado Ute (1959)
Blue Moses (1962)
O Life—A Woe Story—The A-Test News (1963)
Mothlight (1963)
Dog Star Man (1961–1964) and its extended version, *Art of Vision* (1961–1965)

Dog Star Man was selected by the Library of Congress in their first group of historically important films to be preserved. Other films include

Fire of Waters (1965)
23rd Psalm Branch (1966–67)
Scenes From Under Childhood (1967–1970)
The Horseman, the Woman, and the Moth, (1968)
Lovemaking (1968)
The Weir Falcon Saga (1970)
The Machine of Eden (1970)
The Act of Seeing With One's Own Eyes (1971)
The Peaceable Kingdom (1971)
The Process (1972)
The Riddle of Lumen (1972)
The Shores of Phos: A Fable (1972)

The Presence (1972)
The Wold-Shadow (1972)
Sincerities and Duplicities series (1973–1980)
He Was Born, He Suffered, He Died (1974)
Star Garden (1974)
The Text of Light (1974)
The Stars Are Beautiful (1974)
The Governor (1977)
The Domain of the Moment (1977)
Creation (1979)
Murder Psalm (1980)
Arabics (1980–82)
The Garden of Earthly Delights (1981)
Tortured Dust (1984)

The Loom (1986)
Jane (1986)
Confession (1986)
The Dante Quartet (1987)
Kindering (1987)
Faust Series (1987–1989)
Rage Net (1988)
Visions in Meditation 1–4 (1989–1990)
Babylon Series (1989–1990)
Vision of the Fire Tree (1990)
Passage Through: A Ritual (1991)
A Child's Garden and the Serious Sea (1991)
The Mammals of Victoria (1994)

Black Ice (1994)
Chartres Series (1994)
I Take These Truths (1995)
Cannot Exist (1995)
Cannot Not Exist (1995)
Spring Cycle (1995)
Ellipses 1–5 (1998)
Persian Series (1999–2001)
The God of Day Had Gone Down Upon Him (2000)
Love Song (2001)
Panels for the Walls of Heaven (2002)
Chinese Series (2003)

Metaphors on Vision, Brakhage's first book, was published in 1963. The *Brakhage Scrapbook* (1982) contains more of his collected writings from 1964 to 1980. Material from these earlier works was reissued in a publication called *Essential Brakhage* (2001). Another book featuring Brakhage is called *Film at Wit's End: Eight Avant-Garde Film-makers* (1989). He has published numerous articles, some of which were collected in the posthumously published volume *About Time: Essays of a Visionary Filmmaker* (2003).

Brakhage was an instructor at the Art Institute of Chicago from 1969 to 1981. His Art Institute lectures were published as *The Brakhage Lectures* (Chicago: Goodlion, 1972). A larger selection of his lectures was published as *Film Biographies* (Berkeley: Turtle Island, 1977). He began lecturing at the University of Colorado in the late 1950's and taught film history and aesthetics there from 1981–2002. He was made a Distinguished Professor of Film Studies at the University of Colorado in 1994.

Family of Origin

Stan Brakhage was born on January 14, 1933, in the Willows, a home for unwed mothers in Kansas City, Missouri. He tried to search for his origins, but was unable to locate any birth family members:

> The closest success I had is that someone secretly copied the records in the Missouri archives and gave me the name Mirabel Sanders. They declared that she was my mother, that she came out of Indiana, that she was a typist, that she worked in a law office, and that she was allowed to work until the sixth or seventh month of pregnancy, which was unusual in those days, that she was a violinist, that she went to work for the Willows in order to pay for her own internment. The Willows was essentially set up in Kansas City, Missouri, for wealthy, pregnant mothers, young mothers, unmarried mothers, and she went to work for them and helped pay for her own internment, and delivery of myself.
>
> I was told by my adopting parents that my father was killed in an automobile accident, and my mother died of a broken heart. That obviously wasn't true. . . . I don't know if it was true or not, maybe the records were untrue. I don't really know who my parents were. There's always a kind of sense that I'm Moses left among the bulrushes of the Missouri River (Brakhage, personal interview, March 16, 2001).

Adoption and Foster Homes

When he was three weeks old, Brakhage was adopted in Kansas City, Missouri, by a Midwestern teacher and his wife. For as long as he could remember, Brakhage knew he had been adopted. When Stan was six, his parents separated, and he settled in Denver with his adoptive mother and an alcoholic boyfriend. His mother had many subsequent boyfriends, and she would place her young son into foster homes during these relationships. Brakhage was abused by his adoptive and foster parents and by other children in the foster homes:

My adopting parents divorced before I was eight years old, or separated anyway, and then later divorced, so I had a rough upbringing. I think I was adopted in order to try and save a rather hopeless marriage, and my first task on earth was a total failure. They were a respectable couple, but in fact he was a homosexual, a suppressed homosexual, who finally had to break loose of the marriage and go off on his own. My adopting mother was very frustrated, and took a lot of that out on not only him, but on me. So, it was altogether a very bad upbringing and childhood experience. The thing that I remember happily about it was that I was very religious. I chose a church, Episcopalian, and became a choirboy and sang for the St. John's Cathedral in Denver. I had a lot of creative things that I did along the way that were really done for God, in a deep religious sense, and that sustained me very much through my growing up in what was otherwise an almost continually appalling circumstance.

I was put out in a number of homes, including military-type schools, and so on, and I had a really tough childhood in that sense. My mother had separated from my father and took me to Denver. She had a lot of other boyfriends, and I was a hindrance in that regard, so I was put out in a variety of homes—at least seven. I was in most of them for at least a year. The military type home was called Harmony Hall. The kids used to call it "Harmony Hell." It was a really awful situation. Dickens would find it hard to make it believable. There was real abuse, real cruelty to the children. There were seven different families or households, let's put it that way, in which I was raised during this period, including Harmony Hall. In north Denver there were two very unhappy circumstances. I flirted with crime while I was there. At one point, tired of being beaten up by bullies for being the smart kid in the class, and being fat, and wearing glasses, and so on, I stole to hire bullies to protect me, and I ran a gang. I taught children how to shoplift, and I took 50 percent of the take. I had a whole crime scene going in north Denver among the families that I was put out to. One day I just disbanded the gang and decided that crime didn't pay, or whatever, and that this wasn't what I wanted to be. I suffered a great deal from the reprisals from those that I'd been ruling over. So, you can see that this was a really disturbed childhood.

I didn't see my father again until I was 17. I did develop a very fine relationship with him, finally. Whereas with my mother, our relationship came to be very strained because of the way she treated her grandchildren, my grown children. Oh, I took care of all of her additional needs, you know, as she was in an old peoples' home. But I didn't speak to her again and I refused to go to her funeral (Brakhage, personal interview, March 16, 2001).

From age eleven to twelve, Brakhage lived with the Holtman family, where he was well treated. His adoptive mother eventually brought him home when he was in his early teens and he completed high school while living at home.

He earned a scholarship to Dartmouth in 1951, but dropped out to make films, saying:

When I returned to Denver I happened to see Jean Cocteau's *Orpheus* and became very excited to think that a poet could make a movie. Some of my high school friends and I got together with army surplus film and I directed my first film, *Interim.* After that I learned to run the camera and do the editing myself. Still thinking of myself as a poet, I went to San Francisco and met the poets there. After a few months talking with poets, I realized I wasn't one and I threw my thoughts into filmmaking in earnest (*World Film Directors*, 1987).

He studied at San Francisco's Institute of Fine Art and in New York with composers John Cage and Edgard Varese. He also held honorary doctorates from the San Francisco Institute of Fine Art, the California Institute of the Arts, and Bard College.

In 1957, Brakhage married Jane Collom, who had been one of his students. They had five children and were divorced in 1987. He and his second wife, Marilyn Jull, were married in 1989 and had two children, Anton and Vaughn. Says Brakhage:

> I've been very concerned in a way to give my children quite an opposite experience of life than that which I had, and also give them a wholesome sense of love. My first wife and I stayed together clear through till they were graduated and in their late teens or twenties. We had five children, and I photographed much of the upbringing of these children. It permitted me to be what I am in relation to their lives, very directly. So, there's a lot of autobiographical work that was done. I don't do that anymore, but that was a major part of my early filmmaking (Brakhage, personal interview, March 16, 2001).

Stan Brakhage died of cancer on March 9, 2003, at the age of 70. He is survived by his wife, Marilyn Brakhage, seven children, and fourteen grandchildren.

Works Cited

Arts Council of Great Britain. *Stan Brakhage: An American Independent Film-Maker*. London: Arts Council of Great Britain, 1980.

Barrett, Gerald R. *Stan Brakhage: A Guide to References and Resources*. Boston: G. K. Hall, 1983.

Elder, Bruce. *The Films of Stan Brakhage in the American Tradition of Ezra Pound, Gertrude Stein, and Charles Olson*. Waterloo, Ontario: Wilfrid Laurier University Press, 1998.

Hillstrom, Laurie Collier, ed. "Stan Brakhage." *International Dictionary of Films and Filmmakers, Vol. 2: Directors*. Third Edition. Detroit: St. James Press, 1997. 103–107.

James, David E., ed. *Stan Brakhage, Filmmaker*. Philadelphia: Temple University Press, 2005.

Keller, Marjorie. *The Untutored Eye: Childhood in the Films of Cocteau, Cornell, and Brakhage*. Rutherford, NJ: Fairleigh Dickinson University Press, 1986.

MacDonald, Scott. *A Critical Cinema 4*. Berkeley: University of California Press, 2005.

Perry, Ted, ed. *Masterpieces of Modernist Cinema*. Bloomington: Indiana University Press, 2006.

Sitney, P. Adams. *Eyes Upside Down*. New York: Oxford University Press, 2008.

"Stan Brakhage: Correspondences." *Chicago Review* 47:4 (Winter 2001): 11.

BRODKEY, HAROLD (1930–1996)

Novelist
Adoptee

Career, Major Awards, and Achievements

Harold Brodkey was an American novelist. In 1955, he became a staff writer for the *New Yorker*, where many of his short stories and poetic works were first published. His first collection, *First Love and Other Sorrows* (1958), was critically well received. In 1959, Brodkey won a fellowship, the Prix de Rome, from the American Academy of Rome. He also won fellowships from the National Endowment for the Arts and the

John Simon Guggenheim Memorial Foundation. Two of his stories, later published in the collection *Stories in an Almost Classical Mode* (1988), won first place O. Henry Awards in 1975 and 1976. During the 1970s, Brodkey taught literature and writing at Cornell University and at City College, New York. His major work, *The Runaway Soul* (1991), is an autobiographical novel about the life of Wiley Silenowicz, a boy who was adopted in St. Louis during the 1930s. His final book, *This Wild Darkness: The Story of My Death*, chronicles Brodkey's death from AIDS in 1996 and is the intimate self-portrait from which all quotations here were taken. Love-hate relationships in families, especially between parents and children, are Brodkey's most important themes. His works are intensely personal and they have been both praised and criticized for their brutal honesty and autobiographical detail.

Family of Origin

Harold Brodkey was born Aaron Roy Weintraub in Alton, Illinois, on October 25, 1930. His parents were Russian-Jewish immigrants. His mother, Ceil, died when Brodkey was twenty-three months old:

> My mother, my real mother, died, according to family accounts, of a curse laid on her by her father, a wonder-working rabbi. . . . Then Doris, my father's cousin, and Joe came for me and, later on, adopted me. I was told that Doris took me once to the hospital to see my mother, who smelled of infection and medicines and that I refused her embrace, clinging instead to the perfumed Doris; the rescued child was apparently without memory of the dying mother (Brodkey 94–95).

In truth, Brodkey had powerful and recurring reactions to his mother's death throughout his childhood and for a while even refused to walk, talk, or eat:

> I have missed my mother, Ceil, all my life. . . . All children are afraid when their mother leaves the house that she will not return. I dreamed of this throughout my childhood. . . because one day, when I was a year and a half old, it happened—or rather to be exact, it began to happen. . . it was a thing that moved from minute to minute and hour to hour among other events. A mystery (Brodkey 147).

Brodkey was neglected by his birthfather, Max Weintraub, who was "an illiterate local junk man, a semipro prizefighter in his youth, and unhealably violent; I saw him off and on when I was growing up but never really knew him as a father. I was told that after my mother's death, he sold me to relatives—the Brodkeys—for three hundred dollars" (Brodkey 21).

Adoption

Harold was adopted at the age of two by his father's second cousin, Doris Brodkey (known as "Leia," "Leah," or "Lila" in Harold's works), and her husband Joseph ("S. L." in fiction). The Brodkeys also had a daughter, Marilyn, who appears as "Nonie" in her brother's works. Brodkey tried to fit into his new family, but didn't always succeed: "I sometimes see in the mirror the strange rearrangement of an adopted child's face in preparation for entering his new household" (Brodkey 164).

When Brodkey was nine, Joe Brodkey suffered a stroke or heart attack, which made him an invalid for the five years remaining in his life. Doris Brodkey was diagnosed with cancer when Harold was thirteen. According to Brodkey, his adoptive father began to sexually abuse him during the last years of his illness. He went on to say that the abuse grew out of his attempts to comfort his dying father and that this experience led to his own experimentation with homosexuality in the 1960s and 1970s, during which time he believes he became infected with the HIV virus (Brodkey 60–61). In addition to the subject matter and insight for his writing, Brodkey's early experiences seem to have given him a type of nihilism: "I can't remember ever wishing life and death had a perceptible, known, overall meaning. . . . I have accepted since childhood the transience of everything, including meaning—poor orphan that I was. The arrival and departure of significance was something that I was used to"(Brodkey 137).

Education, Military Service, and Significant Relationships

Brodkey graduated at the head of his class at University City High School. He entered Harvard in 1947 as a pre-med student and worked in a shoe store to help support his adoptive mother. Doris died while her son was at college, and after her death, Brodkey changed his academic focus to literature and writing. He married Joanna Brown, a Radcliff graduate, in 1952, and daughter Ann Emily was born in 1953. In 1980, he married his second wife, novelist Ellen Schwamm. On January 26, 1996, Harold Brodkey died of AIDS in Manhattan at the age of sixty-five.

Works Cited

Brodkey, Harold. *This Wild Darkness: The Story of My Death.* New York: Metropolitan Books, 1996.
Moynihan, Robert. "Harold Brodkey." *American Short Story Writers Since World War II. Dictionary of Literary Biography* 130 (1993).

BROWN, RITA MAE (1944–)

Author, Poet
Adoptee

Career, Major Awards, and Achievements

Rita Mae Brown is an American poet, novelist, screenwriter, and activist. She published her first work, *The Hand that Cradles the Rock,* a collection of her poetry, in 1971. She wanted her first novel, *Rubyfruit Jungle* (1973), "to be so witty that even Republicans would be forced to enjoy it" (Brown 13). She received an Emmy nomination for her screenplay *I Love Liberty.* Some of her subsequent novels include *In Her Day* (1976), *Six of One* (1978), *Southern Discomfort* (1982), *Sudden Death* (1983), *High Hearts* (1986), *Bingo* (1988), *Venus Envy* (1993), *Dolley* (1994), *Hotspur* (2003), and *Full Cry* (2004). Sneaky Pie Brown, Rita Mae's cat, is listed as the coauthor for many of her mysteries: *Wish You Were Here* (1990), *Rest in Pieces* (1992), *Murder at Monticello, or, Old Sins* (1994), *Whisker of Evil* (2004), *Cat's Eyewitness* (2005), and *Sour Puss* (2007). Brown's major themes include feminism, civil rights, the American South, lesbianism. The "themes of adoption, of finding one's place in a community, of coming home are important components of Brown's fictions" (Ward 1). One reviewer felt that Brown's early experiences had an important impact on her: "The fact that Brown was an illegitimate and unwanted baby contributes, I believe, to her doggedly determined character. It is no coincidence that Molly Bolt in *Rubyfruit Jungle* shares both her bastard birth and feisty personality" (Levy 1998). Brown's provocative work is especially valued for its humor and originality.

[Will and Deni Mcintyre/Time Life Pictures/Getty Images]

Family of Origin

Rita Mae Brown, who refers to childbirth as "the search for a larger apartment" (Brown 1988, 3), was born on November 28, 1944, in Hanover, Pennsylvania. Her birth mother placed her in an orphanage shortly after her birth. When her adoptive family moved to Fort Lauderdale, Florida, in 1955, Brown claims that the move freed her from an illegitimacy stigma:

> As an adult I know my freedom had to do with more than Florida's fabulous climate. It didn't occur to me until I was in my twenties that our move had freed me from the bonds of my illegitimacy. I was adopted. . . . In a fight at school the first word out of some kid's mouth was "bastard." Sure, I was good with my fists and eventually people let it lie, but I never forgot. In Fort Lauderdale no one cared. I had an equal chance. I made the most of it (Brown 1988, 8).

Brown originally did not wish to locate her family of origin, whom she at one time called her "illegitimate parents" (Ward 1). She did, however, establish her own home in Charlottesville, Virginia, in 1978, where her birthfather's "deep taproots" are. Following the death of her adoptive mother, "Juts," as Brown calls her, she came upon letters from Juliann Young, her birthmother, and decided to call her:

> You might wonder why I didn't hop in the car and drive to see Juliann. . . . It isn't that I wouldn't welcome the sight of her, but I have my pride. I didn't dump her. She dumped me. She has to make the journey. And if she doesn't make it, I'm not angry. . . .
>
> As for me, I wouldn't gain a mother. Juts was my mother and I will be loyal to her until my own death. What I might gain is a friend. . . .
>
> If you are reading this and you, too, have been separated in some fashion from your blood mother or father, you recognize my ambivalence (Brown 1997, 418–419).

During the call to her birthmother, Brown also discovered that she has half-sisters who share her love of horses.

Adoption

Brown's adoptive parents took her at the age of three months to York, Pennsylvania, where her father owned a butcher shop, Brown's Meats. She considers her adoptive parents, Julia Ellen (Buckingham) Brown and Ralph Clifford Brown, her "true" parents (Ward 1). She gives them credit for encouraging her early love of reading and writing and for doing "everything humanly possible to activate my mind" (Brown 3). Brown's gifts were nurtured by her adoptive family, especially her father, "a man with a forty-two-inch chest, a hand that could palm a basketball, and a baritone so deep and rich he made my backbone rattle when he sang" (Brown 4). He died in 1961 when Brown was still a teenager. She maintained a close relationship with her adoptive mother until her death in 1983.

Education and Significant Relationships

Brown graduated from Fort Lauderdale High School and began her studies at the University of Florida. She lost her scholarship there in 1964 because of her involvement in the Civil Rights Movement and her lesbianism. She hitchhiked to New York City and entered New York University, where she earned her BA in 1968 and continued her civil rights and feminist activism. In 1971, Brown moved to Washington, D.C., and completed her PhD in political science there at the Institute for Policy Studies. She had a stormy and highly publicized relationship with tennis star Martina Navratilova in the late seventies and early eighties.

Works Cited

Brown, Rita Mae. *Rita Will: Memoir of a Literary Rabble-Rouser.* New York: Bantam, 1997.
———. *Starting From Scratch: A Different Kind of Writers' Manual.* New York: Bantam, 1988.
Levy, Barbara. "Rita Will: Memoir of a Literary Rabble-Rouser." *The Women's Review of Books* 15 July 1998: 36.
Ward, Carol M. *Rita Mae Brown.* New York: Twayne Publishers, 1993.

BUCHWALD, ART (1925–2007)

Author, Humorist
Home alumnus, multiple foster homes, runaway at age 16

Career, Major Awards, and Achievements

Art Buchwald was a journalist, author, and political humorist. After his discharge from the Marines in 1945 and three years of college, he launched his career in Paris, becoming a regular columnist for the *New York Herald Tribune*. Buchwald later moved to Washington and wrote as a political satirist. He made the cover of *Newsweek* magazine (June 1965), and his column appeared in over 300 U.S. newspapers. His columns have been collected into nearly thirty popular books. He also wrote a play, *Sheep on the Runway* (1969), and an autobiography of his childhood, *Leaving Home*, from which all quotations here are taken. Buchwald won a Pulitzer Prize in 1982 for his journalism and was elected to the American Academy of Arts and Letters in 1986.

[AP Photo/Charles Bennett]

Family of Origin

Arthur "Art" Buchwald was born in Mount Vernon, New York, on October 20, 1925. His mother gave birth at home, attended only by her daughters, Alice, 6, Edith, 5, and Doris, 3. "I like to think that this unusual way of coming into the world played an important part in my developing a positive attitude about life. Maybe it also influenced my decision at an early age that, if I was to survive, I would have to fend for myself rather than wait for help from others" (23–24). Art's mother, Helen Kleinberger Buchwald, was mentally ill and spent much of her pregnancy in a sanitarium. She did not recover after his birth and was institutionalized four months later, until her death in 1960. Buchwald never saw her, and her absence had a permanent effect on him: "As with many children who never knew their mothers, I have been on a lifelong search for someone to replace her. The search has taken more time than my work, and although I know that I will never find a surrogate, I can't seem to stop looking" (13).

Both of Buchwald's parents had been Jewish immigrants from Europe. His mother came from Hungary in 1906 and his father from Austria in 1912. Joseph Buchwald, Art's father, made drapes and curtains for a living. He learned English from the newspapers he found in the subway and was naturalized as an American citizen in 1927. During the Depression, he was seldom able to earn enough money to provide for his sick wife and four children and was forced to place them in various facilities. Although Joseph visited his children faithfully every week and refused to relinquish them for adoption, he was unable to develop closeness with them. His son says, "In going over the relationship, I don't think I ever knew him well. There was no intimacy" (44).

Orphanages and Foster Homes

Art Buchwald was taken as an infant to the Heckscher Foundling Home for care because he had developed rickets. This home for sick children in Flushing, New York, was run by Seventh Day Adventists. His youngest sister, Doris, was also sent to this institution for treatment of osteomyelitis in her leg. Buchwald remained there with his sister for most of his first five years. His two older sisters had been sent to a home called the Shield of David.

Joseph took Doris and Art out of the Heckscher Foundling Home when they began to be influenced by their nurse's religion (32). He then paid distant relatives in the Bronx to board the two youngest children but removed them shortly afterwards when Art was hit and mildly injured by a car. After this incident, Joseph decided to place all four of his children in the Hebrew Orphan Asylum (HOA). The HOA, founded by Jewish Charities in 1860, boarded or supervised foster placements for an estimated 35,000 children before its closure in 1941. Buchwald was a ward of the HOA from the time he was six until he was fifteen, primarily in their foster child program.

All four children went to their first foster home together, two months after their intake in the HOA. The two older girls remained with this family, but after two years Doris and Art were shifted to another family. Buchwald describes this placement as an unhappy one, with friction between other foster children, the family's biological child and the Buchwald children. Doris and Art finally moved to their last placement in February 1936. Although he claims to have been his happiest with this last family, Buchwald's writings suggest that he never felt completely at home anywhere: "When I was small I kept trying to figure out who I belonged to. My father appeared regularly, but he never stayed. The orphanage and the foster homes I lived in were some sort of halfway houses, and no matter how nice the people were, I felt like an intruder using one of their bedrooms" (35).

The long-awaited reunion with his father and sisters came when Buchwald was fifteen. His father and his three daughters moved first into a sparsely furnished apartment, leaving the boy at the foster home. Art says that he felt completely rejected. Joseph eventually sent for his son, but by then Buchwald was very angry. He even refused his father's request to become bar mitzvahed: "the only reason I can give is that I was very mad at my father for what had been done to me, and since it was so important to him, I made the decision not to do it" (45).

Education, Military Service, and Significant Relationships

Buchwald did poorly in school, except in English, and he invested most of his energy in a part-time job with Paramount Pictures. In October 1942, several weeks before his seventeenth birthday, Art ran away and illegally joined the Marines, lying about his age and forging the required permission papers.

Buchwald married Ann McGarry, an American he met in Paris, in 1952. They have three adopted children, Joel from Ireland, Conchita from Spain, and Balmain (Jennifer) from France. Buchwald claims that his childhood experiences were the basis for his career: "I must have been six or seven years old and terribly lonely and confused, when I said something like, 'This stinks, I'm going to become a humorist. . . from then on, I had one goal in mind and that was to make people laugh" (61).

He died January 18, 2007, of kidney failure at the age of 81.

Works Cited

Buchwald, Art. *Leaving Home: A Memoir.* New York: G. P. Putnam's Sons, 1993.

BUNCHE, RALPH (1903–1971)

Statesman, Nobel Laureate
Orphaned at age 12, raised by grandmother

Career, Major Awards, and Achievements

Ralph Bunche was the first African American to win the Nobel Peace Prize. The prize was awarded to him in 1950 for his role as mediator during the Arab-Israeli war that began in 1948. Under nearly hopeless conditions, he patiently and persistently worked for peace between Israel, Egypt, Lebanon, Jordan, and Syria; armistice agreements were concluded in 1949. Bunche began his career as an instructor and codirector of the Race Relations Institute at Swarthmore College, where he conducted important research on colonial policy and race. He wrote or coauthored several influential studies on racial prejudice, including *A World View of Race* (1936) and *An American Dilemma* (1944).

Bunche worked for the National Defense Program from 1941 to 1944 and then became a specialist on Africa for the U.S. Department of State. He wrote most of the trusteeship section of the United Nations Charter, and from 1946 until his retirement in 1971, he served as a peacemaker with the United Nations, becoming Undersecretary-General in 1967. In addition to his efforts during many international crises, including

[Carl Van Vechten Collection/Library of Congress]

those involving the Suez Canal, Cyprus, the Congo (now Zaire), and India-Pakistan, Bunche also actively resisted racial inequality in the United States. He took part in the 1963 demonstrations at the Lincoln Memorial and the 1965 civil rights marches organized by Martin Luther King, Jr., in Selma and Montgomery, Alabama. He refused the job of Assistant Secretary of State offered by President Harry S. Truman as a protest to the segregated housing in Washington, D.C. He also urged the government to use money designated for the War in Vietnam to eliminate American ghettos instead.

Family of Origin

Ralph Johnson Bunch (the *e* on his surname was added later) was born on August 7, 1903, in Detroit, Michigan. His father, Fred, had grown up in the Madison County Children's Home until he was taken in by Absalom and Hattie Roberts Bunch at age seven. Fred, who did not complete grade school, became a barber and "a lovable care-free chap who couldn't sit still" (Urquhart 26). His wife, Olive Johnson, had been the middle child in her family, which Bunche described as "a clan with my maternal grandmother at its head" (Urquhart 25). The couple had a second child, Grace, in 1909.

Fred was often unemployed and the family had severe financial problems. Olive became ill and was diagnosed with tuberculosis, as was her brother, Charlie, who had become an important mentor to Ralph (Urquhart 29). The family relocated to Albuquerque, New Mexico, in the hope that the hot, dry air would help Olive and Charlie recover their health. Fred was unable to find work and finally left his family. The children never saw their father again. Both parents died in 1916 when Ralph was twelve years old:

> Now, more than ever, I seem to regret that I lost my mother when both she and I were so young. I feel cheated to have been deprived of her. I have retained an image of her as a pretty, very sweet and romantic lady, a dreamer, accomplished in music and poetry, and always an invalid. I can never get it out of my mind that on that night of her death in Albuquerque she had asked for milk and there was none in the house because I had drunk it up (Urquhart 29–30).

Olive's brother, Charlie, committed suicide three months after his sister's death. The children were taken to live with their maternal grandmother, Lucy Taylor Johnson, who added the *e* to their last name in 1917, when the family left Albuquerque to make a new life in Los Angeles.

Kinship Care

Lucy, whom Bunche called "Nana," had been the daughter of a house slave and an Irish Catholic plantation owner. She married Thomas Nelson Johnson, a teacher with a fervor for learning. Thomas had been one of the first African Americans to graduate from Shurtleff College in Alton, Illinois, in 1875. He took a position as a rural teacher of black children near Fort Scott, Kansas. Thomas and Lucy had ten children, but five of them died in the harsh frontier conditions. Thomas himself died of malaria at the age of forty, leaving Lucy a young widow with five surviving children and no income. Three of the children, Ethel, Nelle, and Tom, would later help their mother raise Ralph and Grace Bunche.

Bunche attributes the values that distinguished his life and work to his grandmother's influence:

> She instilled in me a desire to do my best in anything I tried to do so that I could have a sense of achievement and experience pride. She taught me the value of self-respect and dignity. She told me to be proud of my origin, of my family and of the society in which I live. I learned from her that hard work can be enjoyed and can be highly rewarding. Although having little education herself, she appreciated the value of education and insisted that I should get as much of it as possible, and the best possible. . . . Nana could be regarded as an optional Negro. She was entirely Caucasian in appearance . . . "White" as Nana was outside, she was all black pride and fervor inside. . . . Nana was fiercely proud of her origin and her race, and everyone in our "clan" got the race-pride message very early in life. It has stuck with me (Urquhart 31–32).

Education and Significant Relationships

Bunche was valedictorian of his class at Jefferson High School, but he nearly dropped out after being excluded from an honor society, the Ephebian Society, because of his race: "I decided to leave school, abandon graduation. Then I thought of my mother's words, 'Ralph, don't let anything take away your hope and faith and dreams.' I decided that I could get along without the honor society" (Urquhart 35). Bunche worked his way through college at UCLA and graduated with highest honors in 1927. He earned his Master's degree (1928) and PhD (1934) from Harvard. He married schoolteacher Ruth Harris in 1930, and they had three children: Joan, Jane, and Ralph Jr. In 1970 Bunche's health began to decline; he became blind and developed kidney disease. He died in New York City on December 9, 1971, at the age of sixty-eight.

Works Cited

Bunche, Ralph. *Ralph J. Bunche: Selected Speeches and Writings*. Charles P. Henry, Ed. Ann Arbor: University of Michigan Press, 1995.

Rivlin, Benjamin. *Ralph Bunche: The Man and His Times*. New York: Holmes & Meier, 1990.

Urquhart, Brian. *Ralph Bunche: An American Life*. New York: Norton, 1993.

BURTON, RICHARD (1925–1984)

Actor
Adoptee

Career, Major Awards, and Achievements

One of the best-known actors of the twentieth century, Richard Burton was acclaimed for both film and stage performances in England and the United States. He began his professional career in London in *The Lady's Not for Burning* (1949) and made his Broadway debut when that play moved to New York in 1950. He continued acting on Broadway and at the Old Vic in London, where he soon established a reputation as a brilliant Shakespearean actor. His most notable roles include Hamlet, Philip the Bastard in *King John*, Sir Toby Belch in *Twelfth Night*, Caius Martius in *Coriolanus*, Caliban in *The Tempest*, Henry V, and alternating roles of Othello and Iago in *Othello*.

[AP Photo]

By 1960, Burton had made more than a dozen American and British films, including *My Cousin Rachel* (1952), for which he received an Oscar nomination for best supporting actor, and *Look Back in Anger* (1959). He was also nominated for Oscar Best Actor awards for his performances in *The Robe* (1960), *Becket* (1964), *The Spy Who Came in from the Cold* (1965), **Edward Albee's** *Who's Afraid of Virginia Woolf* (1966), *Anne of a Thousand Days* (1969), and *Equus* (1977).

Burton began his highly publicized love affair with actress Elizabeth Taylor during the filming of *Cleopatra* (1963). The couple made several more memorable films together, including *Virginia Woolf* and Franco Zeffirelli's *The Taming of the Shrew* (1967).

Burton won the Tony Award for his performance as King Arthur in the musical production of *Camelot* (1960) and a Golden Globe Award for *Equus*. He was made a Commander of the British Empire in 1970. His final appearances were in the mini-series *Ellis Island* (1984), which also featured his daughter Kate, and *1984* (1984).

Family of Origin

Richard Burton was born Richard Walter Jenkins on November 10, 1925, in Pontrhydyfen, South Wales, the twelfth child of Thomas and Edith Jenkins. His father was forty-nine years old and his mother forty-two at the time of his birth. Edith Jenkins died when Richard was two years old, of puerperal fever following the birth of her thirteenth child, Graham. Burton described his father as an alcoholic Welsh coal miner who would take off for weeks at a time.

Following the death of his mother, Richard was taken to Port Talbot to live with his eldest sister, Cecelia ("Cis"), and her husband, Elfed James. He grew up with their two daughters Marian and Rhianon, who were three and six years younger than he was. Burton was "exceedingly dependent" (Bragg 11) on his sister, and she was said to consistently take his side in any quarrel between her brother and husband. Burton grew very close to Cis and she had a lasting influence on him, as he relates:

> Now my sister was no ordinary woman—no woman ever is, but to me, my sister was less than any. When my mother died, she, my sister, had become my mother, and more mother to me than any mother could ever have been. I was immensely proud of her. I shone in the reflection of her green-eyed, black-haired, gypsy beauty. . . . It wasn't until thirty years later, when I saw her in another woman [Elizabeth Taylor] that I realized I had been searching for her all my life (Burton 23–24).

As Burton grew older, his difficulties with his brother-in-law increased. He left school and tried to find work and a home with other members of his family, but was eventually persuaded to return to school, Cis, and Elfed. His relationship with Elfed continued to deteriorate.

Adoption

Richard's emerging dramatic talent came to the attention of an influential BBC director and acting teacher, Philip Burton, and he began to train and mentor the boy. Philip Burton recalls how Richard came to live with him and his landlady, Mrs. Smith:

> One night I was so touched by yet another account of his plight that I said, without realizing the full implications of what I was saying, that there was a spare bedroom in Mrs. Smith's house. . . . He seized on it and asked when he could move in. I immediately

backtracked, and he said with a sorrow that made me feel guilty, "When push comes to shove, nobody wants me" (Bragg 35).

The elder Burton recorded his first meeting with Richard's family:

> Reluctantly Elfed left the room and I said to Cis, "Ritchie is your son much more than your brother, and I know how much you love each other. What do you want me to do?" Her answer, which changed not only Richard's life but mine too, was, "If you take him it would be the answer to my prayers." When Elfed returned with Richard, I told them I would do as they all wished, and the room seemed to be filled with the happiness of relief (Bragg 36).

Philip Burton was not comfortable with the ambiguity of his relationship with Richard (Bragg 41), and he filed to legally adopt him. However, he was twenty days short of meeting an existing requirement that an adoptive parent must be twenty-one years older that the person adopted. Instead, Philip Burton informally adopted him with a deed poll. The document stated: [Richard Walter Jenkins shall] "absolutely renounce and abandon the use of the surname of the parent and shall bear the surname of the adopter and shall be held out to the world and in all respects treated as if he were in fact the child of the adopter." Most biographies claim that Richard's birthfather gave written permission for the adoption, but his brother Graham disputes that (Jenkins 42). Richard always referred to Philip Burton as his father, and when he was told in 1957 that his father (Jenkins) was dead, "his immediate reaction was 'Which?'" (Burton 41). Philip Burton taught Richard to speak English without a Welsh accent and intensively coached him in the skills needed for professional acting. He outlived Richard by eleven years and died of a stroke in 1995, at the age of 90.

Education, Military Service, and Significant Relationships

Richard Burton earned a scholarship to Exeter College at Oxford, but he spent less than a year there before he joined the Royal Air Force in 1944. He was demobilized at the rank of sergeant in 1947. Burton was married five times: to Sybil Williams, with whom he had two daughters, Kate, an actress, and Jessica, who is autistic; twice to Elizabeth Taylor, with whom he adopted a daughter, Maria; to Susan Hunt, and to Sally Hay. He died of a stroke in Geneva, Switzerland, on August 5, 1984, at the age of 58.

Works Cited

Bragg, Melvyn. *Richard Burton: A Life*. Boston: Little, 1988.
Burton, Richard. *A Christmas Story*. New York: Morrow, 1964.
Cottrell, John. *Richard Burton, Very Close Up*. Englewood Cliffs, NJ: Prentice Hall, 1972.
Jenkins, Graham. *Richard Burton, My Brother*. New York: Harper & Row, 1988.

C

CAMPBELL, BEN NIGHTHORSE (1933–)

Congressman
Orphanage alumnus, St. Patrick's Home for Children

Careers, Major Awards, and Achievements

Ben Nighthorse Campbell is a U.S. senator from Colorado. He was elected to the Colorado State Legislature in 1982 and served in U.S. House of Representatives from 1987 to 1992. He was then elected to the U.S. Senate as a Democratic candidate, but joined the Republican Party in 1995. He was reelected to the Senate in 1998 and retired from office in January 2005. Campbell is a member of the Northern Cheyenne tribe in Montana and was the first Native American to serve as a senator in more than sixty years. He considered himself an advocate in Congress for all American Indians and sponsored such legislation as a bill to establish a Museum of the American Indian in the Smithsonian, the renaming of the Custer National Battlefield Monument to the Little Bighorn National Battlefield Monument, and the Colorado Ute Indian Water Rights Settlement Act. In 1982, Campbell was inducted into the Northern Cheyenne's Council of 44 Chiefs in Lame Deer, Montana. His colleagues named him one of the Ten Best Legislators in 1986. In addition to his political activity, Campbell is a rancher, champion quarter-horse trainer, former teacher, and an award-winning jewelry artist. He is an orphanage alumnus.

Family of Origin

Ben Campbell was born in Auburn, California, the second child of Mary (Vierra) Campbell and Albert Valdez Campbell. Campbell's maternal grandfather had been a stowaway from Portugal who found his way west to Sacramento, California and, in 1906, sent for his wife, five sons, and daughter Mary. Mary was diagnosed with tuberculosis in 1917 and began treatment at the Weimar Sanatorium when it opened in 1919. She was a patient and an employee there for twenty-two years. She met her husband at the sanatorium, where he also worked. They married in August 1929. Their first child, Alberta, was born on her father's birthday, July 12, 1930, and their second, Ben, was born on April 13, 1933. When Campbell was two years old, Mary requested permission to place her children in a Catholic orphanage, St. Patrick's Home for Children in Sacramento. Albert, a chronic alcoholic, had deserted the family. She was turned down, as the minimum age for admittance was four.

[AP/Ed Andrieski]

Orphanage

When Campbell was four, he and Alberta were allowed to live for one year at the sanatorium's facility for children of tubercular parents. In 1939, when he was five, his father was in the Placer County jail for drunkenness and failure to provide for his family. Mary, her health failing, received permission to place the children in St. Patrick's Home for Children. Campbell recalls that winter day as his "most vivid memory":

I thought we were just going for a ride. When we got to the place, Mom told Alberta and me to stay in the car. She got out and started talking to these nuns and a priest. I knew something was up. Then she came to get me and left my sister in the car. She took me by the hand and walked me up onto this porch and said I was going to have to stay there. By then I was kicking and screaming and she was crying. She got me inside but I broke loose and managed to scramble out a window. I climbed down through some brush and ran back to the car. The trunk was open so I jumped in and closed the lid on myself hoping they wouldn't find me, but they did. Boy! Talk about abandonment. I think the experience left some real scars. . . . To this day I have a little bit of fear about being abandoned. I don't blame my mother for that. She had nothing. My dad was off drinking. She didn't have any choice" (Campbell 8–9).

The children lived in large dormitories with up to forty to a room, ages four to seventeen, and Campbell remembers being frightened of the older boys and often being hungry (Campbell 10). He remembers a time when a nun threw him into a hog pen for having dirty fingernails (Campbell 9).

Both of Campbell's parents had eighth-grade educations. His father did not acknowledge his Indian ancestry because of existing prejudice. He claims to have run away from home in Colorado to live with Northern Cheyenne relatives in Montana when he was about twelve years old. Albert served in the army and began drinking during World War I. When he returned from the military, he worked at the Weimar Sanatorium as an orderly. It was Albert who showed his son how to work with metal, and by the age of twelve Ben was already designing jewelry. Campbell remembers witnessing some violence between his parents: "One time after Al slapped her, Mary knocked him cold with a heavy frying pan" (Campbell 12). Albert and Mary were legally divorced but resumed living together. Mary opened and ran a small grocery store. Sales increased when a major highway came in near the property. The Campbell family stabilized during the 1940s, despite Albert's continued drinking, and the children returned from the orphanage.

Campbell feels that his orphanage experience ultimately helped him: "As I look back on it I think it was one of the best things that happened to me. It made me very self-reliant and independent. If you have nobody to rely on, then you have got to do it yourself. Another thing people should remember: I wasn't the only one in there. A lot of kids went through those places" (Campbell 11). During their stay at St. Patrick's, the Campbell children were separated from each other. Ben was never close to his sister, who, in 1975, apparently committed suicide from an overdose of alcohol and sleeping pills.

Campbell believes that his orphanage experience is also responsible for his extreme competitiveness and drive: "Part of it has to come from my childhood, an orphan wanting to be as good as the next guy. I have always been a self-driver" (Campbell 71).

Education, Military Service, and Significant Relationships

Campbell dropped out of high school in his junior year to enlist in the Air Force. He became a military policeman and started to learn judo during the MP training. While stationed in South Korea in 1952, he took almost daily judo instruction from two Koreans and earned a brown belt. He also earned his high school equivalency diploma. He entered San Jose City College under the GI Bill and later transferred to San Jose State University, where in 1957 he earned a BA degree in physical education and fine arts. He joined the University's impressive judo team and was eventually the team's captain. Campbell won the Amateur Athletic Association Pacific Coast judo championship four times and became the youngest person in the United States to earn a fourth-degree black belt. In 1960, he enrolled in a demanding judo program at Meijo University in Tokyo, where he earned a sixth-degree black belt. He won the gold medal in the 1963 Pan American Games, open weight division, and competed in the 1964 Olympics.

Campbell's first marriage was annulled, and his second ended in divorce. In 1966, he married Linda Price, a former teacher. They have a son, Colin, and a daughter, Shanan. Campbell worked as a teacher of various subjects, including art, physical education, and shop. In 1968, he began a search for his roots, which led him to the Northern Cheyenne Reservation in Montana. He believes that his ancestor was Rubin Black Horse, a warrior in the Little Bighorn Battle. Although there is no formal documentation, Rubin's descendants, Alec and Mary Black Horse, adopted Campbell into their family: "They accepted me and I accepted them. That was good enough" (Campbell 129–130). Campbell took the middle name "Nighthorse" at the time of his tribal enrollment in 1980, as a tribute to his ancestry.

Works Cited

Barrett, Carole, ed. et al. "Campbell, Ben Nighthorse." *American Indian Biographies.* Pasadena, CA: Salem Press, c2005. 79–80.
Viola, Herman J. *Ben Nighthorse Campbell: An American Warrior.* New York: Orion, 1993.

CAPECCHI, MARIO (1937—)

Geneticist, Professor, Nobel Laureate
Orphanage Alumnus, street child

Career, Major Awards, and Achievements

On October 8, 2007, Mario Capecchi, a professor at the University of Utah, and geneticists Sir Martin J. Evans of Cardiff University and Oliver Smithies of University of North Carolina at Chapel Hill were jointly awarded the 2007 Nobel Prize in Physiology or Medicine for their "discoveries of principles for introducing specific gene modifications in mice by the use of embryonic stem cells." Capecchi developed a technique to target, remove and replace specific genes in mice, discoveries which have vast implications in the treatment of human disease.

His numerous additional awards include the Albert Lasker Award for Basic Medical Research (2001), the National Medal of Science (2001), the World Prize in Medicine (2003), the Pezcoller Foundation–American Association for Cancer Research's International Award for Cancer Research (2003), and the March of Dimes Prize in Developmental Biology (2005). Earlier awards include The Franklin Medal for Advancing Our Knowledge of the Physical Sciences (1997), the prestigious Kyoto Prize in Basic Sciences (1996), for which he presented their traditionally requested autobiographic lecture "The Making of a Scientist," The Gairdner Foundation International Award (1993), and the Alfred P. Sloan Jr. Prize for Outstanding Basic Science Contributions to Cancer Research (1994). He is a fellow of the National Academy of Sciences and holds the Bamberger Endowed Chair in the Health Sciences at the University of Utah.

One interviewer wrote that Capecchi's "genealogy may be at the core of his later proclivity for pursuing scientific paths less traveled" (Gudmundsen J1). His devastating

[AP Photo/Douglas C. Pizac]

childhood experiences also likely had a large part in forming his notable maverick spirit:

> [His] independent streak helped Capecchi weather the biggest crisis of his professional career. In 1980 a panel of reviewers from the National Institutes of Health (NIH) classified his studies on targeted gene replacement (inactivating or modifying a gene in mouse embryos) as "not worthy of pursuit" (Stix 27).

Capecchi continued to pursue his eventual award-winning research, however, using alternative funding. The NIH reviewers would later write: "We are glad you didn't follow our advice" (Stix 26).

Family of Origin

Mario Capecchi was born the illegitimate son of Italian officer Luciano Capecchi and Lucy Ramberg, an American-born poet. He writes:

> I was born in Verona, Italy, on October 6, 1937. Fascism, Naziism and Communism were raging through the country. My mother was a poet, my father an officer in the Italian air force. This was a time of extremes and the juxtaposition of opposites. They had a passionate love affair and my mother wisely chose not to marry him. Considering the times, this took a great deal of courage on her part. (Capecchi, Kyoto Prize Lecture).

Mario's grandmother, Lucy (Dodd) Ramberg, was a painter from Portland, Oregon, who had gone abroad to study art. In 1905, she married German archaeologist Walter Ramberg and the couple had three children, Lucy and her two brothers, Walter and Edward. Ramberg was killed by friendly fire during World War I and the widow and her children made their way to Florence, where she bought a villa and turned it into a finishing school for American girls. When Walter and Edward left to attend college in the United States, Lucy was sent to study at the Sorbonne in Paris, where she later became a lecturer in literature and languages. While in Paris, Lucy joined a group of young artists and intellectuals called the Bohemians. Actively opposed to the Fascists and Nazis, Lucy and her friends retreated to a chalet in the Italian Alps, where she met and fell in love with Mario's father. Eventually the Gestapo caught up with and arrested the Bohemians. Capecchi's mother was arrested at that time and sent to the Dachau concentration camp, where she remained a prisoner until 1945. Before her arrest, she had arranged for Mario to be fostered with a Tyrolean farm family:

> For reasons that have never been clear to me, my mother's money ran out after one year and at age 4½ I set off on my own. I headed south, sometimes living in the streets, sometimes joining gangs of other homeless children, sometimes living in orphanages and most of the time being hungry (Capecchi, Kyoto Prize Lecture).

Lucy was one of the prisoners liberated from Dachau by American troops in the spring of 1945. She located Mario in a hospital in Reggio Emilia, a town in northern Italy, where he had been a patient for nearly a year with malnutrition-related illness. Lucy made contact with her son on October 6, 1945, his ninth birthday. With boat tickets provided by Lucy's brother, Edward Ramberg, and his wife, Sarah, the two soon left Europe to live with the Ramberg family in a Quaker commune they helped to establish in Pennsylvania. Once beautiful and brilliant, Lucy never recovered from her experiences in the concentration camp and, until her death in 1987, she "lived essentially in this world of [her] imagination" (Gudmundsen J1). Mario's uncle Edward was a brilliant physicist whose discoveries helped to build the first electron microscope. He and his wife helped to raise and educate Mario.

Education and Significant Relationships

Mario attended George High School, a Quaker school north of Philadelphia. He worked three jobs during high school in order to save enough money for college. He attended Antioch College and participated in a work-study program in molecular biology at MIT. For his graduate studies, he attended Harvard on a National Science Foundation fellowship and there met his famous mentor, James D. Watson, the 1962 Nobel laureate who codiscovered the structure of DNA. After earning his PhD, Capecchi joined Harvard's department of biochemistry.

Capecchi and wife, Laurie Fraser, live in Emigration Canyon, an area in the Wasatch Mountains outside of Salt Lake City. Fraser, a San Francisco native, and her husband met in 1976 when she worked as an assistant in Capecchi's lab. Their daughter Misha was born in 1984.

In his Kyoto Prize lecture, Capecchi called his early childhood "the antithesis of a nurturing environment, which all of us deeply want to believe is a conducive prerequisite for fostering thoughtful, creative human beings," and he went on to imply that his very gifts came out of "stochastic, chaotic influences." He considers the students he trains "his legacy" and "an extended family" (Dennis 11) and he selects his own protégés on such qualities as curiosity and excitement rather than their credentials:

> Genius should be nurtured in places both high and low. Society must find ways to recruit and nurture its outcasts, even malnourished, illiterate street urchins. "No matter how good you think you are," [Capecchi] remarks, "you don't have the capability to predict who are the people who are going to bloom" (Stix 27).

Works Cited

Capecchi, Mario. "The Making of a Scientist." (Kyoto Prize Lecture, November 1996). *Howard Hughes Medical Institute (HHMI) Research News*. October 8, 2007. October 10, 2007. http://www.hhmi.org/news/nobel20071008a.html

Collins, Lois M. "U. Scientist Capecchi Wins Nobel Prize." *Deseret Morning News*. October 8, 2007. October 10, 2007. http://deseretnews.com/dn/view/1,5143,695216829,00.html

Dennis, Carina. "From Rags to Research." *Nature* 430 (July 1, 2004): 10.

Gudmundsen, Lance S. "Of Mice and Mario: Mario Capecchi Nearly Starved on the Streets of War-Torn Italy. Now He Is Known for Revolutionizing the Study of Human Genetics." *Salt Lake Tribune*. August 31, 1997: J1. October 10, 2007. http://www.lexisnexis.com

Lee, Christopher. "From Child on Street to Nobel Laureate." *Washington Post* 9 October, 2007: A1. October 10, 2007. http://www.washingtonpost.com

"Scientists win Nobel for 'Designer Mice.'" *USA Today* October 9, 2007: 9d. October 10, 2007. http://web.ebscohost.com

Stix, Gary. "Of Survival and Science." *Scientific American* 281 (August 1999): 26.

CASANOVA, GIOVANNI GIACOMO (1725—1798)

Legendary Lover, Writer, Librarian
Raised by grandmother until age 8, then fostered by non-relatives

Career, Major Awards, and Achievements

Casanova was an Italian libertine who is best known for his twelve-volume memoirs, *Histoire de Ma Vie*. His charm and wit gained him entrance into society's highest circles, but the scandals, debt, and intrigues in which he was continuously involved kept him on the move from one European capital to another and led to his several arrests and exiles.

Altera nunc rerum facies.me quero, nec adsum
Non sum qui fueram non putor efse : fui.

JACQUES CASANOVA DE SEINGALT.
a l'âge de 63 ans

[Courtesy of the Library of Congress]

Casanova was originally trained to become an ecclesiastic lawyer, and he achieved a degree in law and took preliminary orders for the priesthood, but was later expelled from the seminary for sexual misconduct. He dabbled with careers in the military, music, occultism, and a dozen other professions, but usually supported himself through gambling, spying, and other shady practices. He ran the royal lottery in Paris, met Voltaire in

Geneva and Catherine the Great in St. Petersburg, fought a duel of honor in Poland, and lived in Naples, Milan, Marseilles, Corfu, Constantinople, Lyon, Dresden, Paris, and Vienna. In 1755, the Inquisition imprisoned him in the Piombi, the state prison at Venice, for being a magician and a Freemason. His daring escape was recorded in his *Histoire de Ma Fuite* (1788). He spent the last years of his life as a librarian in Bohemia, where he wrote his memoirs. The memoirs, considered classics of erotic literature, are also valued for their sweeping first-hand accounts of eighteenth-century Europe.

Family of Origin

According to his own memoirs, Casanova's father was an actor named Gaetan-Joseph-Jacques Casanova, who eloped with his beautiful, sixteen-year-old neighbor, Zanetta Farussi. Zanetta, who became a popular dancer and actress, was the daughter of a shoemaker. Most of Casanova's biographers believe that he was not Gaetan's son, but was instead the illegitimate child of Zanetta and a rich theater owner, Michele Grimani, who arranged for her to marry Gaetan, one of his employees:

> Giacomo's father-by-the-flesh was not Gaetano Casanova but Michele Grimani, of the patrician family which owned the S. Samuele theatre, where Gaetano and later Zanetta played. . . . Zanetta in the end got herself respectably married and at the same time established an obligation by the Grimanis. In the patrician oligarchy of old Venice this would be useful to herself and invaluable to her children. Casanova certainly believed himself to be Grimani's son. He said so in a later pamphlet (Masters 11–12).

Casanova, who referred to himself as Jacques Casanova, Chevalier de Seingalt, was born in Venice on April 2, 1725. He had five younger siblings: a brother Francois (also called Francesco), born in London in 1727 and also illegitimate; Jean (Giovanni), born in 1730; a sister who died in childhood; another sister, Maria Maddalena Antonia Stella, born in 1732; and a brother, Gaetano Alvisio, who was born in 1734 and became a priest. Casanova did not grow up with his siblings or his parents. His nominal father, Gaetano, died in 1733, when Jacques was eight years old. His mother died much later in Dresden on November 29, 1776.

Kinship Care and Foster Homes

When Casanova was a year old, his mother left him in the care of his maternal grandmother, Marzia, who seemed to have been the only relative to ever love the child. The boy was sickly and suffered from continuous nosebleeds: "My disease had rendered me dull and retired; everybody pitied me and left me to myself; my life was considered likely to be but a short one, and as to my parents, they never spoke to me" (Casanova 6). On his ninth birthday he was taken to Padua to live with a Signora Mida, the wife of a Slovenian colonel:

> My small trunk was laid open before the old woman, to whom was handed an inventory of all its contents, together with six sequins for six months paid in advance. For this small sum she undertook to feed me, to keep me clean, and to send me to a day-school. Protesting that it was not enough, she accepted these terms. I was then kissed and strongly commanded to be always obedient and docile, and I was left with her. In this way did my family get rid of me (Casanova 13).

The boy shared a squalid garret room with three other boarded boys and the family servant. Conditions were miserable, and Jacques was constantly hungry, filthy, and bitten by rats, fleas, and lice: "For the first time in my life I shed tears of sorrow and of anger, when I heard my companions scoffing at me. The poor wretches shared my unhappy condition, but they were used to it, and that makes all the difference" (Casanova 17).

The boy's quick mind came to the notice of a teacher at the school, a kindly priest called Doctor Gozzi. When the initial six months at the boarding house were over and Marzia discovered her grandson's piteous condition, she made arrangements with the Gozzi family to board Jacques with them. Casanova wrote in his memoirs that he fell in love for the first time at age twelve, with Gozzi's beautiful fourteen-year-old sister, Bettina, who was placed in charge of the boy. Bettina was, in fact, eighteen years old and Casanova eleven (Masters 14–15) when she "carried too far her love for cleanliness" during his baths and "spent her mornings with me in criminal connection while [Gozzi] was saying his mass" (Casanova 30, 52). Bettina also broke his heart by her preference for a fifteen-year-old rival.

Education, Military Service, and Significant Relationships

In 1783, Casanova's mother left permanently for Dresden, where she became an actress in the service of the King of Poland. Casanova finished his studies in Padua and took the degree Doctor of Civil Law at the age of sixteen. He then entered a Paduan university called "the Bo." While at the university, Jacques went hopelessly into debt from his gambling. When he wrote to his grandmother for more money, she promptly removed him from the university and took him back with her to Venice. After Marzia's death, Jacques became the Grimanis' delinquent ward, and they sent him to the seminary of St. Cipriano to complete his religious education. When the rector found him in bed with another seminarian, he was beaten and expelled. He then set sail east for Constantinople and Turkey, and thus begins his extraordinary and insatiable adult life. He never married: "Casanova loved many women, but broke few hearts. . . . That he knew himself well enough never to take either wife or mistress must be counted as a virtue, such as it was, in this incomparable lover of so many women" (Boyd xi). During his sixties and seventies, Casanova was librarian for the Bohemian Count Waldstein at Dux (now called Duchcov, Czech Republic). He died in Dux on June 4, 1798, of prostatitis and septic infection. He was 73.

Works Cited

Boyd, Madeline, Ed. *The Memoirs of Jacques Casanova.* New York: The Modern Library, 1929.
Casanova, Jacques. *The Memoirs of Jacques Casanova de Seingalt: Venetian Years.* Arthur Machen, trans. New York: G. P. Putnam's Sons, [n.d.].
Masters, John. *Casanova.* New York: Bernard Geis, 1969.
Parker, Derek. *Casanova.* Thrupp, Gloucestershire: Sutton Publishing, 202.

CATHERINE I (Martha Skavronska) (1683–1727)

Empress of Russia
Orphan, adoptee

Career, Major Awards, and Achievements

Catherine was named Empress of Russia after the death of her husband, Peter the Great, in 1725. Born Martha Skavronska, she was the daughter of a Lithuanian slave who had escaped to Sweden. The Czar had been ". . . charmed by her sturdiness, her health, and her cheerful equanimity. She was "like a vivandiere or some junior officer's wife, born to travel in a wagon, sleep in a tent, and take potluck around the campfire. Exactly what he needed, the Czar thought" (Troyat 146).

After Peter's death, Catherine was crowned Empress and stayed informed about matters of state, but appeared at a loss to truly rule. She relied heavily on the advice and recommendations of several of Peter's advisors, most notably Menshikov, the man who had brought Catherine to Peter's attention.

Birth, Adoption, and Upbringing

Both parents died within three years of Catherine's birth, leaving her to be adopted by an aunt. Others raised her brother and sisters. She wouldn't see them again until years later, when she was able to bring them to live in St. Petersburg, discretely supported by the Czar but kept out of Russian public life. Her father, Samuel Skavronski, worked as a gravedigger after his escape to the Swedish province of Livonia.

At the age of twelve Martha was sent to serve in the home of Pastor Gluck, a strict Lutheran who was the Superintendent of the village Marienburg. Her Catholic heritage was filed away, as Martha's life with the Gluck family was a combination of cleaning, sewing, spinning, babysitting, and listening to long sermons. Unlike the Gluck children, Martha was not taught to read or write. She reportedly matured into an attractive young woman who was known for her cheerful demeanor, large brown eyes, upturned nose and ample curves.

She eventually caught the attention of Johann Raabe, a trumpeter in the dragoons. When Martha was nineteen, a marriage was arranged, but her husband left town with his unit shortly thereafter, marching into oblivion and leaving the Russian army to occupy Marienburg. Gluck and his family were granted amnesty, but Martha, who for reasons unknown hadn't fled with her husband, was kept as a prisoner, serving at whatever tasks she was given by the Russian soldiers and Cossacks.

After what may have been several years, she won the attention and protection of Brigadier Bauer. Soon afterward, Boris Sheremetev, the commander-in-chief of the occupying Russian army stationed in Livonia, had her shifted to serve in his household. Within a few months, she was transferred or possibly sold to Major-General Alexander Menshikov, a rising young officer favored by the Czar.

Education and Significant Relationships

Martha's first meeting with Peter the Great came when he visited Marienburg in July 1702. She was waiting tables at a banquet given by Menshikov.

> [The Czar] questioned Menshikov in low tones, turned to Martha, and entered into conversation with her. "He found her clever," wrote Villebois, Peter's aide-de-camp, "and ended his badinage with her by saying that when he went to bed she must bring the torch to his room. This was a decision from which there was no appeal, although it was delivered with a laugh. Menshikov subscribed to it. And the fair one, with the consent of her master, spent the night in the Czar's room" (Troyat 146).

Menshikov had planned all along to bring the Czar a woman who pleased him, perhaps for the long term. He knew that the future Czarina would be forever grateful, and he would have the Czar's ear and even greater favor and influence through her (Longworth 8).

In 1704, the birth of a son led to the christening of baby and mother together. The baby was named Paul and Martha became Catherine. She remained uneducated, though she was instructed in court manners and protocol by women like Princess Natalia, the Czar's sister.

By 1705, Catherine had borne Peter two sons out of wedlock, as Peter was still married but had sent his wife, Yevdokia, to a nunnery. There would be a total of twelve children, but only two would survive: Anna, the future Duchess of Holstein-Gottorp, and Elizabeth, future Empress of Russia.

Most of their relationship was a whirlwind of separation and reunion, punctuated by wars, travels, and Peter's dream of designing and building St. Petersburg in the style of great European cities. In the meantime, they lived in a simple two-room cabin. Later they would set up court in various palaces built to win the respect of European royalty.

As Russia's recognition as a world power grew, so did Peter's influence over the nation's reluctant acceptance of Catherine as his consort, then his wife, and finally their Empress. Many Russians, especially Muscovites, viewed Yevdokia's son Alexei as the true heir to the throne. This gave Catherine considerable anxiety, since her offspring and even her life could be at stake if Peter were to die in battle or due to his heavy drinking and fluctuating health. Alexei, who at one point had become a monk and fled to Italy, was brought back to Russia by the secret police and sentenced to be executed for wishing the death of the Czar. Before that happened, he died mysteriously in his jail cell. Some said that Peter killed him with his own hands.

Catherine's peasant beginnings kept her from being received by a number of European royals, though many did eventually acknowledge her or at least politely tolerate her for diplomatic reasons. With each elevation of status, Peter would launch a new public relations campaign rich with cultural myths about Catherine's heroism, wisdom, virtue, and worthiness.

Shortly before his death, Peter became intensely jealous of an alleged affair between Catherine and her chamberlain, William Mons. Peter flew into a rage and had Mons, along with a number of Catherine's ladies in waiting, interrogated, tortured, and imprisoned or executed, despite Catherine's denials and pleas for mercy for them.

Catherine's final years were spent in increasing excess, hosting lavish dinner parties, buying expensive clothing, and keeping erratic hours. The political machinations of her advisors, as they jockeyed for power and wealth, intensified and carried over after her death in May of 1727. Eleven-year-old Peter Alexeyevich, son of the murdered Alexei, acceded to the throne, but Menshikov, who had persuaded Catherine to name him in her will, continued to rule Russia until political enemies exiled him to Siberia.

Works Cited

Longworth, Philip. *The Three Empresses.* New York: Holt, Rinehart and Winston, 1972.
Troyat, Henri. *Peter the Great.* New York: E. P. Dutton, 1987.

CHANEL, COCO (1883–1971)

Fashion Designer
Orphanage alumna

Career, Major Awards, and Achievements

Coco Chanel created a revolution in the fashion industry in 1919 with her simple but elegant styles. She raised hemlines, banished corsets, and was the first to introduce

[Courtesy of the Library of Congress]

the ease and comfort of jersey knits, blazers, and sweaters: "I invented sportswear for myself. . . . I set the fashion for the very reason that I was the first twentieth-century woman" (Baudot 10). She also replaced nineteenth-century beribboned and feathered bonnets with simple turbans, cloches, and pillbox hats.

Chanel is known best for pairing the simple, classic lines of her fashions with striking costume jewelry. Some of her fashion trademarks include airy and uneven hemlines, the "little black dress," turtleneck sweaters, bobbed hair, camellia flowers re-created in silks or precious metals, and designs in contrasting black and white. She is also well remembered for her popular fragrance, Chanel No. 5. Chanel reigned as the queen of high fashion until she retired during World War II. She made a strong comeback in the early 1950s, however, and her influence on the fashions of that decade is unmistakable. After her death, House of Chanel designers continued to produce her styles in luxury fashion, textiles, fragrances, beauty products, jewelry, and watches. Her legacy company, Chanel, Inc., remains today one of the world's most prestigious fashion and beauty enterprises.

Family of Origin

Gabrielle Bonheur Chanel was born in a charity hospital on August 19, 1883 in Saumur, Maine-et-Loire, France, to Henri Chanel, sometimes called Albert, and Eugénie Jeanne Devolles, known as Jeanne. They were itinerant peddlers: "I was born on a journey. . . . My father was not there. That poor woman, my mother, had to go looking for him. It's a sad story" (Haedrich 21).

Chanel invented many conflicting stories of her childhood and family, making it difficult to determine which circumstances were true: "Come, now, you don't think I'm going to tell you the story of my life!" (Haedrich 49). Documents located after her death, however, have allowed biographers to piece together some of her early story. Chanel was one of five children and her parents' second illegitimate daughter: "Although her parents had married soon after she was born, all her life Chanel worried that her illegitimacy would be discovered. 'She could never live with the truth,' writes Madsen, 'and spent her adult years perpetually revising her life story'" (Felder 175). There are also many versions about how and when she got the name "Coco," including it being her father's pet name for her. Her mother, who had tuberculosis, died shortly after the birth of her youngest child, Antoinette. After his wife's death, Henri deserted his children. He placed his sons, Alphonse and Lucien, into public care, where they became unpaid farm laborers (Felder 175). He took the three girls, Julia-Berthe (the eldest child), Coco, and Antoinette to his mother in Vichy.

Orphanage

Chanel's grandmother, Virginie, had many children of her own, her youngest, Adrienne, being only two years older than Coco. When Coco was six or seven, she was put into a convent orphanage in Moulins or Aubazine. Haedrich, one of Chanel's principal biographers, believes that when Chanel refers to her "aunts' house," she is actually referring to her life in the orphanage: "in her aunts' house, she said, she always wore the same suit, and with complete assurance she added that in the country all the girls were dressed in the same way. 'That was my uniform,' she said another time. For an attentive listener the truth had been merely transposed; unmistakably she was talking about the convent, the orphanage" (Haedrich 43).

The convent had paying students in addition to charity cases. The two types of students were made to dress differently, and the charity students had a lower quality of life. The orphanage girls were distinguished from the paying students by uniforms:

> "Until I was sixteen," she said, "I wore what all the girls of that period wore, a little tailored suit. That was the origin of my suits. I ought to have hated that suit, but I can't wear anything else. . . . For winter I had a kind of cloche, very hard, with a kind of feather on it. . . . There was a little rubber band in the back that went under one's hair, to hold the hat in place when it was windy. I thought the whole business was very ugly. It was my uniform" (Haedrich 34).

Who could foresee that this charity girl would one day re-create her "poor girl look" and little black suit into the very pinnacle of haute couture?

Education and Relationships

Chanel left the convent school around 1913 and opened a millinery shop in Deauville with her sister, Antoinette, and her young aunt, Adrienne. In 1915, she became the mistress of a wealthy horse-breeder, Etienne Balsan, and her fashions began to attract the attention of his stylish friends. Although she went on to other relationships, Chanel never married: "I've had no time for living," she said. "No one's ever understood this. I don't even know whether I've been very happy. I've wept a great deal, more than most people do" (Haedrich 9–10).

Chanel's sisters both died when they were young women. She acted as a guardian for Julia-Berthe's son, André Pallasse. Her brother Alphonse made contact again in 1914, when he went to war, but she avoided seeing her brothers again (Haedrich 41). However, she tried to assist Alphonse's children, Yvan and Gabrielle. Chanel died in Paris on January 10, 1971.

Works Cited

Baudot, François. *Chanel.* NY: Venome Press, 1996.
Felder, Deborah G. *The 100 Most Influential Women of All Time.* Secaucus, NJ: Carol Publishing Group, 1996.
Haedrich, Marcel. *Coco Chanel: Her Life, Her Secrets.* Boston: Little, 1971.

CHAPLIN, CHARLIE (1889–1977)

Comedian, Actor, Filmmaker
Orphanage alumnus

Career, Major Awards, and Achievements

Charlie Chaplin was one of the best known and loved figures in film during the first half of the twentieth century. Chaplin was born in England and remained an English subject throughout his long life, but he lived and worked in the United States for over forty years. He first came to the United States in 1910, touring with an English troupe. He returned in 1912 with the same group and in 1913 was seen by Mack Sennett, who hired him. Within seven years of his first visit, Chaplin was a millionaire, having produced, directed, or acted in more than eighty films. Over fifty were made for Sennett's Keystone Films. Films were made very quickly—the first, *Making a Living,* was released February 2, 1914; *Kid Auto Races at Venice* appeared on February 7, and *Mabel's Strange Predicament* came out February 9. Chaplin created the Little Tramp character for this third film.

He joined the Essanay Company in 1915, making fifteen more films, many with titles including his name, like *Charlie the Tramp.* The following year he went to the Mutual Film Company, making twelve more comedies. In 1918, he opened his own studio to produce higher quality comedies, including *The Kid* and *The Gold Rush.*

Also in 1918, Chaplin joined Mary Pickford and Douglas Fairbanks in supporting the war effort by raising money for the Third Liberty Loan, and the next year the three

[Courtesy of the Library of Congress]

joined forces again, creating United Artists Releasing Corporation to distribute their films. Chaplin's films usually featured the Little Tramp character. In addition to acting, Chaplin wrote, produced, and directed his films, often giving new actors like Jackie Coogan and Paulette Goddard an opportunity to begin their careers.

"Talkies" became possible in 1928, but Chaplin preferred to make silent films after other producers moved on. *City Lights*, released in 1931, and *Modern Times*, released in 1936, were both silent because Chaplin was concerned about losing his international audience if films were made in English only. He was also concerned about how his own voice would sound and whether the Little Tramp, who was essentially a mime, would translate into a speaking character. His first sound film, and the last to use the Little Tramp character, was *The Great Dictator* (1940), in which Chaplin played a Hitler-like character, Adenoid Hynckel, and his double, a Jewish barber.

During the 1940s, Chaplin was investigated by the House Committee on Un-American Activities and the Dies committee for suspected Communist sympathies. Both were unable to connect Chaplin and Communism; however, when Chaplin was on his way to England, his entry permit was rescinded. As a British subject, he could not return to the United States without it. In 1953, he and his family settled in Vevey, Switzerland. Oona Chaplin returned to the States to close the studio and their home and had Chaplin's films shipped to Switzerland where Chaplin built a film vault for them. The films stored there are the principal source for the works available today.

An international figure, Chaplin was a member of the French Legion of Honor, an honorary member of the Norwegian Actors Association, and a member of the British Film Academy. In 1954, he was the recipient of the World Peace Council's Peace Prize. Chaplin came back to the United States to receive a special Oscar in 1972 and went to London in 1975 to become Sir Charles Spencer Chaplin, KBE (Knight Commander of the British Empire).

Family of Origin

Charlie Chaplin was born Charles Spencer Chaplin, the son of Hannah (Hill) Chaplin and Charles Spencer Chaplin, in Walworth, a poor area of London, on April 16, 1889. The Chaplins were music hall performers; Charles senior was a singer of ballads, while Hannah, billed as Lily Harley, played the piano, sang, and acted in skits. Chaplin had two half-brothers on his mother's side. When she was seventeen or eighteen, Hannah ran away with a middle-aged man to South Africa and Sydney, Charlie's elder brother, was born to the couple when Hannah was 18 years old. Sydney, born Sydney John Hill in March, 1885, was named Sydney Chaplin after the Chaplins married in June that year. Charlie's younger brother, Wheeler Dryden, was born in 1892 to Hannah and music hall performer Leo Dryden. Wheeler was taken from Hannah as an infant and raised by his father in India. Chaplin did not know about his younger brother for years, but Wheeler sought out both brothers and later worked for Chaplin at his studio.

Hannah and her husband separated and she became a single parent with little or no child support. Chaplin writes, "I was hardly aware of a father, and do not remember him having lived with us. He too was a vaudevillian. . . trouble was that he drank too much, which Mother said was the cause of their separation" (Chaplin 15).

Hannah was a popular performer and the family lived modestly well until she began to experience problems with her voice. Soon she entirely lost her career and the family's income. One night Charlie remembered being rushed onto the stage to finish his mother's performance after her voice broke:

> It was owing to her vocal condition that at the age of five I made my first appearance on the stage. . . . And before a glare of footlights and faces in smoke I started to sing. . . . That night was my first appearance on the stage and Mother's last. When the fates deal in human destiny, they heed neither pity nor justice. Thus they dealt with Mother. She never regained her voice (Chaplin 19).

Hannah's physical and mental health deteriorated and she was no longer able to keep a home. In 1894, Hannah, Sydney, and Charlie, who was then about six years of age, went into the Lambeth Workhouse:

> How well I remember the poignant sadness of that first visiting day: the shock of seeing Mother enter the visiting-room garbed in workhouse clothes. How forlorn and embarrassed she looked! In one week she had aged and grown thin, but her face lit up when she saw us. . . . She smiled at our cropped heads and stroked them consolingly, telling us that we would soon all be together again (Chaplin 26).

Orphanage

Sydney and Charlie spent three weeks at Lambeth and then were sent to the Hanwell Schools for Orphans and Destitute Children. They were quarantined for "medical and mental observation" (Chaplin 27), then separated, Sydney going to the big boys ward, for children seven to fourteen, and Charlie going to the infants ward:

> On Saturday afternoon the bath-house was reserved for infants, who were bathed by the older girls. This, of course, was before I was seven, and a squeamish modesty attended these occasions; having to submit to the ignominy of a young girl of fourteen manipulating a facecloth all over my person was my first conscious embarrassment (Chaplin 29).

The young Chaplins spent two years in Hanwell and attended their school for paupers, often cold and hungry and frequently severely disciplined. Chaplin always remembered this period of his life as miserable. At age eleven a workhouse boy could join the navy or army and Sydney chose to enter the navy. He was sent to the Exmouth, leaving Charlie alone at Hanwell.

At one time Hannah was able to leave the workhouse and briefly brought her family, including Sydney, back together in a small back room at Norwood. But soon she was sent to the Cane Hill asylum for mental illness and the boys went to live with Charlie's father, his mistress, Louise, and Louise's son, Charlie's four-year-old half-brother on his father's side. Louise resented Hannah's children, especially Sydney, and there were problems of neglect, alcoholism, and violence:

> One day Louise received a visit from the Society for the Prevention of Cruelty to Children, and she was most indignant about it. They came because the police reported finding Sydney and me asleep at three o'clock in the morning by a watchman's fire. It was a night that Louise had shut us both out, and the police had made her open the door and let us in (Chaplin 39).

Hannah eventually was able to recover enough to reclaim her sons. They lived on weekly payments of ten shillings from Charlie's father and moved to a small room at Kennington Cross, where the boys were able to attend school. Chaplin senior died when Charlie was twelve. Hannah died in 1928, in Hollywood, having been brought there by her sons.

Charlie survived by working in a barbershop, as a janitor in the music halls, and performing small dancing or comic parts in vaudeville. By 1906 he and Sydney were supporting actors in the Fred Karno vaudeville troupe, and in 1910 he became the comic star of a second Karno troupe. In 1913 he was seen by Mack Sennett, who offered him a movie contract. That same year, he began work for Keystone Films in Hollywood.

Military Service and Significant Relationships

Though Chaplin had been working in the United States for some time before World War I, the British press criticized him because he did not serve in the military. He had actually been denied because he was both small and underweight. He did raise money for the war through bond drives and made a propaganda film, *The Bond*, which appeared in 1918.

During World War II, the Nazis issued propaganda saying that Chaplin was Jewish. He made a point of refusing to refute these claims during the war or afterward when the FBI investigated his racial origins. He had been baptized in the Church of England but appeared to hold agnostic beliefs.

Chaplin's relationships with women usually began with his discovery of a young actress, followed by close interest in her career. Edna Purviance was his first important leading lady; their romance began in 1916 and ended before his 1918 marriage to Mildred Harris. Purviance continued as a leading actress in Chaplin films and their friendship was lifelong.

Chaplin was twenty-nine when he married sixteen-year-old Mildred Harris, a popular child-actress. Their only child, Norman Spencer Chaplin, died in infancy and Chaplin and Harris divorced in 1921. From 1922 to 1923 Chaplain was involved with and eventually engaged to Pola Negri, though some of Chaplin's biographers believe that the relationship, which was quite public in contrast to his other attachments, was mostly publicity.

In 1924 Chaplin was involved with Marion Davis (best known as the companion of William Randolph Hearst) and sixteen-year-old Lita Gray, whom he had met while filming *The Kid*. She was to star in *The Gold Rush* but was removed when she became pregnant. They married in November and had two sons, Charles Spencer, Jr., and Sydney Earl. Grey filed for divorce in December 1926. The lengthy and bitter law case, the negative publicity, and a tax dispute caused Chaplin to stop work on *The Circus*, his then current film, and go to New York. After the divorce was final (with a record-breaking settlement of $825,000 in addition to extensive legal fees) in August 1927, work on the film was resumed and it was released in 1928.

Georgia Hale, nineteen, was Gray's replacement in *The Gold Rush*. She and Chaplin had an affair that lasted several years, according to an interview given by her in the documentary *Unknown Chaplin*. May Reeves, hired as a secretary, chronicled her affair with Chaplin in 1931 in her book *The Intimate Charlie Chaplin*.

Between 1932 and 1940, actress Paulette Goddard lived with Chaplin in his home in Beverly Hills. Goddard was "discovered" by Chaplin and received leading roles in *Modern Times* and *The Great Dictator*. In 1940, when the relationship broke up, they announced a secret 1936 marriage. The announcement was generally thought to be an untruth constructed to minimize damage to her career. She received a settlement in 1942.

In 1942, a brief affair with Joan Berry, whom Chaplin was considering for a role in an upcoming project, had less agreeable results. Chaplin ended the relationship when Berry began showing signs of mental illness. She filed a paternity suit against him the following year, but blood tests showed that Chaplin was not the father of Berry's child. When her lawyer was able to convince the court that the tests should not be admitted as evidence, Chaplin was ordered to pay child support. The next year, related Mann Act charges were brought against Chaplin, and though he was acquitted, his reputation suffered.

During this time he met Oona O'Neill, the daughter of playwright Eugene O'Neill. After Oona, 18, married Chaplin, 54, on June 16, 1943, her father refused further contact with her. Nevertheless, the marriage was happy. The Chaplins had eight children, Geraldine (1944), Michael (1946), Josephine (1949), Victoria (1951), Eugene (1953), Jane (1957), Annette (1959) and Christopher, born in 1962 when his father was 73 years old.

Charlie Chaplin died in his sleep early on Christmas Day, 1977, in Switzerland. Oona Chaplin died of cancer in 1991.

Works Cited

Chaplin, Charles. *My Autobiography.* New York: Penguin, 1986.

COCHRAN, JACQUELINE (1910?–1980)

Aviator, Business Executive
Former foster child

Career, Major Awards, and Achievements

Jacqueline (Jackie) Cochran is best known as a record-setting aviation pioneer. During her forty years as a pilot, she held more records for speed, altitude, and distance

[Courtesy of the Library of Congress]

than any other pilot in history. Cochran began her flying career in the 1930s as a racing pilot and won her first Bendix race in 1938. Cochran was the first woman pilot to fly faster than the speed of sound (1953) and the first woman to fly a jet across the Atlantic (1962). Her courage and skill won national and international renown.

Cochran became the first woman to fly a bomber across the Atlantic to England, where she organized a group of American women pilots to assist the British war effort. By 1943, she became director of the Women's Airforce Service Pilot (WASP) program. Later, her determination and influence helped to establish the Air Force as a military unit independent of the Army. Among her many awards are the United States Distinguished Service Award, the Air Force Distinguished Flying Cross, France's Legion of Honor, the Harmon Trophy for Outstanding Pilot of the Year (fifteen times), Germany's Pionierkette Winderose decoration, and the Federation Aeronautique Internationale's gold medal. Cochran went on to become the Federation Aeronautique's first woman president from 1958 to 1961. Notre Dame College granted her an honorary Doctor of Science degree in 1970, an astonishing achievement for a woman who left school in the second grade. In 1971, she became the first living woman honored in the Aviation Hall of Fame.

Family of Origin

Jacqueline Cochran wrote that her exact date and place of birth were unknown. According to her autobiographical account, May 11 was a random date chosen by her foster family to celebrate as her birthday. She believed that her birth had taken place near Muscogee, Florida, around 1910: "I was probably born near Muscogee, Florida, but I'll never know the truth of it. . . . I don't think they accurately knew the year of my birth" (15).*

Foster Family

She was raised in poverty in "Sawdust Road," her nickname for the Florida and Georgia sawmill colonies where her foster family lived and worked. Her foster parents had four biological children, two boys and two girls, before they took in "Jackie" as their youngest. She accidentally discovered that she was a foster child around the age of six by overhearing a private conversation:

"Do you hear anything about Jackie's family these days?" a friend of my foster mother's is asking. I'm within earshot but not sight. "Not a word," my mother answers. Silence. My heart beats faster. My mother continues: "And I'm going to keep it that way. Jackie doesn't know she's any different from the others." But I always knew I was different from the others (24).

Education, Military Service, and Significant Relationships

Cochran left school and began working twelve-hour shifts at a cotton mill around the age of eight. She left home when she was approximately eleven years old to begin an

---

*The information Cochran consistently provided in her autobiographies and interviews about her birth and foster family became controversial after the publication of a memoir written by Billie Pittman Ayers and Beth Dees. Ayers, who identifies herself as Cochran's niece, claims that Cochran was born May 11, 1906, in Muscogee, Florida, the fifth child of poor but loving parents, Mary Grant Pittman and Ira Pittman. Ayers claims that Cochran, whose original name she says was Bessie Lee Pittman, fabricated her story about growing up an orphan because she thought it made her seem more interesting, and to give herself anonymity (Ayers x).

apprenticeship with Mrs. Richler, a beautician in Columbus, Georgia. Jackie began her work for the Richler family as a live-in cook and maid, but Mrs. Richler soon began to train the eager teen as a hair dresser. Cochran enjoyed and excelled in the beauty business and eventually established a thriving and innovative cosmetics company of her own, which twice earned her the Associated Press's Business Woman of the Year award.

According to Ayers's memoir, Cochran, then named Bessie Pittman, married Robert H. Cochran, a machinist, on November 13, 1920, when she was fourteen years old (21). Their son, Robert, Jr., died in a house fire at the age of four. The Cochrans divorced a year after the accident, but Bessie retained her married name. She later renamed herself Jacqueline, after choosing the name out of a phone directory. In 1932, Cochran met tycoon Floyd Odlum, her future husband of forty years. She felt a need to search for the truth about her origins before she could marry. Apparently, she feared that confirmation of her suspected illegitimacy might affect her fiancé's regard for her:

> Being an orphan never bothered me until 1936, when I was about to marry Floyd. I thought he should know as much about me as anyone could, so I went south again and got letters from the two people still living who might have more facts than I had. I gave those letters to Floyd in an envelope sealed with a quarter imbedded in wax. On the outside, in my own scrawly handwriting, I wrote, "This is for you, Floyd. I have never read the contents. You can burn it or read it as you wish. I love you very much. Jackie." Floyd chose not to read them then or to burn them either but, instead, handed them back to me.
>
> Truthfully, I didn't want to know what the letters said about me. . . . I realize that might sound strange, but what could the knowledge have added to my life then? More important, what could it have taken away from me? (15–16).

Close friend and mentor General Chuck Yeager, the first person to break the sound barrier, found the sealed envelope after Floyd's death in 1976. He burned the packet unopened, after Cochran decided not to read the contents.

During World War II, Jackie's beauty business had to take a back seat as she became involved in the country's war effort.

Cochran attributed much of her success in life to her childhood experiences. She said that they gave her strength, readiness for anything, and a compulsion to be totally self-sufficient: "If I had had that decent education and a fine family behind me, I probably wouldn't have accomplished half of what I did in my life" (50). She especially wanted to adopt children after a second miscarriage, and once even tried to establish an orphanage at her desert ranch but was prevented by "complications from the state." Cochran died August 9, 1980, of heart disease at her beloved 800-acre ranch at Indio, California.

Works Cited

Ayers, Billie Pittman, and Beth Dees. *Superwoman Jacqueline Cochran: Family Memories about the Famous Pilot, Patriot, Wife & Businesswoman.* [Self-Published] 1st Books Library, 2001.

Cochran, Jackie, and Maryann Bucknum Brinley. *Jackie Cochran: An Autobiography.* New York: Bantam, 1987.

Nolan, Stephanie. *Promised the Moon: The Untold Story of the First Women in Space.* New York: Four Walls Eight Windows, 2002. 31–50.

Rich, Doris L. *Jackie Cochran: Pilot in the Fastest Lane.* Gainesville, FL: University Press of Florida, 2007.

Smith, Elizabeth Simpson. *Coming Out Right: The Story of Jacqueline Cochran, The First Woman Aviator to Break the Sound Barrier* [Juvenile biography]. New York: Walker & Co., 1991.

COLEMAN, FRAN (1945–)

Colorado Legislator, Lobbyist
Orphanage alumna Infant of Prague Nursery and Queen of Heaven Orphanage, Denver, Colorado, adoptee

Career, Major Awards, and Achievements

Fran Coleman was elected to the Colorado House of Representatives as the representative for House District 1 (Southwest Denver) in November 1998 and reelected in November 2000, 2002, and 2004. She is currently an independent lobbyist at the State

[Courtesy of Frances "Fran" Natividad Coleman]

Legislature after serving in the Colorado General Assembly for eight years. Before her election, Coleman worked for thirty years at the Mountain States Telephone and Telegraph Company, now Qwest. She has always been very active in church, political, and community work. She chaired her regional Reading is Fundamental (RIF) program and served on the Colorado Board of Corrections (1992–1997 and 2004 to present). She has served on the advisory board and was chair of LARASA (Latin American Research and Service Agency) and on a community advisory board at Fort Logan, Colorado. Coleman was the chair of her county's Democratic party (1996–1997) and belongs to the National Women's Political Caucus. Her major legislative committee assignments included Information and Technology, Legislative Audit, and Transportation and Energy. In 1999, she sponsored legislation to open adoption records to adult adoptees:

> The natural person to carry the adoption research bill here in Colorado would, of course, be myself and I am committed to see it to the end. . . . As a person, I'm not even angry about it anymore. It just doesn't make sense that I'm a 57 year-old woman who cannot look at her own birth record—that hardly makes sense at all. . . . I think that most people wish to look into their backgrounds and look at their true origins—it is a natural right for anybody, whether you're adopted or not. And that right should not be denied to individuals—it's a fundamental right for all human beings (Coleman, personal interview, June 3, 2002).

Family of Origin

Coleman was born on July 5, 1945, in Denver, Colorado. Although she has the possible names of her birthparents and has been searching for them for several years, she has not yet been able to verify the information. She believes that her biological father is of English ancestry and was in the Air Force at the time of her birth and that her birthmother was of Spanish ancestry. Coleman was twelve years old when she found out about her adoption:

> When I was twelve, I learned that I was adopted. Not my father, nor my aunt or uncle, ever offered that I was adopted. I actually learned it as a result of a cousin who was teasing me. He was calling me the word "coyota," which in Spanish means "half-breed." Of course I was very concerned, because my family was Mexican—the family I grew up in—and that's how I saw myself. I went to talk to Grandpa about it, who would have also been grandfather to this cousin, and I told on my cousin and said that I was very hurt, and couldn't understand why he'd do that. So then Grandpa hugged me and told me that I should go talk to my Dad, that there was more to the story. When I talked to Dad, he said that my father was of English descent and my mother was probably Mexican, but that was pretty much all he knew—and that when they first adopted me all I spoke was English. So they had adopted me when I was three and I'd just chatter away in English. They call me the "little Inglesca"! But with them being a Spanish-speaking family, by the time I was six all I knew was Spanish. In fact, I flunked the first grade because all I spoke was Spanish. That was interesting to me, that I could take on this whole culture I had not known before (Coleman, personal interview, July 12, 1998).

Adoption

Coleman was adopted in 1948, when she was three years old, along with an adoptive brother, David, who was then five years old. Coleman's adoptive parents were of Mexican descent and she has always identified herself with that culture. She grew up on a farm in Gilcrest, Colorado. Her adoptive mother had been unable to become pregnant as a result of smallpox incurred in Mexico. When the family learned on a popular

Spanish radio program that there was a need for Hispanic families to adopt waiting children, they responded. Prior to the adoption, Fran lived in Denver at the Infant of Prague, a Catholic nursery for orphaned or abandoned children, and Queen of Heaven, a girls' orphanage founded by Mother Frances Cabrini, who was canonized as a saint in 1946. Coleman has a vague memory of the day her parents took her home from the orphanage:

> I have one memory, which always used to come to me as a dream, of my adoption. I would see two ladies and a man with a hat standing in this huge room with lots of beds—so I suppose that would have been an orphanage ward where children had their individual beds, and me hanging on to a woman who was wearing black and white, and in retrospect I suppose she was a nun, because I was adopted from the Queen of Heaven Orphanage, here in Denver. In this dream I would hang on to this woman, and these three individuals, a man and two women, were standing there wanting to take me. I imagine that they were my mother and her sister and my father. When Dad finally said that I was adopted, he described that scene exactly as I had known it in my dream. So then I was able to put things together, and make sense of them. Interestingly, I never had that dream again after that. Otherwise, I don't have any memories that I can think of earlier than the age of three. I often have a real sadness that I don't have any pictures of myself as a baby (Coleman, personal interview, July 12, 1998).

Coleman was very close to her adoptive parents, especially her mother, but her mother only lived three years after the adoption before she died in a choking accident while eating:

> I do know that I've always had a deep sense of loss, especially in regards to my adopted mother, of not being able to go to her. Because even though I only knew her for three years, I have a very deep love and deep affection for her—and I get a little emotional here. I feel that the reason I am who I am is because of her and her example. She was a very kind, giving individual. . . . She had enough love in her heart, and determination to be able to make it [the adoption] work—and then to be taken away from us prematurely. I think my hard work and how I love and deal with people comes from her example (Coleman, personal interview, July 12, 1998).

Some months after their mother's death, Coleman and her brother moved in with their maternal aunt and uncle, although their father continued to visit the children when he could:

> For six months Dad tried to hold on to us, but because he was a migrant worker and laborer, he couldn't stay and earn a living. So my aunt kept bothering him, and finally he gave in, and let her take us under her roof. When I talk about my aunt—my aunt and my mother were sisters—they were like Jekyll and Hyde. Mom was very nice and loving, and my aunt was very controversial. Once we went under her roof, she beat us, particularly my brother, every day. I have always been quoted as saying that I was beat up every day from the time I was six until I was eighteen, when I left that home. Every penny we ever earned, once we were able to earn—and each of us had our jobs by the time we were eight, washing dishes for the landlady, or working in her yard, or cleaning her house—we worked for 50 cents an hour—all of that money went into my aunt's pocket. When I turned eighteen, I left home. But the year before I turned eighteen, my father died unexpectedly from a hit and run, so what little support I ever had was definitely gone. . . .
>
> When I lived with my aunt and uncle, I suffered a lot of mental abuse, physical abuse, and some, unfortunately, sexual abuse. I had a lot of anger that I was not aware of and I came to terms with it as a result of someone asking me about looking into my past. That's

when I realized how angry I was and how much I had pushed those feelings down, thus causing me to be driven—to just keep going forward and not look back. However, I always wanted to protect others so that they don't have to suffer like I did. . . .

A lot of the reason why I ran for office is because I feel that I am an individual who is known in the community, who is pragmatic and will get things done—will do their homework and can make changes in peoples' lives (Coleman, personal interview, July 12, 1998).

Education, Marriage, and Children

Coleman earned her Bachelor of Arts degree in business in 1987 from Loretto Heights College in Denver and received her Master's of Science degree in Telecommunications from the University of Denver in 1992. She married in 1965 and has two sons, Matt and Mitch, whom she raised as a single mother after her divorce in 1979. In 1986, she married Ben Coleman and has four stepchildren, Pam, Steve, Craig, and Wayne. Coleman believes that her adoption especially affected her drive and her relationships:

> I think my adoption did affect me and made me a very driven individual, being able to achieve an undergraduate, and then a master's degree, while raising two children as a single mother. To achieve my degrees, and raise my children, and travel, and be a career woman—I would consider that pretty driven—but yet I was really able to balance my life and make sure my children had a good home, a loving home, and got to do a lot of quality things with Mom. When we went to the playground, I went to the playground with them, and guess who played the hardest?—it was usually me. We played sports together and I had my boys involved in football, that sort of thing. That was always really important, that they not suffer like I had, and that they have the love that I didn't have (Coleman, personal interview, July 12, 1998).

Works Cited

Personal interviews with Fran Coleman, July 12, 1998 and June 3, 2002.

CRAWFORD, CHRISTINA (1939–)

Author, Actress
Adoptee

Career, Major Awards, and Achievements

Although she enjoyed an early and successful acting career, Christina Crawford is best known as the author of her first book, *Mommie Dearest* (1978), an autobiography about her traumatic childhood with her famous adoptive mother, Joan Crawford. *Mommie Dearest* was on the *New York Times* bestseller list for nearly a year, and in 1981 it was made into a film (Paramount) starring Faye Dunaway as Joan Crawford and Mara Hobel and Diana Scarwid as Christina. Crawford's additional works include *Black Widow* (1981), which was also a best-seller, *Survivor* (1988), and *No Safe Place: The Legacy of Family Violence* (1995). Crawford established her own publishing house, Seven Springs Press, and brought out several of her works under its imprint, including a twentieth anniversary, expanded edition of *Mommie Dearest* (1997) and *Daughters of the Inquisition* (2003).

[Courtesy of Photofest]

Crawford was a commissioner for Children's Services in Los Angeles. She made child abuse into a national issue and has appeared at numerous conferences as an advocate for the rights of women, children, and adopted persons.

Family of Origin and Adoption

Oscar-winning legend Joan Crawford adopted Christina as a single mother when she was thirty-five years old. Christina had been born in Hollywood and the adoption was arranged through a "baby broker":

> My official papers simply say "girl" born on Sunday afternoon, June 11, 1939. My real mother was a student and my father a sailor, and neither of them wanted to take responsibility for me.

So I traveled from Hollywood Presbyterian Hospital to a baby broker to 426 North Bristol Avenue when I was only a few weeks old (Crawford 20).

Crawford adopted Christina in May, 1940, when she was eleven months old. Three years later, in 1942, Joan Crawford married Philip Terry, and the couple appeared to adopt an infant boy they named Phillip Terry, Jr., in 1943. As it turned out Terry did not formally adopt either Christina or Philip, Jr.

Joan Crawford had earlier attempted to adopt a boy named Christopher, but the baby had been located and reclaimed by his first mother. The incident triggered the first of Christina's recurring nightmares of being kidnapped and prompted Crawford to falsify her subsequent children's birthdates as a precaution:

> Evidently through publicity stories on baby Christopher, which included his real birth date, the natural mother had been able to locate her son. After that episode, Joan Crawford wasn't taking any further chances.
>   From that time on, she changed the birth dates on our certificates. She didn't change mine, but on my brother's she changed the date to October 15, and later, when she adopted two girls she called twins, she changed theirs to January 15 (Crawford 26–27).

Following Crawford's divorce from Terry, Philip Jr.'s name was changed to Christopher. Christina and Christopher shared a room "until we left home as teenagers" (Crawford 26) and they also shared abuse. Actor James MacArthur, Helen Hayes' son and an adoptee,* once found Christopher tied to his bed when he came for a visit (MacPherson E3). Crawford writes the following about her brother:

> He had his share of problems trying to grow up in a houseful of women. He'd run away from home on a number of occasions when he couldn't stand being so cooped up and had been harshly disciplined. . . . What she couldn't control, Mother either dismissed or destroyed. . . . We also found out [after her death] that Mother went to great lengths to adopt Chris by herself in Las Vegas *after* she and Philip separated, although my brother and I both grew up believing that Chris had been adopted by both Philip and Mother (Crawford 168–169).

Christina was eight when two more daughters were adopted, Cathy and Cynthia, were adopted. Crawford decided to raise as fraternal twins, although they were not biologically related (Crawford 47).

> Why in God's name did she adopt all of us in the first place? Sure we served a purpose when we were adorable babies. She got years of prime publicity out of us. . . . Millions of unsuspecting fans thought: "What a wonderful woman. . . to take *four* little orphans into her home." . . . We were the best mannered, best-behaved, most perfect child-mannequins the queen bee could produce (Crawford 197).

Joan Crawford died May 10, 1977. Both Christina and Christopher were disinherited in Crawford's will. Soon after her mother's death, Christina began writing *Mommie Dearest*, which details years of relentless beatings, emotional abuse, alcoholic rages, and a parade of husbands and of lovers of both genders.

---

*James MacArthur was adopted as an infant by Helen Hayes and Charles MacArthur. He appeared in many roles and is best known for his television role of "Danno" on *Hawaii Five-O.*

Education and Significant Relationships

At age twelve, Christina was sent to a California boarding school called Chadwick, which her siblings also attended. She was sent at age sixteen to Flintridge Sacred Heart, a Catholic boarding school near Los Angeles. After graduation, Crawford attended the Carnegie Mellon School of Drama in Pittsburg and the Neighborhood Playhouse Professional School in New York. She received her BA, *magna cum laude*, at the University of California, Los Angeles, in 1974 and her MA in Communication Management from the University of Southern California in 1975.

Crawford married and divorced three times: to Harvey Medlinsky, whom she met during acting school; to writer and producer C. David Koontz, the father of her stepson David; and to Michael Brazzel. She moved to Sanders, Idaho, following a nearly fatal stroke in 1981. There she managed a bed and breakfast called Seven Springs Farms from 1994 to 1999. In addition to publishing and writing activities, Christina Crawford has worked as special events manager at the Coeur d'Alene Resort in Idaho.

Works Cited

Christina Crawford. *Mommie Dearest.* New York: Berkley, 1979.

MacPherson, Myra. "Christina Crawford's Grim Memories of Life with 'Mommie': Hollywood Daughter's Tale of Child Abuse." *Washington Post* 1 November 1978: Style, E1.

DAHLBERG, EDWARD (1900–1977)

Author
Orphanage alumnus, Catholic orphanage 1907–1908, Jewish Orphan Asylum, Cleveland,
Ohio, 1912–1917

Career, Major Awards, and Achievements

Edward Dahlberg was an author and poet. He was hailed as a pioneer of American proletarian writing after *Bottom Dogs,* his first autobiographic novel, was published in 1929. He wrote an additional autobiographic novel, *From Flushing to Calvary* (1932), and an anti-Nazi novel called *Those Who Perish* (1934). His early novels contain coarse and unsentimental descriptions of down-and-out laborers, farmers, and drifters during the Great Depression of the 1930s. In 1935, Dahlberg cofounded the leftist American Writers' Congress and presented his paper "Fascism and Writers" at their convention. He wrote very little during the 1940s and 1950s, undertaking instead an intensive self-study of literature. *Do These Bones Live?* (1941) is a work of literary criticism from that time. A revised edition called *Can These Bones Live?* was published in 1960.

Dahlberg later rejected his early naturalistic style, calling it "dunghill fiction" and the "mediocre manipulations of childhood and young manhood, disfigured by self-pity" (CA). He began to write again in the 1960s; his later style was radically different from his first and was notable for its poetic, biblical, and mythic elements and "queer classical learning" (CA). This later style can be seen in *The Carnal Myth* (1968), *The Sorrows of Priapus* (1973), and *The Olive of Minerva* (1976). Dahlberg's poetry, aphorisms, short stories, and essays were collected into several volumes, including *Reasons of the Heart* (1965), *Cipango's Hinder Door* (1966) and *The Leafless American* (1967). He taught literature at New York University, the University of Missouri at Kansas City, and Columbia University. Dahlberg published two later autobiographies, *Because I Was Flesh* (1964) and *The Confessions of Edward Dahlberg* (1971), from which his commentary in this entry was taken. One critic called *Because I Was Flesh* "a masterpiece of Oedipal obsession, a poetic memoir of primal sunderings and rages" (CA). Dahlberg wrote *Because I Was Flesh*, which is considered his best work, about his wanderings with his mother and his life in the orphanage:

> It is a great pain to divulge the life of a mother, and wicked to betray her faults. Why then do
> I do it? I have nothing better to do with my life than to write a book and perhaps nothing

worse. Besides, it is a delusion to believe that one has a choice. . . . Would to God that my mother had not been a leaf scattered everywhere and as the wind listeth. Would to heaven that I could compose a different account of her flesh. Should I seem to mock that *mater dolorosa* of rags and grief, know that all my laughter lies in her grave (Dahlberg, 1971, 4).

Today, Dahlberg's literary reputation is controversial: he is regarded by some critics as "brilliant" and "a genius," but by others as "a crank" (CA). His biographers suggest that his difficult, "consistently hostile" personality (CA) and contempt for his contemporaries handicapped his literary standing during his lifetime.

Family of Origins

Edward Dahlberg was born on July 22, 1900, in Boston, Massachusetts. His mother, Elizabeth Dahlberg ("Lizzie" in his books), was of Polish descent, with "as many Catholics as Jews" among her ancestors (Dahlberg, 1971, 5). At age sixteen, Lizzie, who had immigrated to New York from Warsaw, entered a marriage arranged by her older brother. The couple had three sons, half-brothers Dahlberg refers to as "feeble seminal accidents" (Dahlberg, 1971, 7). Following the death of one of her children, Lizzie met and ran away with a barber named Saul Gottdank, who was Edward's biological father:

> She abandoned her two sons and fled to Boston. There she bore a child in Charity Hospital. She had been lying in a cheap rooming house where her bastard would have been born had not her groans attracted the attention of a neighbor. She gave me her father's name to hide the fact that I was as illegitimate as the pismire, the moth or a prince (Dahlberg, 1971, 8).

Saul and Lizzie had problems with their relationship and often separated. The family moved from place to place and Saul eventually left for good. Lizzie and her son moved to Dallas, Memphis, New Orleans, Louisville, and Denver before they finally settled into a life of poverty in Kansas City, Missouri, around 1905.

Orphanage

Dahlberg first went to a Catholic orphanage during 1907 and 1908 when his mother became ill following an appendix operation. After several unhappy relationships, Lizzie became the mistress of a retired riverboat captain named Henry Smith. Smith convinced Lizzie to send away Edward, who "attached himself to any man who was interested in his mother" (Dahlberg 1971, 55). Lizzie sent Edward to a Jewish Orphanage where he spent the remainder of his childhood:

> In April 1912, when he was eleven, the boy became an inmate of the Jewish Orphan Asylum in Cleveland, the Forest City. No Spartan ordinances could have been more austere than the rules for the orphans. . . . In the washroom were two long soapstone troughs. Each boy, naked to the navel, with his blue shirt, drawers, and suspenders hanging, stood in front of a faucet, washed his face and body in icy water and scrubbed his teeth with Ivory soap (Dahlberg, 1971, 65–67).

The orphanage children were called by the number assigned to a box in which their few possessions were stored. Dahlberg was "number 92" during his years there. He left the orphanage in the confirmation class of 1917 and, after a few odd jobs, returned to his mother. Smith no longer found him to be "the nuisance [he] had been as a boy who needed a father" (Dahlberg, 1971,106). In her later years, Dahlberg took care of his mother in her later years until her death in 1946.

Education, Military Service, and Significant Relationships

Soon after Dahlberg left the orphanage, he joined the army and served as a private. He attended college at the University of California at Berkeley and graduated from Columbia University in 1923 as a philosophy major. He married seven times, with all but the last marriage ending in divorce: to Ruth Gross and Fanya Fass in 1926; to Sara Mazo in 1930; to Rosa Shuser in 1932; to Winifred Sheehan Moore, with whom he had two sons, Geoffrey and Joel, in 1942; to R'Lene LaFleur Howell in 1950; and to Julia Lawlor in 1967. Dahlberg's health declined from severe stomach ulcers and a series of small strokes. He died of lung congestion on February 27, 1977, in Santa Barbara, California.

Works Cited

CA (Contemporary Authors, 1998). "Edward Dahlberg." *Contemporary Authors Online*. Gale. 15 May 2002.

Dahlberg, Edward. *Because I Was Flesh*. [New York]: New Directions, 1964.

Dahlberg, Edward. *The Confessions of Edward Dahlberg*. New York: Braziller, 1971.

DeFanti, Charles. *The Wages of Expectation: A Biography of Edward Dahlberg*. New York: New York University Press, 1978.

Lethem, Jonathan. "The Disappointment Artist: Edward Dahlberg's Recipe for Crocodile Tears." *Harpers* 306 (February 2003): 49.

Moramarco, Fred. *Edward Dahlberg*. New York: Twayne Publishers, Inc., 1972.

DANILOVA, ALEXANDRA (1903–1997)

Ballet Dancer, Choreographer, Teacher
Adoptee

Career, Major Awards, and Achievements

Prima ballerina Alexandra Danilova performed over one hundred roles during her long and legendary career as a dancer. She was a principal dancer with some of the world's most important companies, including Sergei Diaghilev's influential Ballets Russes, the spinoff Ballets Russes de Monte Carlo, George Balanchine's Young Ballet and his New York City Ballet, and the Metropolitan Opera. Danilova danced onstage until she was fifty-four years old. Some of her most memorable roles include the title role of the *Firebird*, Swanilda in *Coppelia*, the Street Dancer in *Le Beau Danube*, the Doll in *Petrouchka*, the Glove Seller in *Gaîté Parisienne*, and her lovely Odette in *Swan Lake*. After retiring from the stage in 1957, she became a member of the faculty of the School of American Ballet, where she coached, choreographed, and passed on her wisdom to hundreds of young dancers.

Danilova received several major dance awards, including the first Capezio Award for a ballerina in 1958. In 1984, she received the *Dance Magazine* Award. She was the subject of Anne Belle's 1986 documentary *Reflections of a Dancer: Alexandra Danilova, Prima Ballerina Assoluta*, voted one of ten best dance films on video by *American Film* magazine. In 1977, she appeared in Herbert Ross's motion picture *The Turning Point* (1977). She played an aging ballerina teaching her signature role to a young dancer. Danilova published her autobiography, *Choura*, in 1986. She received Kennedy Center Honors in 1989.

[Courtesy of Photofest]

Family of Origin

Alexandra Danilova was born on November 20, 1903, in Peterhof, Russia. She was the younger of two children. Her mother, Claudia (Gotovtzeva), and her father, Dionis Danilov, died when she was two years old. Of her parents, she said, "I have no idea what my father did for a living. I know only that he was out hunting and caught cold. The cold got worse, and my mother looked after him. Then he died. My mother came down with the same disease, and soon she died, too" (Danilova 3).

Adoption

After their mother's death, Alexandra and her older sister, Elena, were taken to live with their grandmother. One morning when Alexandra was four years old, she awakened to find their grandmother dead. The girls were next taken to live with their godmother, Madame Molvo, while she arranged their adoptions to separate families:

> Our godmother, Mme Molvo, took us. She lived on the outskirts of St. Petersburg, in a large, very pretty house. Her children showed us their own rooms first—nursery rooms, decorated with animals, dolls, all kinds of toys. . . . The daughter showed us our room, which was dark and narrow. Our meals were always brought into that room—our morning tea, our dinner.
>
> One day, the children came to fetch me and took me to the drawing room, where my godmother and a lady I'd never seen before were sitting together. . . . I didn't understand what was happening. I turned and looked at the lady, who replied to my godmother, "Yes, I like her. I will take her tomorrow. . . ."
>
> "And Lenochka [Elena], will she go with me?" I asked . . . "No, Lenochka will be taken by another lady. Only you, Chourochka, are very lucky—your new aunt is rich, and you will be happy with her. . . ."
>
> The next day, my new "aunt," Lidia Mstislavna Gototsova, née Nestroeva, came for me. . . . I learned later that she had adopted me to take the place of her own daughter, who had just died (Danilova 4–5).

Alexandra was happy in her new home and grew especially attached to her adoptive father, whom she called "Uncle." Madame Gototsova, however, began divorce proceedings against her husband for drinking and adultery (Danilova 6). She moved to an apartment with Alexandria and placed her under the care of a "despised" German governess (9). Madame Gototsova soon married again, this time to a widower, Mikhail Batianov, who was a high-ranking general. Batianov had eight children from his two previous marriages. Alexandra was resented by the general's children. However, she soon discovered that a budding dramatic talent could relieve her unhappiness:

> Somehow, in the midst of this big family, Aunt Lidia and I remained outsiders. Though initially we were made to feel welcome, we never were made to feel as if we belonged.
>
> My refuge was my imagination. I could pretend that gypsies had kidnapped me and then, feeling sorry for myself, sit and cry" (Danilova 12).

Education and Significant Relationships

When she was eight years old, Danilova was one of 17 out of 250 children chosen to receive ballet training at the Maryinsky, Saint Petersburg's Imperial Ballet School. She was accepted as a boarded student. She continued her training under a scholarship from the Czar, though her school was closed for a year during the 1917 Russian Revolution. She graduated in 1920 and became a member of the corps de ballet of the Kirov, the Soviet State Ballet. Danilova left Russia during a tour in 1924 and, upon Diaghilev's invitation, joined the Ballets Russes.

Danilova was briefly married to an Italian engineer, Giuseppe Massera. She later married Casimir Kokitch, a soloist with the Ballet Russes de Monte Carlo. The marriage was annulled, although she remained friends with him and acted as godmother to his daughter, Kim Kokich. Danilova became a naturalized American citizen in 1952. She died in her Manhattan home on July 13, 1997, at the age of 93.

Works Cited

Danilova, Alexandra. *Choura: The Memoirs of Alexandra Danilova.* New York: Knopf, 1986
Garafola, Lynn. "Alexandra Danilova." *Dance Magazine* 71 (October 1997): 60+.

DAWSON, TOBY (1978–)

Olympic Skier
Adoptee, orphanage alumnus

Career, Major Awards, and Achievements

Toby Dawson is one of the top mogul skiers in the world. He was the bronze medalist in freestyle skiing at the 2006 Olympics. He has been a winner in World Cup, World Championship, and U.S. Championship competitions.

The adopted son of two Vail, Colorado, ski instructors, Toby was skiing at the age of four and racing alpine style two years later. At twelve he switched to freestyle skiing. In 1999, the year he entered his first World Cup race, he placed fifth. The 2004–05 season, when Dawson placed seventh, was his fifth straight season of finishing in the top eight.

Called "Awesome" Dawson for his energetic style, he has been quoted as saying, "I like to go big and jolt the crowd" (Turin 2006 Winter Olympics homepage). In 2003 he was the bronze medal winner in both mogul events in the World Championships and was fifth in moguls in the 2005 Worlds.

Dawson has appeared in four of filmmaker Warren Miller's ski films: *Ride*, *Cold Fusion*, *Storm*, and *Journey*.

Family of Origin

Toby Dawson was born in Korea. As a small child, he was found wandering through the streets of Seoul and taken to an orphanage. He was given the name Kim Soo Chul, which he pronounces "so cool." The orphanage officials estimated his age and assigned the birth date of November 30, 1978, to their new foundling.

As a young adult, he became interested in knowing who his birth parents were. He put his story and posted twelve childhood pictures of himself on the 2006 Turin NBC Olympics Web page, hoping that someone might recognize him. He became discouraged when his success as a skier brought in hundreds of letters from Koreans hoping to claim him. After the Olympics, the story of the adopted Korean-American became front page news in Korea. Both Toby and his adoptive mother, Deborah Dawson, hoped that his win would result in a reunion with his family of origin.

Out of the many would-be parents who came forward was Kim Jae-su, a bus driver from Busan. His three-year-old son, Bong-seok, had disappeared from a market in 1981, the year Kim Soo Chul/Toby Dawson was found. Kim had searched for his son, checking local orphanages where he was told that no child of Bong-seok's description had been found. Genetic tests confirmed that Kim was Dawson's birth father.

[AP Photo/Michael Probst]

They met in Seoul and gave a press conference at a hotel there. Dawson's younger biological brother, Kim Hyun-cheol, accompanied their father. Dawson's birthparents are divorced and Kim would make no public comment regarding Dawson's first mother. Since Kim speaks only Korean and Dawson only English, interpreters translated their comments to journalists and to each other. Kim told reporters that he was happy Dawson had grown up so wonderfully and said, "I am thankful that he has come to look for me even after such a long time." Dawson gave his father a Norwegian ski sweater, which Kim promptly put on, and said, in Korean learned for the event, "I have been waiting a long time, Father" (BBC News).

Adoption

Deborah and Mike Dawson adopted Toby when he was three years old and were told by the orphanage that he had been abandoned. He was traumatized when he first arrived in his new home (NBC Sports) and grew up feeling out of place in Vail, as he explains: "I looked at my parents and I didn't look like them. Then I also felt if I went to Korea I didn't belong there. I felt like I was still lost, stuck between two different worlds" (Herman). Dawson believes that the shyness he felt about not fitting in actually created the aggression he needed to become a world class skier (BBC).

His adoptive parents took him to Korean Heritage Camp so that he would know his birth culture. He was not interested in the camp as a young boy, but developed an appreciation as he grew older and now donates much of his time there. His brother, K. C., also adopted, met his own Korean father in 1997.

Significant Relationships

Dawson married Leah Helmi on April 14, 2007, at a Palm Springs golf resort. His American family and friends attended. Future plans included a second wedding in Korea, to be celebrated with Korean family members.

Dawson is creating a foundation to support agencies who wish to help Korean adoptees and their first families reunite.

Works Cited

BBC News. "U.S. Skier Meets South Korean Dad." *BBC News*. December 27, 2007. http://news
    .bbc.co.uk/2/hi/asia-pacific/6403539.stm

Herman, Burt. "Olympic Skier Toby Dawson Reunites with Korean Family." *USA Today*.
    February 28, 2007. http://www.usatoday.com/. Accessed December 21, 2007.

Jenkins, Lee. "For Dawson, A Bronze and a Chance to Find Birth Parents." *The New York Times*.
    February 16, 2006, D3 (L).

NBC Sports. "S. Korean Claims to be U.S. Mogul Skier's Father." *NBC Sports.ComNews Service*
    July 2, 2008. http://nbcsports.msnbc.com/id/11467660/

Reilly, Rick. "Heart and Seoul." *Sports Illustrated*. 104.9 (February 27, 2006): 86.

DICKERSON, ERIC (1960–)

Football Player
Adoptee, fictitious birth information

Career, Major Awards, and Achievements

During his eleven-year career, Eric Dickerson was selected six times for Pro Bowl and was All-Pro five times. The year he retired he had the second highest career record for rushing. In 1999 Dickerson was inducted into the Professional Football Hall of Fame.

In 1983 Dickerson was a first-round draft choice of the L.A. Rams. At the end of his first season he had broken all rookie records for rushing attempts, rushing yards gained, and touchdowns rushing. Named both Player of the Year and Rookie of the Year, he was also a Pro-Bowl and All-Pro selection that year. In his second season he broke the record of 100-yard-rushing games in a season.

[AP Photo/Bill Janscha]

In 1987 he was traded to the Indianapolis Colts in a major deal that included three teams and ten players. In 1988 he led the league in rushing, the first Colt to do so since 1955. The following season he broke another record when he gained more than 10,000 yards in only ninety-one games; though six backs had equaled his record of yards gained, none had done it in such a short time.

Dickerson played with the Los Angeles Raiders before joining the Atlanta Falcons in 1993. Suffering from a back injury, he was traded to the Green Bay Packers later that year and announced that he had played his last game before the end of the year when he failed a physical and doctors said he would be at risk of serious injury or paralysis if he continued playing.

Family of Origin

Eric Dickerson was born on September 2, 1960, in Sealy, Texas, to unmarried parents. He discovered that he had been adopted at school when he was fifteen years old. A favorite teacher mentioned to him that his father, Richard Seal, a notable college running back, was in town. Confused, he went on to learn that Viola, the woman he had considered his mother, was his adoptive mother, and Helen, the woman he believed to be his older sister, was in fact his birthmother:

> Viola is actually my great-great-aunt, but she is my mother through adoption. Just as a man named Kary, who was Viola's husband before he passed away, was my father through

adoption. My natural mother's name is Helen and my natural father's name is Richard. But Helen was only 17 years old when I was born. She and Richard weren't married, and they had no concrete plans for the future. Still so young herself, Helen felt Viola would be much better equipped to raise a baby. Viola agreed. When I was born, it was Viola who brought me home from Sealy Hospital. . . .

Viola never had any of her own children, but she lent a hand in raising some of her brothers' and sisters' children. That included Helen, my natural mother, who lived with Viola since she was 16 months old. As a result, Helen and I grew up in the same house together. In fact, for a long, long time, I thought that Helen was my sister, Viola was my natural mother, and Kary was my natural father. I didn't find out the entire story until I was 15 years old. . . .

Viola sat me down and told me everything. . . . I have to admit I was shocked. I mean, this was not small news. But I never felt crushed, not even close. To be perfectly honest, I wasn't even sad. I never cried, never considered running away. I just accepted it and went on living my life. It didn't change a thing (9–10).

Dickerson has occasional contact with his birthfather, who lives in Houston. He had been a star running back at Prairie View College in Texas.

Adoption

Viola and Kary Dickerson adopted Eric when he was three months old. A deeply religious couple, they were, Dickerson says, opposites in nature, Viola having a strict and "feisty" nature and Kary having a gentle personality. It was, according to Eric, "a major understatement" to call his upbringing "sheltered" (12). Kary supported his son's football interest and came to every game. He died of heart disease when Eric was in high school.

Dickerson said that he rarely got into trouble as a youth because his mother "could really sling a whip" (12). Viola is still a very important factor in her son's life: "Without a doubt, my mom has been the greatest single influence on my life. Every time I've been faced with a major decision, I've made it a point to get my mother's input" (6).

Education

Dickerson graduated from Sealy High School in Sealy, Texas, and attended college at Southern Methodist University. A running back for SMU, Dickerson was a two time All-America choice by the end of his senior year.

Works Cited

Dickerson, Eric, with Steve Delsohn. *On the Run*. Chicago: Contemporary Books, Inc, 1986.

DUMAS, ALEXANDRE (*FILS*) (1824–1895)

Author, Playwright
Illegitimate child, fostered at Pensions

Career, Major Awards, and Achievements

Alexandre Dumas is the name of two great nineteenth-century French writers. The senior Dumas (1802–1870) is referred to as Alexandre Dumas *père* and is best known as the creator of the literary classics *The Three Musketeers* and *The Count of Monte Cristo*.

[AP Photo]

His son, Alexandre Dumas *fils*, was the most important writer of serious plays in France during the second half of the nineteenth century, becoming even more highly regarded in his time than his respected father. During the twentieth century, tastes changed, and some of the best-known works of the father came back into fashion, often in film or television versions, while the plays of the younger Dumas are now seldom performed, and many have never been translated from the French.

One of his characters, however, has achieved immortality. Marguerite Gautier, the heroine of *La Dame aux Camélias* (1848), has appeared on stage and in motion pictures in many countries and languages, in the novel *La Dame aux Camélias* and in its stage adaptation *Camille*, as Violetta in the opera *La Traviata*, and as Marguerite in the ballet *Marguerite and Armand*, danced by Margot Fonteyn and Rudolph Nureyev for the Royal Ballet.

At the age of twenty, the younger Dumas went to live with his father in Saint-Germain-en-Laye. There he met Marie Duplessis, a young courtesan, who may have been his lover from fall of 1844 through late summer of 1845. Duplessis was lovely, discreet, intelligent, and very successful. The book she inspired, *La Dame aux Camélias*, appeared in 1848, a year after her death of tuberculosis at the age of twenty-three. Dumas was 50,000 francs in debt when he adapted the novel for the stage in 1852, hoping to make some money. The play not only paid his debts but became and has remained an enormous success. In 1853, Verdi made an adaptation of the stage version and called the story *La Traviata*. In 1880, the play became the centerpiece of **Sarah Bernhardt's** first American tour. Altogether, Bernhardt appeared as Marguerite nearly 3,000 times.

Between 1848 and 1887, Dumas *fils* wrote twenty-four plays, of which *La Dame aux Camélias* was the second.

Dumas *fils* was admitted to the Académie Française in 1874. He was made a member of the Legion of Honor in 1894. His influence faded almost immediately after his death because the social issues his plays dealt with resolved themselves or became less important, and as they did, his plays became obsolete.

Family of Origin

Dumas *fils* was the illegitimate son of prominent French novelist Alexandre Dumas (born Dumas Davy de la Pailleterie) and Marie-Laure-Catherine Labay, a dressmaker and seamstress. He was born in Paris on July 27, 1824. At the time of his son's birth, Dumas *père* was twenty-one years old. He was not yet successful, and having few resources, did little to help his son. However, Dumas' financial and social situation soon improved, and he legally recognized the boy. The elder Dumas chose to help his child at a time when fathers had no legal responsibility for their illegitimate children. Such children were also forbidden by law to attempt to gain from their fathers. Dumas *fils* writes:

> And by a happy chance it turned out that my father was impulsive but good. . . . When, after his first successes as a dramatist, he thought he could count on the future, he formally acknowledged me as his son, and gave me his name. This was much. The law did not compel him; and I was so grateful to him for it, that I have borne the name as nobly as I could (Matthews 139).

Education and Significant Relationships

Dumas *père* was largely self-educated. His own father, also an illegitimate son, had died when he was three, and his mother had a great deal of difficulty finding money for schooling. For him, it was important that his young son would have what he himself had not, and when Alexandre was seven, Dumas *père* forcibly removed him from the care of his mother and sent him away. The separation from her son caused Labay so much grief that the younger Dumas never forgot it. One critic wrote:

> Dumas *père* was simply impossible. He gave his son every reason to resent and despise him—and then charmed him out of his resentment. He allowed his son to bear the social stigma of bastardy, though nothing but caste prejudice prevented him from marrying his mistress; and then tore the child, at the tender age of seven, from the arms of his loving mother by force of law and sent him to a pension, where he was scorned for his irregular birth (Auchincloss 25).

He was boarding at a pension run by Prosper Goubaux, of which he wrote: "My torture, which I have depicted in 'Affaire Clémenceau,' and of which I did not speak to my mother, so as not to worry her, lasted five or six years" (Matthews 139). At his second school, the Pension Saint-Victor, Alexandre continued to be teased and taunted by the other students for his illegitimacy. His great-grandmother had been a Haitian woman of African descent and a former slave; it was possible that Dumas was also tormented for racist reasons. Following Saint-Victor, Dumas *fils* attended the College Bourbon. He completed his formal education at the age of seventeen.

The combination of his own suffering at school and his mother's grief influenced the attitudes of the boy in favor of reform, a tendency that appeared later in his work. He felt that his suffering "gave him the habits of observation and reflection" (Matthews 139). His play *Le demi-monde* was one of his first philosophical mouthpieces and it introduced the social realism that earned him a place in the history of French theater. *Le fils naturel* (*The Illegitimate Son,* 1868) is an example of his "thesis plays," which were conceived as opposition to the "art for art's sake" movement. He wished his dramas to teach and moralize. In *Le fils naturel,* Dumas *fils* expressed his belief that the father of an illegitimate child should marry the child's mother and legitimize the child.

Many of Dumas *fils'* pamphlets and plays focused on adultery and prostitution, which he felt had weakened France. He longed for a new age, one built on the moral strength of the nuclear family.

In the meantime, he had produced an illegitimate child of his own, Marie-Alexandrine-Henriette Dumas, in 1860. On New Year's Eve, 1864, he married his child's mother, Nadjeschda von Knorring, the widow of Alexander, Prince Naryschkine, in Moscow. Their second daughter, Jeanine Dumas, was born in 1867.

In 1887 he began an affair with Henriette Régnier de la Brière. His wife was ill at the time, and his infidelity did not end their marriage. Dumas once had argued that divorce should be legalized, believing that it could reduce the practice of adultery. Two months after his wife's death in April of 1895, he married his mistress.

He died on November 27 of the same year at Marly-le-Roi, Yvelines. He is buried at the Cimetière de Montmartre, and his tomb is only a short distance from the grave of Marie Duplessis.

Works Cited

Auchincloss, Louis. "Dumas *fils.*" *The Man Behind the Book.* New York: Houghton Mifflin, 1996. 23–32.

Degen, John A. "Alexandre Dumas *fils.*" *French Dramatists, 1789–1914. Dictionary of Literary Biography* 192. (1998).

Matthews, Brander. "Alexandre Dumas *fils.*" *French Dramatists of the Nineteenth Century,* Third Edition. New York: Benjamin Blom, 1968. 136–171.

E

ELIZABETH I (1533–1603)

Queen of England
Orphaned

Career and Achievements

Elizabeth I ruled England and Ireland from 1558 to her death in 1603. During her forty-five-year reign, England emerged as a leading world power. The queen was famous for her profound and lifelong love of learning, especially theology, languages, and literature. The Elizabethan period was the High English Renaissance, and Elizabeth enjoyed the role of patroness to such literary immortals as Shakespeare, Marlowe, and Spenser, and explorers Walter Raleigh and Francis Drake.

Family of Origin

Elizabeth was born to King Henry VIII and his second wife, Anne Boleyn, in Greenwich Palace on September 7, 1533. She lost her mother at the age of two when the King ordered his wife beheaded on charges of adultery. Anne was executed on May 19, 1536. Most historians believe that the charges against her were fabricated so that the King would be free to marry his third wife, Jane Seymour. Four days before the execution, the Archbishop of Canterbury annulled Anne's marriage to Henry. Elizabeth and her half-sister, Mary, the daughter of Henry's first wife, Katherine of Aragon, were formally declared bastards in the Act of Succession in July 1536. The act also stripped them of the title of *princess*, barred them from succession to the throne, and made it treason to refer to them as legitimate. Henry always acknowledged Elizabeth to be his child, although court rumors, and even Elizabeth's own godfather, Archbishop Cranmer, claimed that she "was a bastard by Mr. Norris and not the King's daughter" (Perry 17). Five men, including Norris, a musician named Mark Smeaton, and Anne's brother, George Boleyn, were convicted of adultery with the queen and executed at the time of Anne's death. Scholars believe that Anne's alleged adultery and its consequences were the reasons why Elizabeth refused to marry and why she encouraged her public image as "The Virgin Queen." Unlike Mary, upon her succession Elizabeth did nothing to legally vindicate her mother, although she did show preferment to those who had at one time defended her mother, and she was said to treasure some of the mementos that had belonged to Anne.

[Courtesy of the Library of Congress]

Fosterage

Elizabeth grew up away from court and was looked after by Lady Bryan, who had also tended her half-sister Mary and the King's illegitimate son, Henry Fitzroy, the Duke of Richmond. Elizabeth regarded her father with reverence and awe but grew up outside of his presence. She did not dare to correspond with him, although she did write to her succession of stepmothers, and her visits to court were rare and stiff with court etiquette. Henry's marriage to Jane Seymour finally produced a legitimate male heir to the English throne, Prince Edward, although the queen died twelve days after his birth. Elizabeth was four years old and carried the elaborate train of his gown at the baby's baptism. The prince became King Edward VI at the age of nine, when Henry died on January 28, 1547. Edward himself died of tuberculosis at the age of fifteen, on July 8, 1553. His will again declared Mary and Elizabeth illegitimate and barred them from succession. Edward left the crown to his cousin, fifteen-year-old Lady Jane Grey. Mary, however, successfully challenged Edward's will and was proclaimed queen on July 19, 1553.

Mary, Henry's firstborn, had been seventeen when Elizabeth was born. At Elizabeth's baptism, she refused to "pay court to her unless compelled by sheer force" (Somerset 5). Thus there existed an early bitterness between the half-sisters. Mary liked to believe that Elizabeth was not her sister at all, and was fond of remarking that "Elizabeth had the face and countenance of Mark Smeaton, who was a very handsome man" (Somerset 33). The dislike between the sisters was especially pronounced with regard to their different religions. Mary was a Catholic and Elizabeth had been raised in Reformation Protestantism.

Mary, later known as "Bloody Mary," tried to force a Catholic revival and restore the relations with Rome that Henry had broken in order to marry Elizabeth's mother. Her subjects rebelled and tried to oust Mary in favor of Elizabeth. Elizabeth, who claimed to be completely innocent of the insurrection, was arrested and imprisoned in the Tower of London on March 16, 1554. Prosecutors were unable to prove any wrongdoing on Elizabeth's part, and she was released in late 1555. When Mary died of cancer on November 17, 1558, Elizabeth was crowned England's queen. The last of the Tudor monarchs, she ruled until her death on March 24, 1603, at Richmond. When the crown passed to the Stuart king, James VI of Scotland, who became England's James I, Elizabeth's land was prosperous and at peace.

Works Cited

Harrison, G. B., Ed. *The Letters of Queen Elizabeth I.* New York: Funk & Wagnalls, 1935.

Levine, Mortimer. *The Early Elizabethan Succession Question 1558–1568.* Stanford, CA: Stanford University Press, 1966.

Perry, Maria. *The Word of a Prince: A Life of Elizabeth I from Contemporary Documents.* New York: Boydell Press, 1990.

Plowden, Alison. *The Young Elizabeth: The First Twenty-Five Years of Elizabeth I.* Gloucestershire: Sutton Publishing, Ltd., 1999.

Somerset, Anne. *Elizabeth I.* New York: St. Martin's Press, 1991.

Starkey, David. *Elizabeth: The Struggle for the Throne.* New York: HarperCollins, 2001.

ERASMUS, DESIDERIUS (1469–1536)

Philosopher, Humanist, Author
Orphaned, raised in a monastery school

[Courtesy of the Library of Congress]

Career, Major Awards, and Achievements

Erasmus was one of the great Renaissance humanists. He promoted tolerance in an age of religious hatred and was skeptical of religious dogmatism. Like Martin Luther, he stood for the purification of the Church, but, unlike Luther, he opposed its division. Although his scholarly contributions are vast and respected, his words could not hold together a religion that was determined to divide into Catholic and Protestant. He was one of the first in the Renaissance era to compile extant Greek New Testament manuscripts into a unified whole.

Family of Origin

Erasmus and his older brother, Peter, were the illegitimate children of Margaret Rogers and a man named Gerrard, who went on to become a priest:

> Legend says that Erasmus was what is called a love-child. The father was a man of some station, well educated—with a singularly interesting and even fascinating character. He fell in love, it is said with a certain Margaret, daughter of a physician at Sieben Bergen. Margaret was equally in love with him. For some unknown reason, the relations, either his or hers, opposed their marriage. They were imprudent, and the usual consequences followed (Froude 2).

Erasmus was born at Rotterdam in 1467; his birth name was Geert Geertsen. Margaret died when Erasmus was thirteen years old, and Gerrard died shortly afterwards.

Guardians and Monastic Life

After the death of their parents, Peter and Desiderius were left in the care of three of their father's friends: a banker, a schoolmaster, and an unnamed man who soon after died of the plague. The banker, busy with his own affairs, left the boys in the charge of the schoolmaster, who stole or squandered the children's respectable inheritance. The boys were then sent by their guardians to a monastery with the Brethren of the Common Life at Hertogenbosch and its school. Erasmus later declared that at both schools the teaching methods were outdated and natural gifts of the students stultified. To avoid an outbreak of the plague, the brothers returned to Gouda, and at their guardians' instigation, entered holy orders. Erasmus was to say later that he felt that his guardians' role in this decision was less than honorable. Nevertheless, at Steyn, the monastery he entered around 1487, Erasmus gained the background for his life's later attainments, studying Virgil, Horace, and Cicero, as well as the humanists of his own century. He was ordained in 1492.

Education

In 1495, Erasmus entered the University of Paris. By this time had had written his *Antibarbari,* which showed his disappointment in the meaningless hardships imposed by the monastic way of life. Paris gave Erasmus an opportunity to study and make rapid progress in Greek, but he was disappointed in the university and he went to England in 1499.

In England, Erasmus met the brilliant Thomas More and John Colet, who directed his attention to Biblical humanism. Neither the Church nor the Protestant reformers appreciated Erasmus' objections to violent reform. He continued to work for conciliation, but his voice was lost at the time in the Reformation. He died on July 12, 1536, at the age of 66, in Basel, at the home of his friend and publisher, Froben.

Works Cited

Froude, J. A. *Life and Letters of Erasmus.* New York: Charles Scribner's Sons, 1895.

ERIKSON, ERIK (1902–1994)

Founding Psychologist
Adoptee, fictitious birth information

Career , Major Awards, and Achievements

During his lifetime, Erik Erikson was one of the most—some said *the* most—influential psychologist in the United States. Trained by Sigmund and Anna Freud, Erikson added his own innovations to the young field of psychology. He moved away from or expanded Freudian theory, developing the idea that important development continued after the first few years and that the ego played a more significant role than the Freudians recognized. While Freud listed five stages of development, Erikson expanded the list to eight, and after his death, Joan Serson Erikson, his widow, added Old Age as a ninth stage, since life expectancy had become so extended in the West. Erikson is given credit for originating the term *identity crisis*. A great deal of his work dealt with the definition and formation of identity, and it is ironic that the person whom some called "the father of identity" (Lifton 206) was never able to discover his own.

Erikson was especially, but not exclusively, interested in child development and believed that the childhood environment was crucial to self-awareness and identity in children. His book *Childhood and Society*, published in 1950, was his most influential work, but he won both a Pulitzer Prize and a National Book Award for *Gandhi's Truth* (1969), a psychohistorical biography that allowed him to demonstrate the ways in which his theories applied to the later, adult stages of life.

In his "Autobiographical Notes on the Identity Crisis" (1970), he says that his interest in child psychology developed out of the combination of his search for his unknown father and his relationships with his adoptive father and with Freud:

> What, in me, responded to this situation was, I think, an ambivalent identification with my stepfather, the pediatrician, mixed with a search for my own mythical father. And if I ask myself in what spirit I accepted my truly astounding adoption by the Freudian circle, I can only surmise (not without embarrassment) that it was a kind of favored stepson identity that made me take for granted that I should be accepted where I did not quite belong. . . . That a stepson's negative identity is that of a bastard need only be acknowledged here in passing. But a habitual stepson might also use his talents to avoid belonging anywhere quite irreversibly (Erikson 744).

In 1933, Erickson and his wife moved to Denmark and from there to Boston, where he established a private practice as a child analyst and acted as a consultant or a staff member at three prestigious institutions: Massachusetts General Hospital, the Harvard Psychological Clinic, and the Judge Baker Guidance Center. The Guidance Center treated emotionally disturbed, delinquent youth from poor families.

Under the influence of Gregory Bateson, Margaret Mead, Ruth Benedict, and other Cambridge intellectuals, Erikson began work toward a PhD in psychology at Harvard, but left in 1936 to accept full-time research work at the Yale University Institute of Human Relations and an opportunity to teach at the Yale Medical School. His 1939 article "Observations on Sioux Education" was the result of time spent the previous year studying Sioux childhood training methods with Yale anthropologist Scudder Mekeel on a South Dakota reservation. This study was the first expression of an interest that

[Jane Reed/Harvard News Office]

would continue through Erikson's life: discovering how universal events in childhood are affected by specific societies.

He spent the next ten years as a faculty member at the University of California at Berkeley, where he was affiliated with the Institute of Child Welfare. He also had a private practice and studied the Yurok (a Native American people) as he had studied the

Lakota. At the end of the decade *Childhood and Society* was published, and Erikson left Berkeley in protest after being asked to sign a loyalty oath. He went back to Massachusetts, to the Austen Riggs Center, a well-known psychiatric treatment center in Stockbridge, to work with emotionally troubled youth. In the 1960s, Erikson returned to Harvard, where he served as a professor of human development. He retired in 1970.

Family of Origin

Erik Erikson was born in Frankfurt, Germany, on June 15, 1902, the son of Karla Abrahamsen, a woman of exceptional beauty and intelligence who was a member of an important family in the Jewish community in Copenhagen. Karla Abrahamson had married Waldemar Salomonsen, a Danish-Jewish stockbroker, but the couple permanently separated on their wedding night and Salomonsen left for the American continent. Young Erik was born "technically legitimate" four years after his mother's separation and was officially named Erik Salomonsen. It is thought that his birth father was Danish: "A persistent Abrahamsen family rumor is that Karla named Erik after the real father, and that he was a Copenhagen court photographer" (Friedman 30).

After Erik's birth, Karla took nurse's training and moved to Karlsruhe, Germany, near the French-German border. In 1904, she married Theodor Homburger, a German-Jewish pediatrician, who made it his only condition for the marriage that Erik would be told that Homburger was his natural father. However, Erik's legal name change didn't come until 1908, and Homburger didn't adopt Erik until 1911. His best childhood friend, Peter Blos, said, "Adoption was the great theme of his existence. He talked about it all the time" (Friedman 28). Another theme in his life was specialness. His mother gave him the sense that he was in some way extraordinary with a unique destiny, but Erikson would say, "[I] felt all along. . . . doubt in my identity" (Friedman 28).

Erik was a "flagrantly tall" (Erikson 743), blue-eyed blonde boy, while both Karla and Homburger were dark. Erik was ethnically Danish and considered the Danish language, which his mother sometimes used with him, special, but, having been born and raised in Germany so that his mother's family could conceal his illegitimate birth from their Copenhagen community, he was for the most part cut off from his extended family. He was teased at his family's synagogue for looking Nordic and at his German grammar school for being Jewish. At home, the Homburgers kept the facts of his birth and parentage from Erik as a "loving deceit" out of a desire to annul the past and start anew. However, even to a small child "there were too many cues to the contrary, including whispers among the adults in the house concerning Erik's paternity" (Friedman 33).

Though Theodor was a caring father, various factors indicate that all three may have felt ambiguous about Theodor's assuming full parental rights and obligations. Did Karla want to give up her special relationship to her son? Did Erik continue to resent Theodor as an intruder into his life and his relationship to his mother? Did Theodor actually want to be the legal parent of, first, the small resentful child and then a somewhat difficult boy who looked nothing like him and whose father might eventually choose to claim him?

Karla and Theodor had three daughters: Elna, who died in infancy from diphtheria, Ruth, and Ellen. Ellen, Erikson's younger half-sister, realized that she would not be allowed to study medicine in Nazi Germany and moved to Palestine in the early 1930s. She later encouraged her parents to join her and her husband. Karla and Theodor Homburger lost much of their income when Theodor was prevented from treating gentile patients, and lost most of their belongings as a result of their move to Palestine.

Erikson sent them $100 a month during their difficult years, a substantial sum during the Depression. His older half-sister, Ruth, and her husband also migrated to Palestine but couldn't make a living and returned to Germany. At once, Erikson made legal arrangements and paid their passage to the United States. He hoped they might stay in Boston, but they chose New York, which had a larger Jewish community, as their new home and soon began a successful business.

According to Friedman, the tension of Erikson's childhood relationship with his adopted father was somewhat relieved by Erikson's ability to support the family when they most needed it. Recognition came in Theodor Homburger's will, prepared in 1942 and executed in 1944, which gave Erikson full equality with Homburger's biological children and formally identified him, for the first time, as Homburger's adopted son.

Education and Significant Relationships

Erik was artistic but not otherwise much interested in his studies at the gymnasium, his German high school. When he left school, he became a wanderer—he worked, drew, and read his way through the Black Forest, the Alps, and Italy, looking for a way to "find himself." In 1927, his friend Peter Blos, who had become a child analyst, invited him to Vienna to teach in an experimental school. The students were children of the patients and acquaintances of Sigmund Freud and his daughter Anna, who, as mentioned earlier, chose Erikson for training. He decided to become a psychoanalyst specializing in child analysis. At the same time, he learned the Montessori method of child education and development. He graduated from the Vienna Psychoanalytic Institute in 1933, just after the Nazis gained control in Germany.

Erikson married Joan Mowat Serson, a native of Canada, in 1930. She would author several books and edit all of Erikson's manuscripts. They had three children, Kai, a sociologist; Jon, a photographer; and Sue, a social anthropologist. The family decided to move to Denmark and then to Boston, where Erikson became the city's first practicing child psychologist.

In 1939, when he became a citizen of the United States, Erikson adopted the name Erik Erikson. Friedman gives several reasons for this. First of all, Erik himself had become a different person from the insecure, unsettled wanderer he had earlier been. He was more solid, established, and confident, a man who could support his wife and children, and help his parents and sisters. His sons suggested the name Erikson, which identified them in the traditional Scandinavian way as their father's sons. At school, they had been called "Hamburger," which pleased no one in the family. In addition, it was a growing custom for Jewish immigrants to take more "American" sounding names, and this was especially true, according to Friedman, for Jewish psychologists, who found that anti-Semitism made finding jobs harder. Erikson's wife liked the change and at that time she also changed her first name, Sarah, to Joan.

Erikson kept his adoptive father's last name as his middle name "out of gratitude" (Friedman 144); Friedman goes on to suggest that the change of his surname was an important symbol of integration and rebirth for Erikson:

> By becoming Erikson, he could see himself as a stepson of sorts in an adoptive land.... Erik had a sense of being special with a destiny of his own. He saw in the missing and romanticized Gentile Nordic father he pursued but never identified an important source of this specialness. In his sometimes acknowledged "fantasy" of his biological father as something of a mythic hero, he seemed to be trying to gather together the various fragments of his

own sense of self, and a new name could mark that effort: "I made myself Erik's son. It is better to be your own originator" (Friedman 146–147).

Erik Erikson died on May 12, 1994, in Harwich, Connecticut. He was 91.

Works Cited

Burston, Daniel. *Erik Erikson and the American Psyche: Ego, Ethics, and Evolution.* Lanham, MD: Jason Aronson, 2007.

Erikson, Erik. "Autobiographic Notes on the Identity Crisis." *Daedalus* 99 (Fall 1970): 730.

Friedman, Lawrence J. *Identity's Architect: A Biography of Erik H. Erikson.* New York: Scribner, 1999.

Lifton, Betty Jean. *Journey of the Adopted Self: A Quest for Wholeness.* New York: Basic Books, 1994.

Welchman, Kit. *Erik Erikson: His Life, Work, and Significance.* Buckingham, UK: Open University Press, 2000.

ESTÉS, CLARISSA PINKOLA (1943–)

Psychoanalyst, Poet, Posttrauma Specialist, Activist
Adoptee, orphanage alumna

Career, Major Awards, and Achievements

Clarissa Pinkola Estés, author of the classic *Women Who Run With Wolves* (1992, 1995, published in thirty-four languages, 145 weeks on the *New York Times* bestseller list), is a Jungian psychoanalyst, practicing clinically since 1971. Three books are forthcoming—*The Dangerous Old Woman: Myths and Stories of the Wise Woman Archetype; La Pasionaria: Collected Poetry of Clarissa Pinkola Estés;* and from Texas A&M University Press, *La Curandera: Walking in Two Worlds.*

Via her dual heritages, "Mexicana by nature, Magyar by nurture," Estés is *cantadora* and *mesemondo,* a keeper of the stories in the old traditions. She has performed at Carnegie Hall and was awarded The Joseph Campbell Keeper of the Lore Award. Her signature healing stories and psychoanalytic commentaries are on audio from Sounds True:

The Creative Fire: Myths and Stories About Cycles of Creativity
Warming the Stone Child: Myths and Stories about Abandonment and the Unmothered Child
The Radiant Coat: Myths and Stories of the Crossing between Life and Death
How to Love a Woman: On Intimacy and the Erotic Life of Women
In the House of the Riddle Mother: Common Archetypal Dreams of Women
The Red Shoes: On Torment and the Recovery of Soul Life
The Boy Who Married an Eagle: Myths and Stories about Male Individuation
The Gift of Story: A Wise Tale about What Is Enough
The Faithful Gardener: A Wise Tale about That Which Can Never Die
Bedtime Stories: A Guided Relaxation for Falling Asleep and Entering the World of Dreams
Theatre of the Imagination, Volumes I and II: Dr. Clarissa Pinkola Estés in Live Performance . . . Stories, Myths, and Poetry

Her most recent live event online is *Mother Night: Myths, Stories, and Commentaries about Living in Two Worlds, and Learning to See in the Dark.*

[Courtesy of Clarissa Pinkola Estes]

Dr. Estés is a post-trauma recovery specialist, most recently serving 9/11 survivor families on both coasts, having served Columbine High School and the Littleton, Colorado, community for three years after the massacre. She has brought messages of hope to those in federal and state prisons for thirty-two years, teaching, among other essentials, "Writing as Liberation of the Spirit." She co-coordinated one of the first safe houses for women in the United States in the early 1970s.

Estés is the director of La Sociedad de Guadalupe, whose mission is to broadcast strengthening stories throughout the world via adult literacy and education. Her thirteen-part live performance series, *Theatre of the Imagination,* has been broadcast on National Public Radio and community radio stations throughout the United States and

Canada. Dr. Estés is deputy managing editor and a columnist on politics, mythos, and culture at the award-winning political newsblog http://themoderatevoice.com. She is a columnist on politics and spirituality at the *National Catholic Reporter* online. Her column is called "El Rio debajo del Rio" (The River beneath the River (http://ncronline .org/blogs/el-rio-debajo-del-rio).

For her lifetime writings and social activism, she has received the Las Primeras Award from MANA, the National Latina Foundation (Washington, D.C.). She was recently inducted into the Colorado Women's Hall of Fame.

Family of Origin

Estés was born in the northern woodlands to parents of Mestizo ancestry, that is, Mexican-Indigenous and Spanish. She has found various members of her "natal" or "life-giving" family—terms she coined in her work, rather than "birth" or "biological." But many family members are still missing. She especially seeks a brother who is a little older or younger than herself, who was also adopted out: "When I perform on stage, I sometimes for a moment look into the faces of the audience for people who might be mine" (Estés, 2002).

Foster Homes and Adoption

Estés' "availability" for adoption was held back until she was an older child. Her natal mother had tuberculosis during pregnancy. When she was surrendered as a toddler, Estés herself was critically ill with pneumonia. She was placed in a foundling hospital, and later moved through several foster homes:

> I know now that rarely does an infant or older child adoption take place anywhere in this world, without a fresh tragedy fully alive and bleeding in the background . . . Jobs were in short supply in the USA when servicemen returned after World War II. Muscle-labor jobs in fields and factories during the war years, were done by impoverished Anglos, newly arrived immigrants, and laborers legally imported from poorest populations in Mexico, Cuba, Puerto Rico, and Tejas. But suddenly those jobs were needed by men who'd come back from war. Many worker-families imported from other countries were suddenly deported. Adoption services, many kinds, some not legitimate, stepped in. Some of our life-giving parents were told since one or more of their children had been born on American soil, the children were U.S. citizens . . . thereby, parents could leave their children here with "a nice family" who'd take care of them . . . Later, "when things got straightened out," the family could come back into the U.S., and claim their blood children again. We will never know how many poor souls did not realize that even if they were brought back into the country to work, even allowed to enter the USA on a worker's visa, that the economy would restabilize for decades afterward—and life-giving parents would never be able to find their children ever again (Estés 2002).

Estés was given to a middle-aged immigrant Hungarian couple who had been turned down for infant adoption because they were "too old," nearing forty years of age. Estés' adoptive father was an old-country tailor from a peasant farm family who could scarcely read or write. Her adoptive mother had worked in factories, not completing school. Estés values the richness of both her natal and adoptive cultures:

> I have to say, even though difficult and torn apart in so many ways in young life, my dual heritages, which have admixtures inside them as well, have a great deal in common. Both my natal and adoptive families have long cultural histories of loving wild music, wild

poetry, fine horses, sharp knives, good-looking men, hard-working women. They love especially the violin *y gitara*, the accordion. In both my cultural [and] spiritual inheritances, there is a madness causing my people to love to dance themselves into the ground. They carry additional insanity—both families love *hot* chiles. Between my natal family [and] my adopted family, except for their mother tongues (neither of which are English), you can hardly tell them apart. They are all eleventh- and sixteenth-century Catholics, evangelized at the blade of a conqueror's sword. They are also often heavy drinkers . . . a polite way of saying "alcoholics." In all, often non-literate, fierce, talented, smart, holy, impossible, cruel, beautiful, generous, eccentric people.

As I have grown to understand more about underpinnings of my destiny, I've come to call myself a "melangeon." It means "to bridge," "to mix," as one would create an infusion . . . two substances, two flavors, two fragrances, making a third. I am both, I am several, I am all of these. No question. Some who carry dual heritages and are bi-racial, like myself, sometimes think we do not belong to either culture—too often, others say out loud, "Hmm, well, you are not completely like us, so you are 'not really us.'"

But that, in my humble opinion, is not true to the heart and soul. *As you wish,* you belong to both and all your families. *As you wish,* you belong to all. "Belonging" has been decided by a Mind far greater than any pea-brained humans. I would advise my sister and brother "melangeons" who have doubts about whether they belong, to become used to grace, used to saying to all sides, "I may seem unusual, and it is true I am quite rare, but I belong to you; yes, I do." You belong, *as you wish,* to all you have been gifted with (Estés 2002).

Estés grew up "amidst blessed green forests, white dunes, blue inland ocean, big skies, lairs, dens and nests of animals, lonely railroad tracks, open fields, and dirt roads—so much God you could hardly stand it." But, her adoptive home was one of constant harshness and upheaval:

I became a profound runaway as a child. There is no way to prettify this, yet I cast few aspersions. These are just difficult facts. My adoptive parents had commendable qualities, especially my adoptive father. But also, circumstances at home were brutal between the adults—and from adult to child. Every egregious act within the family walls was carefully hidden from those outside. We lived in an isolated rural town, population 600. What was called back then "corporal punishment" lapsed daily into incessant physical and verbal abuse. Jerked up out of sleep to be railed at and hit, nights were worse, for in our family, alcohol was one of the four food groups. The first time I ran away, I hid in a window well, covering myself with leaves. I thought I was such a genius 'til I was dragged out and beaten. My little suitcase was packed with the one little blanket I came with sticking out of the side, and it and I were dragged screaming out into the middle of the dirt road, with my adoptive mother ranting, "Go back where you came from!" I learned "to not run away within reach."

I began to run into the thick woods that backed up to the back of the truck farm behind the saltbox I lived in. I often had to run at night, learned to unhook bolts on window screens. I tried running to relatives. No good. Though some pitied you, and others "didn't want to get involved," they always returned you. Eventually, I would run up on the highway to far-away churches, seeking sanctuary. I slept in choir lofts, in naves. As I grew older, I ran over the state line to various juke joints and outdoor warrens where the wandering wounded, the exiled and forlorn, the half-desperate gathered.

Road people, tar-paper shack people, traveling carnival souls, half-mad soldiers, tramps, all stuck together in the woods and on the road. There was danger, but almost never from each other. I knew the road signs of tramps before I was ten . . . upside-down wildflowers tied to a fence meant a kind woman who'd give food lived nearby. Two or three knots of long grass tied to a fence meant, "Bad man, keep away." Many of us child runaways slept together in the woods, huddled against each other at night in old rusted-out model Ts and junked slope-back cars.

I understand deeply about why/how child-gangs are formed; for literal warmth, for love, for loyalty one does not receive elsewhere. We protected each other, stood for each other with passion and gritty erudition, as no one stood for us at school or back [at] home. Most people have *no idea* the huge numbers of children who are alone on the road at night during any given time. Many, many. I learned back then if you asked for help/protection from most adults, they either tried to harm you, or forced you back home without ever examining the family circumstances a child was entrapped in. There was no "child protection agency" then. Not for any child in the boondocks.

Eventually, I saved enough money from jobs selling greeting cards, magazine subscriptions to farmwives, giving shaves and haircuts to farmers on stoops, to not just pay my adoptive mother the weekly rent she demanded "now that you have a job." Finally, in great need, I ran on the railroad all the way to a big city one hundred miles away. Now one might hope at least there'd be no more torment. No more pain. Just turn your back now, never look back, free at last. But that's not how I was summoned.

There were turns for the worse and turns for the better. But almost immediately, even though I was now eighteen, my soul required I gradually turn toward my adoptive parents instead of away from them, not just from pity, but rather in trying to gentle them, to care-give their souls. They were twenty years older than my peers' parents. I was their only child. I know what it was to be alone and without, in far many more ways than one. But I couldn't bear to think of them being all alone in old age too. In my adult years forward, I would learn of my adoptive father's deep childhood wounds that haunted him so in the present. Once educated, I recognized my adoptive mother had an escalating disorder that left her little control over her rages, her deep disrespect and unbearable cruelties toward me and my adoptive father, as well as her thick persona toward others.

In the end, I learned many of the underlying causations of my adoptive parents' choices in life, and their decades of abject unhappiness. I learned my adoption had been a stop-gap measure for their careening alcohol-glutted marriage, to "fill in" my poor adoptive mother's desire "to have my own child out of my own body," as she would often weep to me, and I'd try to comfort her, though, I'm afraid, unsuccessfully so. My adoptive father revealed he had merely acquiesced to "the adoption," trying to appease a woman who would not/could not be pleased, no matter what.

So, as an adult, I stayed near my adopted parents in ways not resentful but honest, heartfelt . . . in ways I hope were honorable, in ways my soul could find peace about *afterward,* in ways I would not defeat my pledge to ever strive to see them as pure souls with imperfect people attached—who were not withholding anything behind their backs, [but] rather, sadly for all concerned, not having it to give to begin with. Thus, I was able to more surely see my adoptive parents through to the ends of their lives, to help them, entertain them, comfort them, assist them financially, even enjoy them sometimes, certainly to love them, especially my adoptive father, [until] they passed away in their late 80s.

I am grateful to have been given opportunity "to learn them better." My desire has been to honor my parents—*all of them*—and my longings for and my blessings over my life-giving family have never ceased.

To honor the most and best I understand in them all; to pray for whatever might be least in them. I hope people will do that for me too, notice/pour *miel,* warm honey over my best and be made glad, to give to me with insight and full heart—without grimacing or ulterior motive—and to pray for the least of me to be transformed.

Some adoption policies have evolved since I was born. I honor people in adoption service who did good, [and I] pray for those who did less than the best for others' souls. There were those who believed [that] taking children from the poor and giving them to those better off was some kind of wonderful social engineering. It wasn't. It was racist to say a Mexican child was "only Spanish" so a Caucasian couple might find that child acceptable. It was racist to try to pass off a light-skinned child who was biracial or Native American, or Black, or Latino, as a Caucasian. But, most of all, by my lights, it was egregiously wrong to separate life-giving parent(s) from child, parents who were merely poor or uneducated, panicked or without resources . . . instead of helping them find all resource to remain holy family together.

There were those in "adoption services" who chronically lied to natal mothers, wanting to pry their light-skinned or "culturally attractive" babies from them; abjectly lying to natal mothers, saying they would "forget"; lying that the mothers were ill-suited to be mothers; lying that a child deserves riches, advantages socially . . . thus misleading naïve and unprotected mothers, thereby sealing those mothers into tombs of unabated grief for life. There are those in "adoption services" who made up falsehoods, half-truths, put forth a luster of lies handed out wholesale to adult adoptees who sought their life-giving parents for decades as well.

Yet, too, there were many in the adoption field who were able to bring children from places where they might have died, culturally, spiritually, emotionally, physically. They brought many to shelter, love, hope instead. The good souls in the adoption field stood up for right, the real, and the visionary.

When I think [of] my own early time on earth, "lost years" from which I've no baby photo, no beloved toy, no bonnet string or tiny clothing to hand down to my children, my grandchildren, no smiling anyone who over decades could give "eye-witness" account of the stories of my lost years, I have this to say:

Whosoever touched me with love during those times in foundling hospital, in foster homes—whosoever might have maybe stopped for a moment to sing me a lullaby—I so hope someone did . . . I appreciate [that] you might have cared, and I thank you for whatever good you did. Although I have not seen your faces since I was a baby and a young child, I have this recurring sense: I remember you—like water remembers wind. The world of adoption turns on such mercies, on such honorable souls as you (Estés 2002).

Education, Marriage, and Children

Estés first went to college at age 26:

a late bloomer by most standards back then. Being a "late bloomer" for many of us means: no financial means, no family encouragement, in fact family scorn . . . it means no mentors, no notice of one's gift by others, no "connections," no guiding person to tell the well-hidden secrets of how to penetrate the thick wall built by the mainstream culture around the daunting castle of higher education (Estés 2002).

At the time, she was "a welfare mother driving an old Ford Pinto held together with duct tape and Bondo. I was fierce: I'm going to get through this wall somehow, dig under until my hands bleed, walk a hundred miles day and night to get around it, make wings of paper and pens to fly over the top. I had to go. I had to" (Estés 2002). She carried her infant daughter to classes in a carrier on her back. She graduated "with distinction" from Loretto Heights College in 1976. She earned her PhD from the Union Institute (1981) and her postdoctoral degree as a certified Jungian psychoanalyst in 1984. Dr. Estés is married and has grown children and five grandchildren.

Reflecting upon her own history and those of other adoptees, Dr. Estés writes,

Adoptees and bi-racial people are often the exact medicine needed for bridging all cultures, certainly for softening the many difficulties of prejudiced hearts and minds. Adoptees, if called to it, have a profound ability to bridge disparate groups, especially those historically hostile to one another. This occurs, in part, because when adopted, in certain ways, our *familiares*, relatives, become everyone. They are everywhere. You are cut from your roots . . . now you can wander, you can belong anywhere. You can be a citizen of the world; you can belong to any and every group—Black, Caucasian, Indian, Asian, Hawai'ian. How? Because the bloodline that matters most, holds strongest, longest, courses fiercely through those who have two disparate families . . . that is, the ability to love one, to love both, and to love all.

Most adoptees have the gift, well-developed or not yet, to bridge two shores . . . whereas others just look at the seemingly impossible spans between two or more ideas, ideals, or groups . . . and perhaps become cynical or give up. But, by living daily as one who has been weirdly, awfully, wondrously, painfully, fabulously adopted, fostered, ably or strangely caretaken . . . in some significant way, we belong to a rare tribe . . . one invested with unusual insights and a strong drive to love, mend, and teach across many boundaries. Because we can often see and love in more than one direction only . . . we are twice-sighted. Together, we most definitely belong to—first and foremost—the Tribe of the Twice Born (Estés, 2002).

Works Cited

Estés, Clarissa Pinkola. *Women Who Run with the Wolves.* New York: Ballantine/Random House, 1992, 1995.

———. *Warming the Stone Child: Myths and Stories about the Abandoned and the Unmothered Child.* Boulder, CO: Sounds True, 1992.

———. Personal interview with Dr. Clarissa Pinkola Estés, September 24, 2002.

Kamp, Jim, and Diane Telgen, Eds. *Latinas! Women of Achievement.* Detroit, MI: Visible Ink Press, 1996.

F

FERLINGHETTI, LAWRENCE (1919–)

Author, Poet, Publisher
Orphanage alumnus, fostered

Career , Major Awards, and Achievements

Lawrence Ferlinghetti is a poet and novelist, artist, publisher, and the owner of City Lights bookstore, a nationally known center for Beat and avant-garde, antiestablishment culture in San Francisco. His poems are known for their clarity, dry humor, and deliberate accessibility.

His awards include the *Los Angeles Times* Robert Kirsch Award, the BABRA (Bay Area Book Reviewers Association, now Northern California Book Reviewers) Award for Lifetime Achievement (1996), the National Book Critics Circle Ivan Sandrof Award for Contribution to American Arts and Letters (1999), and the ACLU's Earl Warren Civil Liberties Award. In 1998, he was named San Francisco's Poet Laureate; in 2003 he was elected to the American Academy of Arts and Letters. In recognition of outstanding service to the American literary community, he received the first Literarian Award, presented by the National Book Foundation, in 2005, and in 2007 he was made Commandeur of the French Academy of Arts and Letters.

In San Francisco, he published his first poem, "Brother, Brother," wrote poetry, painted, and wrote a column for *Arts Digest*. In 1953 he opened City Lights Pocket Book Shop in North Beach as a partner of Peter D. Martin, who was attempting to run a magazine called *City Lights*. The Pocket Books part of the store name came from Ferlinghetti's first publishing project. The bookstore was envisioned more as a cultural and political center than a business. The store soon became a center for what was new in San Francisco, and Ferlinghetti branched out into publishing. His first book, the first volume of the Pocket Poets series, was also his first collection of poetry, *Pictures of the Gone World* (1955). The fourth book in the series would make him famous; this was Allen Ginsberg's *Howl and Other Poems*.

The second printing of *Howl* was intercepted by customs as obscene. The federal attorney declined to prosecute and the case was dropped, but the San Francisco Police Department brought charges of printing and selling indecent material. The ACLU defended Ferlinghetti and won; Ferlinghetti, Ginsberg, *Howl*, City Lights, and the Beats became nationally recognized.

[AP Photo]

In 1957, New Directions published Ferlinghetti's *A Coney Island of the Mind,* which went on to become the largest selling single book by a living American poet and has sold over a million copies. *Coney Island* created a demand for poetry readings, and Ferlinghetti's accessible style made him a favorite among the hippies, who had followed the Beats as the dominant counter-culture group. In 1969, he published *The Secret Meaning of Things,* which was nominated for a National Book Award. In addition to poetry, Ferlinghetti has published novels and descriptions of his travels. Though

Ferlinghetti is strongly associated with the Beats, he has said that he is closer to the Bohemians, the avant-garde group that preceded the Beats. His married, more settled lifestyle contrasted with the on-the-road style associated with the Beats. City Lights Publishers published Beat generation poets but has always included other authors, including international authors, on its list.

Active in anti-Vietnam war protests, Ferlinghetti briefly closed City Lights to protest the Gulf War, then reopened it to make the store a center for antiwar activity. In 2002, Ferlinghetti was one of more than 100 poets who contributed to *An Eye for an Eye Makes the Whole World Blind: Poets on 9/11.*

Family of Origin

Lawrence Ferlinghetti was born in Yonkers, New York, on March 24, 1919. He was the fifth son of Charles Ferling (a name he had shortened from the original Ferlinghetti), a businessman who had emigrated from Lombardy, Italy, and Clemence Mendes-Monsanto Ferling, a second generation American of French and Portuguese-Jewish descent. Charles had died suddenly five months before Lawrence was born. Clemence Ferling was institutionalized at the state hospital with a nervous breakdown when Lawrence was two. Lawrence's brothers were sent to live in a boarding home in Ossining, but Lawrence was taken in by his uncle, Ludovic Monsanto, and his young aunt, Emily. When the Monsanto marriage failed, Emily took Lawrence home with her to Strasbourg, on the French-German border, and did not return for four years. Lawrence always referred to Emily as his "French mother," saying "when I was born the world was still ringing with marching feet. My French mother held me on a balcony in Alsace and waved my hand at the passing parade. A touching gesture, all things considered. Today, it's still happening. I'm still waving, only the expression on my face has changed" (Cherkovski 5).

When Emily returned to the United States, she placed Lawrence in an orphanage in Chappaqua, New York, while she looked for work. He was six years old during his stay at the orphanage, and his only memory of the time is of eating undercooked tapioca pudding, which imagery he incorporated into his novel *Her* (Silesky 7): "He finds himself in his own body in an orphanage to end all orphanages, where in swaddled clothes he eats the undercooked tapioca cat's-eyes of baby reality and puked his way into someone's heart who takes him away and away he goes and the next thing he knows he is walking" (Cherkovski 10–11).

After she found a position as a live-in governess-tutor to the daughter of Presley and Anna Bisland of Bronxville, New York, Emily brought Lawrence to join her, and then left. Lawrence became the informally adopted son of the Bislands:

> The Bislands were kind people and they genuinely wanted Lawrence to remain with them, but they were undemonstrative and reserved. After Emily's departure Lawrence rarely experienced any physical expression of affection. . . .
>
> As for Lawrence, he was obviously starved for affection. Mrs. Bisland often found him crouched next to her bedroom door, sitting on his knees in the hall, his head bent forward, waiting for some attention from the woman who had now become his "mother." But instead of hugging him she would say in a firm but gentle voice, "Lawrence why don't you get up and come downstairs with me," or would suggest that he go out and play. . . .
>
> How often would he find a new home and then, just as the warmth and comfort began to seep through, be snatched away to again be a stranger. . . . He tightened the door on his own privacy, closing off unhappiness and creating mind poems and images of his own. What he could not face in reality he rearranged in his imagination. He drew pictures,

imagined fathers, planned futures, and behind the wall of his growing isolation he emotionally withstood his fate (Cherkovski 10–11).

Education, Military Service, and Significant Relationships

As Lawrence Ferling Monsanto, Ferlinghetti attended the elite Riverdale Country Day School until the stock market crash of 1929 changed the Bislands' fortunes. Lawrence was boarded by the Bislands with another family and attended the Bronxville public schools. He was later sent to Mount Hermon, a prep school in Connecticut. When he graduated in 1937, he changed his name to Lawrence Monsanto Ferling, the name he carried with him through his college and graduate school years and on to California. He discovered his original full name when he received his birth certificate in order to apply for a California driver's license. In January 1955, when he became sole owner of City Lights, he began to identify himself as Lawrence Ferlinghetti.

Ferlinghetti began his writing career at the University of North Carolina, where he was a journalism major. He was a sportswriter for *Carolina* magazine; in his spare time he worked on an unpublished novel and short stories. After graduation in 1941, he joined the navy and was part of the D-Day expeditionary force. Returning to the United States at the end of the war, he enrolled at Columbia, studying Victorian literature and writing his thesis on John Ruskin's criticism of J. M. W. Turner's paintings. After receiving his MA, Ferlinghetti used the rest of his GI Bill benefits to go to Paris, like some of the Lost Generation writers he admired—he was especially influenced by Eliot, Pound, and Hemingway. In addition to studying, he was writing poetry and learning to paint. In 1951 he received his doctorate from the University of Paris (his dissertation was called *The City: Symbol in Modern Poetry: In Search of a Metropolitan Tradition*) and moved to San Francisco.

For twenty years, Ferlinghetti was married to Selden Kirby-Smith, with whom he has a daughter, Julie, and a son, Lorenzo. The marriage ended in divorce.

Works Cited

Cherkovski, Neeli. *Ferlinghetti: A Biography.* New York: Doubleday, 1979.
Silesky, Barry. *Ferlinghetti: the Artist in his Time.* New York: Warner, 1990.
Smith, Larry. *Lawrence Ferlinghetti: Poet-at-Large.* Carbondale, IL: Southern Illinois University Press, 1983.
Theado, Matt. *The Beats: A Literary Reference.* New York: Carroll & Graf, 2001.

FISHER, FLORENCE

Author, Founder of Adoptees Liberation Movement Association (ALMA)
Adoptee

Career, Major Achievements, History, and Awards

Florence Fisher's personal search for her roots and birth identity led to her classic memoir *The Search for Anna Fisher.* She founded one of the earliest adoptee organizations, the Adoptees Liberation Movement Association (ALMA), in 1971. ALMA, now called the ALMA Society, is dedicated to the cause of unsealing adoption records for adult adoptees. ALMA supports search and reunion for those separated by relinquishment and adoption. At its peak, ALMA numbered over 10,000 members. The group began with a simple advertisement that first ran on March 21, 1971, in the *New York Times*: "Adult who was an adopted child desires contact with other adoptees to exchange views on adoptive situation and for mutual assistance in search for natural parents" (Fisher 15).

The number and passion of the responses, both positive and negative, came as a surprise to Fisher. Society at that time generally censured adoptees who wished to search for their families of origin, and portrayed them as ungrateful "bad seeds" or products of inadequate or poor adoptive parenting. Fisher was among the first to challenge this and to claim the right to learn about her origins.

Adoption agencies and state governments began to seal adoption files in the 1930s and 1940s, prohibiting even the persons whose names appeared on the documents from viewing or obtaining them. In 1977, ALMA filed a class action lawsuit against the state of New York (ALMA v. Lefkowitz, et al.), alleging that New York's secretive adoption law was unconstitutional. ALMA challenged a widely misunderstood and inconsistent set of laws that were often intertwined with powerful emotions and biased public assumptions. Though ALMA lost, the suit had been a start. Over time other groups, notably Bastard Nation and the American Adoption Congress, would win access for some adoptees to their original birth certificates through state legislation, ballot initiatives, and state supreme court rulings. As of 2008, eight of fifty states, Alabama, Alaska, Delaware, Kansas, Maine, New Hampshire, Oregon, and Tennessee, uphold an adopted adult's right to obtain or view his or her own original birth certificate. Some other states provide adopted adults with compromised access to their birth records through mutual consent registries or confidential intermediaries.

Following the unfavorable ruling, Fisher decided to turn ALMA's focus towards search and reunion support.

Fisher began her search to obtain her sealed documents in a culture of imposed secrecy. She vividly recalled the time she asked a records clerk for her file:

> He looked up sharply. "Are you kidding, sister?" he said. "This isn't yours. This is a private file and it's sealed. You're lucky you're getting this much."
>
> "Please," I said softly. And then I heard myself say, "It's my life." . . .
>
> I watched him take the envelope, along with the Order of Adoption, to a large machine. While waiting for it to warm up, he leafed casually through the papers in the file. Tears began to fill my eyes. Was it possible that this man could look over my files, could know the facts of my birth—my mother and my father, my origins, everything I hungered for—yet these documents were barred from my sight? Did *he* have a right to this information? . . . [A]ny other person . . . who happened to be born to a legally married couple, and was brought up by them, could come into the Hall of Records and secure any papers pertaining to his own life. Why couldn't I? (Fisher 108–109).

Family of Origin

Named Baby Fisher at the time of her birth at St. Anthony's Hospital in New York around 1928*, she inexplicably acquired the name of Anna Fisher, a combination of her mother's first name and father's last name, on her original records,. Her teenaged

---

*Fisher does not make her date of birth available. In *The Search for Anna Fisher*, she wrote that her mother was born around 1920 and was 17 at the time of Anna's birth, so 1927 or 1928 might be guessed as her approximate year of birth.

parents had been forced to marry in Philadelphia three months prior to their baby's birth, but the marriage was promptly annulled. Anna Sweik Cohen, who was seventeen at the time, was pressured by her parents to place the baby for adoption. Fisher was able to locate her mother at the end of a twenty-year search, and the two reunited in Manhattan, where Anna worked in a large department store. Fisher learned that her mother had married again and that she had two half-siblings, a brother, Robert, and a sister, Marsha.

Fisher also located her father, Frederick Fisher, who had been eighteen years old at the time of his daughter's birth. An actor and stunt man in Hollywood since that time, he welcomed his daughter back into his life in 1971, having himself conducted an unsuccessful search for his daughter via personal ads some time earlier.

Adoptive Family

Fisher was adopted at birth by Harry and Rose Ladden of Brooklyn, New York, in a private adoption arranged by a physician, Dr. Green. Florence's childhood was spent sharing a three-room apartment with her parents, grandmother, and frequently her mother's brother. Her grandmother frequently referred to Florence as the "momser" or "mamzer," which she later discovered meant "bastard" in Hebrew.

Rose Ladden had kept all knowledge of the adoption from Florence and wanted everyone to believe that she was Rose's child by birth. Rose, who was eventually treated for psychiatric illness, infantilized her adopted daughter, feeding her milk from a bottle until she was seven (Fisher 47) and keeping her in a crib until the age of ten. When Florence found a document in a dresser drawer with the name Anna Fisher on it, she asked Rose if she was Anna Fisher, but Rose lied in response. Rose even told her daughter that her labor pains during Florence's delivery were exceptionally bad (Fisher 43).

Rose once showed Florence a razor and then ran into the bathroom, locking the door and telling Florence to watch for blood coming underneath it, and that when it appeared she would know that she had killed her mother (Fisher 39–46). Fisher believed that the lies about her adoption contributed to Rose's illness, saying: "Lies are curious. If the great lie that lived in my home hurt me, condemned me to that sense of emptiness and frustration, how much more did it trap my mother. Now, when the whole drama is done, I think back on all the misery it must have caused her to maintain, over all the many years of my childhood, a lie that became a fantasy—and then a devastating mania" (Fisher 37–38).

Rose died of a brain tumor in 1950, just after the birth of Florence's son. Fisher was able to verify the fact that she had been adopted after Rose's death. Nearly twenty-five years later, Fisher would comment, "Though my childhood had not been pleasant, that was not what motivated my search. Other adoptees I have come to know, who sincerely loved their adoptive families, have no less a desire to know their origins" (Fisher 14).

Education and Significant Relationships

In 1950, Florence left high school to marry a man named Walter, whom she later divorced. The couple had a son named Glenn. Florence recalled repeating the name Anna Fisher over and over again during the delivery. Glenn's birth prompted an observation that adoptees often share—that her son was the first person she knew who looked like her. Fisher married a second time, to a man named Stan. Surnames are not given for Walter, Glenn, or Stan.

Works Cited

Deans, Jill R. "The Birth of Contemporary Adoption Autobiography: Florence Fisher and Betty Jean Lifton." *Auto/biography Studies: a/b* 18.2 (2003): 239–258.
Fisher, Florence. *The Search For Anna Fisher.* New York: Arthur Fields Books, Inc., 1973.

FLAX, CAROL (1952–)

Artist
Adoptee

Career , Major Awards, and Achievements

Carol Flax is a New Media artist who uses technology to explore the ways the personal and the world relate. Memory and history are important motifs in her work, and relationship is a major theme—the relationship between human beings, between human beings and the world, between what is inherent and what is learned, and between the personal subjects of her work and the technology she uses to produce it. Much of her work is interactive and allows the possibility of an unusually dynamic and intimate bond between the artist and the viewer. The viewer is often called on to make choices, and in doing so, they participate in the creation of the work, which changes when another viewer makes other choices.

Flax is the recipient of numerous grants and artist residencies, including a 2000 National Endowment for the Arts Creation and Presentation Grant and nominations for 2005 and 2007 New Media Fellowships through the Program for Media Artists. Her commissioned work *Journeys: 1900/2000* was supported by a residency at the Institute for studies in the arts and was exhibited throughout the United States. In addition, her work has been exhibited and published throughout the world, including the 2001 XXV Bienal de Sao Paulo in Brazil and "Iterations: The New Image" at the International Center of Photography in New York. More than twenty anthologies and catalogs on New Media art include Flax's art, which is also contained in public and private collections. The 2007 *memoria/memoir* has been supported by a co-production residency at the Banff New Media Institute and has been exhibited in Canada and the United States.

[Courtesy of Carol Flax]

From 1997 to 2005, Flax was an art faculty member of the University of Arizona–Tucson, teaching photography and digital media. Her Web site is www.carolflax.net.

(M)Other Stories: A Parent(hetic)al Tale looks at the artist's own adoption. In 1997, Flax collaborated with fellow artist (and fellow adoptee) Ann Fessler, author of *The Girls Who Went Away: The Hidden History of Women Who Surrendered Children to Adoption in the Decades before Roe vs. Wade* (Penguin 2006). Their collaboration, *Ex/Changing Families*, is a multi-media installation that looks at their personal stories along with the larger societal implications of how women and children are viewed in our culture. It was exhibited in 1997 at the UCR/California Museum of Photography in Riverside, California, and in 1998 at the McKinney Avenue Contemporary in Dallas, Texas. Flax's adoption is an important theme in her work:

> As an artist, I try to find those delimiting spaces where the personal and the social come together, where boundaries shift and nothing is quite certain. As an adoptee, I have spent most of my life caught in the transitional state between knowing and not knowing. For years, my work has broached questions of uncertainly in my own identity, extended outward to include larger issues of social and cultural identities (Artist's statement, 2007).

Family of Origin

Carol Flax was born on February 8, 1952, in Los Angeles. The personal information that follows is taken from my May 6, 2002, interview with Flax.

> From what I know, my birthmother got pregnant when she was doing her residency in psychology at Syracuse, New York. She was living in a rooming house and had a relationship with the guy who ran the house, which resulted in her pregnancy. When she told him, he said that he had to think about what he was going to do. He thought about it and said, "I can't do it. I'm not ready to be a father." So, she hopped on a train and went to the farthest city she could find, which was L.A. She wanted to get as far away from her mother as she could. At one point she went to visit her sister and told her sister that she was thinking of moving to California, and her sister said something like, "Well, it's going to really upset Mom, but it's a good thing you're not pregnant because then she would probably kill you." I think she had actually gone to her sister to tell her she was pregnant, and when her sister said that, she decided not to tell her. She went to California, went to L.A., stayed with a friend, then got a job and was working. I was born at L.A. County Hospital.
>
> Apparently they brought me to her—the paperwork got mixed up—so I actually got nursed once—pretty cool. I think she waited the longest they would let her wait to sign the papers, and at some point apparently while she was pregnant with me, she met the man to whom she is still married. She married him shortly after I was born.
>
> He said, "If you want to keep the baby we can get married and you can." But she wasn't quite ready to make that decision. So she signed the papers and gave me up. There's a lot of really fuzzy stuff and much of the information is still sealed, but I was in a foster home for three months, and nobody can tell me why. My birthmother told me she signed the papers, my adoptive parents did everything they were supposed to do, everything was in the works, and nobody knows what the delay was. Apparently it should have been six weeks, according to California law. Nobody can tell me why it took three months.

Adoption

Flax was adopted through the Vista Del Mar agency in Los Angeles, after placement in at least one foster home. She was raised in Los Angeles and her adoptive parents were in the art material business. She was the oldest girl, followed by a second adopted sister and a youngest sister who was born to her adoptive parents. She and her sister always knew that they had been adopted. In my interview with her, she said:

It's so hard to know what the positives were and what the negatives were, because you don't know what life you would have had if you hadn't been adopted. I've had a reasonably good life, I was raised financially more comfortably than I would have been if she kept me. There was good and bad, but mostly it was as good a childhood as anybody else I know.

I believe in open adoption, and I've heard both good and bad stories about that, too. My experience was so easy when I decided to find my birthmother. I mean it took a year, but most of that year was me thinking about each step. Fortunately Ed [her husband] was willing to make phone calls for me. Had he not been, I maybe still wouldn't know. That part was hard, but real exciting. None of it was that difficult. . . . I know a lot of people who really had trouble getting information, and spent a lot of money and angst trying to get that information. It's sort of stupid. Obviously we're entitled to know who we are, and I think the trick is when and how information is given out so that nobody gets hurt. I'm not terribly involved with the politics of searching. I'm more interested in the politics and the social, economic, and cultural issues around adoption in particular: the empowerment and disempowerment of women and children.

I have mixed feelings about all of it. I know being adopted shaped who I am. I know that for a fact. I definitely think a lot of my behavior, although I had no clue at the time, and a lot of decisions, were based on my adoption, in terms of choices I made.

I was a very rebellious kid, and I was also the oldest. So was I rebellious because I was adopted or was I rebellious because I was the oldest? Who knows? I know that a lot of my characteristics come from how I was raised. As an artist, I look for what makes us who we are, and I'm particularly interested in what's genetic and what's environmental—nature and nurture. I don't think I would be as interested in that without the disconnect between nature and nurture created by adoption.

Search and Reunion

Flax found her first mother and two brothers when she was forty years old. Her search took about a year. An astonishing story unfolded as she searched for her mother.

I was seeing a therapist and she kept saying that my adoption is important to my understanding of myself. I kept saying, "I don't know," and she kept pushing it, and finally she convinced me that I should actually do the search and deal with that piece of my life. My husband Ed told me that I used to identify myself as an adoptee pretty early on when I met someone new. I was never aware that I did that. Clearly this piece of my identity was much more important to me than I was consciously acknowledging. Since I found my birthmother, I no longer do that.

In my art practice, I had started making art about family. I had wanted to really talk about my children, and I'd been trying to bring that into my art. I began by making art about parenting, and what I would pass on to the next generation, and in the course of doing that, and looking at what I put out there as a parent, I started looking at what formed me. I went through family snapshots and in the process of doing that realized that my genetic information was clearly a piece that I didn't have. Doing work about my parents led me to realize that I needed more information. That's when I decided to search, decided to find my birthmother, which I did. Shortly after I met her, I went off and did a project in Scotland. While I was there, a curator I had previously worked with called and asked me to do some work about women. That was the point I started making adoption art.

Before I found my birthmother, I was doing some commercial work and wanted to find an agent. I looked through a bunch of directories where artist's reps will take out pages of ads to show the work of the artists they represent. I found this one rep, and I said, "I really like his sensibility." I even liked his name and I liked the artists he represented. I was living in L.A. and he was in San Diego, so I sent him off a bunch of work, and he said "Yeah, I can represent you." I never did a lot of commercial work, but he would call ever so often and say, "Send your book to this agency or send it off here." At some point he moved to San Francisco. He threw these annual parties, which I never attended. We never met in person and we were in irregular communication.

When I found my birthmother I had gone to my adoptive mother and said, "I'm ready to search." I said, "A friend of mine who's adopted has this information, isn't that amazing?" And she said "Oh, I've got it for you if you want it," which I had no clue. I had always been told that "there was no information, that we know nothing, we have no records, nothing."

Once I had my mother's maiden name from these records, I contacted the agency I was adopted from to see if I could get the full story. At the adoption agency, I met with a social worker who went through the files and synthesized a narrative with all the details left out. He gave me that, but to get her first name I had to play this guessing game with him because he couldn't tell me. He wanted to give me the information, so we had to play this little game. I didn't even know what he was doing. He started asking me all these questions that seemed totally unrelated to everything. I got really mad until I finally realized what he was doing, so in the end I had a first and last name.

Once I had the information, I hired a search counselor to try to locate her. She found somebody on the east coast who she thought might actually be her, or could lead us to her. I realized I was too afraid to actually make the calls, so I got my husband to do it. The first person he called turned out to be a cousin of hers. They said, "Well, there's two sides of the family, and they sort of split, but try cousin so-and-so." Cousin so-and-so said, "Well, I don't know her, but I know her sister." So we finally got to the sister, who didn't know I existed. After a great deal of hesitation, she gave Ed my mother's name, her last name, and her son's name. She said, "But she's not home right now, she's visiting her son in San Francisco." And at that point I realized that I'd had a relationship with this same guy for years—my rep turned out to be my own brother! Then when we met, there was an instant rapport. He had not known about me. He accepted me unconditionally the second he heard about me. My other brother, who is older than the brother who is my agent, knew about me, and was actually a little resistant when I showed up. We're now good friends, but when I actually showed up, there was this little sort of push-pull. But the youngest was just like, "Hey, Sis!" There was a real connection.

But it's been good, you know. I hear so many horror stories. I feel very, very lucky and my birthmother's ecstatic that I'm an artist. She said, "If I could've picked anything for you to have been, it would have been an artist." How many mothers say that? And I introduced both my mothers to each other. It was actually really wonderful. I was having an opening in L.A. of one of my adoption installations, and I knew that they would both be at the opening. It was nice.

Flax has contacted some of her biological father's relatives, even though she was not able to locate her father before his death. He left no other known children.

My birthfather died a while before I started the process, but I've had some communication with both of his brothers. And at one point I was getting e-mails from a cousin whose father told him about me. He was aware of me, and I think he was doing a search online and found me, and e-mailed me. And then I met one of my first cousins on my mother's side in Boston.

My birthfather never married, as far as we know. We don't know if there were any other children, but his brothers were not aware of anybody else. He had been a turret gunner during World War II and it seems he was shell-shocked and never fully recovered. From what we could ascertain, he basically drank himself to death. It's too bad—I would have liked to have met him.

Education and Significant Relationships

Flax has an MFA from California Institute of the Arts. She is married to Edmund Fickbohm. She has two daughters, Shana and Reanna, from a previous marriage, and two grandsons, Kyle and Conner.

Works Cited

Flax, Carol, personal interview. May 6, 2002.

G

GEBEL-WILLIAMS, GUNTHER (1934–2001)

Animal Trainer, Circus Superstar
Adoptee

Career, Major Awards, and Achievements

Gunther Gebel-Williams is widely acknowledged as the greatest wild animal trainer in circus history. He began his career in 1947 at the age of twelve, when his mother indentured him to the Circus Williams in Cologne, West Germany. Circus Williams was a family-owned, one-ring company, which then employed about fifty people. Gebel-Williams was one of the first animal trainers to use humane methods and positive reinforcement rather than established "fear techniques," such as whip, chair, water hose, or guns with blanks to control the animal performers. He developed his astonishing acts using food, reassurance, and voice as his main training instruments: "I treated my animals like a part of my family. Maybe that was because I never really had a family of my own when I was a child. I was as protective of my animals as I am of my own children, and I tried to keep them around me, safe and contented, for as long as I could" (69).

Gunther's first work with animals was with horses. After winning international prizes for his horse acts, Gebel-Williams began training lions and elephants, and later tigers and leopards. His first step was to develop trust, to make the animals feel he understood them and to teach them to respect him. He preferred to obtain animals young and jungle born, so that he had charge of their training from the beginning. He could train tigers in six months. Acts using a combination of animals, such as tigers and horses or his famous elephant-tiger pyramid, took much longer to perfect. He always visited the animals before and after each performance to establish a routine that reassured them.

Though he received many offers, he refused to leave the Circus Williams. In 1968, the Ringling Brothers and Barnum & Bailey three-ring circus finally acquired him only by buying Circus Williams. He later became a Ringling Brothers part owner and its vice president for animal welfare, responsible for the care of more than 400 animals. Gebel-Williams made his American debut in 1969. The American Guild of Variety Artists named him "Circus Performer of the Year" in 1973. He was famous for his glamorous appearance, daring rapport with animals, and his capacity for patient, painstaking work. For more than twenty years and 12,000 performances, he never missed a show.

[AP Photo/The National Academy of Television Arts and Sciences]

Family of Origin

Gunther Gebel was born in Schweidnitz, Silesia, the son of Max Gebel, a theater carpenter, and his seamstress wife: "I came into this world on September 12, 1934, when virtually every nation stood at the brink of war. From day one my life was filled with harsh realities, and there was no place in it for daydreams and childish fantasies. The times in which we lived stole any hope for the future from me, and I suppose they did the same to my sister, Rita, and my parents" (71). Gebel-Williams relates in his autobiography that his childhood home was violent and unhappy. He was never able to develop a close relationship with his sister, who was six years older.

His parents eventually divorced, but the brutality in his family did not disappear when his father left: "My difficult life made me tough and pushed me farther away from people and closer to animals" (75–76). After World War II, as Soviet troops advanced towards Schweidnitz, Gunther fled with his mother to Cologne, West Germany. Mrs. Gebel found a job in 1947 as a seamstress with the Circus Williams. She left the circus after three weeks, but first negotiated a contract forcing her twelve-year-old son to stay with the circus and work for the next five years:

> I could not understand why my mother was doing this to me. I tried and tried to figure out what I had done that was so bad to make her want to get rid of me. I was terribly distraught, but she did not change her mind. I do not remember if she kissed me when she left or even said goodbye. All I know is that one day she was gone (96–97).

Gebel-Williams seldom saw his family after he began working for the circus. At first his mother visited him once a year but stopped coming to see him after she remarried. Max Gebel, Gunther's father, only rarely saw his son after the war. He died in 1954.

Adoption

Although the circus owners, Harry and Carola Williams, never sent Gunther to school because they needed him at the circus (109), they grew fond of the boy and taught him a variety of circus skills including tumbling, juggling, trapeze, and wire-walking. The Williams family especially noticed and appreciated his early "uncanny" (106) abilities with animals. Gunther eventually grew close to the entire Williams family, and they became the family he had never had (98).

Harry and Carola had two children, Alfons and Jeanette, and Carola had an older son, Holdy Barlay, from an earlier marriage. Holdy worked with Circus Williams part-time, as he had his own traveling act.

In 1950 Harry Williams was killed in a circus accident. His son, Alfons, died soon after in a car accident. Carola asked Gunther to take over the daily supervision of the troupe while she handled the business side of the circus. Eventually, he became their general manager. In 1956, just before they opened their season in Berlin, Carola informally adopted Gunther and asked him to take their family name.

Marriage and Children

In 1960, Gunther married the Williams' daughter, Jeanette, but they divorced in 1967. In 1968, he married his second wife, Sigrid, a German widow and model, whom he had seen in the circus audience. They have one son, Mark Oliver Gebel. Gunther also helped to raise his step daughter, Tina Gebel-Delmoral, a child from Sigrid's earlier marriage. When Gunther Gebel-Williams retired in 1990, Mark succeeded his father as the Ringling Brothers star animal trainer. When Mark took a leave of absence in 1998 for the birth of his first son, Hunter, Gebel-Williams took his place for more than a dozen performances. A second grandson, Adam, was born in January 2001.

Gunther felt that the violence and indifference of his own parents influenced him as a husband and father:

> The only good that came from this was that I learned how not to treat my own family. I am very protective of my children, and because of that there have been times when I did not give them enough freedom. I love them so much and am so happy to have a family of my own that I try to keep them close to me, and that is not always the best thing for them (72).

Gebel-Williams died of brain cancer in Venice, Florida, on July 19, 2001, at the age of sixty-six.

Works Cited

Gebel-Williams, Gunther, with Toni Reinhold. *Untamed: The Autobiography of the Circus's Greatest Animal Trainer.* New York: William Morrow and Co., Inc., 1991.

GRAHAM, SHEILAH (1904–1988)

Author, Screenwriter, Journalist
Orphanage alumna

Career and Major Achievements

Sheilah Graham was best known as a journalist, columnist, and writer of autobiographical novels, including the best-selling *Beloved Infidel* (1958), which recorded her relationship with novelist F. Scott Fitzgerald. *Beloved Infidel* was made into a movie starring Deborah Kerr and Gregory Peck in 1959.

In 1933 she moved to New York City, hoping to find more writing opportunities, and in 1935 the North American Newspaper Alliance offered her a syndicated column writing about Hollywood. She moved to the Bell-McClure syndicate in 1970 and continued her coverage of Hollywood, international society, and subjects thought to be of interest to women. At the height of her career, her column appeared in 180 newspapers. Graham also appeared on television and radio shows and wrote for popular periodicals. During World War II she returned to England, where she had been born, as a war correspondent.

Graham met Fitzgerald at a party in 1937, and their love affair continued until his death in her arms in 1940. During his relationship with Graham, Fitzgerald remained married to Zelda Sayre Fitzgerald,* who had been institutionalized in 1930 for schizophrenia.

Graham and Fitzgerald immortalized each other in their writings. He modeled Kathleen, the heroine of *The Last Tycoon*, on Graham, and *Beloved Infidel*, her first bestseller, met with a very positive reception from critics, who considered the description of Fitzgerald to be accurate, revealing, and loyal.

The Rest of the Story, which was less successful, continued the story begun in *Beloved Infidel*. *A College of One* described Fitzgerald's guidance of Graham's education and received mixed reviews, though most reviewers felt there was much to be learned about Fitzgerald in the book. Her next book, *Confessions of a Hollywood Gossip Columnist*, was

---

*Zelda was the model for several of Fitzgerald's characters, including Nicole Diver in *Tender Is the Night* and Daisy Buchanan in *The Great Gatsby*. She epitomized the flapper of the American Jazz Age.

[Hulton Archive/Getty Images]

centered on her professional experience. It was less kindly reviewed. In 1976, she wrote again of Fitzgerald, to correct errors, she said, in her own and other's presentations of him. *The Real Scott Fitzgerald* was generally not well received, as it recycled mostly already-known information about Fitzgerald. In 1978 she produced *The Late Lily Shiel*, the story of her own life from orphan to musical comedy star and journalist. In the first four chapters of this book, Graham gives a detailed account of her years in a London orphanage from ages six to fourteen.

Family of Origin

Graham was born Lily Shiel on September 15, 2004, in Leeds, England, to immigrant parents, Louis and Rebecca Shiel. The Shiels were of Jewish descent, and they moved to England from the Ukraine to escape persecution in the *pogroms*. When Lily was eleven months old, her father, a tailor, died of cancer while on a trip to consult a specialist in Berlin. His wife, who could barely speak English, moved her family to London's East End and tried to support them as a cook and by cleaning public lavatories. Although Graham makes no mention of them in her autobiographies, she had five older brothers and sisters, all of whom took anglicized names: Heiman (Henry), Esther (Iris), Sarah (Sally), Meyer (Jack), and Morris (Maurice). The two youngest children, Lily and Morris, were sent to an orphanage known in Graham's autobiographies as the East London Home for Orphans, but Graham's daughter, Wendy Fairly, identified it as the Jews Hospital and Orphan Asylum in Norwood.*

In *Beloved Infidel*, Lily is brought to the orphanage at the age of six by a neighbor she was taught to call "Aunt Mary" (4–5). In *The Late Lily Shiel*, from which all quotations below are taken, she is brought by a male person known only as "The Relative":

> The events of the first day in the Little School are marked indelibly on her mind. . . young newcomers, boys and girls, were herded into a bathroom with steaming water in three big tubs. They were told to remove their clothes, which were then handled gingerly and put into small piles. Lily had never been naked in front of a boy, not that she could remember, and she was somewhat embarrassed, especially as the boys were staring at the girls and whispering and giggling.
>
> Before the bath, three to a tub, the girls as well as the boys were sheared to the scalp by a woman with strong clippers. . . . After the bath they were all dressed alike, in washed-out blue rompers with small knickers attached. And now you could not distinguish boy from girl. They were then marshaled outside and told to say good-bye to whoever had brought them (13–14).

The "Little School" was where children up to the age of eight lived and where they were educated. The Little School children were not permitted contact with family members outside the orphanage: "There were no visiting days for the children in the Little School. It was decided that it was better for them to believe that this had always been their home" (17). At the age of eight, the children were moved to the Big School, where they could receive visits from relatives every six weeks: "They were supposed to bring only cookies and sweets. In a Jewish orphanage? Wherever you looked, there were groups huddled together eating the contraband food" (35). In the Big School, the children were assigned a number, Lily's being 53. At the age of twelve, boys and girls were allowed to grow their hair longer and were allowed to stay up an hour later. The girls' dormitory had three sleeping sections, one for children eight to thirteen years old, one for bed-wetters, and one for girls past puberty.

Graham wrote that the girls never tried to run away from the orphanage, but that a boy would run away about once every year. She went on to say that when the boy

---

*Established by leading Jewish benefactors in 1795, the Asylum was originally a hospital for the aged and later became a home for children known as the Norwood Jewish Orphanage. After the 1960s, it became known as simply Norwood and is now a community-based welfare organization for troubled children and families.

was caught, the headmaster would strip, beat, and humiliate him before the other children:

> The boy was then made to don girl's panties and to stand on a bench—"Up straight now," where all could see his disgrace, wiping his tears with the knuckles of his hands. . . . You wouldn't find the girls running away. They were too timid or too practical. And where was there to run to? If anyone wanted them at home, they wouldn't be here (24–25).

Education and Significant Relationships

Lily loved to read and found solace in books as her escape from the orphanage. She began to excel in her studies and found it a good strategy to avoid punishment and to receive positive attention. She advanced a grade and went on to become head prefect, captain of the cricket team, and the top student in the school. The orphanage offered her a university scholarship to become a teacher, but her family declined the offer. Her mother was ill with cancer and Lily would be needed at home to help. Big School lessons ended at age fourteen: "At fourteen, lessons were over. The boys left to earn their living. But the girls remained for another six months. They were used as servants for the school" (62). Lily left the orphanage in March 1919, at age fourteen and a half. She took a job at an Adressograph factory, where she stamped names and addresses on metal plates for mass mailings. After her dismissal from the factory and a family quarrel, the orphanage helped her arrange work in Brighton as a live-in maid. Her mother died when Lily was sixteen.

When she was seventeen, Lily met Major John Graham Gilliam, an iron and steel manufacturing agent twenty-five years her senior. He encouraged her career as a performer in musical comedies. Lily attended the Royal Academy of Dramatic Art and married Graham in 1926. During their marriage she changed her name to Sheilah Graham and began writing articles about the stage for London periodicals as well as appearing onstage. The couple divorced in 1937.

She was married to Trevor C. L. Westbrook, an aircraft manufacturer, from 1941 to 1946; they had two children, Wendy and Robert. She was naturalized an American citizen in 1947. She married her third husband, Stanley Wojtkiewkz, in 1953. They divorced in 1955. Sheila Graham died in Palm Beach, Florida, on November 17, 1988, of congestive heart failure.

Works Cited

Fairey, Wendy. "Recollections of Sheilah Graham." *Jewish Women's Archive.* September 9, 2007.
    http://www.jwa.org/discover/recollections/graham.html
Graham, Sheilah, and Gerold Frank. *Beloved Infidel.* New York: Quality, 1958.
Graham, Sheilah. *The Late Lily Shiel.* New York: Grosset & Dunlap, 1978.

GREEN, TIM (1963–)

Professional Football Player, Attorney, Author, Media Personality
Adoptee

Career, Major Awards, and Achievements

Tim Green was the number-one draft pick of the Atlanta Falcons in 1986 after a distinguished college career as an all-American defensive end at Syracuse University. Green has also enjoyed a successful and multifaceted post-football career as an attorney, sports commentator, media personality, and author.

Green's nonfiction works include *A Man and His Mother* (1997), an autobiography about his relinquishment, adoption, and subsequent search for his roots, and *The Dark Side of the Game* (1997), a *New York Times* bestseller about the unglamorous aspects of professional football. His novels include *The Red Zone* (1998), *Double Reverse* (1999), *Ruffians* (1999), *The Letter of the Law* (2000), *The Moment of Truth* (2005), *The Fourth Perimeter* (2002), *The Fifth Angel* (2003), *The First 48* (2004), and *Exact Revenge* (2005).

Green is most recently the host of the television show *A Current Affair* (2005), formerly hosted by Maury Povich.

Family of Origin

Tim Green was born in Oswego, New York, on December 13, 1963, to Joanne Heathslide. His maternal grandfather was an Irish Catholic policemen and a minor league baseball player from Syracuse, New York. Joanne had met Tim's birthfather in college, but he denied responsibility for her pregnancy. Joanne married her longtime friend Edward Burgen during her eighth month of pregnancy. The couple settled in Philadelphia after Tim was born and relinquished for adoption, and they had a subsequent son and a daughter. Years later, a social worker would tell Tim that Joanne was the only birthmother who ever returned to the adoption agency to be sure they had placed her son with adoptive parents who both had college educations.

Tim began searching for Joanne at the age twenty-four. He joined the Adoptees Liberation Movement Association (ALMA), signed up for registries, and ran newspaper ads. One woman answered his ad, believing she was his birthmother, and she told him he was the product of a rape by her father when she was eleven. The story initially traumatized him, but important details, including her reported age at the time of relinquishment, didn't match. Tim was able to connect with people who supported his search, including an NFL security agent and the mother of a former girlfriend who revealed that she had given up a son for adoption who would have been about Tim's age. Some key hospital records were obtained through a friend just one week before a fire destroyed everything else in the room, convincing Green that locating his biological family time was "meant to be": "What I felt was too deeply rooted in me to describe with words—or to fully understand, for that matter. Suffice it to say that the thrill of finding her was small by comparison to the knowledge that I would not lose her again" (180). His connection with his birthmother, Joanne, and his half-siblings, Mary and Kenny, completed a vital circle for Green. He later served as best man at Kenny's wedding.

Adoption

Tim Green grew up in Oswego, New York, where he had been born. He was adopted as an infant by Richard and Judy Green. After a difficult pregnancy and birth of a daughter, Laurie, the Greens had been advised not to have any more biological children. They adopted Tim five years after Laurie's birth, and adopted another infant son, Kyle, three years after Tim.

Richard Green was a computer programmer for General Electric, and Judy was a stay-at-home mom. Tim later wrote, "My mother worked to make our house the envy of anyone aspiring to good housekeeping. Every meal was an event" (19). They avidly supported Tim's activities in Boy Scouts and his athletic competitions in football and wrestling. Green acknowledged that sports, school, and scouts helped frame his high achiever mentality: "To me, life was like a scout troop. The aim was to earn badges and advance. The higher you elevated yourself, the more people admired you and the easier it was for them to love you" (18).

Green spent his early childhood sleeping in orthopedic braces in order to correct misaligned legs. He dreamed of becoming a writer and a football player because "football and books were the two things that were revered in our household" (9–10).

He always knew that he had been adopted, but classmates pointed out on his first day at school that the tall boy didn't look like either of his parents. That awareness would follow him through his childhood, a constant reminder that "there is no greater repudiation than to be born and then immediately turned over to the state for redistribution" (14). As Green grew older, he couldn't account for what drove his rage and ferocity on the playing field or caused his seeming inability to develop healthy relationships with women: "The questions I had about who I was, the anger at being cast aside, and the determination to prove I was worthy—all negative things—became assets on the football field. I began to feed off of my own pain as well as the pain I was causing others" (37).

A downward emotional spiral acted out through excessive drinking, casual sexual encounters, and macho bravado, continued through his professional football career until he met his future wife, Illyssa. Green credits her with the tremendous change and redemption in his life, and for giving him the courage to search for his biological family, a decision not initially well received by his adoptive parents.

Education and Significant Relationships

Green credits much of his success in life to his adoptive parents, coaches, supportive family friends, and his wife. He graduated as covaledictorian from Syracuse University in 1984. During his professional football career, he used the off-season to earn his law degree from Syracuse University and Manhattan's Cardozo Law School. Married to Illyssa (Wolkoff) and the father of two children, Green says marriage and fatherhood have provided him with a deeper ability to connect with himself. In fact, when Tim discovered that Illyssa wasn't pregnant after their honeymoon, he nearly panicked and insisted on fertility tests immediately. Despite his doctor's advice to relax and be patient, Green explained: "You don't understand. I don't know where I came from. I don't know if I'll leave anything behind. I'm like a spark from a campfire, flying up into the black night. . . . If I can't leave kids, there's nothing after me. I'm like the spark, coming from nothing, leaving nothing, a meaningless flicker with nothing before it and nothing after" (161).

Works Cited

Green, Tim. *A Man and His Mother: An Adopted Son's Search.* New York: HarperCollins Publisher, Inc., 1997.

H

HAMILTON, ALEXANDER (1755–1804)

Army Officer, Lawyer, Statesman, Congressman, First Secretary of the U.S. Treasury, Author
Orphan at age 13, fostered

Career and Achievements

Alexander Hamilton overcame humble beginnings, the loss of loved ones, and the stigma and consequences of illegitimacy to greatly influence the freedom and formation of the United States. According to Kline, "Illegitimacy, abandonment, poverty, and tragic loss marked the early years of the highly intelligent boy, and undoubtedly did much to supply the urgent drive that characterized his later career" (33).

Hamilton is regarded as one of the greatest thinkers of his day. He was the sole author of sixty-three of the *Federalist Papers*, a voluminous collection of eighty-five articles that advocated ratification of the American Constitution. He coauthored another nine with James Madison and John Jay. Although the *Federalist Papers* are considered Hamilton's greatest achievement as an author, his many additional writings, speeches, and letters provide valuable firsthand insight into the political, economic, and ethical issues of his time.

Hamilton served with such distinction as captain of the New York Provincial Artillery in 1776 that the following year, at age twenty-two, he was promoted to lieutenant colonel in the Continental Army. General George Washington made him an aide-de-camp in March 1777, and he was with the troops as they endured the hellish winter at Valley Forge. Hamilton wrote many of Washington's letters, orders, and speeches, including much of his famous farewell address in 1796. He was appointed Major General and Inspector of the Army in 1798, a post he resigned in 1800 after first using his influence to establish the U.S. Navy.

He began practicing law in 1783, and was involved with several landmark cases including *Rutgers v. Waddington* (1784), which established federal precedence over state, and *People v. Crosswell* (1804), which supported the freedom of the press. He warned that the press must be free to tell the truth or else, "you must forever remain ignorant of what your rulers do" (Randall 423).

Politics was Hamilton's lifelong passion. He was elected a New York Congressman in 1782 and became a New York Assemblyman in 1786. He participated in the 1787 Constitutional Convention and served as the first U.S. Secretary of the Treasury from

[Courtesy of the Library of Congress]

1789 to 1795. He was instrumental in creating Wall Street and the Bank of New York, and his image appears on the American ten dollar bill.

After George Washington's death in 1799, the void in Federalist Party leadership created an internal power struggle between John Adams, Washington's vice president, and Hamilton. Adams publicly referred to Hamilton as a "base-born brat of a Scots peddler"—a bastard. This was a serious slur, a revelation for most people that further damaged Hamilton among New England Congregationalists and Middle States Presbyterians, who refused communion to the illegitimate (Randall 422).

Hamilton's public admission of a thirteen-month extramarital affair with a twenty-three-year-old, along with his opposition to Adams, finally fractured the Federalist party and helped to elect their Republican adversaries Thomas Jefferson and Aaron Burr as president and vice president, respectively. Biographers suggest that Hamilton's strengths and his flaws can be credited to his harsh childhood experiences:

> Once the realities of Hamilton's early years have been allowed credence, we realize to how startling an extent his desperate efforts to handle the situations into which he had been by birth thrown created his adult points of view. . . . Fired by genius, [his] constellation of traits enabled him to recognize in the structure of the emerging United States serious weaknesses which he had the ability and drive to cure. While others cut with the grain, he cut against it. Hamilton's view was always from the outside and it was this that made him one of the greatest of the founding fathers. . . .
>
> Neither Hamilton's admirers nor his detractors realized the truth: the accomplished, smooth, and brilliant man of the world could at any moment change hysterically, invisibly, for the time being decisively, into an imperiled, anguished child (Flexner, 6–7).

Family of Origin

Born January 11, 1755, to Rachel Fawcett Levine and James Hamilton, Alexander was Rachel's third son. Rachel's ancestors were French Huguenots named Faucette who anglicized their name when they fled to the West Indies in the late 1600s to escape Catholic persecution. Rachel's father, John Fawcett IV, was a doctor who owned a sugar plantation on a British island called Nevis.

Seven children were born to Fawcett, of which two daughters survived. The younger, Rachel, was eleven years old when her mother was granted a rare "agreement of separation" from her husband. Rachel inherited her father's entire estate when he died in 1745.

At age sixteen, Rachel married a thirty-eight-year old merchant of Danish or North German and Jewish descent named Johann Michael Levine (spelling varies). The couple moved to an estate called "Contentment" on St. Croix to try their hand at cotton and sugar farming. They had one son, Peter Levine, in 1746. In a biography of his famous father, John Hamilton wrote, "His mother's first husband was a Dane, named Lavine, who, attracted by her beauty, and recommended to her mother by his wealth, received her hand against her inclination" (Hamilton, J. 2). The marriage, unhappy from the start, became even more so. Levine's enterprises failed until, deeply in debt, he eventually hired himself out as a slave overseer and became brutish toward his young wife. Rachel responded to her husband's mistreatment by becoming involved with other men.

Rachel was sentenced and jailed for adultery. Levine believed that this would cause her to reform and return chastened to him. Instead, she ran away. In October 1750, Rachel and her mother "in poverty left the island" (Flexner 13) and moved to St. Kitts. There Rachel met James Hamilton, a Scottish merchant eleven years her senior. James was the fourth son of a wealthy and aristocratic couple from Ayreshire, south of Glasgow. James and Rachel's first son, James, was born in 1753, followed by Alexander two years later. The couple had lived together as husband and wife long enough to qualify them as married under English common law, but Levine refused to divorce Rachel until 1759. The terms of the divorce also made it illegal for James and Alexander to inherit anything from their mother and prohibited Rachel from giving "to her whorechildren what to such a legitimate child alone is due" (Flexner 23).

The divorce, which was granted by the Danish crown, allowed Levine to remarry, but not Rachel, who was liable upon return to be "seized and be further punished." In spite of the danger in St. Croix to Rachel, James Hamilton moved his family there in 1765 in order to collect a debt for his employer. After the desired ruling came in January, 1766, James separated from Rachel and their sons and returned to St. Kitts. Unbeknownst to ten-year-old Alexander, the goodbye to his father was final, and he was never to see him again.

For the next two years, James and Alexander helped their mother operate a small provision store and they attained a moderate prosperity. Then in February 1768, Rachel contracted yellow fever and died. Alexander also developed the disease, but recovered.

Learning of Rachel's death, Johann Levine reappeared to collect her entire estate, as granted in the divorce, for the legitimate firstborn, Peter. Alexander and James were left completely destitute. An uncle, James Lytton, made arrangements for the boys and fronted the funeral expenses. Their cousin, Peter Lytton, was appointed their guardian. Unfortunately, both James and Peter would die the following year without making any provisions for their wards.

Throughout his life, Alexander kept up a correspondence with his brother, James, who spent his entire life in the West Indies. A letter dated a year before his brother's death in 1786 showed that Alexander never lost his concern and regard for their father and that he was still trying to locate him.

Education and Significant Relationships

At age ten or eleven, while his mother was still living, Alexander was apprenticed to two young merchants, Nicholas Cruger and David Beckman. Alexander quickly impressed his benefactors with his exceptional intelligence, diligence, and promise. Following a hurricane on St. Croix in August 1771, a Scottish Presbyterian minister, Hugh Knox, convinced the sixteen-year-old's employers to send him to the mainland for safety and a formal education. Through the help of Reverend John Rodgers, a friend of Knox, Hamilton was enrolled in an Elizabethtown, New Jersey, academy for college preparatory courses. He stayed with the family of Elias Boudinot, a lawyer who would become a surrogate father, mentor, and lifelong friend to Hamilton.

Under the wing of Hercules Mulligan, a prominent New York haberdasher and leader in the Sons of Liberty, Hamilton applied to and was rejected by Princeton University, then a Presbyterian seminary. Princeton's president, John Witherspoon, had often made derogatory public remarks to the fact that his rival William Franklin, Royal Governor of New Jersey, was the illegitimate son of Benjamin Franklin. It was therefore possible, if not likely, that Hamilton was denied a Princeton education because of his illegitimacy. In 1774, Hamilton was accepted at King's College, an Episcopal institution that would later become Columbia University.

Though Hamilton made sincere efforts to comply with the school's code of conduct, he acquired such a reputation in his youth that Martha Washington named their tomcat after him (Randall 124).

In 1780, Alexander married Elizabeth (Betsey) Schuyler, daughter of General Philip Schuyler, who had gained both fame and wealth as a result of the French and Indian Wars. It proved a strategic union for Hamilton and opened many doors throughout his career. Alexander and Betsey had eight children: Philip (who died in a duel in 1801), William, James Alexander, Angelica, Elizabeth, John Church (his father's biographer), Alexander Jr., and Philip II. During their marriage, Hamilton also maintained a thirty-year affair with Betsey's sister, Angelica Schuyler Church. Her husband, John Church, a frequent traveler to England, often left Angelica alone while Betsey and the children stayed in the country (Randall 5). It was Church's pistols that were used in Hamilton's fatal duel with Aaron Burr.

Hamilton died on July 12, 1804, surviving some 36 hours after being shot through the liver in a famous pistol duel with political adversary Aaron Burr. The duel was over an alleged insult for which Hamilton refused to apologize. Though he had accepted Burr's challenge, Hamilton had decided before the duel not to fire his weapon.

Works Cited

Chernow, Ron. *Alexander Hamilton*. New York: Penguin, 2004.

De Ford, Miriam Allen. "The Bastard as Statesman: Alexander Hamilton." *Love Children: A Book of Illustrious Illegitimates*. New York: Dial, 1931.

Flexner, James Thomas. *The Young Hamilton: A Biography*. Boston: Little, Brown, 1978.

Hamilton, Allan McLane. *The Intimate Life of Alexander Hamilton*. New York: Scribner's, 1910.

Hamilton, John Church. *The Life of Alexander Hamilton*. New York: Halsted & Voorhies, 1834.

Hendrickson, Robert. *Hamilton I: 1757–1789*. New York: Mason/Charter, 1976.

Kline, Mary-Jo, ed. *Alexander Hamilton: A Biography in His Own Words*. New York: Newsweek, 1973.

Mitchell, Broadus. *Alexander Hamilton: Youth to Maturity*. New York: Macmillan, 1957.

Randall, Willard. *Alexander Hamilton: A Life*. New York: HarperCollins, 2003.

Roche, John. *Illustrious Americans: Alexander Hamilton*. Morristown, NJ: Silver Burdett, 1967.

HAMILTON, SCOTT (1958–)

Ice Skater
Adoptee

Career, Major Awards, and Achievements

Scott Hamilton won the 1984 Olympic Gold Medal for men's figure skating. He reinvented figure skating style, making it less balletic and more athletic and American.

In 1980, his third place in national competition put him on the Olympic figure skating team. He placed fifth at the 1980 Olympics and at the world championship shortly afterward. Several world class skaters went professional at this point, leaving the amateur titles open to new competition. Hamilton won the 1981 national competition and then the world competition, followed by a gold medal at the first annual Skate American tournament. The U.S. Olympic Committee named him male athlete of the year.

In 1982 and 1983 he maintained his national and world titles. In 1983, he introduced a new costume for male skaters, more like that of a speed skater and less like a ballet dancer. This was part of his campaign to change men's figure skating to emphasize power, precision, and speed over artistry. Going into the 1984 Olympics, Hamilton had won fifteen straight championships and was favored to win the Olympic gold. He did, though his performance was disappointingly below average. A month later, he won a stunning victory at the world championships and then announced his retirement from amateur skating.

[AP Photo/Luke Palmisano]

He accepted a position with the Ice Capades but lost it eighteen months later because organizers thought that female stars were more attractive to audiences. Six months afterwards, he started Stars on Ice and performed as its principal skater for fifteen years.

In 1997, after he was diagnosed as having cancer, Hamilton established a cancer charity, CARES (Cancer Alliance for Research, Education, and Survivorship), and a chemotherapy Web site.

Family of Origin

Hamilton was born on August 28, 1958, in Toledo, Ohio. He made the decision not to search for information about his family of origin after he saw how upset the subject made his adoptive mother. He had first brought up the subject to Dorothy Hamilton, his adoptive mother, during her terminal illness:

> I could tell from the look on her face that I had hurt her feelings. The last thing in the world I wanted to do was offend her.
>
> "Is there something we've done? Have Dad and I let you down in any way?" she said quietly.
>
> I fell silent and regretted bringing the subject up. "We've tried to give you everything," my mother went on. "We love you and have sacrificed for you."
>
> "I know, Mom. I'm sorry. I didn't mean anything by it."
>
> "It's okay," she said, trying to make me feel better. "Can I tell you what I think makes someone a parent? It's the person who changes a child's diapers; feeds him; takes him to school; helps him with his homework; hugs him when he cries and offers advice and perspective. A parent is there to hold a child when he needs stitches and washes his hands when they're dirty. A parent is someone who is there for a child every day."
>
> "You're right," I said. The conversation about the identity of my birth parents ended right there. It was clear to me now. I had just one mother, and I was looking right at her. And as the years went by, I never would pursue my birth parents. I would come to believe what my mother did; that just because you bring someone into the world doesn't make you a parent (Hamilton 78).

Adoption

Hamilton was adopted as an infant from the Lucas County Child and Family Services in Toledo, Ohio. His adoptive father, Ernie, was a biology professor at Bowling Green State University and his adoptive mother, Dorothy, taught second grade and high school home economics. Their daughter Susan was three years old when they adopted Scott. Dorothy had had several miscarriages and a stillborn son prior to Scott's adoption. The Hamiltons adopted a second son, Steven, in 1962.

Referring to himself as "Godzilla in diapers" (17), Hamilton was a small but physically active baby. Around the time of his brother's adoption, Scott developed a mysterious illness, which most biographies call Schwachmann's syndrome, a disorder that caused partial paralysis of the intestinal tract, complicated by respiratory problems. His concerned parents consulted a series of doctors and took him to one hospital after another for tests; Scott was often bedridden and stopped growing. Although Scott was still fragile enough to require a feeding tube, he decided he wanted to try ice skating after watching his sister.

The cool, humid atmosphere of the rink seemed to help his breathing, and he began to recover his health. His natural talent was soon apparent. Impressed by his speed and ability, the rink pros suggested regular lessons. Within six months he was competition skating and within a year the symptoms of his illness were gone and he was growing again. Hamilton's eventual height would be 5′ 4″. As a child, his size, illness, and special diets led to much teasing and bullying in school. In response, Hamilton often acted the class clown. He was also teased about his adoptive status:

> One kid. . . used to make fun of the fact that my birth parents had to give me up. It was cruel, the meanest thing you can say to an adopted child. My mother came up with a line to use in these situations: "My parents got to pick me out, and your parents had to take whatever they got" (25).

Education and Significant Relationships

When he was thirteen, Hamilton moved to Rockton, Illinois, to live and train with Pierre Brunet, a former Olympic gold medalist turned coach. His active training program left little space for a high school education. After graduation, Hamilton decided to leave skating and go to college, but when a wealthy couple volunteered to sponsor him, Hamilton happily returned to the rink. His mother's death of cancer in 1977 gave him the dedication and focus that he needed to overcome his lack of discipline and his national championship rankings began to improve. When one judge told him that he could not be taken seriously internationally because of his lack of stature, he worked on his jumping style, extension, and line, determined to create the appearance of height and the reality of excellence. Hamilton practiced for eight hours a day, six days a week, and worked out at a gym to achieve his peak form. He also concentrated on developing free-skating performances that emphasized athleticism and technique as well as personality and style.

In March 1997, Hamilton was diagnosed with cancer and underwent nine months of treatment, including surgery and chemotherapy. He was assisted in his fight to overcome cancer by his long time girlfriend, Karen Plage. He returned to Stars on Ice on October 29, with his cancer in remission.

Hamilton retired from Stars on Ice in January 2001 and married Tracie Robinson, a former nutrition coordinator for Whole Foods markets, in December 2002. The couple welcomed son Aidan McIntosh on September 16, 2003.

Works Cited

Hamilton, Scott, with Lorenzo Benet. *Landing It: My Life On and Off the Ice.* New York: Kensington Books, 1999.

Shaughnessy, Linda. *Scott Hamilton: Fireworks on Ice* (juvenile biography). Parsippany, NJ: Crestwood House, 1998.

Steere, Michael. *Scott Hamilton: A Behind the Scenes Look at the Life and Competitive Times of America's Favorite Figure Skater.* New York: St. Martin's Press, 1985.

HARRY, DEBORAH (July 11, 1945–)

Singer, Actress
Adoptee

Career, Major Awards, and Achievements

Deborah Harry is the lead singer and cofounder of the punk/new wave "sleaze" rock group Blondie. Harry is known for her style: the dramatic "selling of a song," her trash

[AP Photo]

chic look, and her "pretty come-hither-and-drop-dead" face (Current Biography 191). In addition to her participation in Blondie, Deborah Harry has recorded solo and has had an acting career.

Harry tried painting, writing, acting, and singing careers, supporting herself as a waitress, beautician, and Playboy bunny. She was influenced by the Fugs, a politically oriented prepunk group, and began to be involved in drugs. Feeling endangered by her lifestyle, she left New York City until she felt she was ready to live on her own terms.

When she returned, she became involved with the glitter rock scene and joined a trio called the Stillettoes, who performed in the East Village. Chris Stein attended a performance and joined the backup band. In 1974 he and Harry started their own group and became life partners as well as business partners. Their group began as Angel and the Snakes and evolved into Blondie and the Banzai Babies. Stein and Harry wrote and performed many of the songs that would later appear on Blondie's first album. Blondie and the Banzai Babies became a regular act at CBGB's, a Bowery night club that claims to be the first home of punk rock. Against the background of the group's loud aggressive rock, Deborah Harry, the original two-toned, peroxide blond with black roots, developed her own unique style. She satirized Hollywood and fashion with her trashed-out glamour poses while projecting the real thing as a much-photographed pop icon.

In 1977 Blondie's "Dennis" was number two on the British charts, but "Heart of Glass" was the real breakthrough to world fame. It was number one in both Britain and the United States. Hits that followed included "One Way or Another," "Call Me," "The Tide Is High," and "Rapture." She was largely responsible for Blondie being the most successful 1970s New Wave Band. The band split up in 1984 after Chris Stein became ill with pemphigus, a rare, life-threatening, genetic disease, but Blondie resumed touring and recording again in 1998. In 2006, Blondie was inducted into the Rock and Roll Hall of Fame.

Her first solo album, *Koo Koo*, was at first neither a commercial nor a critical success, though it was to gain popularity with her fans. Her second, more successful album, *Rock Bird* (1986), appeared four years later. The third solo album, *Def, Dumb, and Blonde* (1989), reminded many fans of all they loved about Deborah Harry and went platinum in Australia, doing well in Britain and the United States as well, and was followed by a world tour. A fourth album, *Debravation* (1993), contained a mixture of styles without the necessary cohesion for a successful album. She released her fifth solo album, *Necessary Evil*, in 2007. Harry entered the *Guinness Book of World Records* in 1999 as the oldest female singer to reach number one on the United Kingdom music charts with "Maria." She was fifty-three years old. Her single "Two Times Blue" peaked at number twenty-eight on the American hits chart when she was sixty-two.

Family of Origin

Deborah Ann Harry was born on July 1, 1945, in Miami, Florida. She said in early interviews that she did not wish to search for her family of origin, out of respect for her adoptive parents:

> Well, at one time in my life, it would have been a real emotional thing for me and I hesitated. I couldn't deal with it, but as I got a better perspective on who I was and felt more in touch with myself, I thought, *You know, there are some things in life you should not put off.* I thought I was doing the right thing, and I still feel I did the right thing for me (Che 4).

She changed her mind, however, and initiated a search in the early 1990s. A detective brought back information that her father was dead from heart disease at age seventy-four and that her first mother did not wish to meet her:

> [S]he just wouldn't go into it. The detective tried to ask her a few things but I think her exact words were, "Please do not bother me ever again. I do not want to be disturbed." He didn't even get anything out about who I was. . . .
>
> I'm sure it was hard. I think on my father's side, I have seven or eight half-brothers and sisters. My father was already married and my mother was not married. She got pregnant

and then found out he was married and had all these children. She was heartbroken and she went away, had me and put me up for adoption. I don't know much more than that (Che 5).

Adoption

Harry was adopted when she was three months old by Catherine (Cag) Peters Harry and Richard Harry. She grew up in a working class suburb of Patterson, New Jersey, with a younger sister, Martha, and a cousin, Bill, who lived with the family during his teens. Her parents ran a gift shop and provided a "strict" but "reasonably happy" childhood (Che 4).

Education and Significant Relationships

After graduating from high school, Harry would have preferred not to go to college, but acceded to her parents' wishes until she was old enough to go off on her own and then found an apartment in St. Mark's Place, a center of the 1960s counterculture.

Harry and Stein started their long romantic and creative partnership in 1974 and Harry nursed Stein through his illness. The couple wrote the song "End of the Run," which appeared on Harry's *Def, Dumb, and Blonde* album in 1989, about the end of their relationship. Stein later married actress Barbara Sicuranza and Harry is the godmother of their daughter, Akira.

Works Cited

Che, Cathay. *Deborah Harry*. New York: International, 2000.
"Harry, Deborah." *Current Biography Yearbook 1981*. Ed. Charles Moritz. New York: H. W. Wilson, 191–195.

HAUSER, KASPAR (circa 1812–1832)

Socially Isolated Child, Foundling

Major Achievements

Kaspar Hauser was discovered near a lonely gate by a citizen of Nuremberg, Germany, on May 26, 1828. Barely able to walk or stand, and speaking only a few strange sentences, Hauser soon became the most famous "wild child" of Europe. "Wild" or "feral" children are rare human beings who survive a childhood lived in almost total social isolation. Less than five years after his arrival in Nuremberg as a young teen, Hauser became the victim of murder. His mysterious and tragic life has inspired over three thousand books, fourteen thousand articles, songs, plays, films and other works of art and science (4). Hauser's brief life furthered knowledge in developmental learning, linguistics and child abuse. Those who worked closest with him were struck by his gentleness, compassion and moral purity.

Family of Origin

Hauser was carrying two letters the day he was found—one, probably a fake, from a woman claiming to be his mother. The letter said that he had been born on April 30, 1812, that his father, a soldier of the Sixth Regiment in Nuremberg, was dead, and that she was unable to care for the child, who had been baptized "Kaspar." This letter and the child were supposedly left at the home of a day laborer with ten children sixteen years prior. The laborer supposedly wrote the second letter, which was addressed to the captain of the calvary and which asked that the boy be allowed to join his father's regiment, in fulfillment of the mother's wishes, and that no attempt be made to discover where Kaspar had been living. The boy was taken to the police station where he wrote "Kaspar Hauser" when offered pen and paper.

One theory suggests that Kaspar Hauser was really Prince Gaspard, the legitimate heir to the throne of Baden and the firstborn son of Grand Duke Karl and Stephanie de Beauharnais, Napoleon's adopted daughter. It was believed that the prince was exchanged with a newborn, dying child of one of the gardeners, Johann Blochmann, who was mysteriously promoted in 1812. The duchess did not view her dying newborn child, who supposedly died in October 1812, the same month Kaspar was handed over to "the man with whom he had always been."

Hauser was thought to have been kept in one or more castles until he reached the age of three or four. He was then imprisoned in a tiny, hidden cell in a dungeon, probably the one at Schloss Pilsach, near Nuremberg. Stephanie and Karl had a second crown prince who died a year later, and Karl himself believed at the time of his own premature death that he and both infant sons had been poisoned. Hauser bore a physical resemblance to the Baden royal family and several of its members, including the princesses who would have been his sisters, thought that he was indeed the lost prince. It was rumored that Karl's stepmother, Luise von Hochberg, whose son Leopold inherited the Baden throne, arranged for the kidnapping and the murders (36). Masson's *Lost Prince* presents compelling evidence suggesting this theory. Recent DNA testing on Hauser's blood and blood from two maternal relatives of Stephanie de Beauharnais, however, do not show a relationship. Professor Martin Kitchen's outstanding book *Kaspar Hauser: Europe's Child* presents a detailed, scholarly study of Hauser and examines the many additional theories surrounding him.

Foster Families

The Nuremberg officials kept Kaspar locked in a tower while an investigation was made. Hauser was later released to the family of his teacher, Georg Daumer, on July 18, 1828. Hauser had a painful hypersensitivity to light, sound, metals, and odors. He ran a high fever or lost consciousness if he attempted to eat or drink anything other than bread and water, even in the smallest amounts. His knees were deformed from prolonged sitting and the soles of his feet were soft and looked like he had never walked or worn shoes. Hauser had many unusual abilities, such as an incredible memory. He was able to accurately remember the names and titles of the hundreds of visitors who came to see him during his first months in the tower. He could see clearly and even read in pitch darkness, and his other senses went far beyond the norm. Hauser quickly learned to express himself and began a brief autobiography in September 1828, only four months after his arrival in Nuremberg.

His autobiography described the tiny cell where he had been imprisoned for the past fourteen to sixteen years, and the shadowy figure of the "man with whom he had always been," who daily brought him bread and water. This unseen figure once struck Kaspar with a cane or piece of wood when he made too much noise playing with the two wooden horses, toy dog, and red ribbons that were his only diversions. A first attempt was made on the boy's life soon after it became known that he was writing his history. He was attacked by a veiled man who tried to slash his throat with a butcher's knife. The blow missed his throat and instead injured his forehead. He said that he recognized the voice of his attacker as the man who had imprisoned him.

Kaspar recovered under the careful nursing of the Daumer family. He learned the meaning of family relationships during his happy stay with them. They found him weeping one day, and when asked why, he answered, "I was thinking, why it is that I don't have a mother, a brother, and a sister; it would be so beautiful" (Masson 123). Kaspar had to leave the Daumers in January 1830, after his teacher became ill. He stayed with two other families until he became the legal ward of an English nobleman, Philip Henry, the Fourth Earl of Stanhope, in November 1831. Stanhope expressed a desire to adopt Hauser, and he gave the city money for his upkeep in return for official guardianship. In December 1831, Stanhope sent Hauser to Herr Meyer, an Ansbach teacher who treated Hauser cruelly. Nearly a year later, on December 14, 1832, Hauser was lured to a deserted garden by a man who said he had news of Kaspar's mother. There he was stabbed in the chest and he died of the wounds three days later. In spite of a large reward offered by the King of Bavaria, the murderer was never found. After Hauser's death, Stanhope launched an inexplicable campaign to discredit Hauser as a fraud and claim his death as a suicide. Many scholars, both modern and contemporary, believed that Stanhope was either directly or indirectly responsible for Hauser's death (Masson 218). Those who knew the most about Hauser, including the investigator Anselm von Feuerbach and his early teacher, Daumer, for example, soon also died suddenly and under mysterious circumstances. Both men were believed to have been poisoned.

Works Cited

Kitchen, Martin. *Kaspar Hauser: Europe's Child.* Houndmills, Basingstoke, UK: Palgrave, 2001
Masson, Jeffrey Moussaieff. *Lost Prince: The Unsolved Mystery of Kaspar Hauser.* New York: The Free Press, 1996.

HIGHWATER, JAMAKE (1942–2001)

Author
Adoptee, orphanage alumnus

Career, Major Awards, and Achievements

Native American author Jamake Highwater has earned many awards for his work, including the Newbery Medal (1978), Jane Addams Children's Book Award (1979), Boston Globe-Horn Book Award (1978), the American Library Association's Notable Books for Children Award (1981) and Best Books for Young Adults Award (1978, 1984, 1986), and the Best Books Award from the *School Library Journal* (1980, 1984). Highwater's PBS documentary *The Primal Mind* won the Best Film of the Year Award at the National Educational Film Festival, and the ACE Award from the National Cable Television Association. Highwater's books appeal to both children and adults. They include *Indian America: A Cultural and Travel Guide* (1975), *Song From the Earth* (1976), and his first novel, *Anpao: An American Indian Odyssey* (1977). Other works include *Many Smokes, Many Moons: A Chronology of American Indian History Through Indian Art* (1978), *Moonsong Lullaby* (1981), *Journey to the Sky* (1978*)*, and *The Sun, He Dies*

(1980). Both *The Sun, He Dies* and *Anpao* are considered by critics as Highwater's best works. Anpao, which means "dawn," and his difficult twin brother, Oapna, search for their parentage in a world where characters suddenly change, vanish, and reappear. Highwater's recent works include *The Language of Vision: Meditations on Myth and Metaphor* (1994), *Dance: Rituals of Experience* (1996), and *Rama: A Legend* (1997).

Family of Origin

The son of Amana (Bonneville) Highwater, a Blackfoot, and Jamie Highwater, a Cherokee, Jamake Highwater was born in Glacier County, Montana, around February 1942.* Amana was a mix of French Canadian and Blackfoot ancestry and her teachings were an important part of her son's early life: "Her vivid teachings were my access to the Indian world, for I grew up constantly on the move and never had the advantages of the extended family life which mark the training of most primal peoples" (Highwater xvi–xvii).

The family was always on the move because of his father's work. The elder Highwater was a rodeo clown and a movie stuntman in Westerns. Highwater said that sometimes he would accompany his father to work and sit "under walnut trees in the San Fernando Valley while my dad was out being killed by John Wayne" (Shirley 361). Jaime Highwater died in an automobile accident when Jamake was about seven years old, and the boy was placed in an orphanage.

Adoption

His father's closest friend, Alexander Marks, and his wife Marcia, who were not Native American, adopted the boy and Jamake began calling himself "J Marks." He would later use both Jamake Highwater and J Marks as pen names. His teen years were spent in the San Fernando Valley, California:

> I was adopted as a child and grew up as "J. Marks" in Southern California, at a time when adoption was still a covert matter. I do not know exactly where or when I was born. All records of my birth were permanently sealed. In my home we didn't talk about the past. My natural curiosity about my heritage was ignored or rebuffed. When I did manage to prod a bit of information from someone, what I was told usually contradicted something else I had been told earlier. Nothing about my life seemed to match. And being the adopted son of a motion-picture family that used four of five different professional names also didn't help my sense of identity. By the time I reached adolescence I urgently wanted to use my original name, Jamake Highwater. My friends at school in the San Fernando Valley were the offspring of parents so often divorced and remarried that they found my identity crisis just a bit quaint (Wilson).

Education

Highwater began to write "compulsively" (Shirley 361) at around the age of eight. During the 1960s, he helped found and administer the San Francisco Contemporary Theatre, and he traveled extensively throughout the United States and Canada. In

---

*Several authorities have challenged Highwater's claims of native ancestry, and his associated dates, names, ages, and parentage, are controversial. Highwater has himself given several versions of his birth and adoption stories to interviewers, but that does not necessarily prove intentional fraudulence on his part, as some critics have contended. It very common for adopted people to need to revise their personal histories as they encounter or are given varied and sometimes falsified information about their origins. Highwater's "father/parents died in a car crash" story represents a particularly classic fabrication that many adoptees have been told.

1986, he received an honorary Doctor of Fine Arts from the Minneapolis College of Art and Design.

Highwater's adoption has had an important impact on his work: "It is little wonder that so much of my writing focuses upon the drama of familial and cultural histories. The greatest mystery of my life is my own identity. So I have always been fascinated by people who recall the kind of intimate biographical information that is utterly alien to my experience" (Wilson). An important theme in Highwater's writing is the struggle of living in dual cultures with conflicting values.

On March 29, 1979, Highwater went through a naming ceremony reserved for *minipoka,* or favored children of the Blackfeet nation. At Lethbridge University in Alberta, Canada, Ed Calf Robe conferred on Highwater the name Pittai Sahkomaapii, meaning "Eagle Son." Highwater wrote that the ceremony was an important part of reclaiming his identity and a way to honor his mother: "This name-ceremony was the vindication of my mother's constant efforts to keep my heritage alive within me. Sadly, she had passed away and could not see the embrace of my people for which she had longed for [sic] all her life" (Highwater xviii).

Jamake Highwater died from a heart attack at his home in Los Angeles on June 3, 2001.

Works Cited

Forester, C. S., and Joan Lowery Nixon. *Cyclopedia of Young Adult Authors, Volume 2.* Pasadena, CA: Salem Press, 2005.

Highwater, Jamake. *The Primal Mind: Vision and Reality in Indian America.* New York: Harper, 1981.

"Jamake Highwater." *Wilson Biographies Plus* (online). August 23, 2001. http://hwwilsonweb .com.skyline.cudenver.edu/

Shirley, Carl L. "Jamake Highwater." *Dictionary of Literary Biography 1985 Yearbook.* Detroit, MI: Gale, 1985. 359–366.

HILL, FAITH (1967–)

Singer
Adoptee

Career, Major Awards, and Achievements

Faith Hill is an American country and crossover singer who has sold over thirty million records and has had eleven number one singles in country music as of 2007. She has received several Grammies including Best Country Album (*Breathe,* 2000), Best Country Collaboration with Vocals ("Let's Make Love" with Tim McGraw, 2000), and Best Country Vocal Performance—Female (for *Breathe* in 2000 and for *Cry* in 2002).

Hill has also received honors from the American Music Awards, the People's Choice Awards, the Country Music Association, and the Academy of Country Music. *Ladies Home Journal* called her one of the thirty most powerful women in the United States in 2001.

Her first album, *Take Me as I Am* (1993), sold three million copies. It was followed in 1995 by *It Matters to Me,* which also sold three million copies. Hill then took a three year break to begin a family with her husband, country music star Tim McGraw. Her 1998 album, *Faith,* contained her first pop chart hit, "This Kiss," which also made number one on the country list. *Faith* sold six million copies, and was followed by

[AP Photo/Art Foxall]

Breathe, an album of songs about love. It was less country in style than previous albums but started at number one on the *Billboard* country chart. It also moved Hill away from her "girl next door" image. Her 1999 tour showed that she hadn't left the girl next door that far behind. The tour gave support to a national children's book drive and netted 35, 000 books to be given to hospitals, day care centers, schools, and libraries. Literacy is an important cause for Hill, and in 1996, she founded the Faith Hill Family Literacy Foundation in honor of her adoptive father, who left school in the fourth grade to help support his fifteen member family.

In 2000, Hill began to branch out, appearing in the TV special *Behind the Music* and the Lifetime Channel's *Intimate Portraits*. She performed at the Grammy and Academy Awards shows, endorsed Cover Girl makeup, sang the national anthem at the Super Bowl, began the tour called Soul2Soul with Tim McGraw, was named one of the ten best dressed women of the year, and won the Country Music Association's Female Vocalist of the Year award. The award caused some controversy, since to some it appeared that Hill was moving away from country toward pop.

After the 2001 *There You'll Be: The Best of Faith Hill* came *Cry*, which won a Grammy and sold over three million copies. The singles from the album, which was nearly completely pop, got less country radio air time than her earlier singles. In 2004 Hill made her film acting debut in the remake of *The Stepford Wives*.

In 2005, *Fireflies* returned Hill to country themes and styles. It was Hill's third consecutive album to debut at number one on both country and all genre album charts, and the biographical "Mississippi Girl," written by John Rich and Adam Shoenfield, was her highest starting single to date. The album restored her place and air time on country radio.

After Hurricane Katrina in 2005, Hill and McGraw, who had been raised in Louisiana, were hosts for charity concerts for the benefit of hurricane victims and started a foundation called Neighbor's Keeper, which helps community charities provide for basic needs during and after natural disasters.

The Hill-McGraw Soul2Soul II concert of 2006 was the highest grossing country tour to date. Hill's 2007 album was *The Hits*, a greatest hits album.

Family of Origin

Faith Hill was born September 21, 1967, in Ridgeland, Mississippi, to a young unmarried mother. Her adoptive parents told her that her mother had become pregnant by a married man and that she had no choice but to put the baby up for adoption. Hill fantasized about her first parents and described her origins as "that little mystery inside of me" (Dickerson 11). After she left home, she began to actively search for her birth mother, with the help of her adoptive brother, Wesley. Hill's adoptive parents had provided her first mother's social security number and other details, but even with this information, the search took three years to complete. Hill contacted her first mother through a court appointed intermediary in 1990, "I was a potent mixture of nerves and excitement and anxiety, so many things" (Dickerson 41). Hill drove to Jackson, Mississippi, where she met her first mother, a tall blonde like Faith herself, in a city park:

> I found out that she is a painter, an artist, and she has an incredible sense of style. . . . She's a sweet, sweet woman. I have a lot of respect for her, and I had no feelings of anger or any of that. . . . I know she must have had a lot of love for me to want to give me what she felt was a better choice. Thank God she let me live (Dickerson 42).

Hill has not divulged names or specifics about her family of origin for privacy reasons. She has a younger full biological brother, Zach, who met her adoptive brothers, Wesley and Steve, during Hill's fortieth birthday celebration in Greece in 2007.

Adoption

A local doctor arranged a private adoption for the three-day-old baby with Ted and Edna Perry, a Baptist couple with two biological sons, Wesley and Steve. Wesley, then eight, wanted to name his new sister Audrey, after a favorite television character, Audra, on *The Big Valley*. She was christened Audrey Faith Perry and raised in a very Christian home.

Ted Perry worked at the Presto Manufacturing Company, a cookware factory in Jackson, Mississippi. Edna worked at a bank. The family moved from Jackson to a small town called Star, Mississippi, when Faith was eleven years old.

Education and Significant Relationships

Hill's first performance was a 4-H luncheon when she was seven, and by the time she was in her teens, she was singing at many local churches. She was a popular cheerleader, school council member, and homecoming queen at the McLaurin Attendance Center, Star's High School. When she was seventeen, she formed her own band to play at area rodeos.

At nineteen, she dropped her studies at Hinds Community College and moved to Nashville, hoping to become a country singer. Instead she found a job as a secretary at a music publishing firm. After a coworker heard her singing to herself, she became a demo singer for the company and began singing backup vocals for Gary Burr, a songwriter who often tried out his new songs at the Bluebird Café in Nashville. A Warner Brothers executive heard her at the Bluebird and offered her a recording contract.

In 1988, she married Dan Hill, a music executive and songwriter. They divorced in 1996.

Faith Hill met country music star Time McGraw in 1996 on their Spontaneous Combustion tour and married him later that year. McGraw learned at age eleven that the man he thought was his father was actually his stepfather. His biological father was baseball legend Tug McGraw. Biographers suggest that shared issues surrounding their births were an important influence in their relationship:

> Tim's attraction to Faith had many of the same psychosocial ingredients. Tim had abandonment issues with his father and trust issues with his mother for not telling him the truth. . . . When Faith poured her heart out about her situation, Tim knew exactly how it felt. He didn't tell her to get over it the way her first husband had. . . . People could gossip all they wanted, Faith and Tim had found their soul mates (Dickerson 89).

The couple has three daughters: Gracie Katherine, born in 1997; Maggie Elizabeth, born in 1998; and Audrey Caroline, born in 2001.

Works Cited

Dickerson, James L. *Faith Hill: Piece of My Heart*. New York: St. Martin's Guide, 2001.

Ginsberg, Leah. "Faith Renewed: Wife, Mother, Superstar." *Good Housekeeping* 242.1 (January 2006): 134+.

Griffiths, John. "I Know How Lucky I Am." *McCall's* 128.2 (November 2000): 20–33.

Helligar, Jeremy, and Mary Green. "Faith Accompli." *People Weekly* 52 (July 12, 1999): 95+.

JOBS, STEVE (1955–)

Business Executive, Computer Pioneer
Adoptee

Career, Major Awards, and Achievements

Steve Jobs, the cofounder (with Steve Wozniak) and CEO of Apple Inc., is one of the few businessmen whose name is a household word. In the late 1970s and early 1980s, he was one of the visionaries who first saw the possibilities of the personal computer and its commercial potential. He is also the founder of Pixar Animation Studios, which was purchased by Walt Disney Company in 2006 in an all-stock deal, making Jobs the largest single stockholder in Disney.

In 1987 he received the National Medal of Technology from President Ronald Reagan; also in 1987 he was the recipient of a Jefferson Award for Public Service and of the Samuel S. Beard Award for "Greatest Public Service by an Individual 35 Years or Younger." In recognition of his roles at Apple Inc. and Pixar, *Fortune* magazine named him the most powerful person in business in 2007. The same year, he was inducted into the California Hall of Fame.

While in high school, Jobs began attending after-school lectures at the Hewlett-Packard Company, located in Palo Alto. As a Hewlett-Packard summer employee, he worked with Steve Wozniak, who was only a few years older.

In 1974 he attended meetings of the local computer club where Wozniak was considered the genius in residence. Jobs worked at that time for Atari, the video game company, and with Wozniak briefly built "blue boxes" that allowed purchasers to make illegal long-distance phone calls. Then he took off to backpack in India with Daniel Kottke, who would become Apple's first employee.

Jobs was only twenty when he persuaded Wozniak to join him in a company that would market a computer Wozniak had designed for himself. Apple Computer Co. was founded on April 1, 1976. The partners planned to sell printed circuit boards, but instead they developed the Apple I, a completely assembled computer, which they sold to electronics enthusiasts. They made enough money to develop a second version, and the following year Apple II, designed for inexperienced and general users, made Apple a

[AP Photo/Remy de la Mauviniere]

big-time player in the new personal computer industry. In December 1980, Apple went public. Shares sold out in minutes and Jobs was a multimillionaire.

During the next years, Apple developed several computers, including the technologically advanced LISA, which was too technical for the popular market. In spite of problems in development, in 1983 Jobs was able to convince John Sculley of Pepsi-Cola to move to Apple as CEO. In 1984 Apple introduced the Macintosh, a LISA descendent, innovative because of its user-friendly interface and, more influentially, its use of a "mouse" that allowed buyers to use the computer without knowing a complicated command system.

The following year, after an internal power struggle, Sculley removed Jobs from control of the Mac division. Jobs said, "something slowly began to dawn on me. I loved what I did. . . . I had been rejected, but I was still in love. And so I decided to start over" (Jobs, Stanford Commencement Address, 2005).

Jobs sold all but one share of the business he had founded and promptly created his new computer company, NeXT. NeXT became relatively popular in academic and scientific circles but, because of its high price, never achieved mainstream popularity. Jobs marketed it as a technologically superior intrapersonal computer, designed to allow communication and collaboration. The NeXT e-mail system, for example, included embedded audio and graphics. In 1993 NeXT moved entirely to software development, releasing NeXTStep/Intel.

NeXT technology made contributions to the development of the World Wide Web, which had been developed on a NeXT workstation by Tim Berners-Lee at the European Organization for Nuclear Research (CERN). NeXT was also influential in the development of *Doom,* the computer game voted in 2004 by industry insiders to be the greatest game of all time, and in the return of the Apple computer.

In 1996, Apple, in financial trouble, bought NeXT and returned Steve Jobs to Apple. Soon afterwards the directors fired Apple's chief executive and appointed Jobs the interim CEO. He abandoned several company projects and brought NeXT technology to Apple, increased sales, and introduced iMac and additional new products, giving particular attention to his trademark aesthetic detail. In 2000, Jobs became permanent CEO. In the 2000s, Apple moved into the music business with the iPod portable player and iTunes software, joined the cell phone industry with iPhone, developed a growing recycling program for computer products, and introduced Apple TV. In 2007 Apple Computer Inc. was renamed Apple Inc. Jobs has remained an active leader for his company in spite of serious health problems. He has been fighting a rare form of pancreatic cancer since 2004 and received a liver transplant in January 2009.

Family of Origin

Steven Paul Jobs was born February 24, 1955. His parents, Joanne Carole Schieble and Abdulfattah Jandali, were graduate students at the University of Wisconsin. Jandali was from Syria. They went to San Francisco for the birth of their child, whom they wished to be raised by college-educated adoptive parents.

In a 1984 interview, Jobs said:

> I think it's a natural curiosity for adopted people to want to understand where certain traits come from, but I'm mostly an environmentalist. I think the way you are raised, your values, and most of your worldview come from the experiences you had growing up. But some things aren't accounted for that way. I think it's quite natural to have a curiosity about it. And I did (Young 16).

Jobs' birthparents later married each other, and Jandali became a political science professor. Mona Simpson, the novelist (*Anywhere but Here* and *A Regular Guy*), is their daughter and Steve Jobs' full biological sister. Jobs located Mona when he was twenty-seven and has said that he considers her one of his best friends.

Adoption

Steven was to have been placed as an infant with a lawyer and his wife. At the last minute, however, the potential parents decided they'd prefer to adopt a girl. Paul and Clara Jobs, who were next on the waiting list, became the boy's new parents. Discovering that Clara had not graduated from college and that Paul had not completed high school, Joanne Schieble refused to sign the final adoption papers until the prospective parents promised that Steve would be able to go to college (Jobs, Stanford Commencement Address, 2005).

Paul was a machinist and Clara an accountant. Both have been described as straightforward and without pretense. Steve Jobs' first home was in an area of small rented homes filled by young families.

Education and Significant Relationships

When Steve said he wouldn't go back to his old junior high school because he wasn't learning anything there, Paul and Clara moved to Los Altos so that he could attend Homestead High School in nearby Cupertino. Intense and single-minded even as a young teenager, Jobs had the advantage of attending school where a new emphasis was being put on science in the curriculum.

In 1970, Jobs moved to Portland, Oregon, to attend Reed College. Though he dropped out after his first semester, he continued to audit classes at Reed and became part of the 1960s counterculture.

Jobs met his wife Laurene in 1989, when she was a graduate student at Stanford and he gave a talk to business students there. They were married in 1991, and have two children, Reed and Laurene. Jobs also has a daughter, Lisa, from an earlier relationship.

Works Cited

Butcher, Lee. *Accidental Millionaire: The Rise and Fall of Steve Jobs at Apple Computer.* New York: Paragon House, 1988.

Jobs, Steve. "You've Got to Find What You Love." Stanford Commencement Address, June 12, 2005. *Stanford News Service.* February 19, 2008. http://news-service.stanford.edu/news/2005/june15/jobs-061505.html

Young, Jeffrey S. *Steve Jobs: The Journey is the Reward.* Glenview, IL: Scott, Foresman and Co., 1988.

K

KARLOFF, BORIS (1887–1969)

Actor
Orphan

Honors, Achievements, and Awards

A performer in radio, film, and on the stage in both the United States and Britain, Boris Karloff acted in 163 films. He is known to contemporaries for his roles as Frankenstein's monster in horror films, but he also exhibited a softer side through his passion for children's stories. Thousands of children grew to know him as the narrator of *How the Grinch Stole Christmas*. However people recall him, "Every filmgoer's memories include Karloff limping, leering, and lurching through dozens of films; some good, some bad, and some mediocre" (Underwood 163).

As for awards, Karloff received relatively few for a man of his fame and longevity in the acting business. He received two Ann Radcliffe Awards for his contributions to the "Gothic" genre and a "Count Dracula" award was presented to him posthumously.

Family of Origins

Born in south London as William Henry Pratt on November 23, 1887, to Edward and Eliza Sara (Millard) Pratt, Karloff was the youngest of eight sons and one daughter. Eliza was Edward's third wife (the previous two had died), and roughly the age of his eldest daughter Emma at the time they married.

Eliza's family had lived in Bombay for a time and there has been some conjecture that Eliza's mother (or even Eliza herself) may have been Indian. (There is also a rumor that Boris was the illegitimate offspring of a shipboard romance between Eliza and an Egyptian man.) A similar theory about Indian ancestry has been attributed to Karloff's father. This type of speculation is often invoked when discussing the fact that Boris Karloff had such dark eyes and skin coloring (Buehrer 2).

He never knew his father, who worked for the Indian Salt Revenue Service and died while Karloff was a baby. His mother followed Edward in death while Karloff was still young and he was raised by his siblings.

[AP Photo]

His older brother George was the first person to expose him to theater, taking him to Christmas plays and shows put on by their cricket club. His first role in a play was the Demon King in *Cinderella*. "'I was about nine years old then,' Karloff [said in] 1967, a mildly enthusiastic smile lighting up his avuncular features. 'I had no idea that I had struck oil!' Right then and there he knew acting was the only thing he really wanted to do for the rest of his life"(Underwood 18).

Young Pratt left home in 1909 after flipping a coin to determine his destination: heads, Canada—or tails, Australia. Heads it was, so he sailed for Montreal on a second-class ticket with £150 in his pocket, a failure in his brothers' eyes and something of a family black sheep for eschewing expectations that he would enter the consular corps or government service like most of the rest of his siblings. Instead, he found odd jobs as a laborer, real estate agent, and coal shoveler, while trying out for parts in small traveling theater companies.

It was in Canada that he first used the name Boris Karloff, on an application for a part with the Ray Brandon Players of Kamloops, British Columbia. He had recalled that Karloff was a name buried somewhere deep in his mother's family heritage. It apparently served him well because he got the job. When World War I broke out in 1914, he tried to enlist in the British Army, but a heart murmur disqualified him.

Working with nomadic theater troupes eventually led him to California and Los Angeles. After more than a decade of stage and small film roles, Karloff's Frankenstein's monster was "a role which would attract the attention of several influential movie people, including Howard Hawks who then cast him in the movie made from the play" (Buehrer 221).

Education and Significant Relationships

Educated at King's College, University of London, Karloff admitted that he attended more plays than classes after enrolling in 1907 (Underwood 20). With brothers in such prestigious positions as legal advisor to the Governor of Bombay, governor of an Indian province, and Consul General of Tsinan, China, young William was expected to follow a similar path. "He tried telling his family that he would prefer a career on stage to that of the Foreign Service, but whichever brother was home at the time told him bluntly that he did not have the good looks nor the talents of his older brother George. They felt the goal was ridiculous, and they would not countenance it" (Buehrer 3).

Like his father, Karloff married three times. His first wife was Helene Vivian Soule, a dancer known as "Polly," whom he married in 1923 and divorced in 1929. Next he married Dorothy Stine, a University of Southern California graduate and public school librarian. They had a daughter, Sara Jane, who was born on Karloff's fifty-first birthday during the filming of *Son of Frankenstein*. The Karloffs created a lavish Los Angeles estate with a distinctly British flavor, exhibiting their love of cricket and gardening. They divorced in 1945.

In 1946, Karloff married Evelyn Helmore, an Englishwoman from Putney. She was an assistant story editor to producer Darryl F. Zanuck. They relocated from Los Angeles to New York City in 1951 and moved back to their native England in 1959. They were a very private, almost reclusive couple.

Karloff remained close to a number of his colleagues, including actors Lon Cheney and Bela Lugosi, and socialized with such notables as Noel Coward, Robert Kane, Michael Balcon, Karloff's brother Sir John Pratt, Lady Montague, and other members of high society. His declining health forced him to use a portable oxygen tank and a wheelchair.

He died February 2, 1969, while still under contract for a film. He was cremated and his ashes were quietly interred in the lawn of the Garden of Remembrance with only four people in attendance at the funeral. "He died, one of only two or three actors to have declined to send a biographical note to *Who's Who in the Theatre*, and as incurably stage-struck as he had been when he played the Demon King in a church pantomime seventy years before" (Underwood 167).

Works Cited

Buehrer, Beverley Bare. *Boris Karloff: A Bio-Bibliography*, Westport, CT: Greenwood Press, 1993.

Nollen, Scott Allen. *Boris Karloff: A Critical Account of His Screen, Stage, Radio, Television, and Recording Work*. Jefferson, NC: McFarland and Company, Inc., 1991.

Underwood, Peter. *Karloff*. New York: Drake Publishers, Inc., 1972.

KEAN, EDMUND (1787–1833)

Actor
Fostered

Career, Major Awards, and Achievements

Edmund Kean was a gifted and popular tragic actor on the nineteenth-century stage. He received international acclaim for his Shakespearean roles, which included Shylock, Richard III, Hamlet, Othello, Lear, Coriolanus, and Iago. Kean made his reputation at the Drury Lane Theater, but later appeared in New York, Paris, and Canada. He gave several performances at Windsor for George III. Among Kean's admirers were some of the era's greatest literary figures, notably Lord Byron, Keats, and Coleridge. Kean's considerable merits as an actor were thought to have been tempered by his violent recklessness and weakness for drink.

Family of Origin

Edmund Kean was born on March 17, 1789, in London to an unmarried, itinerant actress, Anne Carey, also known as "Nance or Nancy." His father was a theater builder, also named Edmund Kean, who committed suicide when he was twenty-two years old. The baby stayed with his mother for the first four or five months and then was given to another actress, Miss Tidswell, who unofficially adopted him:

> He was even then much neglected, and was afterwards more so; and when Miss Carey declined being troubled any longer with the maternal offices, Miss Tidswell took him, as we have stated, generously offering him, however, in the first instance to "Aunt Price" [Edmund's father's sister]. "Why not take care of him?" said she, "it will be much better." But Aunt Price, a prudent mantua-maker, declined this proposal, and replied that "she did not wish to have him." In the end, after having been pushed about and rejected like "the mark" at school, the father put out the poor child to nurse with a woman in the neighbourhood of London, who very speedily evinced her qualifications for that tender office, by allowing her charge to become crooked (Proctor 9–10).

Kean wore leg braces for part of his childhood to correct the physical problems caused by early neglect and malnutrition. Sometimes Kean's birthmother, Ann Carey, would go door to door selling flowers, powders, and balms. She would retrieve her son from Miss Tidswell and take him with her "because of his appearance, which was in a high degree interesting, and promoted the sale of her wares" (Proctor 12). Kean often ran away, "'because,' as he said, 'she took all my money.' On such occasions, when he thought fit to quit his mother, on account of her affection for his salary, he deserted to Miss Tidswell,

[Hulton Archive/Getty Images]

whom he left, in turn, because she beat him: he then went over to Aunt Price, and again quitted her, when, as it is said, 'everything was not to his taste'" (Proctor 38).

Foster Home

Miss Charlotte Tidswell was the mistress of Edmund's father's older brother, Moses Kean. She raised Edmund and sent him to a day school in London, where he consistently played truant. An actress herself, she also began to train him in theater arts. Her efforts to create a home for Edmund were continually foiled by his attempts to run away. Miss Tidswell at last had a brass collar welded around his neck; it carried an inscription asking that the boy be returned to her at Theatre Royal, Drury Lane. Many persons thought that Miss Tidswell was Edmund's biological mother, including Edmund himself:

> "Why did she take so much trouble about me," he would say, "if I was not related to her? She did not like me; or, if she did, she didn't appear to do so. She kept me, indeed, but she used to thump me often enough, and tie me to the bed-post; and, at last she put a collar round my neck, as though I had been a dog." He was himself very doubtful of "Miss Carey's" claim to the honour of being his mother. Her utter indifference towards him in his childhood, added to her habit of fleecing him of every penny that he earned, in some degree, it must be owned, justified this unfilial skepticism (Procter 42).

Marriage and Children

Kean married a woman ten years his senior named Mary Chambers. They lived the life of wandering actors, and their first son, Howard, died at a young age of tuberculosis. Their second son, Charles, survived the family's early poverty and grew into a notable actor himself.

An acute alcoholic, Kean collapsed on March 25, 1833, at Covent Garden, during a performance of *Othello*. Kean was playing the title role with son Charles in the role of Iago. He died on May 15, 1833, at the age of 46. Charles Kean and his wife, a distinguished actress named Ellen (Tree) Kean, adopted a daughter who became the acclaimed nineteenth-century American actress, Agnes Robertson.

Works Cited

Phippen, Francis. *Authentic Memoirs of Edmund Kean of the Theatre Royal, Drury Lane.* London: J. Roach, 1814.

Procter, Barry Cornwall. *The Life of Edmund Kean.* NY: Benjamin Blom, 1969.

Skinner, Otis. *Mad Folk of the Theatre.* Freeport, NY: Books for Libraries Press, 1970.

KEATS, JOHN (1795–1821)

Poet
Orphan

Career, Major Awards, and Achievements

John Keats is considered a leading poet of the Romantic Movement in England. His literary reputation began with the publication in 1817 of his first volume of poetry. This edition contained his famous work "On First Looking into Chapman's Homer," written when Keats was only nineteen years old and which today is considered one of the finest sonnets ever written. Keats's poetry is prized for its rich imagery, haunting beauty, and intensity of feeling. His most beloved works include the odes "To a Nightingale," "On a Grecian Urn," "To Psyche," "To Autumn," and the longer works "Endymion," "Fall of Hyperion," "The Eve of St. Agnes," "La Belle Dame sans Merci," and "Lamia."

Family of Origin

John Keats was born on October 31, 1795, in Moorfields, outside London. He was the oldest of four children born to Thomas and Frances "Fanny" (Jennings) Keats. Thomas was the head stableman at the Swan and Hoop, a large livery stable and ale house owned

[Courtesy of the Library of Congress]

by Fanny's father. John Keats was described as a "violent and ungovernable child" (Rosetti 13), and his parents eventually placed him and his brothers in a respectable school at Enfield. Keats lost both his parents while a student there. His father, after a visit to his boys at the school, stopped to dine at Southgate, returned very late and, as described by Richard Abbey, Keats's future guardian, was "riding very fast, and most probably very much in Liquor" (Hewlett 17) when an accident occurred. He died the next evening, on April 16, 1804. Keats' mother, Fanny, left with four small children and her invalid father's prosperous business, made a hasty and unhappy second marriage to a fortune-hunter, Mr. Rawlings, less than three months after the accident. The couple sent the four children to live with their maternal grandmother, Mrs. Alice Jennings. Rawlings became the sole proprietor of the Swan and Hoop after the death of Fanny's father in 1805.

Fanny soon left her second husband, and accounts vary widely as to what next became of her. By some accounts, she went to live with her mother and children but others say she took to drink and ran away with another man (Hewlett 18). There is some support for the latter: in April 1805, Rawlings and Fanny filed a lawsuit against her mother over an ambiguity in her father's will. This hostility may have made it unlikely that Fanny would return to her mother until she became reconciled with her in 1809, at that time being ill and "in great distress" (Gittings 28). Fanny, whom Abbey and others described as an impulsive woman of ardent physical passions and an irregularity of conduct (Hewlett 16), was an affectionate mother and John Keats was devoted to her. Fanny became confined to her bed with rheumatism and tuberculosis. Keats helped to nurse his mother and was "passionately inconsolable" (Rosetti 16) when she died in February 1810.

Guardians

Keats's grandmother, who was seventy-four when Fanny died, placed John, aged fourteen, and her other grandchildren into the care of two guardians, John Sandell, a merchant, and Richard Abbey, a tea merchant. Sandell took little part in the trusteeship and after the death of their grandmother in 1814, Abbey became the sole guardian of the Keats children.

Education and Significant Relationships

At Abbey's instigation, Keats left his school at Enfield, where he had made a fortunate and lifelong friendship with Cowden Clarke, who would one day introduce him to England's leading literati. Abbey apprenticed John to a surgeon and intended that he be trained as an apothecary. Keats's brothers were taken to work in Abbey's London counting house, and his little sister, Fanny, went to live with Abbey, his wife, and their adopted daughter. John and Fanny regarded Abbey as a tyrant. Abbey withheld funds from them and even attempted to keep their legacy when they came of legal age, to cover his "business reverses" (Rollings 63). Keats was very unhappy with what he considered his gruesome medical training (Hewlett 38), and he decided to leave medicine in 1817 and become a poet. When he announced this to his guardian, Abbey "called him a Silly Boy, & prophesied a speedy Termination to his inconsiderate Enterprise" (Hewlett 53).

Keats then lived with siblings and friends, and sometimes in solitary retirement, and dedicated himself to his poetry. His genius and poetic works developed quickly. Through Cowden Clarke, he became acquainted with and was able to impress the leading poets of his age, among them Shelley, Leigh Hunt, and Wordsworth. While staying with his friend Charles Armitage Brown, he met and began a turbulent love affair with Fanny Brawne, and they became engaged. Under the strain of overwork, love, and money trouble, Keat's health began to break down, and on February 3, 1820, while being helped into bed with a fever, he coughed up a single drop of blood. Keats told Brown: "I know the colour of that blood. It's arterial blood. I cannot be deceived in that colour.

That drop of blood is my death-warrant. I must die" (Hewlett 287). Keats went to Italy at the invitation of his friend Joseph Severn, who nursed him in through the final stages of tuberculosis. He died in Rome on February 23, 1821, at the age of twenty-five.

Works Cited

Gittings, Robert. *The Keats Inheritance*. New York: Barnes & Noble, 1965.

Hebron, Stephen. *John Keats*. NY: Oxford University Press, 2002.

Hewlett, Dorothy. *A Life of John Keats*. New York: Barnes & Noble, 1970.

Rollings, Hyder Edward. *The Letters of John Keats 1814–1821*. Cambridge, MA: Harvard University Press, 1958.

Rosetti, William Michael. *Life of John Keats*. New York: AMS Press, 1971.

LENNON, JOHN (1940–1980)

Singer, Songwriter
Fostered with relatives

Career, Major Awards, and Achievements

John Lennon was the lead singer, guitarist, and songwriter for the Beatles, the immensely popular and influential British quartet that became a prominent cultural force in the early 1960s. The Beatles (Lennon, Paul McCartney, George Harrison, and Ringo Starr) won many Gold Record awards for their music, as well as the 1964 British Song Writers Guild award. In 1965, the Beatles received a Grammy and were named members of the Most Excellent Order of the British Empire (M.B.E.) by Queen Elizabeth. The Beatles starred in three films: *A Hard Day's Night* (1964), *Help!* (1965), and *Yellow Submarine* (1968 animated feature). He also published two volumes of his poetry and sketches.

Family of Origin

John Winston Lennon was born on October 9, 1940, in Liverpool, England, to Alfred "Freddie" and Julia (Stanley) Lennon. Lennon said that his mother "just couldn't deal with life" (Beatles 7). John's parents' marriage ended soon after his mother became pregnant during the lengthy time her husband was working away at sea. The baby, whom Julia named Victoria, was born June 19, 1945, and was taken to a nearby Salvation Army orphanage named Strawberry Fields. From there she was adopted, and all traces of her were lost (Goldman 31–32). Lennon's father left the family home in Penny Lane, and Julia moved in with John Dykins, with whom she had two more children, Lennon's half-sisters. Lennon's mother sent him to be raised by her older sister, Mary Smith, called "Aunt Mimi." Julia became like an aunt or older sister to her son (Beatles 10), and Lennon grew very resentful toward Dykins. He became increasingly hostile until he was finally expelled from his kindergarten at age five for attacking other children (Goldman 33).

When Lennon was seventeen, his mother was killed by a drunken off-duty police officer, who ran over her with his car while she was waiting at a bus stop. Said Lennon: "I lost her twice. Once when I was moved in with my auntie. And once again at seven-

[Courtesy of the Library of Congress]

teen when she actually, physically died. That was very traumatic for me. That was really a hard time for me. It made me very, very bitter. The underlying chip on my shoulder that I had got really big then. Being a teenager and a rock'n'roller and an art student and my mother being killed just when I was reestablishing a relationship with her" (Beatles 13).

Lennon's father had lost his own father at sea and had grown up in a Liverpool orphanage, the Blue Coat Hospital. John was told that Freddie simply abandoned the family, but biographers dispute this (Goldman 32–33). Lennon's Aunt Mimi told him that his parents had "fallen out of love. . . . I soon forgot my father. It was like he was dead. But I did see my mother now and again and my feeling never died off for her. I often thought about her, though I'd never realized for a long time that she was living not more than five or ten miles away" (Beatles 7). After an unsuccessful attempt to gain custody of John in 1949, Freddie did not try to contact his son until 1964, at which time Lennon refused to reestablish the relationship. Freddie died of stomach cancer in 1975.

Kinship Care

Aunt Mimi, a nurse, and her husband, George Smith, brought Lennon up in a middle-class neighborhood in Liverpool. He was a difficult and disturbed child, and Mimi, a no-nonsense, matriarchal woman (Goldman 40), raised her nephew with strict discipline and routine. Lennon had mixed feelings about growing up without his parents: "The worst pain is that of not being wanted, of realizing your parents do not need you in the way you need them. When I was a child I experienced moments of not wanting to see the ugliness, not wanting to see not being wanted. This lack of love went into my eyes and into my mind" (Beatles 7). He also saw it as an advantage: "Sometimes I was relieved to have no parents. . . . I never had that fear of, and adulation for, parents" (Beatles 7). Lennon believed it was even a factor in his rise to stardom: "I was never really wanted. The only reason I am a star is because of my repression. Nothing would have driven me though all that if I was 'normal'" (Beatles 7).

Education and Significant Relationships

Having displayed an early talent in art, Lennon was sent to the Liverpool College of Art, where he met his first wife, Cynthia. He had always been musical but was unable to afford lessons (Beatles 8). Lennon met Paul McCartney in 1958, and George Harrison the following year and the young men formed a band. Peter Best was their drummer when they began performing in Hamburg, Germany. He was replaced by Ringo Starr in 1962. During an engagement at a cellar club known as "the Cavern" in Liverpool, the group came to the attention of promoter Brian Epstein. Epstein became their manager in early 1962 and groomed them with the neat, collarless suits and mop haircuts that would become their signature during the early years of their popularity. "Beatlemania" was well underway by the time the group performed at the London Palladium in October 1963, and their single hits and LP's sold millions of copies. The Beatles made several American tours, beginning in late 1963, with appearances on the Ed Sullivan Show and at Carnegie Hall. Their recording "I Want to Hold Your Hand," a Lennon and McCartney composition, sold more than four million copies and became America's top hit, even before their arrival in the United States. To Lennon, the former lonely child who always considered himself different (8), performing became a way to gain love: "I was always a rebel because of whatever sociological thing gave me a chip on the shoulder. But on the other hand, I want to be loved and accepted. That's why I'm on stage, like a performing flea. Because I would like to belong" (Beatles 9).

Lennon and his first wife, Cynthia (Powell) Lennon had a son, John Julian, who was born in 1963. They divorced in 1968 and Lennon married Yoko Ono in early 1969. Their son, Sean, was born in 1975. John Lennon was killed when a mentally ill fan, Mark David Chapman, shot him to death outside his apartment in New York City, on December 8, 1980.

Works Cited

Beatles. *The Beatles Anthology*. San Francisco: Chronicle Books, 2000.
Goldman, Albert. *The Lives of John Lennon*. New York: William Morrow & Co., 1988.
Henke, James. *Lennon Legend: An Illustrated Life of John Lennon*. San Francisco: Chronicle Books, 2003.

LEONARD, HUGH (1926–)

Playwright, Author
Adoptee

Career, Major Awards, and Achievements

Hugh Leonard is a prolific Irish playwright, author, and screenwriter. He is best known for his autobiographical play *Da*, which took four Tony awards in 1978: best

[AP Photo]

play; Bernard Hughes for best actor; Lester Rawlins for best supporting actor; and Melvin Bernhardt for best direction. The same year *Da* also won the New York Drama Critics Circle award, the Drama Desk award, and the Outer Critic's Circle award. *Da* was made into a movie starring Bernard Hughes and Martin Sheen in 1988. The play is about Leonard's relationship with his adoptive father and is set at the time of his father's funeral. Many of its scenes are also included in his first autobiography, *Home Before Dark* (1979). Leonard published a second autobiography, *Out After Dark*, in 1989.

He worked for over fourteen years in the Land Commission as "the world's longest-serving temporary clerical assistant" (*Out After Dark* 25). During his civil service years, he began to write and became involved with an amateur theater group. His second play *The Big Birthday* was accepted and produced at the Abbey Theater in 1956. Leonard took his pen name from a character named Hughie Leonard in his first play, *The Italian Road*, which the Abbey Theater had rejected in 1954:

> If I had paused to think, what I needed least in all the world was another name. Legally, I was John Joseph Byrne: at least on my birth certificate . . . [my mother] gave me a legacy of twenty years of utter misery by putting the stroke of a pen across the box headed 'Name of Father' . . . My adoptive parents' name was Keyes, and in Dalkey, I was known as Jack Keyes and still am. . . . Now, to John Joseph Byrne, Jack Keyes, and John Keyes Byrne, I was about to add a fourth name and . . . a fifth. . . . The quack psychoanalysts might suggest that I was in search of an identity. I prefer to think, and it may be the same thing, that I did not have a name I cared to lay claim to as my own (*Out After Dark* 186).

According to the *Dictionary of Literary Biography* (286), out of Leonard's numerous plays his most important are *The Poker Session* (1963), *The Au Pair Man* (1968), *The Patrick Pearse Motel* (1971), *Da* (1973), and *Summer* (1974). He is also a gifted screenwriter who won a Prix Italia Award for Original Dramatic Programme in 1967 for *Silent Song* (BBC). His works are valued for their wit, humor and technical excellence.

Leonard was literary editor for the Abbey Theater in the 1970s and became program director for the Dublin Theater Festival in 1978. He also wrote a regular humor column called "The Curmudgeon" for the Irish *Sunday Independent* newspaper until his retirement in 2006.

Family of Origin

As partially discussed in the quotation above, Leonard was born in Dublin on November 9, 1926, to Annie Byrne and an unknown father. It is clear from his autobiographies that Leonard's illegitimacy created many difficulties for him and that what he was told or overheard about his first family frightened him as a child:

'Da, do you know the thing I'm worst afraid of?'

'What's that?'

'Me mother. Not mammy: me real one. Aunt Chris says that when it gets dark she comes and looks in at me through the window.'

'Is that a fact?'

It had been in the back of his mind like a spider. . . (*Home Before Dark* 59–60).

When Leonard's adoptive mother "had drink on her," she would threaten to send him back "if he is bold" (*Home Before Dark* 22), and he often overheard her telling visitors that his first mother had damaged the child's health in an attempted abortion:

'She tried to get rid of him.'

'Get rid?'

'Before he was born. Whatever kind of rotten poison she took. Sure Dr. Enright told me, plump and plain. "Ma'am," he said, "that child will never make old bones"' (*Home Before Dark* 171).

Adoption

When he was ten days old, Leonard was adopted from the Holles Street Hospital by Nicholas Keyes, a gardener, and his wife Margaret (Doyle) Keyes. He grew up in Dalkey, a suburb south of Dublin, with his parents and his mother's sister, Mary. Hugh writes that both Mary and he were brought into the family by Margaret Keyes without consulting her husband: "When my mother adopted me, ten days old, she did not even consult him in advance, but simply arrived home by tram one day with a *fait accompli* wrapped in several blankets" (*Out After Dark* 136–137).

Leonard was able to turn his relationship with his adoptive father into his prize-winning play, *Da*, but he found it harder to write about his adoptive mother. His autobiographies reveal her problems with alcohol, her pride, and her cruel tongue, but they also clearly show her devotion to her son and that "love turned upside-down was love for all that" (*Home Before Dark* 131–132).

Education and Significant Relationships

Leonard attended Loreto Convent as a young boy, followed by Harold Boys' school. At Harold, he won a scholarship to Presentation College, and although he had greatly looked forward to attending, his two years there were marred by his "outsider" status and by his concerns about illegitimacy and class.

He joined the Land Commission in 1945 and married Paule Jacquet, a Belgian national, in 1955. They have a daughter, Danielle.

Works Cited

Gallagher, S. F. *Selected Plays of Hugh Leonard.* Gerrards Cross, Buckinghamshire: Smythe, 1992.

Leonard, Hugh. *Home Before Night.* New York: Atheneum, 1980.

Leonard, Hugh. *Out After Dark.* London: Deutsch, 1989.

Kosok, Heinz. "Hugh Leonard." *British Dramatists Since World War II. Dictionary of Literary Biography* 13 (1982).

Pearce, Sandra Manoogian. "Hugh Leonard." In *Irish Playwrights, 1880–1995.* Bernice Schank and William W. Demasters, eds. Westport, CT: Greenwood Press, 1997. 145–158.

LIFTON, BETTY JEAN

Author, Adoption Counselor
Adoptee

Career, Major Awards, and Achievements

Betty Jean Lifton is a leading authority on the psychology of the adopted child, birth parents, and adoptive parents, as well as the complexity of search and reunion. She is considered a pioneer in the adoption reform movement and has been a strong advocate for the adoptees' right to their original birth certificate.

[Courtesy of Betty Jean Lifton]

Her memoir *Twice Born* (1975) was the first of a trilogy dealing with the difficulties of putting together a healthy sense of self when a person doesn't know his or her family of origin.

Lifton discovered that she was unprepared to find her mother, and her mother was unprepared to be found: "That was our tragedy. We didn't understand the trauma we had each experienced by our separation or the defenses we had developed to survive. We didn't understand anything" (Lifton, e-mail interview April 8, 2008).

Because of the lack of guidance, they had difficulty forming a sustained relationship. "Mother and daughter—after all they had been through—would remain taboo to each other. Society had done its job well," she wrote in *Twice Born* (151). It was the realization of the emotional cost of trying to break the taboos inherent in the adoption system that set Lifton on a life course to understand the psychological dynamics of growing up adopted and the complications as well as the rewards of the reunion process.

Twice Born was followed by *Lost and Found: The Adoption Experience* (1979), which introduces the concepts of the "Good Adoptee and Bad Adoptee" and "Waking up from the Great Sleep." *Journey of the Adopted Self: A Quest for Wholeness* (1994), the last book in her trilogy, developed the concepts of the "Artificial Self" and the "Forbidden Self," and identified the ghosts that trail the adopted child: the ghost of the child he or she might have been, the ghost of the child the adoptive parents might have had, and the ghost of the birth mother. She also identifies ghosts that accompany birth mothers and adoptive parents.

As a journalist, Lifton wrote books about children who had been orphaned or separated from their families by war. *Return to Hiroshima*, with the renowned Japanese photographer Eikoh Hosoe, documented the lifelong impact on child survivors of the atomic bomb and won the *New York Herald Tribune* Award in 1970. *Children of Vietnam*, which she coauthored, documents the fate of children whose lives were torn apart by the war and was nominated for the National Book Award in 1973. *The King of Children* (1988), her biography of Janusz Korczak, the legendary hero who voluntarily went to his death in Treblinka with the orphans of the Warsaw Ghetto, was nominated for the Jewish National Book Award in 1989. It received the Joel H. Cavior Literary Award (1989), the International Janusz Korczak Society Literary Award (1989), and Eli Wiesel wrote the introduction to the book.

Lifton has also written many books for children: *Kap the Kappa*, the story of a Japanese river elf adopted by a fisherman's family, won the Herald Tribune Award (1960) and *Tell Me a Real Adoption Story* won the Praise Award from Pact, an adoption alliance (1994).

In addition to her books and clinical practice, Lifton has lectured and held workshops throughout the United States and abroad on the psychology of the adoptive family.

Among her numerous awards for her adoption work, she received the Emma Villardi Award from the American Adoption Congress (1995) and a Recognition Award from St. John's University (2008) for her outstanding contribution to the understanding of the adoption experience. She is a founding member of its biennial adoption conferences.

Family of Origin

Lifton was born in Staten Island, New York, to an unmarried teenager who struggled to keep her against the wishes of her own mother, who was the daughter of a prominent Orthodox rabbi in Bensonhurst, New York. Defiantly taking a chance that the birth father would change his mind, Lifton's mother placed her in the Hebrew Home for

Infants in the Bronx. After two years, however, she gave up hope and reluctantly placed her with the Louise Wise Adoption agency in New York City. Lifton learned later that the trauma of relinquishing her child caused her mother to go temporarily blind. She married and divorced twice and lived as a recluse with her son in her later years. Lifton's birth father had died by the time she identified him, but she was able to make contact with members of his extended family.

Adoption

Betty Jean, who goes by the nickname "BJ," was adopted by a couple in their late thirties and grew up with them as an only child in Cincinnati, Ohio. When she was seven and quarantined in bed with scarlet fever, her mother told her that she was adopted and that her birth parents were married and deceased, which she believed. She was made to promise that she would never tell her father that she knew about her adoption, that it would break his heart: "'He wants you to think he is your real daddy.' . . . The child just lies in the room. Now she is truly in quarantine. The sign tells it as it is: she is someone different, tainted, dangerous to society" (*Twice Born*, 8). Lifton would come to realize the destructiveness of secrets and what she refers to as a "conspiracy of silence" which isolates the adopted child and make it difficult to form a healthy sense of self.

Education and Significant Relationships

Lifton attended Barnard College in New York, where she majored in English literature and drama and acted in the Columbia Players. She met and married her husband, psychiatrist and writer Robert Jay Lifton, shortly after graduation. For the next fifteen years, they lived alternately in Japan, Hong Kong, and America. A son, Kenneth Jay, was born in Tokyo in 1961, and daughter Karen Natasha was born in 1965 in New Haven, where Robert Lifton had a research chair at Yale. During that time Lifton formed a professional theater company, The Jugglers, in New York City, which performed her multimedia plays for children at City Center in Manhattan and the Brooklyn Academy of Music.

After two of her adoption books were published in the 1970s, Lifton was sought after by many adoptees for advice and support. She took a PhD in adoption counseling at the New York campus of the Union Institute and opened a clinical practice to serve all members of the adoption triangle. A close friend of **Erik Erikson**, Lifton was influenced by his identity theory, which stresses the importance of continuity with one's past in the service of one's future. She also made use of theories of the self and concepts of trauma for she believes that all members of the adoption triangle have been traumatized by their losses.

Lifton relocated with her husband in 2001 to Cambridge, Massachusetts, where she continues her adoption practice. Her adult children and four grandchildren live in the area. She commutes monthly to Manhattan to see clients there and does telephone counseling across the country. She writes and has an additional counseling practice in Wellfleet, Massachusetts, during the summers. The Liftons observe a silent Quaker vigil every August 6, the day the bomb fell on Hiroshima, in remembrance of those who died that day: "My focus shifts back and forth," she says, "from my concern with healing in the adoption world to healing in the larger world that we all share" (Lifton, e-mail interview April 8, 2008).

Works Cited

Lifton, Betty Jean. *Twice Born: Memoirs of an Adopted Daughter.* New York: Penguin, 1977.

————. *Lost and Found: The Adoption Experience.* New York: Dial, 1979.

————. *Lost and Found: The Adoption Experience.* Third edition, expanded and updated. Ann Arbor: U of Michigan Press, 2009.

————. *Journey of the Adopted Self.* New York: Basic Books, 1994.

Book Chapters:

Lifton, Betty Jean. "The Inner Life of the Adopted Child: Adoption, Trauma, Loss, Fantasy, Search, and Reunion" in *Handbook of Adoption: Implications for Researchers, Practitioners, and Families* by Rafael Art Javier et al. Thousand Oaks, CA: Sage, 2007: 418–424.

————. "The Adoptee's Two Mothers." *The Source of the Spring: Mothers through the Eyes of Women Writers* by Judith R. Shapiro. Berkeley, CA: Conari Press, 1998: 33–47.

————. "Shared Identity Issues for Adoptees." *Clinical and Practice Issues in Adoption: Bridging the Gap Between Adoptees Placed as Infants and as Older Children* by Victor Groza and Karen Rosenberg. Westport, CT: Praeger, 1998. 37–48.

————. "The Adopted Self." *Trauma and Self.* Charles B. Strozier and Michael Flynn, eds. Lanham, MD: Rowman & Littlefield, c1996. 19–28.

————. "Bad/Good, Good/Bad: Birth Mothers and Adoptive Mothers." *"Bad" Mothers: The Politics of Blame in Twentieth-Century America.* Molly Ladd-Taylor and Lauri Umansky, Eds. New York: New York University Press, 1998. 191–197.

LILI'UOKALANI (1832–1917)

Queen of Hawai'i
Adoptee

Career, Major Awards, and Achievements

Lili'uokalani was the last of Hawai'i's hereditary rulers. She came to the throne on January 29, 1891, as the successor to her brother, King David Kalākaua, who died in San Francisco where he had gone hoping to recover his health. Kalākaua, who had no children, had designated Lili'uokalani as the next ruler. From the early 1880s, Lili'uokalani had been increasingly involved in government as a thirty-year power struggle to control Hawai'i's land, wealth, and political structure began. In 1881, she served as regent while the king went for a nine-month world tour. Her government was faced with a smallpox epidemic almost immediately, and she won praise for her behavior during this and other difficult situations. As crown princess, she held public receptions to allow the Hawai'ian people to get to know her.

When she became queen, Hawai'i was governed by a constitution which had been accepted in 1887. Opponents called it the "Bayonet Constitution" because King David Kalākaua had signed it under threat of military force. Written by Hawai'ian Interior Minister Lorrin A. Thurston, the Constitution was supported by the Honolulu Rifles, an armed militia group, by politicians who favored annexation by the United States, and by members of the Hawai'ian League, a secret society desiring annexation. It tended to favor the rich and influential.

Supported by public opinion, the new queen decided to oppose the 1887 Constitution and to write a new Constitution that would have restored some powers to the monarchy and re-enfranchised Native Hawai'ians and Asians who had lost influence under the then current Constitution.

[Courtesy of the Hawaiian Historical Society]

Numerous American and European residents of the kingdom supported annexation of Hawai'i to the United States. Sugar producers were especially interested in annexation so that their sugar would have the same trade advantages as that produced on the mainland. Some of the Americans and Europeans living in Hawai'i formed a Committee of Safety on January 14, 1893, in order to express concern about the safety of non-Hawai'ians, such as themselves, living in Hawai'i. Two days later the U.S. Minister, John L. Stevens, ordered a company of Marines and two companies of American sailors to take up strategic positions in the city to keep the peace.

On the following day the Queen was deposed and a provisional government instated. On February 1, Hawai'i was declared a protectorate of the United States by the American Minister.

In the United States, President Grover Cleveland and members of his administration asked for an investigation. The new American Minister, James H. Blount, was sent to Hawai'i to listen to both sides and concluded that the people of Hawai'i supported the queen. The Blount Report and the Cleveland administration found the deposition of the queen illegal and criticized the actions of Stevens and the American troops. On November 16, 1893, Cleveland proposed that, in return for amnesty for everyone involved, Lili'uokalani would be restored to the throne. The queen's initial position was that the people involved should be executed for treason, and Cleveland turned to Congress for a solution. When the queen decided not to press for executions, the new U.S. Minister demanded that the Provisional Government reinstate her. The Provisional Government refused, and the U.S. Congress instituted its own investigation, which produced the Morgan Report on February 26, 1894. The new report declared all parties involved not responsible for the overthrow of the Queen and her government. The fairness of the findings of both reports is still questioned by supporters of both sides.

The Republic of Hawai'i was proclaimed on July 4, 1894, with Sanford B. Dole as President, and the United States recognized it as a protectorate.

In early January, Robert Wilcox, a longtime supporter of Lili'uokalani, led a revolutionary movement that failed in a matter of days. The former queen was arrested on January 16—weapons had been found in her gardens, though she stated that she was unaware of them. She was fined and sentenced to five years at hard labor, but the sentence was commuted to imprisonment in the 'Iolani Palace. Eight months later she abdicated, thus securing the release of Wilcox and others who supported his revolution and were under sentence of death for treason.

In 1898, after the Spanish-American War, Hawai'i, along with Puerto Rico, Guam, and the Philippines, was annexed by the United States. Hawai'i became the fiftieth state in 1959.

Lili'uokalani is widely known as the last queen of Hawai'i, though few outside of Hawai'i know much about her short and difficult reign. Her influence remains strong because she composed over 150 Hawai'ian songs, many of them famous, including perhaps the best known of all, the lovely "Aloha Oe," and the second Hawai'ian national anthem, "He Mele Lahui Hawai'i," written in 1868 at the request of King Kamehameha V.

Family of Origin

Born September 2, 1838, Lili'uokalani was the daughter of Analea Keohokalole, a wealthy high chiefess who was one of the fifteen counselors of King Kamehameha III, and her cousin and husband, Caesar Kaluaiku Kapa'akea, also a high chief but of lesser rank than his wife. Lili'uokalani was their third child.

The English name given to her at baptism was Lydia Paki, and she was registered as the adopted daughter of Abner and Laura Paki. Her original Hawai'ian name was given to her at birth by Kinau, the king's half sister and one of the highest ranking woman in Hawai'i. The custom was to name a child after an important event, which helped place the child in time. The name Kinau chose, Lili'u Loloku Walania Kamaka'eha meant "smarting, tearful, burning, sore eyes," given because Kinau had a painful eye infection at the time of Lydia's birth. The future queen's brother renamed her Lili'uokalani when he chose her as crown princess.

Adoption

Lili'uokalani was adopted at birth by Laura Konia, a granddaughter of King Kamehameha I, and her husband Abner Paki, a chief who held high political status as an advisor to the king.

Traditionally, Hawai'ian parents with many children* would give a child or children to friends or relatives, often those who were childless or had few children. Children were given in *hana'i* not only out of generosity and in friendship but also to improve the child's station in life. Perhaps more important, *hana'i* solidified the relationships among the *ali'i*, Hawai'i's upper and royal class.

Hana'i was a commonly practiced form of open adoption, especially among the *ali'i*. No stigma was involved in *hana'i* adoptions. A child often knew his or her first parents and had contact with them if they lived close by. On the other hand, a *hana'i*-adopted child could also lose track of his or her family of origin.

Lili'uokalani benefited from this system, since it put her in line for the throne. Of her own experience she said:

> I knew no other father or mother than my foster parents, no other sister than Bernice. I used to climb up on the knees of Paki, put my arms around his neck, kiss him, and he caressed me as a father would his child; while on the contrary, when I met my own parents, it was with perhaps more of interest, yet always with the demeanor I would have shown to any strangers who noticed me. . . . I knew. . . my own brothers and sisters, yet we met throughout my younger life as though we had not known our common parentage. This was, and indeed is, in accordance with Hawai'ian customs. It is not easy to explain. . . but it seems perfectly natural to us. As intelligible a reason as can be given is that this alliance through adoption cemented the ties of friendship between the chiefs. It spread to the common people, and it has doubtless fostered a community of interest and harmony (*Hawaii's Story* 4).

However, she also told the story of Prince Lot (later Kamehameha V), who sent a messenger to his sister, telling the messenger, "You must go back and tell my sister that on no account is she to give that child to another. I am an adopted child myself, deprived of the love of my mother, and yet I was a stranger in the house of my adoption" (*Hawaii's Story* 26). He was too late; the message arrived an hour after the child had been given to another.

Education and Significant Relationships

Lili'u's wet nurse, Kaikai, introduced her to the ways of traditional Hawai'i. Her *hana'i* mother, Konia, accepted Lili'u as her child and heir. Konia's biological daughter,

---

*Lydia's parents eventually had ten children.

Bernice Pauahi, was the *hanaʻi* daughter of high chiefess Kinau, who had given her own biological sons in *hanaʻi* to Kamehameha III, providing him with heirs.

Liliʻu and Bernice (later Bernice Pauahi Bishop, the founder of the Kamehameha Schools), played and attended school together. Much later, in 1884, Liliʻuokalani wrote "Chant," which put Hawaiʻian music to verses from the book of Job, for her *hanaʻi* sister's funeral. This is the only piece of music she is known to have composed that year.

They attended the Royal School (formerly the Chiefs' Children's School) with Liliʻu's biological older brothers, James Kaliokalani and David Kalākaua.

On September 16, 1862, Liliʻu married John Owen Dominis, a *haole* (nonnative Hawaiʻian) who became private secretary and confidential advisor to King Kamehameha V and the Governor of Oʻahu and Maui. Later, as husband of the queen, he was given the title of Prince Consort. Dominis died in August 27, 1891, only months after Liliʻuokalani became queen. Though Liliʻuokalani paid tribute to him in her book *Hawaii's Story*, most sources say that the marriage was not especially happy.

The queen loved children and, according to an article in the *Honolulu Advertiser*, had large pockets sewn into some of her dresses so that she could carry supplies of candy for the children she met. Her *hanaʻi* daughter, Lydia Kaʻonohiponiponiokalani Aholo, was adopted in 1878. In 1883 she adopted two boys: Kaiponohea ʻAeʻa, the son of one of her household staff members, and John Dominis ʻAimoku, the illegitimate son of her husband, John Owen Dominis.

Liliʻuokalani was 79 when she died in 1917 from complications after a stroke. She died at Washington Place, the Dominis home which had been her principal private residence and is now the home of the governors of Hawaiʻi. In 1909 Liliʻuokalani had put her estate into a trust to provide care for orphaned and destitute children in Hawaiʻi, especially native Hawaiʻian children, and today her legacy funds the Queen Liliʻuokalani Children's Center.

Works Cited

Allen, Helena G. *The Betrayal of Liliuokalani: Last Queen of Hawaii 1838–1917*. Glendale, CA: Arthur H. Clark, 1982.

Liliʻuokalani. *Hawaii's Story, by Hawaii's Queen*. Honolulu: Mutual Publishing, 1990.

Serrano, Zenaida. "Celebrating the Life of Queen Liliʻuokalani." *Honolulu Advertiser*. August 29, 2007. June 12, 2008. http://the.honoluluadvertiser.com/article/2007/Aug/29/il/hawaii708290373.html

LINKLETTER, ART (1912–)

Humorist, Radio and Television Host, Broadcaster, Producer, Businessman
Adoptee

Career, Major Awards, and Achievements

Art Linkletter is best known as the host of two of the longest-running shows in television and radio history: *House Party* (CBS), which ran for nineteen years, and *People Are Funny* (NBC), which ran for twenty-six years. He also starred in *Life with Linkletter* (ABC) and appeared in two movies, *Champagne for Caesar* (1950) and *People Are Funny* (1981). He won four Emmy nominations, two Emmy Awards, and a Grammy Award.

[AP Photo/Damian Dovarganes]

He has written over twenty books, including two autobiographies, *Hobo on the Way to Heaven* (1980) and *I Didn't Do it Alone* (also 1980). His humor books include *People Are Funny;* a top American best-seller, *Kids Say the Darndest Things; Confessions of a Happy Man; Wish I'd Said That; Women Are My Favorite People; Kids Sure Rite Funny; Oops! Life's Awful Moments;* and *A Child's Garden of Misinformation.* In addition, Linkletter has produced numerous books and videos on more serious topics, such as aging, drug abuse, family violence, poverty, public speaking, and business. Examples include *Old Age Is Not for Sissies: Choices for Senior Americans*; *Drugs at My Doorstep*; *My Child on Drugs? Youth and the Drug Culture*; and *Yes You Can! How to Succeed in Business and Life*. His *Linkletter Down Under* is a travel memoir of Australia, where President Reagan appointed him the Ambassador and Commissioner General of its 150th Anniversary Celebration.

At 97, he continues to run Linkletter Enterprises, and he is on the board of directors of such notable companies as Metro-Goldwyn-Mayer, Western Airlines, YMCA, and Kaiser Hospitals. Linkletter Enterprises comprises a variety of family businesses, and he was the original promoter for the hula-hoop and the game of *Life*. His picture was on the $100,000 bill in early versions of the game. Throughout his career, Linkletter has been a popular speaker and was the national spokesperson for the United Seniors Association, American Leprosy Missions, and World Vision, among others. He has been a conservative activist for many years, serving on presidential commissions and as a humanitarian volunteer, especially for causes that benefit children and older persons.

Family of Origin

Art Linkletter was born in Moose Jaw, Saskatchewan, Canada, on July 17, 1912, to Effie Brown, an unmarried woman, and a married man named Kelly or Kalle from nearby Regina. Listed as Arthur Gordon Kelly on his birth record, Linkletter never intended to pursue a search for his birth relatives: "it wouldn't be fair to everyone concerned for me suddenly to descend on a mother, probably with her own family, who had once disowned me and announce my true identity" (*Hobo* 156–157).

His search was forced upon him, however, in an unusual way: in wartime 1942, a federal grand jury indicted him as an illegal alien and for illegally voting in an election. Linkletter, who became naturalized as a U.S. citizen, pleaded *nolo contendere* to the charges and was fined $500. Linkletter was three years old when he moved to the United States with his adoptive family: "I had chosen to assume that mother and father Linkletter had become naturalized Americans, making me automatically a citizen. . . . Who would have thought that a grand jury would have found anything sinister in the fact that I was born in Moose Jaw?" (*Hobo* 153–154).

As part of their case against him, the grand jury investigators provided detailed evidence regarding his birth and birthparents. Although Linkletter once wrote that he did not approve of adoptee searches except for valid medical reasons (*Hobo* 71–72), he did locate and visit the house in which he was born, his orphanage, and his original birth records during a trip to Canada:

> After some diligent searching we found my birth certificate, from which my father's name had been erased, obviously to avoid the scandal of siring me out of wedlock. However, by holding the aging document up to the light I could see enough of the original writing to learn, for the first time in all these years, that my name was in fact not Kelly. I cannot say for certain, but to the best of my ability to make out erased and faded handwriting my father's name was Kalle or something very similar (*Hobo* 160).

Adoption

Art Linkletter describes his adoptive parents, John and Mary (Metzler) Linkletter, as "the most kindly people I have ever known" (Linkletter *Hobo* 28). The couple adopted him as a one-month old baby in Moose Jaw. He was their only child. John Linkletter failed in various Canadian and American business ventures before he finally settled in San Diego and successfully established a shoemaker's shop, a trade that he had learned as a child. A devout member of a local Pentecostal church, John Linkletter, to his son's discomfort, often brought home, fed, and sermonized the area's drifters and derelicts. Linkletter credits his father for his faith, which "shielded and comforted me in times of trouble" (Linkletter *Alone* 2) and his spirit of adventure.

Linkletter discovered that he was adopted by finding a letter:

> When I was quite young (I don't recall my exact age, maybe eight or nine) I learned I had been adopted. I found out about it by snooping in John Linkletter's mail and reading something from the adoption agency that brought my world crashing down. Someone didn't want me. My real mom and dad had gotten rid of me; they had dumped me, it seemed then, onto anyone who would take an unloved, unwanted kid. I didn't know that I had no legal father. I didn't learn about that until my federal indictment many years later, but it wouldn't have mattered, really. I was a castoff, and in the face of that shocking discovery, all the real affection that the Linkletters had shown me was temporarily forgotten" (Linkletter *Hobo* 52).

Education, Marriage, and Children

Linkletter left home at age sixteen, traveling with a high school friend, Denver Colorado Fox. The boys "rode the rails" and worked odd jobs across the country, until they arrived in New York in 1929. There, they took jobs on Wall Street as a stock clerk and typist, jobs which soon were lost in the October 1929 stock market crash. After stints as cadets on a passenger vessel, the *S.S. American Legion*, Art and Denver returned to San Diego. Art lived with Denver's family and attended San Diego State College, where he studied Voice and Drama and graduated with a Bachelor of Arts degree in 1934.

During his senior year at college, Art began his broadcast career and fell in love with Lois Foerster, the woman to whom he would be married for over sixty-six years. The Linkletters had five children, Jack, Dawn, Robert, Sharon, and Diane, nine grandchildren, and fourteen great-grandchildren. Their daughter Diane, while under the influence of LSD, committed suicide in 1969 and thus became the impetus of her father's longtime campaign against drug abuse. Son Robert Linkletter died in a car accident in 1980. Son Jack Linkletter died of lymphoma in 2007.

Art and Lois Linkletter unwind by taking ski trips to Colorado and surfing in Hawai'i. Although he has received fourteen honorary doctorate degrees and recognitions too numerous to list, Linkletter considers his family to be his "greatest success in life" (Selle 2) and his favorite award is "Grandfather of the Year" (sterlingspeakers.com).

Works Cited

Linkletter, Art, with George Bishop. *Hobo on the Way to Heaven.* Ottawa, IL: Caroline House, 1980.
———. *I Didn't Do it Alone.* Ottawa, IL: Caroline House, 1980.
Selle, Robert R. "Linkletter: Man of Many Riches." *World and I.* May 2002: Expanded Academic ASAP (Infotrac/Gale database), July 26, 2002.

LIOTTA, RAY (1955–)

Actor
Adoptee, orphanage alumnus

Career, Major Awards, and Achievements

Ray Liotta is an American actor who began his career with the role of Joey Perrini on the NBC soap opera *Another World* (1978–1981). He was nominated for a Golden Globe

[AP Photo/Frank Franklin II]

Award and a Boston Film Critics Award for best supporting actor for his intense, critically acclaimed performance as Ray Sinclair in *Something Wild* (1986). His major film roles include Eugene in *Dominick and Eugene* (1988); Shoeless Joe Jackson, the ghost in *Field of Dreams* (1989); and Henry Hill in *GoodFellas* (1990). Liotta also appeared in *Article 99* (1992), *Domestic Dilemma* (1992), *Unlawful Entry* (1992), *No Escape* (1994), *Corrina, Corrina* (1994), *Operation Dumbo Drop* (1995), *Unforgettable* (1996), *Turbulence* (1997), *Cop Land* (1997), *The Rat Pack* (1998), *Inferno* (1999), and *Muppets From Space* (1999). His recent work includes *Forever Mine* (2001), *Hannibal* (2001), *Heartbreakers* (2001), *Blow* (2001), *John Q* (2002), *Narc* (2002), *Identity* (2003), *Anger Management* (2003), *The Last Shot* (2004), *Powder Blue* (2009), and *Crossing Over* (2009).

Family of Origin

Ray Liotta was born in Newark, New Jersey, on December 18, 1955, and was placed in an orphanage for the first six months of his life. He is of Italian, Scottish, and Irish ancestry.

Liotta met his birthmother for the first time when he was 43, after his wife found her through a locating service. He learned that she had been a single mother who felt unable to care for a second child. He said in an *A&E Biography* interview that the reunion brought him relief and happiness: "For me, I found out the reasons why she did what she did, and I realized it was out of love. And that was very comforting for me" (A&E).

Adoption

Alfred and Mary Liotta adopted Ray as an infant. Alfred Liotta owned a chain of automotive parts stores. Both of his adoptive parents were active in local politics and enjoyed international traveling. Mary Liotta died June 17, 1989, while Liotta was filming *GoodFellas*.

Liotta said that his parents told him early that he was adopted: "I knew right off the bat that I was adopted. I did a report on it in show-and-tell in kindergarten" (Cunningham 104). When he was three years old, his parents let him help select their second child, a baby girl: "I remember coming home, being so proud, thinking that's how it was done. I just picked out a sister! She was my little trophy" (Cunningham 104). His interviewers consistently agree on Liotta's reticence to discuss his youth: "'It was fine. Nice life. I grew up nice.' End of story" (Kaylin 294).

Education, Marriage, and Children

Liotta graduated from the University of Miami with a BA degree in Theatre and Fine Arts. While in college, a friend said that Liotta used to draw on his feelings about being adopted and channel them on stage (A&E). He met his future wife, Michelle Grace, at a baseball game, and they married in 1997 with two wedding ceremonies, one in Las Vegas and one in Thailand. They have a daughter, Carson.

Works Cited

A&E Biography. "Ray Liotta: Hollywood GoodFella." Arts and Entertainment Television. 15 January 2003.
Bishop, Kathy. "Ray Liotta." *Rolling Stone*, Nov. 1, 1990, 62.
Cunningham, Kim. "The Unmarried Man." *People*, March 30, 1992, 104.
Kaylin, Lucy. "Wise Guise." *GQ*, April 1990: 104.

LOUGANIS, GREG (1960–)

Diver
Fostered, adoptee

Career, Major Awards, and Achievements

Greg Louganis is considered one of the greatest divers in history. When he was only sixteen years old, he won a silver medal at the 1976 Olympics for ten-meter platform diving. In the 1984 Olympics, he won gold medals for both three-meter springboard and ten-meter platform diving. He won an additional two gold medals at the 1988 Olympics, even after an accident in which he hit his head on the diving board during a reverse dive. He has won six world championships and holds forty-seven national title wins. Additional awards include six gold medals at the Pan Am games, the 1985 Sullivan Award for most outstanding amateur athlete, and the 1988 Maxwell House/United States Olympic Committee Spirit Award. In 1985, Louganis was inducted into the Olympic Hall of Fame, and in 1993 into the International Swimming Hall of Fame.

Louganis has also made a name for himself as an actor, dancer, and author. Some of the productions he has appeared in include *Move Over* (1988), *The Mighty Ducks 2* (1993), *Jeffrey* (1993), and *The Only Thing Worse You Could Have Told Me* (1995). He published his autobiography *Breaking the Surface* in 1995. It was first on the New York Times Best-Seller list for five weeks. His second book, *For the Life of Your Dog*, was published in 1999. Greg Louganis is also a spokesman and activist for a number of organizations that benefit youth.

[AP Photo/Bob Galbraith]

Family of Origin

Greg Louganis was born on January 29, 1960, in El Cajon, California, to unmarried teenagers. His birthfather was Samoan and his birthmother was of Northern European ancestry. During an especially difficult time in his life around the age of twelve, he learned more about his original family from the adoption agency:

> It was comforting to know that thought went into the decision to put me up for adoption. I had always assumed that my biological parents didn't love me. There were so many blank spots in the story, and I had chosen to fill them in as negatively as I could imagine, a pattern I repeated often in my life. I assumed that my biological parents had simply wanted to unload me. I never thought of two teenagers knowing they wouldn't be able to provide the opportunities they wanted me to have. I never thought that giving me up might have been a difficult decision for them (44–45).

Adoption

Greg was adopted by Pete Louganis, a bookkeeper of Greek ancestry, and his wife Frances, a housewife. They named their son Gregory Efthimios Louganis. He was their second adopted child. The Louganis family adopted a daughter, Despina, in 1958. She was of Native American and European ancestry.

Greg had been hard to place at that time because of racial reasons, as he relates:

> For my first nine months I lived with a foster family. The adoption agency was having a tough time placing me because of my coloring. The family that took care of me called me Timmy, which might have been the name my natural parents had given me. . . .
>
> I don't even remember asking Mom if I was adopted. It was something I always knew. I remember her saying that she couldn't have children, so adoption gave her the chance to have kids, which made perfect sense to me. It was also the perfect way to tell us we were adopted (28).

Physically gifted, Louganis joined his sister Despina's three-days-a-week dance and acrobatics classes at the age of eighteen months. By the age of three he was performing in competitions with another child, Eleanor Smith, who became his regular partner: "Even as a kid I was a perfectionist. . . . I've thought a lot recently about why it was so important to me that I do everything perfectly: I wasn't good in school, particularly in reading, and this was the one way to prove that I wasn't retarded" (18).

Greg's father was not supportive of his son's interest in dance and acrobatics, but he was in favor of diving and hired former diver John Anders as a coach. When he was ten, Louganis competed in his first national diving event, the Junior Olympics, in Colorado Springs. His youthful competitiveness, he says, sprang from his need to be loved: "Even then, winning was a way of making sure that they loved me" (23).

One of the people who saw Louganis perform in the Junior Olympics was the 1948 and 1952 Olympic diving gold-medalist, Dr. Sammy Lee. He was so impressed by the boy's talent that he later agreed to become his coach for the 1976 Montreal Olympics.

In spite of his remarkable abilities, Greg had a very difficult childhood, and he struggled with severe bouts of depression. He had problems in school, especially from his dyslexia, which was not diagnosed until college, and he was also teased and bullied over his skin color and for being a "sissy." In his autobiography, Louganis describes an especially vicious neighborhood fight that was quietly witnessed by his father: "I remember now that he let it happen and that I knew at the time he was there. He might as well have been the one throwing the punches" (37).

Greg described his father as a good provider for his family, but as chronically angry, authoritarian, and a heavy drinker. He did not establish a positive relationship with his father until after both men had contracted life-threatening illnesses. When his cancer progressed, Pete Louganis, who had by now divorced, moved into Greg's home and was nursed there until his death in 1990.

Education and Significant Relationships

Greg began college at the University of Miami on a diving scholarship but transferred to the University of California in 1981 in order to train with diving coach Ron O'Brien. In 1983, he earned his Bachelor of Arts in Theater, with a minor in Dance.

Louganis made his homosexuality public at the 1994 Gay Games and revealed that he has AIDS in his 1995 autobiography. He was in a long physically and emotionally abusive relationship with his business manager, Jim Babbitt, known as Tom in the book. After they separated and in defiance of a restraining order, Babbitt, who has since died, continued to threaten and stalk Louganis. Louganis then commenced a four-year relationship with Steve Kmetko, a television anchor, who also appears in *Breaking the Surface*.

Works Cited

Craig, David Cobb, and Vicki Sheff-Cahan. "A New Leash on Life: Retired from Diving, a Healthy Greg Louganis Now Spends His Time Coaching Canines." *People Weekly* 25 June 2001: 113+.

Louganis, Greg, with Eric Marcus. *Breaking the Surface*. New York: Random House, 1995.

M

MACY, ANNE SULLIVAN (1866–1935)

Teacher for the Blind and Deaf (Helen Keller's Teacher)
Orphanage alumna (Almshouse)

Career, Education, and Achievements

Anne Sullivan Macy, often called Annie Sullivan, is best known as Helen Keller's teacher, the woman who enabled Keller, who had become deaf and blind as the result of an illness when she was less than two years old, to acquire language and education and live a remarkable life.

At age fourteen, Sullivan, who had lost much of her sight as a child, began attending the Perkins School for the Blind. While there, she regained some of her sight through surgery. She also learned the manual alphabet in order to communicate with a deaf-blind friend. Sullivan was twenty when she graduated as valedictorian of her class in 1886 and was engaged as governess and tutor to Helen Keller, with the encouragement of the director of the Perkins School.

Helen, then seven years old, had created a sign language communication system of about 60 signs with the young daughter of the Kellers' cook, allowing her to communicate to some degree with her family, but she was highly undisciplined. Sullivan took Helen to live with her in a cottage on the Keller property in order to teach her the manual alphabet so that she could communicate more effectively with others. Sullivan began by teaching Helen words, signing the names of the things around them into Helen's palm. Annie was an instinctive and innovative teacher: "At a time when the concept was revolutionary, she emphasized the importance of permitting children to find their own gait and follow their own interests" (Lash 237).

By 1888, Keller, accompanied by Sullivan, was ready to attend the Perkins School (then known as the Cambridge School for Young Ladies) in New York City, and then go on to Radcliff. At each school, Sullivan spelled the lectures and demonstrations into Keller's hand. When Keller graduated from Radcliffe in 1904, she was the first deaf-blind college graduate in the United States.

Sullivan and Helen Keller moved to a farm at Wrentham, Massachusetts, around the time of Sullivan's marriage to John Macy. They later moved to a house in Forest Hills, New York, and were joined by Polly Thompson, who acted as a secretary to Helen Keller

[AP Photo/Archives of the American Foundation for the Blind]

and an assistant to Sullivan, whose health began to decline in 1916. Nevertheless the three women traveled throughout the United States during the war and in other countries later. They lectured and gave vaudeville performances until 1920, when Sullivan's health became too fragile. Beginning in 1924, both Sullivan and Keller worked for the American Foundation for the Blind.

Helen Keller earned many honors in her lifetime, including the Presidential Medal of Freedom (1964), the United States' highest civilian honor; she was an "example of courage to all mankind, she has devoted her life to illuminating the dark world of the blind and the handicapped." However, one biographer wrote that "a question remained as to how much of what was called Helen Keller was in reality Annie Sullivan. The answer is not simple. During the creative years neither could have done without the other" (Lash 3). A well-known play about Annie Sullivan's work with Keller, *The Miracle Worker,* by William Gibson, won the Tony Award for Best Broadway Play in 1959. In the film adaptation, directed by Arthur Penn. Anne Bancroft and Patty Duke won the 1962 Best Actress and Best Supporting Actress Oscars, respectively, for their portrayals of Sullivan and Keller.

Family of Origin

Annie Sullivan was born to Irish "potato famine" immigrants on April 4, 1866, in Feeding Hills, Massachusetts: "I knew very little about my parents. . . . There were no Bible records of births and deaths in my family. A few facts have been dug out of church and municipal records. I know that Limerick, Ireland, was their birthplace" (Lash 4).

Annie's mother, Alice Cloesy,* had tuberculosis and needed a crutch to walk. She bore five children, the fourth and fifth children, Nellie and John, died in infancy. Annie's father: "red-haired Thomas Sullivan, was not only illiterate and unskilled but a drinker and a brawler, and shiftless" (Lash 4). Annie contracted trachoma around the age of five; it gradually damaged her vision. When she was eight, her mother died, leaving Annie, a seven-year-old son, Jimmie, and a younger daughter, Mary. An uncle took in Jimmie, who had been born with a tubercular hip, and Mary. Annie tried to keep house for her father in a "dilapidated little cabin on her uncle's farm" (Lash 5), but eventually Thomas abandoned the family and no one could ever discover what became of him.

Almshouse

Mary went to live with an aunt, while Annie and Jimmie were sent to the State Infirmary (almshouse) at Tewksbury:

> Annie [was sent there] because she was difficult to manage and too blind to be useful, Jimmie because he was becoming helplessly lame with a tubercular hip.
>   They entered the almshouse [on] February [22], 1876, and Jimmie died in May. Annie stayed four years. No one outside was interested in her and she had no friends but her fellow paupers. It was one of them who told her that there were special schools for the blind, and as time went on—she lost track of time in Tewksbury—her desire for an education grew. To escape from the pit of degradation and disease in which she lived seemed impossible and the stench from the almshouse rose so high that the State Board of Charities ordered an investigation. . . when the committee members arrived she flung herself towards them, unable to distinguish one from another, and cried out, "Mr. Sanborn, Mr. Sanborn, I want to go to school!" (Keller 9–10).

The almshouse, which housed an average of 940 men, women, and children, had a men's ward and a women's ward. Annie was desperately attached to her brother and the two avoided separation when they arrived in a "Black Maria":

> The attendant who received them proposed to separate them, sending Annie to the women's ward and Jimmie to the men's; but Annie, whose whole childhood had been one

---

*Alice's name was also spelled Cloahassy in some records.

abandonment after another, protested with such passionate sobs that the attendant relented and sent them both to a woman's ward. No matter that it was unpainted, overcrowded, peopled with misshapen, diseased, often manic women; they were together (Lash 7).

One night, however, she awoke to find that Jimmie had been taken to the "dead house." When she crept to the poorhouse morgue, where the resident children were often allowed to play, she found Jimmie's small body:

> [I] kissed and kissed and kissed his face—the dearest thing in the world—the only thing I had ever loved. . . . When I got back, I saw that they had put Jimmie's bed back in its place. I sat down between my bed and his empty bed, and I hoped desperately to die. I believe very few children have ever been so completely left alone as I was (Lash 8).

Annie's own isolation and loneliness may have been the driving force behind her extraordinary lifelong desire to "deliver" those even more isolated than herself: the deaf-blind. Helen Keller wrote this about her teacher:

> She would often remind me of the deaf-blind throughout the world waiting for deliverance. "Hold out your arms to them, forget yourself in them, and be faithful to their cause. That will be your true memorial to me, Helen. There may be a wall between you and them, but hammer it down, stone by stone, even if you are broken by the effort, just as some of Florence Nightingale's nurses died of exhaustion" (Keller 217).

In February 1877, Annie was sent to the Hospital of Les Soeurs de la Charité in Lowell, Massachusetts, for eye surgery. When she recovered, she worked in Boston doing light housekeeping for a family until she left for additional surgeries at the city infirmary. Following those, the Boston family would not take her back, and Annie returned to the women's ward at Tewksbury. She wrote:

> Very much of what I remember about Tewksbury is indecent, cruel, melancholy. . . gruesome in the light of grown-up experience; but nothing corresponding with my present understanding entered my child mind. Everything interested me. . . . I often wonder. . . how I escaped contamination in that slum—that "rookery." . . . There are nascent in the child-mind countless pure immunities that prevent it from being harmed (Lash 10–13).

On October 7, 1880, Annie was accepted at the Perkins School for the Blind.

Significant Relationships

Sullivan married John A. Macy, a Harvard professor, in May 1905. Macy assisted with Keller's autobiography, *The World I Live In*, first published in 1908, and it was Macy who first introduced Keller to socialism. She became a dedicated party member in 1909. The Macys separated in 1913, but never formally divorced. John Macy died in 1932.

From 1927 to 1930, Sullivan's sight deteriorated seriously, and by 1935 she was completely blind. Late in her life, she became determined to adopt a "neglected deaf and blind baby" she had learned about from Louisville, Kentucky, but was persuaded against it. Keller explained, "It was only after many an unwilling argument that we who knew of her failing health induced her to give up the idea of adopting the baby. But her darkness throbbed with the hidden fire of that longing"(Keller 217).

On October 20, 1935, Annie died of heart disease in Forest Hills. Helen died in 1968. The ashes of Anne Sullivan Macy and Helen Keller are interred together at the Washington National Cathedral.

Works Cited

Keller, Helen. *Teacher: A Tribute by the Foster-Child of Her Mind.* New York: Doubleday, 1955.

Lash, Joseph P. *Helen and Teacher: The Story of Helen Keller and Anne Sullivan Macy.* New York: Delacorte/Seymour Lawrence, 1980.

MANDELA, NELSON (1918–)

Human Rights Leader, President of South Africa, Nobel Laureate
Adoptee

Career, Major Awards, and Achievements

On February 11, 1990, Nelson Mandela walked out of the maximum-security prison in South Africa, after what he has described as twenty-seven years of prison and silence, and immediately took a place as one of the world's political and moral leaders. Four years later he was elected President of South Africa, and today he serves as a world-ranking diplomat and elder statesman.

In 1993, with South African President F. W. de Klerk, Mandela won the Nobel Peace Prize. During his years in prison, Mandela received the Bruno Kreisky Prize for Human Rights (1982), was named an Honorary Citizen of Rome (1983), and received the Sakharov Prize (1988) and the Gaddaff Human Rights Prize (1989). He shared the Houphouet Prize in 1991.

Mandela and others helped create the ANC (African National Congress)Youth League, which looked toward "the overthrow of white supremacy and the establishment of a truly democratic form of government," according to Mandela. Eventually the Youth League would dominate the ANC party, gaining strength from opposition. In 1948 the National Party (the Nationalists) had come to power and began establishing "apartheid," a system of racial segregation that changed prevailing custom to law. The Nationalists outlawed Communism, using a definition so encompassing that nearly anyone could be considered a communist. The ANC demanded that the new laws be repealed and Mandela helped organize the Campaign for the Defiance of Unjust Laws. Protesters entered "white only" areas, used "white only" entrances, and participated in strikes. Mandela and others were convicted of "statutory communism" (Mandela was not a member of the Communist Party) and "banned"—prohibited from attending gatherings—for several months.

In late 1956 Mandela and 155 others were charged with treason, accused of trying to replace the government with a Communist government. The government was unable to prove that ANC members had plotted violent revolution and the defendants were acquitted. Shortly afterward, a warrant for Mandela's arrest was issued. In 1960 the government had made membership in the ANC illegal, and Mandela was a member, now living as a fugitive. In the early 1960s, the government began meeting ANC-sponsored nonviolent actions with violence, and Mandela was chosen to organize an armed branch of the ANC called Spear of the Nation. In 1962 he was arrested for inciting workers to strike and for leaving the country without valid documents. Having qualified to practice law ten years earlier, Mandela argued his own case, not denying the charges, which were true, but declaring that the government had used the law to make him an outlaw. He was sentenced to five years in prison without the possibility of parole.

[Courtesy of the Embassy of South Africa]

Shortly afterward, authorities raided ANC headquarters at a farm in Rivonia; the raid provided them with evidence that the ANC planned to use guerilla tactics against the government. ANC leaders, including Mandela, were tried for treason. The defendants were found guilty and sentenced to life in prison with no chance of parole. The Rivonia Trial focused media on South Africa and generated sympathy for the ANC leaders, with a *New York Times* editorial pronouncing the government the "ultimate guilty party" and maintaining that the South African government was guilty in world opinion.

For the next eighteen years, Mandela was imprisoned in a maximum security facility on Robben Island, off the coast of South Africa. His first cell was seven feet square; he could receive one short letter and one visitor every six months. Conditions slowly improved; though prisoners were forbidden to read newspapers (they nevertheless did), they were permitted to take correspondence courses from the University of London. Beginning in the 1970s, political study groups were sometimes permitted, and in 1980, the *Johannesburg Sunday Post* printed a petition for the release of Mandela and other ANC leaders. A new generation of young black South Africans was making apartheid an important political issue and the government was beginning to recognize that there would have to be some accommodation.

In 1985 President P. W. Botha offered to free political prisoners if they agreed to unconditionally repudiate violence. Mandela refused, believing that the government's use of violence against the ANC left the ANC no alternative but to use violence in return. However, Mandela sensed a change in government attitude and began working toward the idea of conducting secret talks with the government in the hope of reaching a compromise between the government and the ANC. In 1988 Mandela was transferred to Victor Verster Prison, near Cape Town, where talks continued. The following year Botha stepped down, to be replaced by F. W. de Klerk. Mandela soon realized that de Klerk recognized that change was inevitable. Mandela was correct; shortly after becoming president, de Klerk began overturning many of the laws that enforced apartheid and in February 1990 lifted the ban on opposition organizations, including the ANC. Mandela was released on February 11.

A few months later, he embarked on a world tour, meeting world leaders and being welcomed as a world leader himself. He returned to South Africa to work with de Klerk as leaders of the Convention for a Democratic South Africa, which directed that a freely elected constitutional assembly would draft a new constitution for South Africa and that the first elections open to all South African citizens would be held in April 1994. For their work, de Klerk and Mandela were awarded the Nobel Peace Prize for 1993.

Mandela became the ANC candidate for president, and the ANC carried 62.6 of the vote. Mandela included members of the ANC and its rival Inkatha Freedom Party, as well as Nationalists, in his cabinet in order to advance tolerance and understanding among South Africa's diverse ethnic and political groups. At the end of his five year term, Mandela left office and now serves as an elder statesman and diplomat addressing the problems of the world.

Family of Origin

Mandela was born July 18, 1918, in Mvezo, a village on South Africa's southeast coast. His father, Gadla Henry Mphakanyiswa, was a member of the royal house of the Thembu tribe and was the chief of Mvezo. Mandela's mother was his father's third wife:

> All told, my father had four wives, the third of whom, my mother, Nosekeni Fanny, the daughter of Nkedama from the amaMpemvu clan of the Xhosa, belonged to the Right Hand House. Each of these wives—the Great Wife, the Right Hand wife (my mother), the Left Hand wife, and the wife of the Iqadi or support house—had her own kraal [homestead]. . . my father sired thirteen children in all, four boys and nine girls. I am the eldest child of the Right Hand House and the youngest of my father's four sons. I have three sisters, Baliwe, who was the oldest girl, Notancu, and Makutswana. . . .
>
> My mother presided over three huts at Qunu which, as I remember were always filled with the babies and children of my relations. . . . In African culture, the sons and daughters

of one's aunts or uncles are considered brothers and sisters, not cousins. We do not make the same distinctions among relations practiced by whites. We have no half-brothers or half-sisters. My mother's sister is my mother; my uncle's son is my brother; my brother's child is my son, my daughter (Mandela 5–6).

Adoption

Mandela's father died of lung disease when the boy was nine years old. After a brief period of mourning, his mother took him to the capital of Thembuland, Mqhekezweni, where he became the ward and adopted son of the regent Chief Jongintaba Dalindyebo:

> I later learned that, in the wake of my father's death, Jongintaba had offered to become my guardian. He would treat me as he treated his other children, and I would have the same advantages as they. My mother had no choice; one did not turn down such an overture from the regent. . . . Children are often the least sentimental of creatures, especially if they are absorbed in some new pleasure. Even as my dear mother and first friend was leaving, my head was swimming with the delights of my new home (Mandela 15).

Mandela's mother visited him in prison in the spring of 1968. She had made a long journey in ill health from the Tanskei and the prison granted her a forty-five-minute visit with her son. She died of a heart attack several months later.

Education and Significant Relationships

Though his education at Methodist primary and secondary schools taught him to think of himself as a "black Englishman," Madela was also lastingly influenced by the training of his mentor and guardian, Jongintaba, who taught that a leader is like a shepherd who directs his flock from behind. Mandela credited this mentor for his belief in leadership through consensus.

In spite of the respect Mandela had for his guardian, his western education made him unwilling to submit to marriage with a woman of his guardian's choice in accordance with tribal tradition, and in 1941 he ran away to Johannesburg, where he took a job as a law clerk for a liberal Jewish firm. At that time, he began a correspondence course from the University of South Africa, which awarded him a BA in 1942. In 1943, he began work on a Bachelor of Law degree at the University of Witwatersrand, where he found people of a wide variety of political thought. Friends urged him to consider joining the Communist party and the African National Congress. Mandela considered carefully and decided that his own ideas and interests were most similar to those of the ANC, which he joined in 1944. He has received a great number of honorary doctorates, including a joint honorary degree from thirty-eight traditionally black American universities (1990), presented during a ceremony at Morehouse College in Atlanta.

From 1944 until their divorce in 1956, Mandela was married to Evelyn Mase, a nurse. The marriage produced four children (one died in infancy). In 1958 he married Nomzamo Winnie Madikizela, a young social worker. They lived together for four years before Mandela was imprisoned and have two daughters. Winnie Mandela served as principal spokesperson for her husband and became well known in her own right. Her reputation was badly damaged by charges of criminal involvement, and Mandela distanced himself from her; they separated in 1992. In 1996, Graca Machel became Mandela's "official companion." Machel, a lawyer and freedom fighter, is the widow of former President Samora Machel of Mozambique, and served as that country's education minister. She and Mandela married in 1998.

Works Cited

Lodge, Tom. *Mandela: A Critical Life.* New York: Oxford University Press, 2006.

Maharaj, Mac, et al. *Mandela: The Authorized Portrait.* Kansas City, MO: Andrews McMeel, 2006.

Mandela, Nelson. *Long Walk to Freedom: The Autobiography of Nelson Mandela.* Boston: Little, Brown, 1994.

MCDANIELS, DARRYL (1964–)

Singer, Songwriter
Late-discovery adoptee

Career, Major Awards, and Achievements

Hip Hop pioneers Darryl "DMC" McDaniels, Joseph "Rev Run" Simmons, and Jason "Jam Master Jay" Mizell established the group Run-D.M.C. in 1983 with their debut single "It's Like That." With their subsequent albums, *RUN-D.M.C.* (1984), *King of Rock* (1985), *Raising Hell* (1986), *Tougher Than Leather* (1988), *Back from Hell* (1990), and *Down with the King* (1993), the group is credited with breaking down existing barriers and bringing rap into the music mainstream. Their Web site (www.rundmc.com) notes a number of "firsts" the group achieved. They were the "first rap act to earn RIAA gold, platinum, and multiplatinum albums." Theirs was the first rap group to appear on the cover of *Rolling Stone*, receive a Grammy nomination, appear on Saturday Night Live, and perform at Live Aid. In celebration of the Fiftieth Anniversary of Rock, *Rolling Stone* magazine produced its "Immortals" edition, which honored "the fifty greatest artists of all time." In it, Run-D.M.C. is called "the Beatles of hip-hop," and is credited with creating "the first true rap album" and directly influencing more than two decades of hip hop artists (D. 138).

McDaniels struggled with a serious depression that intensified during a Run-D.M.C. European tour in 1997. He had a history of drug and alcohol abuse, including several arrests for driving under the influence and public intoxication. During the tour, he began to experience problems with his voice, later diagnosed as spasmodic dysphonia, a disorder that features involuntary spasms in the larynx and was caused, he believes, by a combination of heavy drinking and his aggressive vocal performances. Separated by the tour from his wife and newborn son, McDaniels says that he was on the verge of suicide when he heard Canadian music star Sarah McLachlan's song "Angel" on a car radio. He felt a powerful connection to her music, which he credits with literally saving his life at that time (Frauenhofer). What he would discover three years later was that both he and Sarah McLachlan were adopted.

McDaniels experienced creative differences with other members of Run-D.M.C. and appeared on only three songs of their 2001 *Crown Royal* album. The group retired following the death of Jason Mizell, who was gunned down in a Queens recording studio in 2002. The trio has brought out successful remixes and Greatest Hits collections, and McDaniels and Simmons have both gone on to release solo albums. On McDaniels' first solo, *Checks, Thugs and Rock N Roll* (2006), he collaborated with Sarah McLachlan on the song "Just Like Me," an adoptee remake of Harry Chapin's "Cat's in the Cradle." "Just Like Me" also appears on McLachlan's 2008 album *Rarities, B-sides & Other Stuff.*

[AP Photo/Daron Cummings]

McDaniels was thirty-five years old when he found out that he had been adopted. He had called his parents to ask for basic details about his birth to be included in his auto-biography, *King of Rock: Respect, Responsibility, and My Life with Run-D.M.C.*, published in 2001. They gave him a few facts, hung up, and an hour later called back to tell him that he had been adopted. Stunned and setting out with only his birthday and a partially correct name for his mother, McDaniels began to seek his origins in October 2000. He asked VH1 to film his search and the result is a remarkable documentary entitled *DMC: My Adoption Journey*. In a *PopMatters* interview, McDaniels says:

> Up until the point that DMC found out that he was adopted, I was living my life from chapter two, it was a whole new beginning. . . a whole 'nother life, a whole 'nother purpose, and once I got to the beginning of it, everything's finally starting to make sense, but there's still a lot of emotions, naturally. . . .
>
> I'ma do the documentary, the first three days was cool, but by the third day I was ready to quit, because all of the emotions and the issues that was coming up. . . but then, I had to keep going, 'cause I kept meeting young little kids, women, birth mothers, birth fathers, they said, "D, what you're doing is a good thing, this is gonna help me." . . . So it got really scary, 'cause I'm not a role model. . . it was very hard, but it was easy, because it wasn't just all about me, it was about *all the people* (Frauenhofer).

Other adopted persons can relate wholeheartedly as the camera captures McDaniel's excruciating progress through information roadblocks, sealed records, support groups, and the paralyzing fears that precede initial contact with birth families. With the help of Pamela Slaton, a fellow adoptee and professional searcher, McDaniels succeeded in locating his first mother and the film concludes with their reunion. *DMC: My Adoption Journey* won a 2007 Emmy Award for "Outstanding Arts and Culture Programming." Even before winning his Emmy, McDaniels was passionately involved with adoption reform and helping children in foster care. He writes on his Web site (http://www.me-dmc.com/index.cfm/):

> It is now confirmed that the responsibility of being put here to be DMC, blessed with the culture of Hip Hop as my foundation, the journey has not ended, but now has just begun. DMC means Deliver My Children! And I'm gonna do exactly that! . . . There's going to be someone there reppin to the fullest for them! I'm bringing truth and justice for all these kids now, and for the ones already laying in the graves! And for my fellow adoptees, I am going to remove the guilt and the shame from the triad, birth-mom, adoptee, and adopted parents, and thus will remove the pain. If you thought this documentary changed a multitude of lives, my next project will change lives again, change laws, change history, and change the world!

In 2006, McDaniels coestablished the Felix Organization: Adoptees For Children (http://adopteesforchildren.org/) with fellow adoptee Sheila Jaffe, the *Sopranos* casting director. Their mission is to help enrich the lives of children in foster care. The organization operates a summer camp, Camp Felix, in Putnam Valley, New York. In September 2006, McDaniels was recognized for his work with foster children and adoption by a Congressional "Angels in Adoption" award. In 2008, McDaniels became a partner with Children's Aid and Family Services and he continues to contribute his time, resources, and celebrity to promote adoption.

Family of Origin

McDaniels was born on May 31, 1964, in Harlem to Berncenia Lovelace, who was a teenager at the time of his birth. They were reunited on November 19, 2005. Lovelace did not know that her son was famous until their first meeting. He has two half-brothers and a half-sister.

Adoption

Byford and Bannah McDaniels adopted Darryl when he was one month old and raised him in Hollis, Queens. His brother, Alford, is three years older than Darryl. In his autobiography, McDaniels describes his parents as "always hard working, on time, on point, never failed, taking care of business" (103) and says that his childhood was a very happy one. His adoptive family was upset by his decision to search for his first family.

Education and Significant Relationships

Although neither of his parents were Catholic, McDaniels was educated entirely in private Catholic schools, including an all boys' high school where he earned straight A's, graduating in 1982. He attended St. John's University in New York City as a business management major, but left college after two semesters to pursue his music career.

McDaniels married Zuri L. Alston on September 28, 1992. Their son, Darryl M. McDaniels, Jr., known as "DSon," was born July 27, 1994, in Queens, New York. The family lives in New Jersey.

In January 24, 2008, McDaniels appeared before a New Jersey state Senate panel. His testimony supported a bill that would allow adult adoptees access to their original birth records.

Works Cited

D., Chuck. "The Immortals # 48: Run-D.M.C." *Rolling Stone* 946 (April 15, 2004): 138.

Frauenhofer, Michael. "Just Like Me: An Interview with DMC." *PopMatters.* June 30, 2006. http://www.popmatters.com/music/interviews/dmc-060630.shtml

Heffernan, Virginia. "After the Hit Records, a Search for His Roots." *New York Times.* February 25, 2006: B11. *Lexis Nexis Academic.* February 14, 2007 www.lexisnexis.com.skyline.cu denver.edu/us/lnacademic/

McDaniels, Darryl, with Bruce Harring. *King of Rock: Respect, Responsibility, and My Life with Run-D.M.C.* New York: St. Martin's Press, 2001.

MCKENZIE, RICHARD B. (1942–)

Educator, Author
Orphanage alumnus, Barium Springs Home for Children 1952–1959

Career, Major Awards, and Achievements

Richard McKenzie is the Walter B. Gerken Professor of Enterprise and Society at the University of California at Irvine's School of Management. He currently teaches courses for MBA students on microeconomics, management, and economics. He has won numerous teaching awards and has written more than twenty books, and he is the author of over a hundred scholarly articles, pamphlets, and news articles.

McKenzie became actively involved in the orphanage debate of 1994, headed by Newt Gingrich. Critics assailed orphanages for having damaged the children in their care, an assessment McKenzie considers grossly unfair, as he wrote in the *Wall Street Journal*:

> Most critics would like the public to believe that those of us who went through orphanages were throttled by the experience. No doubt, some were. However, most have charged on. In many ways, we represent the best of what this country is about—plumbers and nurses, ministers and managers, teachers and baggage handlers—in the main, good, well-meaning Americans who have answered the call to rise above expectations.

McKenzie is an advocate for the reestablishment and reform of children's institutions and is a prominent scholar of adult orphanage alumni. He draws on his early experiences for writings such as *The Home: A Memoir of Growing Up in an Orphanage* (1996), *Rethinking Orphanages for the 21st Century* (1998), congressional testimony on child welfare options (July 1999), and numerous articles.

Family of Origin

Richard McKenzie was born March 7, 1942, in Raleigh, North Carolina, to alcoholic parents who let him run wild on the streets of Raleigh. When he was ten years old, his mother committed suicide and he, along with a younger brother, was placed in the Barium Springs Home for Children ("The Home") at Piedmont, North Carolina.

Orphanage

McKenzie remained at the home until high school graduation night, when orphanage residents were expected to move out of the facility. He regards his experiences in the home as imperfect, but overall very positive:

> For most of us, The Home was a place to change course. It offered a set of experiences that were life-focusing. It gave us constraints, direction, purpose, and inspiration. The Home in rural North Carolina is no longer a place, although a few of the old buildings still stand. Now it represents a state of mind, a past we cannot forget and would not if we could (7).

McKenzie credits his success in life to advantages provided by his institution and its facilities, which included a working farm, hundreds of wooded acres, a pool, and a gymnasium. At The Home, he was imbued with a work ethic and sense of personal responsibility and was given a chance to go to college at The Home's expense.

Education and Significant Relationships

McKenzie earned his PhD in Economics at Virginia Tech in 1972. He married and is the father of four children.

Works Cited

McKenzie, Richard. *The Home: A Memoir of Growing Up in an Orphanage.* New York: Basic Books, 1996.

MENDIETA, ANA (1948–1985)

Artist
Operation Pedro Pan Refugee, orphanage alumna, and fostered person

Career, Major Awards, and Achievements

Ana Mendieta was a Cuban-American artist best known for her feminist art, especially her performance art, and for the controversy surrounding her untimely death. Like Frida Kahlo, her art was both personal and political, and she used her body as her chief inspiration, but unlike Kahlo, she did not use paint as her principal medium.

When her alma mater, the University of Iowa, opened a video art program that became a center of avant-garde expression, Mendieta enrolled and was introduced to state-of-the-art technology and the newest ideas and concepts. Simultaneously, she sought a return to her roots. She studied Caribbean and Latin culture, art, literature, history, anthropology, and sociology. In 1971, she participated in an archaeological dig in Mexico, returning in 1973, 1974, 1976, and 1978. She also became interested in and influenced by the rituals of Santeria, a Caribbean religion with African origins, which was reflected in her work throughout most of the 1970s.

Mendieta became an American citizen in 1970 and began performance art the same year, documenting her performance pieces on film and in photographs. Violence against the female body, including sexual abuse, was one of her major themes. Many of her performances made disturbing use of quantities of animal blood, which she claimed connected her with "Ochun," a Santeria goddess of feminine power (Cabañas 13). Some of her blood art includes *Bird Transformation* (1972), *Rape-Murder* (1973), *Sweating Blood* (1973), *Blood Writing* (1974), and *Body Tracks* (1974).

In 1975, she participated in a group show in New York City, and the following year the same gallery, the 112 Greene Street Gallery, gave her a solo show. In the late 1970s Mendieta "moved from a direct presentation of her body to a more focused search for identity and connectedness" (Cabañas 14). She fused multimedia with performance art to imprint her small* third-world woman's body into the land, claiming a place for it and the people it represented. Her *Silueta* pieces involved carving or impressing her silhouette into mud or sand or using her body to paint her image or movements onto walls. In 1977, she traced her image onto a mound of earth using gunpowder and set it on fire. Her work was admired for its mixture of the ephemeral (sand, gunpowder, or other materials which did not last) with relative permanence (photos or film, which were used in shows later) and for her mixture of beauty and danger. Altogether she created over 200 works using earth as her medium (Blocker 45). After completing her MFA, Mendieta moved to New York City in 1978, where she worked as a waitress to make ends meet. It was not long, however, before she became a notable member of the art community there.

In 1980, Mendieta received grants from the National Endowment for the Arts and the Guggenheim Foundation, and with an invitation from the Cuban government, she returned to her native land for the first time since 1961, feeling "afraid before I went there because I felt I've been living my life with this obsessive thing in my mind—what if I find out it has nothing to do with me? But the minute I got there, it was this whole thing of belonging again" (Cabañas 15).

When she returned to the United States, she served as a co-curator of a *The Dialectics of Isolation*, a show which featured the work of third-world women artists living in the United States. Mendieta made a second trip to Cuba in 1981, with the support of the Ministry of Culture, to take the *Silueta* series "to its source" (Cabañas 15). In Cuba, she created her *Rupestrian* series (1981) by carving archetypal goddess images into the natural limestone formations at the Jaruco State Park near Havana. The series includes *Guabancex* (Goddess of the Wind), *Guanaroca* (First Woman) and *Atabey* (Mother of the Waters). In New York, she exhibited life-sized black and white photos of the carvings at the A.I.R. Gallery in November, 1981.

---

*Mendieta's autopsy report listed her height as four feet, ten inches, and her weight as ninety-three pounds. (Katz 17)

The new decade marked a time of change for Mendieta. She moved away from the ephemeral and began to make lasting works. She was commissioned to produce a permanent public piece in Hartford, Connecticut, and she created a female form, *Arbitra*, from a seven-foot log burned with gunpowder. She next worked with bark, paper and dry leaves to make small portable "totems" of female forms and labyrinths. In 1983, she accepted a fellowship from the American Academy in Rome and began working in a studio for the first time, dividing her time equally between Italy and the United States. She expressed her desire to take her art in a new direction: "I don't feel that I can emulate nature. Installation is a fake art. So I've given this problem to myself—to work indoors" (Marks 256). In Rome, she created the mosaic-like *Stonewoman* series (1983) using marble chips. She also experimented with some less successful sand and binder floor reliefs, which one critic called "giant biscuits" (Marks 256). In 1984, she was working with freestanding sculpture, creating tree trunks in which human forms were burned or carved or both. She was preparing seven of these pieces for an outdoor exhibit in Los Angeles at the time of her sudden death.

Family of Origin and *Operation Pedro Pan*

Ana Maria Mendieta was born in Havana, Cuba, on November 18, 1948, to Raquel (Oti) Mendieta, a scientist educated at the University of Havana and a former "Miss Varadero" beauty queen, and Ignacio Alberto Mendieta, a lawyer with family connections to highly placed political people. Ana's maternal great-grandfather, Carlos María de Rojas, had been a famous general in Cuba's War of Independence and her grandfather had been consul to Spain. Following Batista's coup in 1934, Ana's uncle, Carlos Mendieta, served as the provisional president of Cuba until he resigned in 1935.

Ana's father initially aided Castro's 1959 revolution against Batista. However, when Castro identified the revolution as Marxist-Leninist, Ignacio Mendieta, a Catholic and anti-Communist, became an active counter-revolutionary. When Castro abolished private schools and instituted a program to send school children fourteen years and older to the country to teach rural people to read and write, the Mendietas feared that Raquelín, Ana's fourteen year old sister, would be recruited, sent away, and indoctrinated with Socialist thought. After a seventeen-year-old friend of the girls was sentenced to thirty years in prison for distributing antigovernment leaflets that the Mendieta sisters had also distributed, the family made a decision to try and get the girls out of Cuba.

In 1961, Ana and Raquelín left for the United States through a program called *Operation Pedro Pan*, which brought 14,048 Cuban children to the United States in "the largest recorded exodus of unaccompanied minors in the Western Hemisphere" (www.pedropan.org). The program was funded through U.S. corporations, citizen donations, and Catholic Charities. About half of the exiles were taken in by their family members and friends, while the other half went to facilities located for them through the Catholic Services Bureau, under the direction of Father Bryan O. Walsh.

Orphanages and Foster Homes

Raquelín had just turned fifteen and Ana was twelve when they arrived at the Miami International Airport on September 11, 1961. The sisters had no American family or friends to come for them, so they spent three weeks awaiting relocation at Camp Kendall, a Miami refugee camp. On October 5, 1961, they were sent to St. Mary's Home in Dubuque, Iowa, which was then a home for disturbed and delinquent girls. The language barrier was only one of many problems the girls faced in their new home, as Raquelín explains:

> We had never heard of Dubuque, we didn't even know how to pronounce it. . . . We really didn't want to leave Kendall, we felt safe there, we felt we knew the language. There were six of us scheduled to leave, three sets of sisters, and none of us wanted to leave, but we had no choice, we were not asked whether you wanted to leave. . . . [At Saint Mary's, one] of the girls in our dormitory had stabbed her mother with a pair of scissors. Another had thrown someone down a well. Another had tried to strangle a counselor and push her over the balcony. . . . One had committed armed burglary of a gas station, one had been raped by her stepfather, ran away from home, and requested to be taken in. Another girl was picked up in the streets for having switchblade fights with men.
>
> These were the people that we went to live with. We came from middle-class homes in Cuba, and we had lived a very sheltered life. Our culture calls for young girls to be chaperoned everywhere they go. We went from living that kind of life to living in this kind of environment where every second you didn't know whether you were going to be killed or someone was going to beat you up or what was going to happen to you (Conde 119–120).

St. Mary's had a policy to switch roommates and furniture around every few weeks (Conde 121), which only added more insecurity to the girls' environment. After nine months at St. Mary's, the sisters were sent to a foster home, the Butlers, but were returned to the orphanage seven months later. They were next sent to a boarding school, Our Lady of the Angels Academy, in Clinton, Iowa. When the school year was over, the girls went to the city children's home in Cedar Rapids, which was also a half-way house for youth coming out of the Mitchellville reform school (Katz 134). The girls were separated when Raquelín graduated from high school and began to attend and room at college during their third year in Iowa. Ana became interested in art during this year, which her sister called "the worst year without our family. . . [we] had, by then, suffered many levels of abuse at the hands of our keepers" (Moure 228).

Ana, who had three foster homes by the time she graduated, was finally sent to live with a foster family she liked, the Saddlers, a young couple and their new baby. She, however, had many difficulties at Regis High School, which she entered her junior year. The Mendieta sisters, whose prominent family claimed Spanish ancestry, were unprepared for the racism they encountered at their schools. As Raquelín said, "It never entered our minds that we were colored" (Blocker 53). Called "nigger" and "whore" and told "go back to Cuba" (Cabañas 12), the girls soon dissociated themselves from the white Midwesterners.

Raquelín, who also became an artist, wrote: "In a strange way, I believe Ana and I were able to become artists because we left Cuba" (Moure 223). Ana also realized that her profound alienation and her search to recover identity and roots were critical aspects of her art. She said:

> My art is grounded in the belief in one Universal Energy which runs through everything from insect to man, from man to spectre, from spectre to plant, from plant to galaxy. . . . There is no original past to redeem; there is the void, the orphanhood, the unbaptized earth of the beginning, the time that from within the earth links upon us. There is above all the search for origin (Blocker 34).

Biographers and critics agree that Mendieta's youthful exile is the key to understanding her mature art:

Friends say such turmoil on the cusp of adolescence was the reason Mendieta, who died in 1985, spent the rest of her life trying to claim a sense of belonging through her art.

In an exhibit. . . at the Des Moines Art Center, Mendieta's photographs, sculpture, drawings, and performance art convey her deep longing to define her identity.

"For Ana, the longing to find a place or an identity is something you cannot avoid in her work," Fleming said. "It's a direct attempt to connect with her past. . . . She lived between cultures, between languages, and this is something every displaced person goes through" (Dvorak).

Ana was seventeen when she reunited with her mother and her seven-year old brother, Ignacio, when they emigrated from Cuba on January 29, 1966. Ana's father had been arrested in 1965, accused being a spy for the CIA. He spent eighteen years of his twenty-year sentence in prison. In order to petition the U.S. government to help him, his family needed to be U.S. citizens. Ana, and especially Raquelín, had become disillusioned with the United States and were not happy about declaring allegiance to it, but Ana convinced Raquel that they needed U.S. passports if they were going to be able to leave the United States, and Ana longed to travel. Ana's father was finally able to join the rest of the family, who had settled in Cedar Rapids, in 1979.

Education and Significant Relationships

Ana attended a Catholic school, El Apostolado del Sagrado Corazón, before she left Cuba. She graduated from Regis High School in Cedar Rapids, Iowa, in 1965.

She initially attended Briar Cliff University in Sioux City, but transferred to the University of Iowa, where she earned a BA in 1969 and a master's degree in painting in 1972. She enrolled in University of Iowa's experimental Intermedia Program for the New Performing Arts, where she was mentored by Hans Breder, with whom she also had a romantic relationship. She completed her MFA there in 1977. In the mid-1970s she taught elementary school art while developing her own style, a unique combination of civil rights, feminism, and advanced technology that "pushed the boundaries of art" (Dvorak 2).

At a Soho exhibit in 1979, Mendieta met Carl Andre, an American minimalist artist and poet. Andre, who was thirteen years Mendieta's senior, was already an established sculptor with works in the Guggenheim, Whitney, and Tate museums. The couple married in Rome in January 1985. On September 8 of that year, Mendieta fell from their Manhattan apartment window and plunged thirty-four floors to her death. Andre claimed that Mendieta committed suicide, but a grand jury indicted him for her murder. Although Ana's sister (now Mrs. Raquel Harrington) and her mother were convinced of his guilt, Andre was acquitted at his nonjury trial on February 11, 1988, by Judge Alvin Schlesinger, who found that guilt could not be proven beyond a reasonable doubt.

Mendieta's ashes are buried in Cedar Rapids, Iowa.

Works Cited

Blocker, Jane. *Where Is Ana Mendieta? Identity, Performativity, and Exile.* Durham, NC: Duke University Press, 1999.

Cabañas, Kaira M. "Ana Mendieta: Pain of Cuba, Body I Am." *Woman's Art Journal* 20 (Spring/Summer 1999): 12–17.

Conde, Yvonne M. *Operation Pedro Pan: The Untold Exodus of 14,048 Cuban Children.* New York: Routledge, 1999.

Dvorak, Todd. "Collection of Works by Cuban Exile Who Settled in Iowa on Display." *Associated Press State and Local Wire,* February 16, 2005. Campus Research (Westlaw). Auraria Library, Denver CO. January 23, 2008.

Katz, Robert. *Naked by the Window: The Fatal Marriage of Carl Andre and Ana Mendieta.* New York: Atlantic Monthly Press, 1990.

Marks, Claude, Ed. "Ana Mendieta." *World Artists 1980–1990.* New York: H. W. Wilson, 1991.

Moure, Gloria. *Ana Mendieta.* Barcelona: Ediciones Polígrafa, 1996.

MICHENER, JAMES A. (1907–1997)

Author, Educator, Philanthropist
Foundling, adoptee, fictitious birth information

Career, Major Awards, and Achievements

Between 1947 and his death in 1997, James A. Michener wrote forty-nine books that together sold 100 million copies and were translated into approximately fifty languages. Several of his books became successful motion pictures (*Hawaii*), theatrical productions (*South Pacific*), or television mini-series (*Centennial*).

Michener began his career writing a sports column for the local newspaper and editing his high school newspaper. Scholarships took him through college. He earned degrees at Swarthmore and the Colorado State College of Education (now the University of Northern Colorado, where the library is named after him). In 1931, a Lippincott grant provided money for travel and study in Scotland, England, Spain, and Italy. Altogether he attended nine colleges and held nineteen honorary doctorates.

After receiving his MA, Michener taught first English and then history, and later worked for a textbook company as an editor. During World War II, he served with the Navy in the Pacific and began writing fiction. *Tales of the South Pacific* (1948) won a Pulitzer Prize and was adapted for the stage as the tremendously successful musical *South Pacific. Sayonara* (1954) was made into a movie, and in 1959, *Hawaii* was published.

Michener had settled in Hawai'i in 1949. While he worked on other projects, he researched and wrote the book that would become his breakthrough novel, creating a format that was to become characteristic for him. *Hawaii* was a huge book, beginning with the volcanic origins of the islands and containing novella length sections about every group that settled there: the first Hawai'ians, the missionaries, the Chinese, the Japanese, and the mixture of cultures that make up the modern population. Michener combined personal knowledge, factual research, and good storytelling to produce a blockbuster best-seller. Over forty years later, it is still in print. Most of his subsequent books followed the same geographical/historical fact mixed with fiction pattern.

Caravans (1963) and *The Source* (1965) combined the monumental scope of *Hawaii* with a typical Michener theme of Americans in exotic places, and *Centennial*, published in 1974, celebrated Colorado on the same scale. Michener was interested in the lives of young Americans, both in fiction (*The Drifters*, 1971) and fact (*Kent State: What Happened and Why*, 1971). His social concerns were reflected in his political activities. In 1960, having moved back to Pennsylvania from Hawai'i, he was chairman of the Bucks County Citizens for Kennedy. In 1962 he tried for a seat in the House of Representatives

[AP Photo/Marty Lederhandler]

and in 1968 he ran for elector. The last experience produced a book on electoral reform, *Presidential Lottery: The Reckless Gamble in Our Electoral System.*

In the early 1980s, Michener moved to Texas at the invitation of the governor, to write about Texas. *Texas* was published in 1985, *Alaska* came out in 1988, and his auto-biography, *The World Is My Home,* in 1992. Michener earned $117 million dollars from his writing. Much of it was given to colleges, libraries, and museums, making him one of the great twentieth-century philanthropists. The books that Michener believed would live longest are those about Asian art, which include *The Floating World*, a history of the art of Japanese prints, and *The Hokusai Sketchbook*, which he edited. It is based on 257 plates of prints from Michener's personal collection.

Family of Origin and "Adoption"

Michener's foster mother, Mabel (Haddock) Michener, was a widow who took in many foster children, especially infants born to unwed mothers, whom she raised along with her son, Robert. Mabel worked finishing buttonholes, doing laundry, and cleaning houses for a real estate company, and she and the children lived in poverty, moved often, and were often shunned by the Doylestown, Pennsylvania, community where they lived. James's bones did not develop properly as a result of malnutrition and there was frequent illness in the home. When Mabel became seriously ill, she sent James to be looked after by her sister, Hannah, whose husband ran the local poorhouse. Michener called his six-week stay in the poorhouse "the end of the line," and he vowed to never end up there again:

> I had very bad moments. We don't have poorhouses like that now. When you go through the kind of childhood I had—the kind that does kids in—you harden up a bit. I was just a tough little son of a bitch. The hard years were from zero to fourteen* (Grobel 4).

Michener grew up believing that he was the son of Mabel and her late husband, Edwin. In fact, most of the children she fostered thought so, as one girl later remarked: "We were just a bunch of happy little kids. I think there were seven of us, and we all got along. We all thought we were brothers and sisters and that Mabel was our mother" (Hayes 16).

Biographers May and Hayes write convincingly that James's "foster" mother had in fact given birth to him, although she never acknowledged it during her lifetime. Her son Robert, five years old at the time, actually recalls being in the same room when the birth occurred, on or near February 3, 1907, at Arthur Haddock's home in Mount Vernon, New York:

> Strange how vivid this one memory is. . . . I remember Hannah Haddock, mother's youngest sister, a young nurse in training, doing all the chores for mother—alone. I remember lying on a cot in the same room with Arthur Haddock, mother's youngest brother, lying on his side and shielding me from any view of the proceedings. Also trying to quiet me. It was thus that James Albert [Michener] entered this world, so help me God (Hayes 13).

Of all the fostered children Mabel raised, only Robert and James were given her married name and only James and Robert inherited her small savings. James also had a resemblance to Mabel.

One day, when James was nineteen years old and in his junior year at Swarthmore College, Edwin's brother Louis clarified that Edwin could not have been his father, since he had died in 1902, five years before Michener's birth. When James then asked Mabel

---

*At fourteen, Michener was offered a summer job at the Willow Grove Amusement Park. He had taken his first paying job at the age of nine, cultivating phlox for the Burpee Seed Farm, which he did not enjoy: "If my birthday were tomorrow and someone were to give me a bouquet of the horrid flowers, I would punch him in the nose" (Severson 2).

for the truth about his origins, she told him that he was adopted, brought to her in February 1907 as a foundling infant, one or two weeks old, and that no further information was known about him.

Mabel Michener was the saving grace of James Michener's childhood, but pride must have prevented her from telling the truth about his birth. When Louis revealed her secret, she twisted the facts. Someone—she said she could not remember who—told her James had been born in Mount Vernon, New York, several days before she claimed him. But she knew nothing more. She insisted that she had "adopted" him—though never officially—named him James Albert after a favorite uncle, and loved him like her own son.

There were many crises in James Michener's childhood, but none could have troubled him more than Louis's and Mabel's revelations. After nineteen years of believing he was the child of a father he never knew and a mother he cherished, he was suddenly no one. For weeks he asked questions and searched for information. Who was he? What was his nationality? Were his parents still alive? Was he abandoned? Should he feel ashamed or betrayed? He asked Mabel's two sisters to help him, but they volunteered nothing, saying they did not know the circumstances of his birth. He looked for a birth certificate, but found none. Finally, convinced that he could learn nothing more about his birth, he vowed to accept Mabel's upsetting story. "I decided to hell with it," he explained years later. "I was never going to know what really happened, and I wasn't going to worry about it again. I put it out of my mind when I was nineteen" (Hayes 12).

He was never able to "put it out of his mind," however, and his foundling status and lack of official records were often an "acute" problem in his life. He writes:

> Although the extensive Michener clan has always welcomed me, and although I have appreciated their friendship and have maintained close association with them... I am not a Michener, I am not related to them. Actually, I do not know who my parents were, or where or when I was born. I never had a birth certificate. The problem became acute in 1931, when I wished to get a passport for travel in Europe. At that time my foster mother, Mabel Michener, took me to a local notary public and told him that I was a foundling whom she had taken care of since birth. The notary said I would not be able to get a passport on that statement, so in my presence he and my mother worked out a statement to the effect that I was the son of Edwin and Mabel Haddock Michener, and on these terms I got the passport.
>
> The same problem recurred in 1942 when I wished to enlist in the Navy. Again my mother testified that I was a foundling, and again it was found advisable to revert to the passport story, which was already in the government files. So again I became the son of Edwin Michener.
>
> The facts in the case are very clearly set forth in the official Michener family history. This establishes that Edwin Michener was dead long before I was born. The date, locale, and parentage of my birth I have never known (Day 15–16).

Not all of the Michener clan "always welcomed" James, as he says. Edwin's two sisters gave James "the ugliest memories of my childhood" (Michener 483). They would bring candy for their nephew Robert and deny any to James or the other children, for example, and make cruel comments when Mabel was out of earshot. Michener's identity crisis grew to become a prominent feature of his personality, as one biographer writes, "He has never been able to understand himself. This is the tragedy of James Albert Michener. Although he is an enigma to everyone who knows him, he is especially an enigma to himself. He was born an enigma, and any understanding of him begins there" (Hayes 10).

As a positive result, Michener's foundling status created in him a curiosity and admiration for people of all ethnicities and races. His numerous biographers often refer to him as "citizen of the world" or "citizen of all mankind," and this interest in other cultures has been a rich source out of which have sprung his extensive travels, the exotic details and settings for novels, and his pronounced hatred of racism or cultural discrimination of any kind:

> When you grow up at the bottom of the totem pole, you see things from a different perspective, and with me there's always the circumstances of my birth. If I really don't know who I am, I can hardly look down on anyone. I seem to have a Germanic turn of mind, but I may be Jewish or Lithuanian or part black. With the uncertain background, one's attitude becomes quite liberal (Hayes 11).

In spite of his own thwarted search for the truth about his origins, Michener was not in favor of open adoption records. The statement below, however, taken from a 1996 interview, reveals that he followed the adoption rights movement with interest:

> I've done a lot of work on this recent move to uncover all records—a very bad idea, really. I doubt that much good will be accomplished. I've followed a hundred cases: everyone handled in a different way, all of them handled it wrong. I don't think there's a right way to do it. If you tell the kid from the beginning, I've seen that work very poorly. If you don't tell him, as in my case, you run a great risk.
>
> Naturally you can't help but speculate.... One day I suddenly thought, Jesus, I'm penalizing myself twice. I'm experiencing this unfairness and now I'm brooding and bitching about it and I'm losing double. From that moment on I never bitched about anything.
>
> In psychological profiles on me it's been speculated that my drive to research objects is really a search for my own parents, but I'm not wise enough to answer that.... There is a great deal about me that I don't want to know... I have stabilized my life. I get by. I have no belief at all that it is as good as it could be, but I sure as hell don't want somebody messing around with it when I am reaching a kind of stabilization, pitiful as it is (Grobel 14–15).

In 1987, on Michener's eightieth birthday, a childhood friend, Helen Gallagher, wrote him a letter saying she had overheard as a girl that a prominent citizen of Doylestown had been his father and that Michener also knew him well. Although she gave the man's name, Michener calls him "Mr. Blank" in his memoir and goes on to say:

> If Mr. Blank had been my father, so be it. He'd given me a sturdy body and a clear mind, and a boy can wish for little more.... But when I think of my mother slaving as she did, toiling at the most menial jobs, unable to give her children the things she knew they needed, I find it incomprehensible that a man of means and position who was in major part responsible for her condition should have refused to help her.... It was fortunate... if he was my father, that I never knew it... had I known that he was treating Mrs. [Mabel] Michener in the way some said he did, I would surely have killed him (Michener 495).

Significant Relationships

Michener married Patty Koon in 1935 and Vange Nord in 1948. Both marriages ended in divorce. In 1955 he married Mari Yoriko Sabusawa. She died in 1994.

Although he never fathered* or adopted children, Michener had a keen desire to help young people and he designated over $14 million of his royalties for scholarships:

---

*Michener believed that a severe case of childhood mumps left him sterile for life.

I feel a deep commitment to helping talented people and a keen sense of responsibility to the new generations, so I have plowed my money into these various channels (Hayes 8).

In 1997, Michener made the decision to go off dialysis and died of kidney disease. He was 90.

Works Cited

Becker, George J. *James A. Michener.* New York: Frederick Ungar, 1983.

Day, Grove. *James Michener.* Boston: G. K. Hall: 1977.

Grobel, Lawrence. *Talking with Michener.* Jackson: U of Mississippi P, 1999.

Hayes, John P. *James A. Michener: A Biography.* Indianapolis: Bobbs-Merril, 1984.

May, Stephen J. *Michener: A Writer's Journey.* Norman: U of Oklahoma P, 2005.

Michener, James A. *The World Is My Home: A Memoir.* New York: Random House, 1992.

Severson, Marilyn S. *James A. Michener: A Critical Companion.* Westport, CT: Greenwood Press, 1996.

MONAGHAN, TOM (1937–)

Founder of Domino's Pizza
Fostered child, orphanage alumnus

Career, Major Awards, and Achievements

In 1960, Tom Monaghan bought a financially troubled pizza parlor, DomiNick's, in Ypsilanti, Michigan, with his younger brother, Jim. Jim, busy with a full-time job, soon sold his share to his brother. Tom Monaghan's hard work, entrepreneurial spirit, and imaginative innovations would soon turn the business, which he would rename Domino's, into a successful, multimillion dollar industry. Free home delivery, one of Monaghan's earliest innovations, was to make Domino's a serious competitor to Shakey's, Pizza Hut, Little Caesar's, and the other top pizza franchises of the 1960s and 1970s. Dominos created a unique campaign in which the pizza was guaranteed delivered within thirty minutes or it was free. The practice was eventually retired amid concerns that the deadlines encouraged reckless driving during delivery. Other Monaghan innovations that allowed fast delivery and a high quality product included conveyor ovens, corrugated cardboard pizza boxes, dough trays, vans with warming ovens and insulated carriers.

Monaghan weathered several crises in his business, including a devastating fire in 1968, a trademark lawsuit in 1979, and a near bankruptcy caused by too rapid expansion. Monaghan made arrangements whereby he paid all creditors back in full.

Monaghan's outspoken political and religious views often created repercussions for the company, an example being an ongoing boycott called in 1989 by the National Organization of Women in response to Monaghan's outspoken opposition to legalized abortion.

In 1989, Monaghan turned the Domino's presidency over to P. David Black, his operations vice president. At the time he stepped down, Domino's had grown to over 5,100 US restaurants and over 250 international ones. He fully retired in 1998 and sold the company, but he remains a significant shareholder. Monaghan told his employees that the secret to being successful is "to have a good product, give good service, and apply the

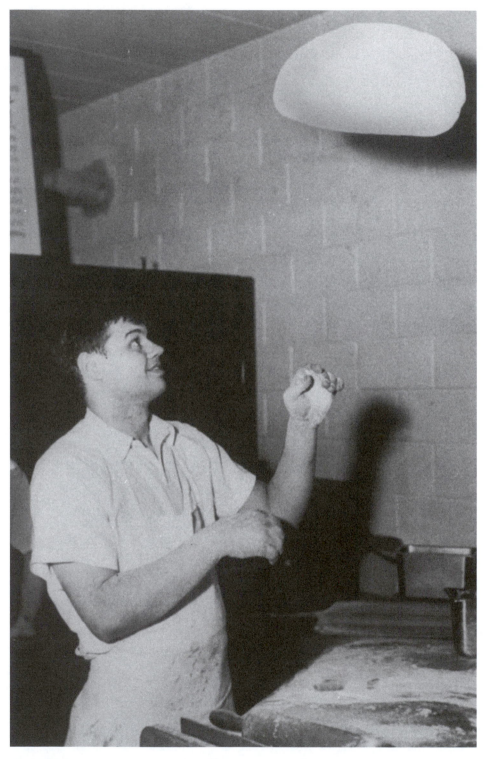

[Taro Yamasaki/Time Life Pictures/Getty Images]

Golden Rule" (Monaghan 9). He wrote in his autobiography, *Pizza Tiger*, that he learned these important values from Sister Berarda, one of the nuns at his orphanage. He called her a great inspiration and "my surrogate mother" (29):

> Unfortunately, most people don't have the importance of being nice to others instilled in them by their parents. I had only a brief taste of it myself, from a nun named Sister Berarda in the orphanage. But I never forgot it, and I don't think it's ever too late to learn (Monaghan 10).

Monaghan's successes allowed him to fulfill his youthful passions for baseball, cars, and architecture. In 1983, he bought the Detroit Tigers baseball club. The Tigers won the World Series the following year. He built a large business complex, Domino's Farms, for his company headquarters. It is located only a few miles from the house his father built in Ann Arbor. Domino's Farms has on display Monaghan's large collection of classic cars. The National Study Center for Frank Lloyd Wright is located in the center of the complex. It houses one of the world's largest artifact collections of Frank Lloyd Wright, Monaghan's favorite architect. One of the designers who worked for Monaghan, David Hanks, said in a July 1989 *GQ* interview that he was "pursuing a toyless boyhood with his monumental acquisitions" (Landrum 102).

In 1984, Tom Monaghan won the Harvard Business School Entrepreneur of the Year Award. He was also given The Horatio Alger award and the Napoleon Hill award in 1984. He holds six honorary doctorate degrees.

Family of Origin

Thomas (Tom) Stephen Monaghan was born in Ann Arbor, Michigan, on March 25, 1937, the eldest son of Francis Monaghan, a truck driver, and Anna (Geddes) Monaghan, a nurse's aide. A second son, Jim, was born to the couple in August, 1939. Francis died on Christmas Eve 1941 of peritonitis brought about by gastric ulcers. Tom was four years old at the time of his father's death. He describes himself as a "strong and restless" child (26), and Anna found that she could not leave him unattended even for a moment. She also realized that her earnings of $27.50 a week were inadequate to support her family, so she decided to put her sons into foster care and return full-time to school to become a registered nurse. She intended to bring the boys home when she found a good job.

Foster Homes and Orphanages

The boys lived with a couple of foster families before they went to the orphanage, the longest stay being with an elderly German couple, Mr. and Mrs. Frank Woppman.

They entered St. Joseph's Home for Boys in Jackson, Michigan, when Tom was in the first grade. St. Joseph's was a Catholic orphanage run by Felician nuns. Tom felt out of place and unhappy at St. Joseph's, as he wrote:

> I soon discovered there were two prisons in Jackson: the Michigan State Penitentiary and the one I was put in. . . . Life in the orphanage was stifling. In the six-and-a-half years I spent there, I never got over the feeling that my existence was abnormal, that my lot in life was unjust (27).

Anna Monaghan was able to finally bring her sons home when Tom was in the seventh grade, but he and his mother could not get along. Tom tried to busy himself with summer jobs, but the relationship grew more strained until Anna finally applied to the state Children's Home and Aid Society, and Tom was sent for fosterage to several farming families: the Beaman family in Interlochen, the Johnson's near Traverse City, and the Crouch family near the Boardman River.

Education and Significant Relationships

While in high school, Monaghan decided that he wanted to become a priest and was allowed to enter the St. Joseph's seminary in Grand Rapids. Less than a year later, the superior explained to Tom that he "lacked the vocation" (Monaghan 36) and he was expelled:

> The problem, as I see it now, was the similarity between the discipline of the seminary and that which I had disliked so much in the orphanage. I had grown adept at sidestepping rules in the orphanage, and I didn't take the regulations of St. Joseph's seriously enough. I couldn't avoid getting involved in pillow fights in the dorm or whispering during the "Grand Silence" (36).

After being expelled from seminary, Tom returned to live with his mother and Jim, but the conflicts became worse. At last Anna had Tom arrested after he took her car without permission and he spent six months in a detention home.

Tom's paternal aunt, Peg, and her husband, Dan Mahler, asked for and were granted custody of Tom the summer before his high school senior year and the placement was a happy one, according to Tom: "I was treated like a member of the family, and that's what I had craved ever since I first went to the orphanage" (Monaghan 39). Dan gave Tom a summer job in his construction company. Tom later worked as a busboy at the country club where Peg was a waitress. Tom graduated from St. Francis High School in Ann Arbor in 1955 "by the skin of my teeth" (40), finishing forty-fourth in his class of forty-four students.

Monaghan hoped to study architecture at the University of Michigan, but poor grades and inadequate finances prevented this, so he briefly attended Ferris State College and then joined the Marine Corps, intending to find a way to finance college. After boot camp, he was stationed at Okinawa, Japan, and Camp Pendleton, California. After his discharge in 1959, he twice enrolled at the University of Michigan and twice dropped out within the first three weeks.

Monaghan met his wife, Marjorie (Margie) Zybach, while he was delivering a pizza to her college dormitory at Central Michigan University in February 1961. A few days later he brought her a large heart shaped pizza for a Valentine's Day gift. The couple married on August 25, 1962, and Margie worked as a waitress and school librarian before joining the Domino's business as bookkeeper. The Monaghans have four daughters, Mary, Susan, Margaret, and Barbara.

Works Cited

Landrum, Gene N. *Profiles of Genius: Thirteen Creative Men Who Changed the World.* Buffalo, NY: Prometheus Books, 1993.

"Monaghan, Tom." *Current Biography Yearbook 1990.* Ed. Charles Moritz. New York: H. W. Wilson, 1990. 450–454.

Monaghan, Tom, with Robert Anderson. *Pizza Tiger.* New York: Random House, 1986.

MONROE, MARILYN (1926–1962)

Actress, Model
Fostered, orphanage alumna

Career, Major Awards, and Achievements

Marilyn Monroe rose out of a traumatic and unstable childhood to become one of the most photographed and widely recognized icons of the twentieth century. Much has been written about how her childhood privations helped to both develop and destroy the adult she became. Monroe was a teenaged military wife working on an assembly line when her legendary career began. Private David Conover of *Yank* magazine first photographed her while she worked at the Radio Plane Company in Los Angeles. Conover, who was under the command of then Captain Ronald Reagan, had been instructed to take pictures of pretty girls to boost military morale. Later she joined the Blue Book modeling agency, where manager Emmeline Snively coached her to adopt many of her future hallmarks, such as her pale blonde hair and quivering upper lip.* Between 1949

[Courtesy of the National Archives and Records Administration]

---

*Emmeline Snively told Monroe to draw down her upper lip when she smiled, to compensate for a long nose and short upper lip. The effort caused her upper lip to quiver and became one of her signature expressions (McCann 43).

and 1983, *Life* magazine published thirty articles about her, with her photo appearing on eleven covers.

As an actress, Monroe had an active film career with Twentieth Century Fox and Columbia Pictures. Her credits include

The Dangerous Years (1947)	*Don't Bother to Knock* (1952)
Scudda Hoo! Scudda Hay! (1948)	*Monkey Business* (1952)
Ladies of the Chorus (1948)	*O. Henry's Full House* (1952)
Love Happy (1949)	*Niagara* (1953)
A Ticket to Tomahawk (1950)	*How to Marry a Millionaire* (1953)
The Asphalt Jungle (1950)	*Gentlemen Prefer Blondes* (1953)
All About Eve (1950; winner of the 1950	*There's No Business Like Show*
Academy Award for Best Picture)	*Business* (1954)
The Fireball (1950)	*River of No Return* (1954)
Right Cross (1950)	*The Seven Year Itch* (1955)
Hometown Story (1951)	*Bus Stop* (1956)
As Young as You Feel (1951)	*The Prince and the Showgirl*
Love Nest (1951)	(1957)
Let's Make it Legal (1951)	*Some Like it Hot* (1959)
Clash by Night (1952)	*Let's Make Love* (1960)
We're Not Married (1952)	*The Misfits* (1961)

Monroe was fired from *Something's Got to Give* just two months before her untimely and widely scrutinized death in 1962.

Monroe's awards range from the prestigious to the humorous. She won three Golden Globe Awards: World Film Favorite (1953 and 1961) and Best Actress in a Comedy (1958). In 1959, she won the Donatello Prize (Italian Oscar) and the Crystal Star Award (French Oscar) for Best Foreign Actress, for *The Prince and the Showgirl*. The Los Angeles Press Club named her "Miss Press Club" (1948), and *Look Magazine* voted her "Most Promising Female Newcomer" (1952). She won additional recognition from *Photoplay* magazine, *Redbook* magazine, and the military periodical *Stars and Stripes,* which named her "Miss Cheesecake of the Year" (1951 and 1952).

In an unpublished 1962 interview with Margaret Parton, writing for *Ladies Home Journal,* Monroe confirmed her painful struggle with public perception, saying, "People didn't take me seriously, or they only took my body seriously. . . . Please don't make me a joke" (McCann 2). In spite of her Hollywood "dumb blonde bombshell" image, Monroe was intelligent, articulate and a voracious reader. Her friends and acquaintances recall her compassion even at the height of her fame and stardom. She was known to rescue animals and offer money or a kind word to people on the street. An active Democrat, she was very interested in politics and had a strong sense of social justice. Passionately opposed to the atom bomb, she sponsored the National Committee for a Sane Nuclear Policy in 1960. She was invited to meet several heads of state, including Queen Elizabeth of England, Soviet Premier Nikita Kruschev, and the President of Indonesia. She loathed McCarthyism, red-baiting, and J. Edgar Hoover, the FBI chief at the time.

Family of Origin

Born Norma Jeane Mortenson on June 1, 1926, and baptized Norma Jeane Baker, she was given her most famous name by Ben Lyon, the head of casting at Fox Studios. Monroe confessed: "I've never liked the name Marilyn. I've often wished that I had held out that day for Jean Monroe. But I guess it's too late to do anything about it now" (Riese 363). During her life Monroe used over twenty five different names and aliases.

Norma Jeane's mother, Gladys Pearl Monroe, had already married and divorced twice by the time Norma Jeane was born. Her first husband was a gas station attendant named Jack Baker. Their children, Hermitt Jack, born in 1918, and Bernice, born in 1919, went with their father when he divorced Gladys in 1921. Hermitt Jack died of tuberculosis before Norma Jeane was born and Bernice did not meet her half-sister until after she was famous:

> In 1961, after her split from Arthur Miller, Marilyn invited Bernice to come and visit her in New York. Reportedly, the two sisters got on quite well, and when Marilyn visited Joe DiMaggio in Florida, she also stopped by to see Bernice, who was living in Gainesville, Florida. Following Marilyn's death, Bernice worked in tandem with DiMaggio in making the burial arrangements. . . . Somewhat surprisingly, Bernice was named as a primary beneficiary in Marilyn's will (Riese 331).

In 1924, Gladys married Edward Mortenson, a Norwegian baker who had left a wife and three children in Norway. That relationship also didn't last, and Mortensen would die in a motorcycle accident in 1929.

Monroe believed her father was C. Stanley Gifford, a coworker at Consolidated Film Industries, where Gladys worked as a film cutter. Gladys and Gifford had an affair during 1925 and 1926, but it ended abruptly with the news that Gladys was pregnant. In later years, Monroe attempted to contact Gifford by calling him, but Gifford reportedly hung up. By the fall of 1951, through a hired private detective, Marilyn tracked Gifford to Hemet, California. With Natasha Lytess (her drama coach and mentor) in tow for support, Marilyn drove from Hollywood to Riverside, where she abruptly pulled the car over and called Gifford from a pay phone. Reportedly, Gifford's wife answered the phone and told Marilyn, "He doesn't want to see you. He suggests you see his lawyer in Los Angeles if you have some complaint. Do you have a pencil?"

In 1961, after Marilyn Monroe was an international superstar, Gifford tried to make amends by sending Marilyn a card that said "Best wishes for your early recovery. From the man you tried to see nearly ten years ago. God forgive me." Upon receiving the card, Marilyn confided to a friend, "It's too late."

According to biographer Fred Lawrence Guiles, Gifford made one last attempt to contact Marilyn. A Palm Springs nurse telephoned Marilyn in Brentwood in 1962 to say that Gifford had had a heart attack and wasn't expected to survive. He wanted to talk to Marilyn before he died. Marilyn responded by saying, "Tell the gentleman I have never met him. But if he has anything specific to tell me, he can contact my lawyer. Would you like his number?" That was the last time Marilyn heard from Gifford, and vice versa. Gifford survived his heart attack and outlived his daughter—if she was indeed his daughter (Riese 175).

Monroe usually told people her mother was an invalid who couldn't care for her and that her father had died in a car accident.

After the birth of her last child, Gladys continued to work, and she paid Wayne and Ida Bolender five dollars each week to care for Norma Jeane. Wayne was a mail carrier, and Ida looked after children they called "the twins," their adopted son, Lester, and Norma Jeane. Gladys visited every Saturday and finally saved enough to mortgage a bungalow in Hollywood, rent out rooms, and bring Norma Jeane to live with her in

1934. She had a breakdown some months later and was committed to the Norwalk State Asylum, where she remained until 1945. Marilyn's grandmother, Della Monroe, also suffered from mental illness. Della died from heart disease and manic-depressive psychosis in the Norwalk asylum when Norma Jeane was a year old.

Gladys emerged from the asylum in 1945 and lived with her daughter for seven months before returning to Norwalk. In 1952, Monroe had her transferred to the luxurious Rockhaven Sanitarium in Verdugo, California, and established a trust fund for her mother's ongoing expenses. Gladys twice attempted suicide after Marilyn's death, using hairpins to stab herself on one occasion and shoving bed sheets down her throat on another. In 1967, Gladys moved to Gainesville, Florida, under the guardianship of her daughter, Bernice. She died on March 11, 1984.

Foster Homes and Orphanages

During her childhood, Norma Jeane passed through twelve foster homes. In several there were allegations of sexual molestation:

> I was almost nine, and I lived with a family that rented a room to a man named Kimmel. He was a stern-looking man, and everybody respected him and called him Mr. Kimmel. I was passing his room when his door opened and he said quietly, "Please come in here Norma. . . ." He smiled at me and turned the key in the lock. "Now you can't get out," he said as if we were playing a game. I stood staring at him. I was frightened, but I didn't dare yell. . . . When he put his arms around me I kicked and fought as hard as I could, but I didn't make any sound. He was stronger than I was and wouldn't let me go. He kept whispering to me to be a good girl. When he unlocked the door and let me out, I ran to tell my "aunt" what Mr. Kimmel had done (McCann 41).

Her foster parents (and some biographers) did not believe her. Her foster mother told her, "Don't you dare say anything against Mr. Kimmel. Mr. Kimmel is a fine man. He's my star boarder!" (McCann 41). Other biographers believe that these were precisely the traumas that created the "child in a woman's body" which epitomized Monroe:

> The very qualities resulting from Monroe's childhood abuse were further exploited by Hollywood film-makers and publicists. She became a "sex goddess," a child to be worshipped in a woman's body. . . as her clothes designer Billy Travilla so graphically describes: "She was both a woman and a baby. . . . A man wouldn't know whether to sit her on his knee and pet her, or put his arms around her and get her in the sack" (McCann 42).

After Gladys was institutionalized, the county appointed Grace McKee, Gladys's best friend and coworker at Columbia Pictures, Norma Jeane's legal guardian. Grace, a film librarian and unmarried at the time, placed her in the Los Angeles Orphans Home Society on September 19, 1935. McKee visited every week and typically took Norma Jeane out for a movie and ice cream. Norma Jeane lived at the orphanage for three years, from nine through eleven years old. She slept in bed twenty-seven, facing the RKO Studios water tower. A girl named Maria, who lived in the orphanage at the same time, recalled her as a "very quiet, very gentle girl":

> I'll never forget how good and kind she was to me. So even today if I hear people putting her down, it's like a knife in my heart. She was a very generous person who would never say no to you if you asked her for something. I remember her sitting quietly at a piano we had there and playing for us. She always reminded me of a doe. A funny thing: In 1962, I got

the feeling that I should write to her. Whether she'd remember me or not, I wanted to let her know she had a friend. I did write the letter and a month later, she passed away (Riese 279).

The Los Angeles Orphans Home Society was rebuilt in 1956 and changed its name to Hollygrove. It remains a children's institution at its old location near Paramount Studios.

In 1937, Grace McKee married Erwin Goddard and they brought Norma Jeane to their home. Although Grace loved the child and had paid for all of her singing, dancing, and piano lessons, Monroe harbored resentment towards her guardian. She developed one of her strongest attachments, however, to Grace's aunt, Ana Lower, to whom she went after Erwin reportedly came home drunk one night and made advances to the young teen. Erwin, a research engineer, transferred to West Virginia and Grace joined him. Before the move, Grace arranged for her fifteen-year-old ward to marry a twenty-one-year-old neighbor, Jim Dougherty, on June 19, 1942. Monroe always felt that Grace had arranged the marriage to get rid of her (Riese 179). Grace died in 1953 from an overdose of barbiturates.

Education and Significant Relationships

Norma Jeane attended eight different schools in ten years while bouncing between foster families. Although her early studio biographies implied that she graduated from Van Nuys High School, she actually attended Van Nuys High School from September 1941 through February 1942, then University High School. She dropped out when she married. Jim Dougherty had been a football star and high school class president. With the war on, he joined the merchant marines and soon sailed away from his young wife.

In 1947 and 1948, she attended the Actors Lab in Hollywood. In 1951, Monroe took evening classes in art appreciation and literature through UCLA's extension program and was simultaneously coached by Michael Chekhov and Natasha Lytess. In 1955, she moved to New York to study at the Actors Studio under Lee Strasberg, the father of Method Acting.

Monroe was romantically linked to a long list of actors and international luminaries and she married twice after her divorce from Jim Dougherty in 1942: to baseball great Joe DiMaggio in 1954 (divorced in 1955) and to playwright Arthur Miller in a civil ceremony June 29, 1956, and a Jewish ceremony July 1, 1956. They divorced in 1961. Monroe described her relationship difficulties, saying:

> Me, myself, I'm not as mature as I should be. There's a part of me that has never developed and keeps on getting in the way, getting me in lousy situations, screwing up relationships, stopping my rest. I think about it all the time. My mother wasn't strong-minded. Maybe what I'm talking about is a weak-minded quality I inherited from her (Weatherby 184).

Perhaps most significant to her were the children she so desperately wanted but either lost or never bore. Both Monroe's maid, Lena Pepitone, and her closest friend, Amy Greene, recall Marilyn saying she had given up a son in her mid-teens as the result of a molestation/rape. Actress Jeanne Carmen also remembered Marilyn saying she had given up a child but recalled it was "after the marriage to Dougherty and before the real Hollywood breakthrough, when Marilyn was about twenty-one" (Summers 22–23). There was always some question, however, as Marilyn would make things up sometimes, just to create a reaction (Summers 19, 23).

After lifelong, severely painful gynecological difficulties and multiple miscarriages, Monroe finally discovered that she was pregnant by Arthur Miller. It was a tubal pregnancy and ended in emergency surgery:

> She would never entirely recover from this experience and, ironically, she would die five years hence on the anniversary of this miscarriage. The desire to have children was intense for Monroe; her body would at last be her own, since she felt it would exist for the child who belonged to her, a physical exclamation of blood, spirit, and soft, warm flesh. . . . She could never truly stop herself from longing for a child of her own . . ." (McCann 148–149).

The theory that Marilyn Monroe became pregnant by one of the Kennedy brothers, most likely Robert, and had an abortion in Mexico shortly before her death, has been neither confirmed nor refuted by medical evidence. Some believe that to be the source of her dramatic emotional decline and increased use of drugs, culminating in her accidental death or suicide on August 4, 1962. Others have theorized that she was murdered by any of several men of power.

Tributes to Monroe abound, such as this one by Favius Friedman in the December 1962 issue of *Silver Screen* magazine:

> If she lived in anything, it was the desperate knowledge that she wanted love more than anything else in the world. . . . She fought until the last to forget that most of her life she was a lost child, afraid and insecure, and when peace still eluded her, at 36, she vanished with a sigh, unaware how the world would forever miss her.

Works Cited

McCann, Graham. *Marilyn Monroe.* New Brunswick, New Jersey: Rutgers University Press, 1988.

Riese, Randall, and Neal Hitchens. *The Unabridged Marilyn: Her Life from A to Z.* New York: Bonanza Books, 1987.

Summers, Anthony. *Goddess: The Secret Lives of Marilyn Monroe.* New York: MacMillan, 1985.

Weatherby, W. J. *Conversations with Marilyn.* New York: Mason/Charter, 1976.

N

NICHOLSON, JACK (1937–)

Actor
Fictitious birth information

Career, Major Awards, and Achievements

Jack Nicholson won the Oscar for Best Actor in 1975 for his performance in the film adaptation of Ken Kesey's novel *One Flew over the Cuckoo's Nest*. He won an additional Oscar for Best Supporting Actor in 1983 for his work in *Terms of Endearment*. He has been nominated for eleven academy awards and has won many additional honors from the New York Film Critics Circle, National Society of Film Critics and the Screen Actors Guild. He was presented with the Cecil B. DeMille award in 1999. His unique, middle-aged antiheroes are unforgettable mixtures of vulnerability, humor, evil, and sexuality, all topped off with his signature Mephisto smile. Nicholson has produced over three decades of impressive work. Some of his best-known films include *Easy Rider* (1969), *Five Easy Pieces* (1970), *Carnal Knowledge* (1971), *Chinatown* (1974), *The Shining* (1979), *Prizzi's Honor* (1985), *The Witches of Eastwick* (1987), *Ironweed* (1987), *Batman* (1989), *Hoffa* (1992), *Wolf* (1994), *As Good As It Gets* (1997), *About Schmidt* (2002), *The Departed* (2006), and *The Bucket List* (2007).

Family of Origin

Nicholson was raised by his grandmother, Ethel May Nicholson, whom he believed to be his mother. He was thirty-seven years old when he first learned that June, the woman he thought was his sister, was, in fact, his mother. Nicholson's grandmother had raised Jack and her two daughters, June and Lorraine, as a single, working mother. Her husband John, Jack's namesake, left the family because of a serious drinking problem when Jack was still an infant. Ethel May was a beautician and supported her family with earnings from her beauty salon, located in the family's New Jersey home. Nicholson reportedly hated school (Downing 9) but was a very bright and popular student with straight A's and a few deportment problems. Upon graduating high school, Nicholson visited his "sister" June in Hollywood in 1954, and afterwards moved to California to begin his acting career.

[AP Photo/Michael Tweed]

Fictitious Birth Information

In 1975, Nicholson learned that June had given birth to him out of wedlock when she was seventeen years old. An investigator doing a cover story on him for *Time* magazine uncovered the truth and Lorraine later confirmed the story. Nicholson was at work on the film *The Fortune* when he got the reporter's phone call:

> I was stunned. Since I was at work, I went to Mike Nichols, the director and said, "Now Mike, you know I'm a big-time method actor. I just found out something—something just came through—so keep an extra eye on me. Don't let me get away with anything" (Collins 17).

June had been a talented young dancer when she gave birth to Jack on April 22, 1937, in Neptune City, New Jersey. Nicholson admired June, with whom he lived when he first came to California. She died of cancer shortly before Jack discovered that she was his mother. He says of her:

> June and I had so much in common. We both fight hard. It didn't do her any good not to tell me, but she didn't, because you never know how I would've reacted when I was younger. . . . I'm very contra my constituency in terms of abortion because I'm positively against it. I don't have the right to any other view. My only emotion is gratitude, literally for my life. If June and Ethel had been of less character, I would never have gotten to live. The women gave me the gift of life. . . . They trained me great, those ladies (Collins 17).

Nicholson never learned the identity of his biological father, claiming that the only persons who knew were his now deceased mother and grandmother (Collins 17). He explained in a later interview, "I'm not overly curious. . . . I've always said I had the most fortunate rearing. No one would've had the courage to design it that way, but it was ideal. No repression from a male father figure, no Oedipal competition" (*Current Biography* 433).

Significant Relationships

Nicholson has a daughter, Jennifer Nicholson, from his marriage to Sandra Knight, which ended in 1968, and a grandson, Sean. He also has two children, Lorraine and Raymond, from his relationship with Rebecca Broussard. His other important relationships include a long-time romance with actress Angelica Huston and a recent romance with the young actress Lara Flynn Boyle.

Works Cited

Downing, David. *Jack Nicholson: A Biography*. New York: Stein & Day, 1984.
Collins, Nancy. "Jack Nicholson: The Great Seducer." *Rolling Stone* (March 29, 1984): 15+.
"Jack Nicholson" *Current Biography Yearbook 1995*. New York: H. W. Wilson, 1985. 433–437.

O

OAKLEY, ANNIE (1860–1926)

Sharpshooter, Performer
Poorhouse alumna, indentured

Career, Major Awards, and Achievements

Annie Oakley is best known as a star of Buffalo Bill's Wild West Show. She was a sharpshooter of amazing talent who could split a playing card at 90 feet, then put more bullet holes in it before it touched the ground. She was also a philanthropist and, according to her great-niece, Bess Edwards, a woman who "believed in and campaigned for women's rights to hold paid employment, earn equal pay, participate in sports, and defend themselves in their homes and on city streets."

After her 1882 marriage to fellow sharpshooter Frank Butler, Annie took Oakley as her stage name and served as Butler's assistant. When he realized that she was the better performer, Butler took on the roles of assistant and business manager.

They joined the Wild West Show in 1885. Oakley's main rival was Lillian Smith, another rifle sharpshooter, who maintained that she was younger (and therefore more talented) than Oakley. Oakley first took six years off her age (the youngest age she could claim and still be her father's child), then left the show, returning when Smith left. The missing six years have caused confusion among biographers: some have written that she met Frank Butler when she was 16, not 21, for example.

As a Wild West Show star, Oakley performed incredible feats. In Europe, she performed before Queen Victoria and, at the request of the queen's grandson, the future Kaiser Wilhelm II, she shot the ashes off a cigarette he was holding. This was a trick she usually performed with Butler, who held the cigarette in his mouth. In the United States, she was honored by Sitting Bull, also a member of the Wild West Show, who gave the five-foot-tall cowgirl the name *Watanya Cicilla*, translated as "Little Sure Shot."

A railway accident left Oakley temporarily paralyzed in 1901, but after five spinal operations, she made a complete recovery. However she left the Wild West Show not long afterwards and began acting and touring in *The Western Girl*, a play written for her.

In 1903, Annie Oakley made the news in a different way. The Hearst newspapers brought out a story that Oakley had been arrested after stealing money to buy cocaine. A woman in Chicago had been arrested on those charges and did tell the police that her

ANNIE OAKLEY.
Famous Rifle Shot and Holder of the Police Gazette Championship Medal.

[Courtesy of the Library of Congress]

name was Annie Oakley, but the arrested woman was not the sharpshooter. Most papers that had carried the story printed retractions and apologies, but Oakley sued others, winning all but one of the fifty-five libel cases. Since her expenses were greater than the amounts she received, she lost money but felt her reputation was worth more than what she spent.

An automobile accident resulted in serious injuries to her right leg, for which she needed a steel brace. In later years she toured less often, but she continued to set sharp-shooting records throughout her life.

Oakley preferred to avoid publicity for the parts of her life that did not involve sharpshooting. She believed in and supported women's rights, including the right to exercise and be healthy, and she contributed funds to support young women whose needs she discovered. Her niece, Bess Edwards, said that there is evidence she provided the money for college and professional education for at least twenty young women. She helped widows and orphans with money and by giving exhibitions to raise funds for them. After Annie Oakley's death, it was found that all of the money she had made had gone to charity.

Family of Origin

Oakley was born Phoebe Ann Mosey on August 13, 1860, but was always called Annie. She was the fifth of seven children born to Quaker parents Jacob Mosey (also recorded as Mosee and Moses) and his wife Susan (Wise) Mosey. Her parents married in 1850 and kept a tavern in Blair County, Pennsylvania. They moved to Ohio after a careless guest upset an oil lamp and the tavern burned. The family moved to a cabin near Willowdale (then called Woodland), Ohio, where Annie was born. Jacob rented a farm and drove a postal route. When Annie was six, her father died of pneumonia.

Poorhouse and Indenture

Shortly after her father's death, Annie was taken to the county poor farm, called the Darke County Infirmary, where Matron Edington taught her to sew, knit, darn, and embroider—skills that came in handy later, when Oakley created and tailored her own costumes—in return for help with odd jobs and the resident children. One biographer wrote of the poor farm:

> Many persons incapable of attending to their own wants were housed at the infirmary and a shortage of rooms compelled the children to associate with these unfortunates, whose habits of life and language were not intended to exert that influence for good that should always surround the child.
>
> Apparently the infirmary was the dumping ground for the elderly, the orphaned, and the insane. Perhaps this early experience, working at such a place, aroused in Annie the tremendous compassion she had for children wherever she went (Sayers 1).

Annie next became a hired girl with a family she referred to as "the wolves" because of the harsh treatment she received from them. The family wrote to her mother saying that she was making progress in school and had a light workload. In reality, however, the child began her workday at 4:00 A.M., taking care of livestock, a garden, and a baby, milking, churning, cooking, cleaning, and hunting:

> Not surprisingly, Annie eventually seized the opportunity to run away and to hitch a train ride back to Susan. Annie later wrote that "for years" she asked "God each night" to bless

the stranger who had helped her escape the "wolves" by buying her a train ticket. Although she never spoke directly of it, Annie also indicated that she had suffered physical mistreatment, and perhaps sexual abuse as well, at the hands of her employer (Riley 95).

In the meantime, her mother remarried, had another child, and lost her second husband. Annie rejoined the family when she was nine, about the time that her mother married for the third time. When Annie returned, she took up hunting on a scale that allowed her to sell to local people for money to support her family. She seldom attended school, probably because she needed the time to hunt, but also by preference. In time she was able to pay off the mortgage on the family home and earn a reputation as an excellent shot: "Oh how my heart leaped with joy," she wrote. "I handed the money to mother and told her that I had saved enough from my trapped game" to pay off the mortgage (Riley 96).

Significant Relationships

When sharpshooter Frank (Francis E.) Butler brought the Baughman and Butler shooting act to Cincinnati in 1881, he bet a local hotel owner $100 that he could outshoot any local talent. The hotel owner set up a shooting match between Butler, then thirty-one, and twenty-one-year-old Annie Mosey. Butler lost the match when he missed on his twenty-fifth shot. He married Annie the following year, on June 20, 1882. For a short time they lived in Cincinnati, in a neighborhood known as Oakley, from which Annie probably took her stage name. They would remain happily married and good business partners for nearly fifty years.

Annie Oakley died of pernicious anemia on November 3, 1926. She was buried in Greenville, Ohio. Frank Butler died twenty days later.

Works Cited

Edwards, Bess. Annie Oakley Foundation. 24 October, 2007. http://www.annieoakleyfoundation .org/bio.html

Etulain, Richard W. *Western Lives: A Biographical History of the American West.* Albuquerque: University of New Mexico Press, 2004.

Riley, Glenda and Richard W. Etulain, eds. *By Grit and Grace: Eleven Women Who Shaped the American West.* Golden, CO: Fulcrum, 1997.

Sayers, Isabelle S. *Annie Oakley and Buffalo Bill's Wild West.* New York: Dover, 1981.

P

PATON, JEAN (1908–2002)

Mother of the Adoptees' Rights Movement
Adoptee

"But what is any knowledge in this field worth if it has no connection with the *maturing* adopted?" (Paton, *The Adopted Break Silence* 3)

Career, Major Awards, and Achievements

Jean Paton is considered the mother of the adoptees' rights movement and was the first scholar to study the adopted in adulthood. During her forties, Paton was employed as a social worker in Baltimore in the fields of foster care, child placement, and psychiatric service. During that time, she developed both an interest in adoption reform and a great sympathy for her fellow adopted adults, whom she called "the most neglected group of people in America today" (Kittson, *Orphan Voyage* 10):

A person may leave his home and never see it again, but he remains confident of where his origins lie, and where his roots remain.

But the person who, at birth, sees nothing but the turned backs of his kindred people, whose birth is not welcome, for whom there is no baby shower, who is not entered into the family Bible, who is forgotten by almost all of the relatives, such a person has no refuge that has depth and that remains. He has a wall to climb, and even if he is able to scale it he is forever invested with the character of the stones which he has climbed. . . .

In Cedaredge I have an old log cabin which houses a collection of books that were written by orphaned people. This reveals that almost all of the great literature of the world was written by people who were orphaned—whether by death, illegitimacy, exile, or neglect of parents, whatever. When you are outside the settled order of things you have a different perspective. It's open out there, the air is thinner and there are fewer clouds. You can find universal values which you can give back to society. But also if you are on the margin, it is a little scary. . . . I had an advantage in that I was first on the scene, but I was also very much alone. . . . Almost from the beginning I put out releases. . . gathering living communications from people out on the margin as I was (Paton, *Influence of Sealed Adoption* 14–15).

Paton resigned from social work in 1951 and in 1953 she entered the University of Pennsylvania, determined to pursue an original study of adopted adults. On April 28,

1953, Paton established the Life History Study Center in Philadelphia and began to solicit interviews from adults who had been adopted as children via personal advertisements in the *Saturday Review*. Sixty-four adoptees responded, and the results from their subsequent interviews and correspondence formed the case studies for Paton's first book, *The Adopted Break Silence* (1954). Paton wrote that her own adoptee status allowed her subjects to freely discuss their illegitimacy, relinquishments, and adoptions, all profoundly stigmatized during the 1950s, with unaccustomed candor (Kittson, *Orphan Voyage* 40). She published subsequent writings on the subject, sometimes using variations of her birth name. Her writings include *They Serve Fugitively* (1954), *The Vocabulary of Social Orphanhood with Focus on Adoption* (1964), *Orphan Voyage* (1968, 1980), and *The Influence of Sealed Adoption on the Individual and on Society* (1987). Paton later moved to a cabin in Cedaredge, Colorado, where she established the Orphan Voyage organization and museum.

Paton tirelessly advocated adoption reform, and she especially campaigned for access to sealed records for adult adoptees and their first parents. Her influence on later reform organizations, most notably **Florence Fisher**'s ALMA (Adoptees Liberation Movement Association) and CUB (Concerned United Birthmothers) was considerable. Paton's final letter to CUB, dated five days before her death on March 27, 2000, clarifies her legacy:

> [A professor] said the movement started in the 70s? Whatever was I doing in 1953? The adoption rights movement took a different form after Florence Fisher got into it, but without the work of forming groups, the massive correspondence with individuals, the field trips, plus my own influence on Fisher, there would have been no movement. If [the professor] wants to know the true antecedents, tell her to get in touch with me. I think she might be surprised. We are in another Civil War, and it is not at all pleasant (Vedder 2).

Family of Origin

Jean Paton was born Ruth Edwina Kittson in Detroit, Michigan, on December 27, 1908. Edwina was the name of a doctor in the hospital where she was born. Her parents, who were unmarried, placed her for adoption. In 1942, Paton went to a Detroit court where she was given access to her first parents' names on her adoption records, but she did not begin her own search until 1954. Paton hired a detective who located an Aunt Viola in Detroit on February 18, 1955. The aunt was still living in the family home, built by Paton's grandfather around 1900. Viola soon facilitated an emotional reunion between Paton and her mother, Emma, who was living nearby.

Although Paton knew her father's name, her mother was reluctant to discuss what Paton calls her "mysterious sire": "The ease with which he is tossed out of memory by the family into which he so ingloriously intruded is moderated by the way he lingers within my bones" (Kittson, *Orphan Voyage* 88). Paton was able to verify the spelling of his name and that he was born in 1878. Although she was never able to meet him, she was able to trace "slender facts" about his employment history and learn that he was of Celtic ancestry and had also been adopted (Kittson, *Orphan Voyage* 233).

Adoption

Paton was adopted twice. Adopted as an infant and named Madeline Viola, she was returned for another placement after the death of her first adoptive father. She was next adopted in 1911 at the age of two by a doctor and his wife, Thomas and Mary Paton, who named her Jean Madeline Paton and raised her in Ypsilanti, Michigan.

Education

Paton earned her Bachelor of Arts degree from the University of Wisconsin and received her Master of Arts in Social Work from the Philadelphia School of Social Work.

Paton died on March 27, 2002, in Harrison, Arkansas, of heart disease. At ninety-three she was working on a new book about adoption at the time of her death.

In addition to her adoptive name of Jean Paton, she used variations of her birth name, Ruth Edwina Kittson, as her pen names.

Works Cited

Kittson, Ruth. *They Serve Fugitively*. Acton, CA: Life History Study Center, 1959.

Kittson, Ruthena. *The Vocabulary of Social Orphanhood with Focus on Adoption*. Hasty, AR: Orphan Voyage, 1964.

Kittson, Ruthena Hill. *Orphan Voyage*. Reprint of 1968 edition. [United States]: Country Press, 1980.

Paton, Jean. *The Adopted Break Silence*. Philadelphia, PA: Life History Study Center, 1954.

———. *The Influence of Sealed Adoption on the Individual and on Society*. Cedaredge, CO: Orphan Voyage, 1987.

Vedder, Karen. "Jean Paton, Mother of Adoption Reform, is Honored by CUB." *CUB* [Concerned United Birthparents] *Communicator* Spring/Summer 2002.

PLUM, DAMSEL (Alfia Vecchio Wallace, 1964–)

Linguist, Web Designer, Cofounder of Bastard Nation
Adoptee

Career, Major Awards, and Achievements

Damsel Plum cofounded and designed the colorful adoptee activist Web site *Bastard Nation*. The Web site grew out of an Internet Usenet group called alt.adoption and was created by "founding foundlings" Damsel Plum, Shea Grimm, and Marley Greiner in 1996. A pioneer adoptee Web site, *Bastard Nation* advocates adoption reform in terms of greater transparency and accountability in the adoption industry, adoptee civil rights, and unconditional access for adopted adults to their original vital records. It also provides a forum for persons who have experienced difficult or abusive adoptions or reunions. The Internet has done much to help adopted persons, an otherwise invisible minority, mobilize as a community. *Bastard Nation*'s irreverent, angry, and humorous content has earned both applause and criticism, but at its core, searchers find helpful and reliable resources and unflagging support.

Plum edited the related newsletter, *Bastard Quarterly*, from 1997 to 2002, when she retired from the Web site, and in 1996 cofounded *The Adoption Ring*, a collection of Internet links that help members of the adoption triad. She was given the 2000 Forbes *Best of the Web* Award for *Bastard Nation* and *The Adoption Ring*. She helped found and administer two additional and innovative programs: TIES (terminal illness emergency search), which helps expedite adoption searches for terminally ill seekers, and CARE (coalition for adoption registry ethics), an organization that opposes unethical or predatory adoption registry practices. She has presented numerous workshops for *Bastard Nation* and *American Adoption Congress* conferences and has administered special events, such as Adoptee Rights Day (1998–2001) and Regday (1998–2000), an annual day of awareness regarding mutual consent registries.

Plum located her family of origin in 1990 after a difficult search. She advocates self-empowered searches for adoptees who wish to search:

Society still treats adopted adults like chattel, like people who were lucky enough to be given not only life, but somebody to change their diapers, and therefore they don't have a right to their original birth certificate. They don't have a right to any genealogy other than that of the people who raised them; they don't have a right to their adoption file or anything that might be contained therein.

Once I got involved with the adoptee rights movement I found out that all this was systemic. States sealed records in 1914 so that there wouldn't be shame associated with being adopted and that adoptees would be able to inherit just like biological children. The end result was that adoption practitioners were able to operate, especially private practitioners, in a zero accountability environment. A big part of our message is that adoption needs to serve the adopted person and the family. Once the person is an adult, that person needs to be considered independently of the family. That person is a citizen. That person pays taxes and is not a criminal. That person needs to be treated equally under the law the same as every other person.

Bastard Nation has worked hard to get people out of the closet, using the Internet, which is a revolutionary activist tool, to bring people together who are disenfranchised, who may have shame issues, or who may have never told anybody. To be able to bring people together is incredibly empowering and incredibly effective. Mind you, bastards are beautiful, and we are fabulous. I think there is something to be said for celebrating our unique and wonderful heritage—our patchwork heritage (personal interview, June 12, 2002).

Family of Origin

Damsel Plum is the *nom de plume* of Alfia Vecchio Wallace. She was born December 17, 1964, in New York City to a college art student from North Carolina. I interviewed Damsel Plum on June 12, 2002, and her birth, adoption, and adoption search stories are given below.

My birthmother named the wrong guy as the birthfather and therefore I was put into a family that was Sicilian and Jewish, Anglo-Jewish. When I got off the plane, and my birthmother looked at me, she said, "Oh my God, it was Herb!" She had some explaining to do.

I talk to my birthmother a few times a year, and she comes to visit every few years. I probably talk with my birthfather a little less, although I get along with him.

I have a half-sibling, a brother ten years younger. We had really, really, really, really different upbringings. Really different. My birthmother became a missionary and a born-again Christian. She runs a foster home for wayward boys in the North Carolina woods. I was raised by hippie intellectuals in New York City . . . a very different scene.

[Our relationship] is cordial. You know there's a tie there. It's just that we don't have common experiences behind us, so it's hard. My birthfather lives in the South, and grew up in this Pentecostal family. In my adoptive family, everybody wore their heart on their sleeve, said what they thought, and were into the free exchange of ideas. It is very different in my birth family, but we get along fine.

I didn't search until I was twenty-six. When I was eighteen, my [adoptive] dad gave me my adoption papers with my original name and he told me that I could go to the agency and find out some information. I got all the nonidentifying information and felt really overwhelmed. I was just starting college and I didn't do anything with it. I went back once after graduate school and got slightly different information. I got out of graduate school and started thinking, "Well, I'm twenty-six, I'm going to start thinking about having a family, and I should really find out about my family, my biological background." That's when I decided to search in earnest. I went to the agency with my parents and I found out all about roadblocks. I joined Adoption Circle with **Joe Soll** and learned a little bit about adoption activism, started compiling stuff, joined ALMA [Adoptees' Liberty Movement Association], and just started reading about how to do it.

New York is really, really hard [to search]. It's not like it is in California, where it's relatively easy. I found somebody who was willing to give me a clue that I needed, and that was the profession of my maternal grandfather. So I left work that day, and went to the Fifth Avenue Library. I looked up everybody with the last name on my adoption decree who belonged to that profession in the *Who's Who in Science*. Then I pretended to be a genealogist with the National Genealogical Society. I asked very mundane questions about male scions of the family and when I got the answers that I wanted, I called and said, "Did you have a daughter in New York City in 1964?" and they said, "Oh, who is this?" I had to really tip-toe around. I mean, it's all very humiliating and you feel like some sort of Peeping Tom or somebody creeping around, and all you want to know is "Who the heck is the person who gave birth to me?"

I would not say I'm very glad I searched. Yes, I feel more whole. Yes, that shadow, that cloud of uncertainty has lifted and I'm glad I did it, but it was hard.

Adoption

I was adopted in New York City in 1964, through the Spence Chapin Agency, and I lived in a foster home for two months with an older lady who adored babies. I was raised in Jackson Heights, Queens, New York, in a middle class, melting pot, semiurban kind of neighborhood. My [adoptive] mother grew up in boarding schools in England, a daughter of privilege, and my dad was the child of Sicilian immigrants. They met in Italy when he was doing his PhD and she was in finishing school. Her father opposed the marriage, but they got married anyway.

I was well placed based on educational background of the family and the desire for travel. My birthmother's father is a world-class nuclear physicist and writes books on how to build nuclear power plants. Her mother was a homemaker. I grew up in a family that was very academic. My [adoptive] mother's father was a world authority on Dutch and Portuguese colonization and her mother was a journalist for *The New Yorker* who has published over fifty books. My [adoptive] dad was a history professor. I traveled a lot as a kid and young adult but I didn't look anything like my parents, you know. They all had black curly hair and dark eyes, and I have blonde hair, blue eyes and am very fair. So they were constantly having to make excuses for the way I looked.

I always knew I was adopted. They read me the *Chosen Baby* book, and it was all "you were chosen, you're special," then they had a daughter two years after they got me and she looks like them. You often hear these stories of people feeling like they were treated second best when they had other siblings that were not adopted, but that was definitely not the case with us. She's my sister—we grew up together.

If anything I felt that my dad, I don't want to say he pitied me, but he really went out of his way to make me feel special. When I was in third grade, for some reason it came up, and I said, "Oh, I'm adopted," and some kid said, "Oh, you mean your mother was a whore, and she didn't want you?" and I was like "WHAT? No! It means I'm chosen and special," and they laughed at me. I went home crying and my dad told me that those kids were ignorant jerks. This was a very empowering phrase for me, "ignorant jerks," and I had plenty of opportunities to use it. I feel like the parents who raised me are my parents, and my allegiance is to them. My dad lived with me for the last three years of his life while he was sick. He passed away in 1998. My mother lives in New York City. This is my family.

Education and Significant Relationships

Plum attended the High School for Performing Arts in New York City. She completed a double major in linguistics and Russian at SUNY, Stony Brook. She earned a Masters degree in Slavic languages and literature at Yale University. She studied additional languages, including Spanish, Greek, Latin, Italian, and Arabic at the University of California, Berkeley.

She and her husband, Dr. Arthur Wallace, live in northern California and have two sons, Alfred and Andrew. Plum does selective freelance Web design and maintains her own Web sites *Plumsites* and *Bay Area Moms*. She teaches technology and foreign languages to Marin county school children.

Works Cited

Babb, L. Anne. *Ethics in American Adoption.* Westport, CT: Bergin & Garvey, 1999.

Carp, E. Wayne. *Adoption Politics and Ballot Initiative 58.* Lawrence, KS: University Press of Kansas, 2004. 26, 28, 31, 103, 106–107, 113, 141.

Foreman, Gayle. "Are You My Mother? Adopted Teens Search for Their Families, Their Histories, and Their Identities." *Seventeen Magazine* 59 (November 2000): 182.

Garfinkel, Simson. *Database Nation: The Death of Privacy in the 21st Century.* Sebastopol, CA: O'Reilly & Assoc., 2000. 146–147+.

Shaw, Randy. *Reclaiming America: Nike, Clean Air, and the New National Activism.* Berkeley: University of California Press, c1999: 282–286.

Sullivan, Randall. "The Bastard Chronicles." *Rolling Stone* February 15, 2001: 53.

POE, EDGAR ALLAN (1809–1849)

Author, Poet
Fostered

Career, Major Awards, and Achievements

Edgar Allan Poe is best known for his dark and haunting stories and poems. He is considered a major figure in world literature and is the founder of the modern detective story and the modern horror story. He was a pioneer of the short story and is a forefather of such literary genres as psychological realism, science fiction, and surrealism. His use of symbolism had a great influence on modern poetry. In 1843, two of his works won first prize for fiction: "Manuscript Found in a Bottle," published in the *Baltimore Saturday Visitor* and "The Gold Bug" in the *Philadelphia Dollar Newspaper*. His poetic works were first published in the following collections: *Tamerlane and Other Poems* (1827), *Al Aaraaf, Tamerlane, and Minor Poems* (1829), *Poems* (1831), *The Raven and Other Poems* (1845), and *Eureka: A Prose Poem* (1848). His short stories include *Tales of the Grotesque and Arabesque* (1840), *The Murders in the Rue Morgue* (1843), *The Man That Was Used Up* (1843), and *Tales* (1845). Poe also wrote essays and short novels. He was posthumously considered one of the finest literary critics of his time. He was editor or editorial staff member for several journals, notably the *Southern Literary Messenger* (1835–37), *Burlington Gentleman's Magazine* (1839–40), *Graham's Lady's and Gentleman's Magazine* (1841–42), *Evening Mirror* (1845), and the *Broadway Journal*, which he owned (1845–46). Poe published his works in these journals and gained some national recognition during his lifetime. Even so, Poe's earnings remained meager and much of his adult life was spent in poverty.

[Courtesy of the National Archives]

Poe's numerous works are now available in many collected editions. His stories have been made into plays, recordings, and popular movies, such as *The Raven* (1912, 1915, 1935, 1963, 1973), *The Bells* (1913), *The Murders in the Rue Morgue* (1914, 1932, 1954, released as *Phantom of the Rue Morgue*, 1954), *The Black Cat* (1934, 1941), *The Premature Burial* (1935, released as *The Crime of Dr. Crespi*, 1962), *The Tell-Tale Heart* (1941, 1950, released as *Heartbeat*, 1953, two versions in 1959, 1971), *Masque of the Red Death* (1954, 1964, 1970), *Tales of Terror* (1962), *The Haunted Palace* (1963), *The Pit and the Pendulum* (1961, released as *The Pit*, 1964, 1966, 1975), *The Tomb of Ligeia* (1965), *City in the* Sea (1965, released as *War-Gods of the Deep*), *The Fall of the House of Usher* (1960, 1969), *The Oblong Box* (1969), *Spirits of the Dead* (1969), and *Annabel Lee* (1973). Musician Lou Reed created a thirteen-song work called POEtry (2001), based on Poe's works.

Family of Origin

Edgar Allan Poe was born in Boston, Massachusetts, to David Poe, Jr., an Irish-American actor, and Elizabeth (Arnold) Poe, an English-born actress. David Poe had a promising law practice, but, to the strong disapproval of his family, he decided instead to become an actor. In the six years he performed on stage, David was cast in 137 different roles, but a growing alcoholism and his tendency to make violent threats to unfavorable critics began to undermine his successes.

Poe's mother, Elizabeth, known as "Eliza," had immigrated to America as a young girl with her widowed mother, notable Theatre Royal actress Elizabeth Arnold. Eliza made her own stage debut in Boston at the age of nine and enjoyed a promising career on the stage. Her husband was eventually given only minor roles, if any, and so Eliza's inadequate earnings alone had to sustain the couple's growing family. Their first child, William, was born in 1807, followed by Edgar on January 19, 1809, and a sister, Rosalie, in December 1810. David Poe deserted his family before the birth of Rosalie. Edgar's autobiography claims that both his parents died within weeks of each other from consumption (Harrison 344).

Adoption

After Eliza's death on December 8, 1811, her children went into separate homes. Their grandfather, David Poe, took in William. John Allan and his wife Frances (known as Fanny), took Edgar, who was barely three years old at the time. Rosalie was seriously ill as an infant and initially not expected to live. She was taken in and eventually adopted by the Mackenzie family, who lived near the Allans. Although Rosalie survived, she was permanently frail and developmentally injured.

The Allans were wealthy theatergoers and had learned of the last illness of Eliza Poe, one of their favorite actresses. Although the Allans never formally adopted Edgar, he grew up as Edgar Allan and his name was recorded into the family Bible. Allan also provided for at least one illegitimate son, Edwin Collier, who was a few years older than Edgar. Edgar was especially close to his foster mother, who had herself been orphaned at the age of ten and raised by a guardian. Fanny and her older sister, Anne, known as "Aunt Nancy," doted on Edgar. Fanny had many health problems, and she passed away in 1829 at the age of forty-four, while Poe was away at West Point.

Poe's foster father, John Allan, was a stern, self-educated, self-made man who created his fortune as an exporter. Allan had emigrated from Scotland when he was sixteen years old and became the clerk of his rich merchant uncle, William Galt. Galt sponsored liberal educations for his eight adopted and fostered children, but kept his nephew "tight to business" (Silverman 12). Poe's relationship with his foster father became worse as he grew older: "In being John Allan's ward, he became dependent on the care and generosity of someone who despised dependence and felt that he had been cheated of care and generosity himself" (Silverman 11). Poe's final break with his foster father occurred after Fanny's death, as he explains in his brief autobiography:

In about 18 months [after Fanny's death] Mr. A. married a second time (a Miss Patterson, a near relative of General Winfield Scott)—he being then 65 years of age. Mrs. A. and myself quarreled, and he, siding with her wrote me an angry letter, to which I replied in the same spirit. Soon afterwards he died, having had a son by Mrs. A., and although leaving a vast property, bequeathed me nothing. The army does not suit a poor man—so I left W. Point abruptly, and threw myself upon literature as a resource (Harrison 345).

A Richmond friend, Susan Archer Talley, discussed the quarrel mentioned: "after Louisa [the second Mrs. Allan] had emphasized Poe's dependent position and reminded him that he was 'an object of charity in her house,' he retaliated by accusing her of having married for money" (Meyers 54). Indeed, Allan had inherited his Uncle Galt's fortune and was thought to have been one of the wealthiest men in Virginia. His rift with Edgar not only left the young man destitute, but "caused great psychological as well as material damage. The death of Frances Allan reflected the death of his mother; the rejection by John Allan mirrored the desertion of his father; and the adopted orphan, having lost his foster parents, was orphaned once again" (Meyers 55).

Education, Military Service, and Significant Relationships

In 1826, Allan sent Poe to the University of Virginia with $110 but refused to let him return to school after the first year. Allan sabotaged Poe's numerous attempts to find work by unfailingly contacting the potential employer and giving them negative reports about his ward. Edgar tried to supplement his meager allowance by gambling and accrued many "debts of honor," which Allan refused to pay:

> He knew that an inexperienced boy of seventeen with $110, in a university in which the minimum annual expenses were "$350, plus room, bed, blankets, and ordinaries at $149 per annum, was assuredly committed to confusion, misery and failure. So that when Allan sent this arrogant, brilliant, stylish young man as a beggar among the wealthiest young men in Virginia, it was a calculated and cruel mortification, unforgettable and unforgivable in any circumstances. For one as delicately balanced as Poe, it produced strains and tensions with which he could not begin to cope rationally (Mankowitz 35).

Hounded by creditors, in 1827 Poe enlisted in the army under the name Edgar A. Perry and became a regimental sergeant-major. He was honorably discharged in 1829. He attended the U.S. Military Academy at West Point in 1829–1831.

Poe moved to New York City and found his aunt, Mrs. Maria Clemm, whom he called "Muddy," and came to regard as his mother. Mrs. Clemm was the sister of Edgar's father, David Poe, and had lost her own son as an infant. Edgar formed an intense attachment to Mrs. Clemm and her nine-year-old daughter, Virginia, whom Poe called "Sissy" and would marry when she was thirteen years old. Virginia died of consumption on January 30, 1847, at the age of twenty-four. Poe, who had become addicted to alcohol and other drugs, died on October 7, 1849, in Baltimore, Maryland. His death at age forty was believed to have been caused by either a lethal amount of alcohol or encephalitis.

Works Cited

Bittner, William. *Poe: A Biography*. Boston: Little, Brown, 1962.

Harrison, James A. *The Life of Edgar Allan Poe*. New York: Haskell House, 1970.

Kennedy, J. Gerald. *A Historical Guide to Edgar Allan Poe*. New York: Oxford University Press, 2001.

Mankowitz, Wolf. *The Extraordinary Mr. Poe.* New York: Summit Books, 1978.

Meyers, Jeffrey. *Edgar Allan Poe: His Life and Legacy.* New York: Charles Scribner's Sons, 1992.

Quinn, Arthur Hobson. *Edgar Allan Poe: A Critical Biography.* New York: D. Appleton-Century, 1941.

Silverman, Kenneth. *Edgar A. Poe: Mournful and Never-Ending Remembrance.* New York: Harper-Collins, 1991.

Sova, Dawn. *Edgar Allan Poe, A to Z.* New York: Facts on File, 2001.

R

REAGAN, MICHAEL (1945–)

Author, Talk Show Host, President's Son
Adoptee

Career, Major Awards, and Achievements

An avid campaigner for Ronald Reagan during his bids for the presidency, Michael Reagan began his career as a boat salesman and was later a record-setting, world-champion speedboat racer. By the mid-1980s, he began hosting a weekly Sunday afternoon radio talk show. In 1986, he landed character roles in television soap operas like *Capitol* and *Falcon Crest*, which starred his adoptive mother, Jane Wyman. He played small parts in several movies, such as *Over the Top* and *Cyclone*, and he briefly hosted a Canadian television game show, *Ricochet!*

Today, as a nationally syndicated radio talk show host and author of six books, Michael Reagan is heard daily by over five million listeners via more than 200 stations across the United States. Known for his conservative and colorfully expressed viewpoints, he often champions the policies and perspectives of his adoptive father, former president Ronald Reagan, through his provocative on-air political and social commentary and through his books, which include *On the Outside Looking In* (1988), *Michael Reagan Making Waves* (1996), *The City on a Hill: Fulfilling Ronald Reagan's Vision for America* (1997), *The Common Sense of an Uncommon Man: The Wit, Wisdom, and Eternal Optimism of Ronald Reagan* (1998), and *Twice Adopted* (2004).

Reagan served on the Board of Directors of the National Association of Radio Talk Show Hosts and is a member of the Board of Directors of the John Douglass French Alzheimer's Foundation. President George W. Bush appointed him to the National Moment of Remembrance Committee.

Family of Origin

Michael Edward Reagan was born March 18, 1945, in Los Angeles to Irene Flaugher, 28. She named him John after his biological father, Corporal John Bourgholtzer, a tall, athletic soldier of German-American descent. Bourgholtzer was a Catholic and married; Flaugher was a Protestant divorcée.

[AP Photo/Michael Sohn]

The couple had met in Ohio, but after they discovered Irene was pregnant, she followed Bourgholtzer to Arizona when the army transferred him there. When he was transferred to France, he gave Irene $400 and asked that she go to California to deliver their baby. Bourgholtzer would not meet his son until 1990, 45 years later, after settling in Florida and fathering two more children.

Flaugher moved into a home for unwed mothers and worked as a waitress in Los Angeles at the time her son was born. Before relinquishing custody, she insisted on meeting the baby's prospective adoptive parents, actors Jane Wyman and Ronald Reagan. Wyman later told Michael that he was adopted through an agency and did not disclose that she had met his birth mother.

Irene eventually returned to Ohio and had another son, Barry Lange. Barry learned the truth about his half-brother around 1981, shortly after Ronald Reagan became president. Irene died of a heart attack in 1985 at age 69. Though she died before reunion with Michael, she left Barry a scrapbook documenting everything the local newspapers had recorded about the Reagan family's activities.

Michael and Barry met each other in 1987, after Michael unexpectedly received information about his birthmother's family through a mutual friend. Michael Reagan attended a Flaugher family reunion in 1990 and met a large group of extended family members who had gathered in New Castle, Pennsylvania. The man who had spent years wondering about his origins finally discovered more birth family than he had ever imagined.

After they met, Barry told Michael: "Mom actually took you and placed you in Jane Wyman's arms. It must have almost killed her to do that, but she wanted to do the best thing for her baby" (*Twice Adopted* 292).

Michael's birthfather died after a series of strokes in 1993, but he also passed on a box of photographs and newspaper clippings about Michael Reagan. Terry Dougela, Reagan's half-sister, later told him, "He had regrets about giving you up for adoption, but he felt it was best to let you live your life and not intrude. He was probably afraid that you wouldn't accept him and forgive him. . . . He was very proud of you" (*Twice Adopted* 302).

Adoptive Family

Doctors had advised Ronald Reagan and Jane Wyman that it would be a health risk to have more children after the birth of their first child, Maureen. A family anecdote credits four-year old Maureen for initiating Michael's adoption when she surprised her father on a shopping trip by dumping her piggy bank contents on the counter and asking the clerk for a brother. "The story is undoubtedly apocryphal. . . . The fact that I was adopted was probably going to be withheld from me as long as possible in keeping with the custom of the time. Little did my adoptive parents know how much pain the fact that I was adopted would soon cause me" (*On the Outside Looking In* 14). When Michael was four, Maureen told him the secret that he had been adopted. Reassured by his parents, he shared his adoption story at school and was afterwards often teased about being illegitimate. Soon his initial feelings of "being special" and "chosen" changed to worry and shame.

Michael spent his summers at a day camp and was the victim of a sexual assault while there. The molestation, which included nude photographs, and Michael's own belief that "bastard" children would go to hell, were to cripple his life for decades to come:

> At the age of seven I was sexually molested by a camp counselor. I told no one. Jane and Ronald were divorced by then, and I suffered alone and in silence as I have all the other traumas of my life. It is only in the light of recent discovery that I have come to realize that my memory has been selfishly selective. My parents—birth as well as adoptive—were not villains, and I hobbled through my early years on the crutches of adoption and sexual abuse (*On the Outside Looking In* 8).

After Ronald Reagan and Jane Wyman divorced, Michael stayed with his adoptive mother. Wyman won many awards during her busy film career, including the Best Actress Oscar in 1949, and she chose to educate Michael and Maureen at boarding schools. Later Michael moved with his mother to Newport, where he attended a day school. This allowed him a brief period of living at home, which he craved. After Michael had spent several months making new friends and settling in to the day school, Wyman abruptly told her son that she was sending him to Loyola High School in Los Angeles. Loyola was a boarding school, and had a reputation as one of the highest rated Catholic schools in the area. Michael's rage over the event led him to destroy a bicycle, which had been a gift from his mother, with a ball peen hammer. He later wrote, "All I could think of was that the bike was a gift from mom and it didn't like me either. . . . With every smashing blow I thought of that bike as my mother, hoping if I somehow destroyed it I was also destroying her" (*On the Outside Looking In* 69). Michael's one oasis seemed to be his weekend visits to Ronald Reagan's Malibu ranch, where he had a chance of getting his father's attention.

Ronald Reagan had remarried to Nancy Davis in 1952. Nancy had also been adopted as a child, by her stepfather, and it was she who, after an argument with Michael, first discovered and told him his birth name. During the family's White House years, serious rifts developed between Michael and the rest of the first family, but these were eventually resolved. One source of the rift was Michael's first autobiography, *On the Outside Looking In,* published during his father's administration, and which gives an intimate account of adoption by parents who would attain the absolute pinnacle of fame: "The odds against an adoptee ending up as a child of the President of the United States are staggering. But then, so are the odds against a movie actor becoming president" (*On the Outside Looking In* 7).

Education, Marriage, and Children

Abysmal grades forced Michael to repeat his junior year of high school. In a bargain struck with his father, Michael transferred to Judson, a boarding school in Arizona. For the first time, his outlook rose with his grades. He lettered in football, basketball, and baseball, becoming the top pitcher for the team. When Michael graduated in May 1964, he was a member of the National Honor Society. Medically disqualified for the Viet Nam war draft, he briefly attended Arizona State University.

Michael married Pamela Putnum in 1970, but the couple divorced in 1971. He married his second wife, Colleen, in 1975. They have a son, Cameron, and a daughter, Ashley.

Reagan credits three events with finally bringing relief from his inner turmoil: searching for his birth family and finding out about his roots, telling his wife Colleen and adoptive family about being molested, and finding peace with God.

Works Cited

Reagan, Michael. *The City on a Hill: Fulfilling Ronald Reagan's Vision for America.* Nashville: Thomas Nelson, 1997.

———. "From Grief to Optimism." *U.S. News and World Report* June 21, 2004: 58 (Michael Reagan's eulogy for President Ronald Reagan).

———. *Making Waves: Bold Exposés from Talk Radio's Number One Nighttime Host.* Nashville: Thomas Nelson, 1996.

———. *On the Outside Looking In.* New York: Kensington, 1988.

———. *Twice Adopted.* Nashville: Broadman & Holman, 2004.

ROWELL, VICTORIA (1959–)

Dancer, Actress, Author
Orphanage alumna, fostered person, foster child activist

Career, Major Awards, and Achievements

Victoria Rowell is probably best known for her roles as Drucilla Barber Winters on the daytime drama *The Young and the Restless* and Dr. Amanda Bentley on *Diagnosis Murder*, but she is becoming equally well-known for her work with foster children.

[AP Photo/Gus Ruelas]

Rowell was eight when she received a Ford Foundation Scholarship to the Cambridge School of Ballet. By the time she was sixteen, she had received scholarships to study at the School of American Ballet and the American Ballet Theatre. She danced professionally with several companies before becoming a guest-artist teacher at New England area schools, but found that the ballet world was very difficult for African American women. As she grew older and taller, she also felt pressured to keep her 5' 7" body under 100 pounds.

She became a guest artist and teacher at New England area schools, and at the same time she began a second career as a model, appearing in *Seventeen* and *Mademoiselle* before she moved on to acting. She auditioned for *The Cosby Show* and was given a recurring role, playing Paula, the biological mother of Olivia Kendall. Bill Cosby also chose her to play his daughter in the feature film *Leonard 6*. She moved to Los Angeles to continue her acting career.

Relentlessly cast as wholesome "Suzy Homemaker" types, Rowell relates that she arrived following baby-sitter problems "with seconds to spare" at an audition for the *Young and the Restless* (Gregory 78). Her cranky mood turned out to be a gift in disguise, as it helped her land the role of Drucilla Barber, a delinquent street girl with a bad attitude. Viewers wrote to express disapproval of negative African American stereotyping,* but Rowell felt that their disapproval would be short-lived, as the character was scripted to get an education, find a good job, and study ballet. From one season to the next, Drucilla moved up in the world, eventually marrying successful advertising executive Neil Winters. Rowell was nominated for an Emmy award and won eleven NAACP Image Awards, the 1993 and 1994 awards for her role as Drucilla. At Rowell's suggestion, a foster care and adoption storyline was integrated into *The Young and the Restless* and the storyline received local and national honors.

Never content with one job, Rowell played pathologist/medical examiner Dr. Amanda Bentley on *Diagnosis Murder* for eight seasons, costarring with television legend Dick Van Dyke, all the while continuing her role on *The Young and the Restless*, which she finally left in 2007. During this time she was influential in a program to employ Los Angles foster youth, called Foster Youth Connection. She has been able to help some of her protégés break into the entertainment industry: "I wanted these kids to see someone successful who has been in their shoes" (Gregory 128).

Rowell has appeared in feature films such as *The Distinguished Gentleman* (1992) with Eddie Murphy, *Eve's Bayou* (1997) starring Diahann Carroll, and *Home of the Brave* (2006) opposite Samuel L. Jackson and rap artist 50 Cent. She played Josette Metoyer, an elderly Haitian plantation owner, in the Showtime mini-series *Feast of All Saints* (2001). Additional roles in television shows include *The Fresh Prince of Bel Air*, *Herman's Head*, and *Deadly Games*, and in the films *Dumb and Dumber* (1994) and *Barbed Wire* (1996).

In 1990, Rowell established and funded a scholarship program to help children in foster care participate in the arts and sports. Her successful advocacy program became the Rowell Foster Children's Positive Plan (RFCPP), a nonprofit organization that helps to enrich the lives of foster children through the arts, sports, job mentorship, and other types of support. It is located on the web at www.rowellfosterchldren.org. RFCPP, which has helped hundreds of foster children, has earned important political, social and cultural endorsements from a variety of groups and organizations, including the Clinton administration, congressional and municipal partners, the Ford Foundation, American

---

*Nearly a quarter of daytime drama watchers are African-American. *Essence*, September 1995.

Ballet Theatre, School of American Ballet, the NAACP, New Yorkers for Children, the Alliance for Children's Rights, and the Children's Defense Fund.

Family of Origin

Victoria Rowell was born on May 10, 1959, in Portland, Maine, the fifth of six children of Dorothy Mabel Collins Rowell, a white Mayflower descendant who was later institutionalized with schizophrenia:

> First there were two boys, then three girls—of whom I was the youngest—and then another boy. We were each of different paternity but all given the last name of Dorothy's first and only husband, Norman Rowell, Sr. . . .
> Eventually Dorothy's family and the law interceded, deeming Dorothy unfit to raise her four younger children, all born out of wedlock. Whether this had mainly to do with the different fathers being Hispanic and African American was never admitted (Rowell 6–7).

Dorothy gave birth to Norman Jr. in 1943 and David in 1952. She and her husband separated and Dorothy moved with her sons to Brunswick, Maine, but Norman Sr. fought to regain custody of their eldest boy. In 1956, Dorothy gave birth to Sheree, whose father was Puerto Rican, and in 1957 to Lori, whose father was African American. Victoria Rowell believes that her father was "a dashing young black sailor" (Rowell 26) whom Dorothy had dated during the summer of 1958.

Neighbors began to voice their concerns about Dorothy, who was manifesting symptoms of mental illness. When it was time for Victoria's birth, Dorothy took a taxi to the nearest hospital, leaving David (age 7), Sheree (3), and Lori (2), completely unattended. The landlady contacted social services about her tenant's crying children, and when the state officers arrived, they found the children hungry, frightened, and living in a "deplorably filthy" home (Rowell 27). When Victoria was sixteen days old, her mother lost custody of the remaining children. Dorothy had a sixth child, a son whom she raised on her own, "despite some interruptions" (Rowell 28).

Rowell saw her mother only three times in her life, two of the visits were arranged by Agatha Armstead, who fostered Victoria. Dorothy, who was often institutionalized, died of lung cancer in 1983. Rowell's half-brother, David, brought her to say goodbye to their dying mother, but their mother's sister Lillian, who was caring for Dorothy at the time, would not let Victoria into the house. Although she was also not invited to attend her mother's private funeral, Rowell went anyway: "After a lifetime of exclusion and denial, I had found the courage to show up. It was the courage to reveal a family's secret that I was the human stain on the blue-blood pedigree" (Rowell 14).

Rowell's father's name, she believes, was Wilson, and his family was from Washington, D.C. (Gregory 128,132). She came across this information in 1983 when she found one of her mother's letters:

> I read it, frenzied, following her handwriting that took up the front and the back. . . then I froze, reading what she said was my father's name. My validation, that two people, each of whom had names, had created me, a father and a mother, was there in black and white, literally. After folding the letter, exactly as I found it, I returned it to its dark vault and never touched it again (Rowell 243).

Orphanage and Foster Homes

Following Social Service's intervention, Norman Sr. came and took custody of David. Sheree and Lori were taken to an orphanage until a suitable African American foster or adoptive family could be found for them. Victoria boarded at Mercy Hospital for five days then was sent to the Holy Innocents orphanage.

Victoria was placed with Bertha and Collins Taylor on June 8, 1959. The Taylors were a white family who adored the child and wished to keep her with them. Social services wanted the baby to be placed in an African American home, so, when she was two-and-a-half, Victoria was removed from the Taylors and given to Robert and Agatha Armstead, an older couple who were already fostering her sisters, Sheree and Lori.

Victoria and her sisters grew up on the Armstead farm, called Forest Edge, in Maine. Robert Armstead, Rowell's foster father, had been a black orphan with whom Victoria felt a special bond. He died shortly before Victoria turned three. His wife Agatha Wooten Armstead, whom Rowell called "Ma," was a very accomplished woman of African American and Native American ancestry. Rowell writes, "Every day that unfolded around her was Ma's personal celebration of life, nature, art, music, language, family, and work. Not necessarily in that order" (Rowell 42). Ten children were born to the Armsteads, nine survived to adulthood. Since they were grown when the Rowells came, the girls called the Armstead children "aunts" and "uncles." Agatha was influential in seeing that Victoria stayed with her sisters rather than being placed in a solo adoption "with an excellent, young, childless Negro family" (Rowell 51), which was her case worker's preference. Agatha recognized and tutored Victoria's special abilities and the child joyously responded to one willing to teach her. She relates:

> Like many children who grapple with instabilities in their home and family lives, I depended on my early observational powers for stability, as a way to give me a desperately needed connection—not just to other human beings but to all that was certain and tangible (Rowell 57).

When she was nine, Rowell moved to Dorchester, Massachusetts, to live with Agatha's son, Richie Armstead, a Boston police officer, his wife, Laura, and their daughters. This enabled Rowell to attend the Cambridge School of Ballet and study under her mentor, Esther Brooks. While at this home, Rowell began to experience a physical complaint that would continue to plague her: her palms and feet became suddenly excessively wet with perspiration. Victoria believed at the time that this was a type of "stigmata" connected to her having been born out of wedlock or to her being a foster child (Rowell 129). She would later have surgery to correct this condition, called hyperhidrosis, which is caused by a nerve abnormality near the spine.

Barbara Sterling, originally from Jamaica, was the mother of Victoria's friend in ballet school, Jackie Legister, and her home became Rowell's unofficial "weekend respite dwelling" (Rowell 162). Rowell called Sterling "an earth mother to me, a root woman" (164).

For two years, beginning when she was fourteen, Rowell stayed in Roxbury with the parents of her best friend, Lauren Turner. In the mid-1970s, Rowell began to live at the home of another ballet friend, Robyn Silverman. Silvia Silverman, Robyn's mother, was a teacher from middle class suburbia; her father, Maurice, ran a drapery business. The Silverman's was Victoria's last foster home before she emancipated from state care at age eighteen. When Rowell left for New York, the Silvermans made a gift to her of the money Social Services had sent them for her care, which they had put aside for her.

Rowell honored her mother, Dorothy Rowell, her five foster mothers—Bertha Collins, Agatha Armstead, who died in 1982, Rosa Turner, Barbara Sterling, Silvia Silverman—and her dance mentors and other personal heroes in her memoir, *The*

Women Who Raised Me, published in 2007 by William Morrow. The book is a tribute to the memorable women who raised, supported, and mentored her in her journey from foster child to widely recognized actress and mentor to other foster children.

Education and Significant Relationships

Rowell, who received eight years of formal training at the Cambridge School of Ballet, graduated from Shaw Preparatory School in Boston in 1979. In addition to her studies at the School of American Ballet and the Dance Theatre of Harlem, she also studied with the American Ballet Theater and the Julliard School of Music in their Dance Extension program. In 2006, Rowell was given an honorary Doctorate of Humane Letters from the University of Southern Maine for her work with foster youth.

In 1989, Rowell married Tom Fahey, with whom she had a daughter, Maya, named after the Russian ballerina Maya Plisetskaya. Maya, who is blond and blue-eyed, inherited her grandmother and father's English and Celtic features. The couple divorced in 1990.

Rowell also has a son, Jasper Armstrong Marsalis, with jazz musician Wynton Marsalis. Jasper played his mother's television son "C.J." on *Diagnosis Murder*.

In 1994, Rowell arranged the first reunion of her brothers and sisters. She remains in contact with her three brothers, who live and work in Maine, and her two sisters. Lori is married with four children; she is a police officer and forensic photographer in Boston. Sheree works as an accounting supervisor for a government agency. She lives in Colorado.

Works Cited

Gregory, Deborah. "Victoria's Secret." *Essence* 26 (September 1995) 76.
Rowell, Victoria. *The Women Who Raised Me: A Memoir*. New York: William Morrow, 2007.

S

SACAGAWEA (ca. 1788–ca.1812)

Interpreter and Guide
Captured, sold

Major Achievements

The young Shoshone mother who accompanied the Lewis and Clark Expedition from 1804 to 1806 is a figure of much historical contention. Scholars argue over her age, names, role in the expedition, and her death. A written record of her first appears in William Clark's journal on November 4, 1804, when he notes the visit of Toussaint Charbonneau and his two Snake (Shoshone) wives to Fort Mandan, the expedition's winter camp, built near the mouth of the Knife River in North Dakota. President Thomas Jefferson and the U. S. Congress had authorized a corps of thirty-three men, headed by Captains Meriwether Lewis and William Clark, to explore a possible water route along the Missouri and Columbia rivers to the Pacific Ocean. The corps hired Charbonneau, a French-Canadian trader who spoke French and Hidatsa, as an interpreter, provided that he also bring one of his wives to interpret the Shoshone language. The explorers hoped to buy horses and supplies from the Shoshone, and Sacagawea, Charbonneau's second wife, became the chosen interpreter.

Sacagawea was pregnant with her first child when she joined the expedition, and was thought to be around sixteen years old when she gave birth to a son on February 11, 1805, after what Lewis described as a tedious and violently painful labor (February 11, 1805). The baby was named Jean Baptiste Charbonneau and called "Pomp" by William Clark, who later legally adopted him. He accompanied his mother in a cradleboard. The explorers quickly lost respect for Charbonneau and recorded several examples of his cowardice and brutality toward his wife (May 14 and August 5, 1805). The journals also reflect, however, a deepening appreciation for Sacagawea's courage and merit. The June 1805 journals record her recovery from a severe illness and near drowning in a flash flood. She used her knowledge of plants to find, gather, and prepare wild edibles for the corps. She was the expedition's symbol of "friendly intentions" toward the native peoples the expeditionary group encountered. Lewis remarked: "a woman with a party of men is a token of peace" (September 13, 1805). The corps named a "handsome river" in Montana after her in recognition of an event in which the boat she was riding nearly capsized during a storm. While her husband cowered in the boat, Sacagawea swam out and rescued "papers, instruments, books, medicine, and a great proportion of our merchandise" that had washed overboard (May 14, 1805).

Sacagawea's role as a guide is sometimes disputed. However, Clark himself recorded, during the return journey, "the Indian woman, who has been of great service to me as a pilot through this country, recommends a gap in the mountains more south which I shall cross" (July 13, 1806). The expedition followed the Columbia River and reached the Pacific Ocean near present-day Astoria, Washington, on November 7, 1805, and returned to Saint Louis, Missouri. Sacagawea has many memorials, including her river, three mountains, and two lakes. Although no authentic portrait of her exists, a U.S. dollar, first coined in 2000, and many statues and paintings carry her imagined image.

Family of Origin

Sacagawea was born sometime around 1788 in the Shoshone village near the Salmon River in eastern Idaho. Her father was chief of the Lehmi band. Her Shoshone name was Boinaiv ("Grass Maiden"). In 1800, when she was between the ages of ten and twelve, her band was camped at the Three Forks area of the Missouri River in Montana when a Hidatsa war party attacked.

Captivity and Significant Relationships

The girl was taken captive during the Hidatsa raid, along with several other children, and was taken to their camp, where she was renamed Sacajawea ("boat-launcher") or Tsakakawia ("Bird woman"). She and another girl were later sold to Charbonneau, or were won by him in a gambling match. He later claimed them as his wives.

During the expedition, on August 17, 1805, Sacagawea reunited with her long-lost relatives near Beaverhead Rock in Montana. She had a joyful and tearful reunion with her brother, who was now the Lemhi-Shoshoni leader Chief Cameahwait. He told her that only one other brother and her elder sister's son remained alive in her family. According to the customs of her nation, Sacagawea immediately adopted her nephew, whose name was Bazil, but left him in the care of his two uncles.

There are two main accounts of Sacagawea's death. Biographer Grace Hebard of the University of Wyoming believed that a woman recorded as Sacagawea, Bazil's mother, who died in 1884 at around the age of 100, was the expedition's guide. Hebard claims that she left Charbonneau, married a Comanche man, bore five more children and eventually returned to the Shoshone people at Wind River, Wyoming, where she became a tribal elder. This Sacagawea is buried at Fort Washakie, Wyoming. The more compelling, if sadder, version comes from a written account by an employee of the Missouri Fur Company, John Luttwig. On December 20, 1812, he recorded the death of "the Wife of Charbonneau, a Snake Squaw," who died of a "putrid fever" and who left a "fine infant girl," Lizette. This Sacagawea was around twenty-five years old when she died and was buried at Fort Mandan, North Dakota. William Clark recorded Sacagawea as deceased in his account book for 1825–1828 and legally adopted both of her children, Jean Baptiste and Lizette.

Works Cited

Kessler, Donna J. *The Making of Sacagawea: A Euro-American Legend.* Tuscaloosa, AL: University of Alabama Press, 1996.

Lewis, Meriwether, and William Clark. *The Journals of the Lewis & Clark Expedition.* Lincoln: University of Nebraska Press 1997.

Lindenmeyer, Kriste. *Ordinary Women, Extraordinary Lives: Women in American History.* Wilmington, DE: 2000.

Morris, Larry E. *The Fate of the Corps: What Became of the Lewis and Clark Explorers after the Expedition.* New Haven: Yale University Press, 2004.

SAFFIAN, SARAH (1969–)

Author, Journalist, Educator
Adoptee

Career, Major Achievements, and Awards

Sarah Saffian is the author of *Ithaka: A Daughter's Memoir of Being Found* (1998), an intimate and expressive chronicle of her emotional journey following unexpected contact from her family of origin—both parents and three full siblings—when she was twenty-three years old.

Saffian's family of origin hoped that she would contact them soon after she turned eighteen. When that did not take place by the time she had turned twenty-one, they registered with a search organization and with her adoption agency. Eventually, they hired a private investigator who located her and they made contact:

> I guess the reason my birth parents sought me out and contacted me is because they had learned in a support group that it can be beneficial to an adoptee to be found. The people who left returned, which counteracts that feeling of abandonment. For me, it did eventually do that, but what I had to do first was to get over the initial feeling of being reminded that they'd left in the first place, which I'd never really given much thought to. I'd known I was adopted from a young age, but I hadn't really thought about it that much, and my

[Courtesy of Sarah Saffian]

birthmother contacting me reminded me that she gave me up for adoption, and then six years later my [adoptive] mother died, and I hadn't really processed either of those losses very much at all. So, the phone call triggered this retroactive contemplation of these events and how they might have affected me. (Saffian, personal interview).

Saffian articulates and examines many of the quandaries adopted persons share, such as issues of identity and loyalty, but *Ithaka* resonates with anyone trying to balance multiple relationships:

In terms of this idea of multiple families, and coming to understand how they can coexist, when I've been with my birth family I have observed what a wonderful mother Hannah [her first mother] is. It's touching to me to see her with the three children she raised. It's mainly a positive feeling. I mean there may be a little feeling of nostalgia, in the literal sense, that kind of yearning. But what I've come to realize is that I can feel that about her and it doesn't have to do with my parents, who raised me. It doesn't disqualify them. I wouldn't have wanted to grow up in any other family and, frankly, I can't imagine having grown up in any other family. I can't imagine Hannah having kept me and marrying Adam and having three other kids who I would have grown up with. I can't imagine it because it's just not my reality. I can't imagine not knowing and not having been raised by the parents who did raise me and having the siblings I have. So, it takes time to see these various families as not mutually exclusive. But once I do, I'm able to have all these feelings. I can have relationships with both, and it doesn't have to be confusing and it certainly doesn't have to be disloyal to anyone (Saffian, personal interview).

A writing professor at Eugene Lang College at the New School University, where she teaches journalism to undergraduates, Saffian has previously worked as a senior editor for *Entertainment Weekly*, a contributing editor for *Rosie*, a senior writer for *Us* magazine, and a staff writer for the *New York Daily News*. She has written for the *New York Times*, the *Village Voice*, the *San Francisco Chronicle, Harper's Bazaar, Redbook*, and slate.com, among other publications, and has created an online course about identity through Harvard Law School.

She has appeared extensively on television and radio, including CNN, MSNBC, *Today, A&E Biography, The Rosie O'Donnell Show*, Leonard Lopate, and BBC Radio, and at such live events as the *Los Angeles Times* Festival of Books, the Modern Language Association, and the American Adoption Congress. Saffian serves on the Board of Directors of the New York City-based adoption agency Spence-Chapin Services and on the editorial advisory board of *Adoptive Families* magazine (which featured *Ithaka* in its 2005 round-up of best adoption literature), and has been a writer-in-residence at the Atlantic Center for the Arts and the Millay Colony for the Arts. Saffian recently completed an essay about her father, who died in April 2006, to be included in an anthology on parent loss that will also feature pieces by Rick Moody, Amy Bloom, David Gates, and others.

Family of Origin

There are several unusual twists to Saffian's story. She was born Susan Morgan on February 23, 1969, at Staten Island Hospital, New York. Her first parents, Hannah Morgan and Adam Leyder, met in college during their sophomore year at the University of New Hampshire. Hannah became unexpectedly pregnant with Sarah soon after graduation and the couple decided that they were not yet ready to become parents. They placed their baby for adoption through the Louise Wise Adoption Agency, a Jewish service in New York City. In 1971, Hannah and Adam reunited and they married in March, 1977. The Leyders had three more children: Renee, born in 1978; Lucy, born in 1982; and Sam, born in 1986. Saffian and her Leyder siblings have been able to develop warm relationships:

> One thing that's been funny—and it hasn't troubled me, we've actually laughed about it— is how to refer to my birth parents to their other kids. . . . I don't feel comfortable saying "Mom and Dad," because they're not my mom and dad in the same way that they're their mom and dad. But then to say "your mother and father" feels like "I'm just this friend of the family and Hannah and Adam aren't connected to me at all," which also isn't true. So, I tend to say "your mom and dad," but it's not ideal. I mean, do I refer to them as Hannah and Adam to their kids? That would be weird, too—they don't call them that. It's been interesting, the semantics. It's funny to talk about it with them. My birthmother said that there's really no model for this relationship, that it's an ongoing improvisation. I thought that was a really good way to look at it.
>
> The relationship does continue to evolve, and as easy and positive as the initial reunion can be, things can come up later that surprise you in that they affect you so deeply. An example was my birth brother's bar mitzvah in 1999. I'd had my reunion with my birth parents three years before that and we were in regular contact through phone and e-mail. He was having his bar mitzvah the weekend after my [adoptive] sister Rachel was graduating from high school, and so I went directly from one family event to the other: I went to Rachel's high school graduation with my family, and then I got on a bus and went to my birth family's house for the weekend, for my birth brother's bar mitzvah. . . . This was my first big birth family event, and I told my parents I was going, of course, but I worried about how they would feel about it. In making the plans I hadn't anticipated it being so emotional. It was wonderful, but it was more intense than I thought it would be (Saffian, personal interview).

Adam Leyder had been orphaned as a child. He was born in Los Angeles and his father died in a hunting accident when Adam was two weeks old. His mother died of breast cancer when he was six. The Smiths, friends of his mother, became Adam's guardians, and he was brought up with their son Mike. At first, Saffian felt that her connection with Adam as a fellow adoptee made their relationship "more loaded" and "uncomfortably close" (*Ithaka* 176):

> The other unusual part of my story is that Adam is also an adoptee, and I think that it informed the way that he interacted with me, not only as my birthfather, but as a fellow adoptee who resisted dealing with his being adopted. He waited a long time to search for his biological relatives and regretted having waited so long to make that connection. I think that he didn't want me to make that same mistake—he wanted to make sure that I was dealing with it, and not just sweeping it under the rug.

Even though Saffian has a good relationship with both families now, contact with the Leyders initially gave her a profound sense of isolation:

> I wasn't really a part of my birth family, because even though we were blood-related, I didn't know them; and at the same time, the fact that I wasn't biologically related to the family that I did know was now emphasized. I was caught between two "normal" families—one I was linked to by nature, the other by nurture, but neither by both (*Ithaka* 100).

Adoption

Sarah Ruth Saffian was adopted by Marvin and Nancy Saffian in April 1969. Her father told her that she had been adopted when she was about seven, and had found different notations for her birth and the day she was brought home in a datebook:

I mulled over the two-month discrepancy for several seconds before calling to my father to ask why I had taken so long to come home from the hospital. . . . Then for the first time, he told me the story of my adoption.

"Mommy and I tried to have you on our own, but we weren't able to," he began. I didn't yet know exactly how babies were made, but I had seen pregnant women before—on the street, mothers of friends. "So we adopted you, which means that someone else gave you to us to be our daughter."

"We were asking for you in particular—you were meant to be with Mommy and me," he said, and I did have the sense of being carefully selected, deliberately ordered, as if I were a Saffian because I met their specifications. The message that I was supremely wanted overrode any potential feelings of being unwanted by my original set of parents. . . . Mostly, however, I absorbed this new information the same way that I had taken in my mother's death, turning numb in the face of its enormity—as though the revelation belonged to someone else (*Ithaka* 4–5).

Sarah's adoptive mother, Nancy, died of cancer on December 26, 1975, when Sarah was six years old. Her father remarried when Sarah was ten, and the couple had two children, Maxwell and Rachel Anne. Concerning her stepmother, Sarah writes, "Kathy, whom I considered Mom, had picked up where Nancy left off and mothered me devotedly, with strength and sensitivity" (*Ithaka* 9). And about her adoptive father, Marvin, who died in April 2006, Sarah says, "He was actually the person I felt the most related to in the world" (Saffian, personal interview).

Education and Significant Relationships

Saffian earned her BA in English and American literature with honors from Brown University and has an MFA in creative writing from Columbia University. She married editor and writer Charles Leerhsen on October 2, 2004.

Works Cited

Saffian, Sarah. *Ithaka: A Daughter's Memoir of Being Found*. New York: Basic, 1998.
Saffian, Sarah. Personal interview. September 20, 2002.

SAINTE-MARIE, BUFFY (1941–)

Singer, Songwriter, Educator, Actress
Adoptee

Career, Major Awards, and Achievements

Buffy Sainte-Marie began performing in New York City coffeehouses and nightspots such as the Bitter End soon after her graduation from college. Her first recording contract was with Vanguard, the same company that recorded the work of Joan Baez. Sainte-Marie's first recording was *It's My Way* (1964). Her work was praised for its polish, vibrancy, and originality. Before 1970, Sainte-Marie had made five more recordings: *Many a Mile* (1965), *Little Wheel Spin and Spin* (1966), *Fire and Fleet and Candlelight* (1967), *I'm Gonna Be a Country Girl Again* (1968), and *Illuminations* (1969).

Sainte-Marie appeared on the scene at exactly the right time, as folk merged with rock and music merged with politics. "Now that the Buffalo's Gone," "Universal Soldier,"

[Courtesy of Photofest]

and "My Country 'Tis of Thy People You're Dying" were some of Sainte-Marie's most popular songs. Sainte-Marie considers herself more a representative of Native peoples than a political person. She has lived on reservations across the United States and several in Canada.

In the early 1970s, Sainte-Marie produced two greatest hit albums and four new albums and then left recording to become a mother and a visual artist, though she continued to write songs. From 1976 to 1981, she and her son, Dakota "Cody" Wolfchild Starblanket, appeared regularly on Sesame Street "to let little kids and their caretakers know that Indians exist and that we are not all dead and stuffed in museums" (Caldwell 142). In 1982 she was honored for her work with indigenous people as recipient of the Queen Elizabeth II Jubilee medal and received an Academy Award as cowriter of "Up Where We Belong," written for *An Officer and a Gentleman.*

The album *Coincidence and Likely Stories* came out in 1992, her first album in fourteen years, and she toured internationally. She won the Charles de Gaulle Grand Prix in 1993 and in 1995 was inducted into the JUNO (Canada's Emmy) Hall of Fame. *Up Where We Belong* (1996) covered new songs and new versions of old songs.

Even though she likes to perform with her mouthbow, one of the very oldest known musical instruments, Sainte-Marie was also one of the first artists to incorporate digital technologies, rare among folk musicians, out of "her curiosity and interest in sound" (Caldwell 139):

> I'm not the only native person who was real early in computer technology. People thought I was out of my mind, even as recently as two years ago, for talking about Indian people and computers. White people were laughing up their sleeves, thinking, "That's a funny idea." That was really insulting. I said, "Okay, I'm writing an article"; so I did. It's called "Cyberskins" (Caldwell 140).

Though Sainte-Marie is often thought of as a singer and activist, she is also an educator. During the 1990s she lived in Hawaii but worked as an adjunct professor at Indian Federated College in Saskatchewan and York University at Toronto, taught digital art as an artist in residence at the Institute of Indian Arts in Santa Fe, and lectured at Evergreen State College in Washington. She invested a large portion of her time to the Cradleboard Teaching Project, sponsored by the Kellogg Foundation, which helps develop accurate native curricula for reservation and mainstream schools. She also endowed a scholarship for native peoples, the Nihewan Foundation, with proceeds from her concerts.

Family of Origin

Sainte-Marie was born on the Piapot Reservation in Craven, Saskatchewan, on February 20, 1941, to Cree parents. Her biographies say she was orphaned as an infant and taken to Massachusetts for adoption. Her new town was an all white community, except for her adoptive mother and one Chippewa resident: "He was wonderful to me. He was really the only person who gave me a sense of native reality" (Caldwell 136). She visited her native lands as a young girl and has a formal membership in the Cree nation:

> I visited [Saskatchewan] when I was a child, and in my teens I used to go back and forth. My adopted mom was part Micmac, but it's not as though she was living in the community. I was the first person in that family to really connect, and explore the deeper meaning of a whole additional culture (Caldwell 136).

Adoption

Albert C. Sainte-Marie, who worked as a mechanic, and his wife, Winifred (Kendrick) Sainte-Marie, had lost their first child. They adopted "Buffy," whose given name was Beverly, when she was a few months old. Buffy was given U.S. citizenship through her adoption and grew up in Wakefield, Massachusetts, with summers at Sebago Lake, Maine. She was a "shy and withdrawn" child (Braudy 17):

> "I wanted above all to be a blond," she recalls. "I always wanted to be like the other girls in my school. If they cut their hair short, I cut mine. But when I went to parties I didn't enjoy myself. What was wrong with me? I used to ask myself. Now I know I simply felt bored, but then I blamed myself (Braudy 17).

Saint-Marie's musical gifts were apparent very early and were encouraged by her adoptive parents. She taught herself to play her parents' piano when she was four years old. As a child and young woman, she enjoyed writing poems and setting them to music. Her father gave her a second-hand guitar when she was seventeen, and she developed her own style of playing. Eventually she taught herself thirty-two different ways of tuning the guitar. Her singing style was also self-taught, and she has said that she cannot sing a scale.

Education and Significant Relationships

Sainte-Marie registered at the University of Massachusetts with the intention of studying veterinary medicine but switched to Oriental philosophy and education:

> I got a teacher's degree so I would have a way to make a living. The combination of philosophy and teaching has been perfect for my own sense of communication in learning from other people and passing on what I have learned. In the native community there are so many people who are "under-recognized" but who are very important teachers (Caldwell 137).

An exchange program allowed her to take classes at Smith, Amherst, and Mount Holyoke. By the time she graduated in 1963 with a degree in philosophy, she had gained a reputation as a folk singer on campus and was playing in nearby coffeehouses. She was rated as one of the ten most outstanding members of her class. In 1983 she completed a PhD in digital art.

Sainte-Marie has indicated that she likes to maintain privacy in her personal life: "The songs are as public as I get. I feel that's enough contribution, so I don't feel bad keeping my personal life personal (Braudy 18). It is known that in 1967 she married Dewain Kamaikalani Bugbee, a man of mixed Hawaiian-American and Indian-white ancestry. Her son was born in 1976.

Works Cited

Bataille, Gretchen M., ed. "Sainte-Marie, Buffy." *Native American Women: A Biographical Dictionary*. New York: Garland, 1993: 224.

Braudy, Susan. "Buffy Sainte-Marie: 'Native North American Me.'" *Ms.* 111 (March 1975): 14.

Caldwell, E. K. "Up Where We Belong: Buffy Sainte-Marie." *Dreaming the Dawn: Conversations with Native Artists and Activists*. Lincoln, NE: University of Nebraska, 1999. 135.

Johansen, Bruce E., and Donald A. Grinde, Jr. "Sainte-Marie, Buffy." *The Encyclopedia of Native American Biography*. New York: Holt, 1997.

Malinowski, Sharon, ed. "Buffy Sainte-Marie." *Notable Native Americans*. New York: Gale, 1995. 377.

SARGON I (ca. 2334–ca. 2279 B.C.E.)

King of Akkad (also transcribed as Accad or Agade)
Adoptee

Career and Achievements

Sargon I, also known as Sargon the Great, was an early king of the Akkadians, a Semitic people who lived in ancient Sumer, the northern Mesopotamian land between the Euphrates and the Tigris rivers (now located in the area known as Iraq). He was trained by his adoptive father to be a gardener, but later became the cup-bearer of Ur-ilbaba, the king of Kish. After Sargon defeated the king's enemy, Lugalzaggesi, the king of Erech, who had overthrown and killed Ur-ilbaba, he became commander of the Akkadian court and army, at that time numbering 5,400 men (Kramer 61). Because Sargon's legitimacy was dubious, he and his supporters credited his rise to kingship to the favor and will of the goddess Ishtar. Sargon built the city of Akkad near Kish and established the world's first empire through military conquest of much of the Near East, from the Persian Gulf to the Mediterranean. He was the "first dynamic leader of men to emerge from the twilight of prehistory into the full light of the written record" (Cottrell 199). He was also the earliest recorded adopted person. Sargon's two sons, Rimush and Manishtushu, succeeded him.

Family of Origin

The text of what is known as *The Sargon Legend* or the *Sargon Birth Legend* was found during an excavation of Ashurbanipal's library at Nineveh during the 1800s. The inscriptions had originally been carved on two columns. Although Sargon I was a real king, some scholars believe that his birth legend is a later literary composition rather than the royal contemporary inscription it appears to be (Longman 54). How much of the legend is biographical and how much is fiction has not been determined. A translation of the first fourteen passages on the first column is given here:

> I, Sargon, strong king, king of Agade, am I. My mother was a high priestess, my father I do not know. My paternal kin inhabit the mountain region. My city [of birth] is Azupirānu, which lies on the bank of the Euphrates. My mother, a high priestess, conceived me, in secret she bore me. She placed me in a reed basket, with bitumen she caulked my hatch. She abandoned me to the river from which I could not escape. The river carried me along; to Aqqi, the water drawer, it brought me. Aqqi, the water drawer, when immersing his bucket lifted me up. Aqqi, the water drawer, raised me as his adopted son. Aqqi, the water drawer, set me to his garden work. During my garden work, Ishtar loved me [so that] fifty-five years I ruled as king. The black-headed people I took over and governed (Lewis 24–26).

In some translations "paternal kin" is translated as "uncle," or "my father's brother," and "Aqqi the water drawer" is "Akki the irrigator" (Cottrell 199). Further, other reputable translations interpret the description of Sargon's mother in the second and fourth lines as "humble" rather than "high-priestess," thus: "my mother was humble, I knew not my father." Lewis argues convincingly, however, that the transliteration of Sargon's mother as a "priestess" or "high priestess" rather than "humble" makes more sense, as it would explain the necessity for relinquishing her son, as priestesses were prohibited from bearing children and "in the eyes of this tradition, Sargon was considered illegitimate" (Lewis 38–42). Since priestesses usually came from the nobility, Sargon's promotion from simple gardener to a royal office also seems more credible with Lewis's interpretation.

Adoption

Like Moses, Sargon was pulled out of the river by a person who adopted and raised him—in this case a gardener named Aqqi. The theme of an adoptive parent or parents who rescue an infant exposed to danger from animals, rivers, or other elements, may have been part of early adoption rituals. Because of the frequency of such phrases as children "at the mouth of the dog" and "at the mouth of the raven," some scholars of ancient legal texts believe that a staged exposure and subsequent rescue of the child by the adoptive parent were part of ancient adoption rituals:

> It seems likely that this text ["at the mouth of the dog"] actually refers to an adoption ceremony in which the participants acted out the roles that will determine the future of the child. . . . Essentially, in any case of adoption, one party relinquishes claim to a child and the other party assumes it. The person abandoning the child in the ceremony (here the lady) surrenders all claims to him by exposing him to die. The person who first gave him life takes it away thereby terminating her rights as parent. The adopter rescues the child from danger, which is tantamount to giving him life. In so doing he symbolically becomes the natural parent and the child belongs to him (Lewis 55).

Although infant exposure was a literal practice throughout history, Sargon's adoption story seems to be either a description of such an adoption ceremony as mentioned above or else a mythic account. A genuine foundling would not know the type of details about his original family that Sargon knew.

Works Cited

Cottrell, Leonard. *The Quest for Sumer.* New York: G. P. Putnam's Sons, 1965.

Kramer, Samuel Noah. *The Sumerians: Their History, Culture, and Character.* Chicago: The University of Chicago Press, 1963.

Lewis, Brian. *The Sargon Legend: A Study of the Akkadian Text and the Tale of the Hero Who Was Exposed at Birth.* Cambridge, MA: American Schools of Oriental Research, 1980.

Tremper, Longman III. *Fictional Akkadian Autobiography: A Generic and Comparative Study.* Winona Lake, IN: Eisenbrauns, 1991.

SARRAZIN, ALBERTINE (1937–1967)

Author
Adoptee

Career, Major Awards, and Achievements

Albertine Sarrazin, a French author writing from prison, became popular during the 1960s. An intelligent and outspoken critic of the social conventions that incarcerated her, she particularly appealed to the feminists of that era. Gloria Steinem wrote in a *New York Times* book review that Sarrazin's young and tragic death transformed her into a "kind of James Dean for the intelligent girl rebel" (Steinem 4).

Those of Sarrazin's works that were published in her lifetime include *La cavale* (translated as *The Runaway*), 1965; *L'astragale* (*Astragalus*), 1965; *La traversière* (*The Crossing*), 1966; and *Poèmes* (1969). *La cavale* was awarded the Tunisian *Prix des quatre jurys* in March 1966. Posthumous works include *Journal de prison 1959* (1972); *Le passe-peine 1949–1967* (*Doing Time 1949–1967*), 1976; and *Œuvres* (*Works*), 1985. Her short stories, letters, and a travel diary were also published following her death. Sarrazin's fiction is autobiographical: she always appears as the character "Anne" or "Anick." And although most of her novels are set in prison, their themes are always about her "search for psychic and emotional wholeness" (Gelfand 1988, 267).

Family of Origin

Sarrazin was born on September 17, 1937, in Algiers. Her mother, who was of Spanish origin, was unmarried and fifteen years old at the time she left her newborn daughter with the Algerian Assistance Publique. Sarrazin was given the name Albertine Damien at the welfare office, but it is unclear who named her. Very little information is known about her first parents. Critics believe that her relinquishment had a major impact on Sarrazin's life and work:

> The mother she never knew haunted Sarrazin all her life: direct invocations to this adored but absent figure appear in her journals and in *La cavale*; and more indirect insistence on her felt incompleteness, her sense of detachment from normal coordinates of human identity, marks all of Sarrazin's works. The recurrent themes of solitude, deracination, and the journey to acceptance, as well as the cyclical structure of all her novels, bespeak her quest for unity (Gelfand 1988, 266).

An example of the type of invocation to the "adored but absent" mother to which Gelfand refers above can be seen in these lines from *The Runaway*:

> I think of your youth of those days, mother, little sister, you who were not even as old as Maria; under your dress, under your skin, I was warm too, and you carried me like one of those summer fruits you craved. . . oh, mother, how I adore you for having remained unknown! (Sarrazin 79).

Adoption

Albertine was adopted by a middle-aged French couple when she was eighteen months old. Her father, a doctor and colonel in the colonial army, and his wife took her to their home in Aix-en-Provence following the end of World War II. They renamed her Anne-Marie R—— (only the first letter of the adoptive family name has been given in sources). Her adoption was an unfortunate one, and Sarrazin eventually "bitterly exposed the tyrannical father and humiliated mother who had raised her" (Gelfand 1988, 267) in her novel *La traversière* (*The Crossing*).

A forty-year old uncle, Albert R——, raped the ten-year-old girl on September 27, 1947. Sarrazin, who was a brilliant but undisciplined child, became uncontrollable. Her parents brought her first for psychiatric examination and at last asked the police to commit her to a reform school, the Bon Pasteur (Good Shepherd) disciplinary school in Marseilles. In 1953, Albertine was taken under guard from Bon Pasteur to a different school, where she was given the *baccalauréat* exam. During the exam, she successfully escaped through the school's kitchen and hitchhiked to Paris, where she survived through prostitution and false identification. In Paris, Albertine and Emilienne, her lover and school friend from Bon Pasteur, were arrested for a botched armed robbery of a dress shop on December 21, 1953. Albertine's adoptive parents refused to provide a lawyer for her, and she was sentenced to seven years in prison. She served her sentence at the Fresnes, Doullens, and Amiens prisons.

In October 1956, her adoptive parents had their daughter's adoption officially annulled, and they disowned her. *La traversière*, which was never translated from the French, begins with her adoptive family's renunciation and Albertine's subsequent suicide attempt: "The adoption story is crucial because, when the colonel pronounced the nullification, Albertine experienced a loss of faith in any normalcy in her family life" (Gelfand 1975, 199).

Education and Significant Relationships

Sarrazin successfully completed her baccalauréat in philosophy in July 1955, while she was a prisoner at Fresnes.

Sarrazin broke out of Doullens prison in 1957 by jumping from a thirty-foot wall. In the process she broke her astragalus, a bone that connects the ankle to the foot. She would later name *L'Astragale*, which she called her "little love novel" (Gelfand 1988, 269), after the incident. A passing motorist named Julien Sarrazin rescued, cared for, and hid the fugitive. Julien, who also had a criminal record, and Albertine committed several burglaries together, and Julien was arrested in March 1958 and incarcerated in the Pontoise and Soissons prisons. Albertine was discovered and rearrested in September 1958. She was released on October 5, 1960, but was arrested again in 1964 for stealing a bottle of whiskey. She spent four more months in prison before her final release in August 1964.

Albertine and Julien Sarrazin married on February 7, 1959, while Albertine was still in prison. She had health problems relating to both her earlier ankle injury and to a 1960 car accident that had killed Julien's mother and seriously injured the couple. On July 10, 1967, Albertine died of cardiac arrest on the operating table during kidney surgery. In 1970, Julien successfully brought a malpractice suit against his wife's doctors at Saint-Roch Clinic in Montpellier. With the settlement award, he established a publishing house, the Éditions Sarrazin, in honor of his wife's writings.

Works Cited

Gelfand, Elissa. "Albertine Sarrazin." *French Novelists since 1960. Dictionary of Literary Biography* 83 (1989).

Gelfand, Elissa. *Albertine Sarrazin: The Exorcism of Prison.* Diss. Brown University, 1975.

Sarrazin, Albertine. *The Runaway.* Trans. Charles Lam Markmann. New York: Grove Press, Inc., 1967.

Sartori, Eva Martin, and Dorothy Wynne Zimmerman, eds. *French Women Writers.* Lincoln, NE: University of Nebraska Press, 1994.

Steinem, Gloria. "Inside Story: *The Runaway* and *Astragal.*" *New York Times Book Review* 9 (June 1968): VII:4.

SHABAZZ, BETTY (1936–1997)

Educator, Civil Rights Activist
Adoptee

[AP Photo/Patrick J. Cunningham]

Career, Major Awards, and Achievements

Dr. Betty Shabazz is best remembered as the wife and widow of Malcolm X. Dr. Shabazz was also known and honored in her own right as an educator and an advocate of civil and human rights.

While Shabazz was attending nursing school in New York City, a school friend invited her to hear Nation of Islam leaders Elijah Muhammad and Malcolm X and, following their lecture, introduced her to the speakers. Shabazz was impressed with Malcolm X and his passionate ideals.

Once Betty decided to become part of the Nation of Islam, she adopted the dress and diet of followers and changed her name to Betty X. Elijah Muhammad encouraged followers to use X as a last name to represent the African names they had lost when their ancestors were brought to the Americas. Betty X taught classes and traveled on behalf of the Nation of Islam.

Black Muslim men and women did not date, but instead spent time together in the company of friends. Betty and Malcolm started seeing each other in this manner, and about the time of Betty's graduation from nursing school, Malcolm called her from Detroit and asked her to marry him. Less than a week later, on January 12, 1958, Betty and Malcolm were married in Lansing, Michigan. She was twenty-three, and he was thirty-two. The marriage lasted seven years, until Malcolm's murder.

In 1964 Malcolm split with Elijah Muhammad and the Nation of Islam. He went on pilgrimage to Mecca and Medina, the *Hajj* which is required of Muslims who have the health and financial ability to make the trip, and met traditional Muslims. When he converted to Sunni Islam, he took the name El-Hajj Malik El-Shabazz and Betty became Betty Shabazz. During this brief period, Malcolm came into his own as a major black civil rights leader, but in February 1965, the Shabazz home was firebombed, and on the February 21, at the Audubon Ballroom in Harlem, Malcolm X was assassinated. Most reports say that Betty and their four daughters witnessed the murder and others say that Betty, who was pregnant with twins, used her own body to shield her young daughters in the confusion that followed the shooting. The three assassins were members of the Nation of Islam.

A month after Malcolm's death, Betty went to Mecca on her own *Hajj* pilgrimage, which she considered a transforming experience. She remained a practicing Sunni Muslim for the rest of her life and raised her children in that tradition.

The decade after Malcolm's death was a time of personal growth and achievement for Betty. As the champion of her husband's legacy, Shabazz became affiliated with two other notable widows whose husbands were assassinated because of their civil rights activities, Myrlie Evers-Williams, the widow of Medgar Evers, and Coretta Scott King, the widow of Martin Luther King, Jr. Friends and supporters helped Betty and her children find a new home in Mount Vernon, New York, and Betty worked hard to maintain the lifestyle she wanted for her children.

Having earned her doctorate, Shabazz accepted a position as assistant professor at Medgar Evers College in 1976 and later became head of institutional advancement and public relations there. She also traveled as a speaker for racial tolerance, civil rights, and the importance of African American self-determination, and served on a number of boards. Nina Sudarkasa, former president of Lincoln University and a friend of Shabazz, said Shabazz was "a tireless and resolute voice on behalf of economic, social, and political justice for the dispossessed and downtrodden from Selma to Soweto" (Rickford xix).

In 1994 Shabazz finally spoke publicly about her belief that Louis Farrakhan, the controversial leader of the Nation of Islam, was linked to the assassination of Malcolm X. Her daughter Qubilah was arrested for soliciting someone to kill Farrakhan when the would-be hit man turned out to be a government informant. Many well-known members of the African American community gathered around Betty and her daughter, whom Betty thought had been manipulated. Then Farrakhan surprised many people when he charged that Qubilah had been led into criminal action by the government, which intended, he said, to create animosity between the Nation of Islam and the rest of the African American community. At a May 1995 fundraiser sponsored by Farrakhan to help defray Qubilah's legal fees, Betty Shabazz formally shook Farrakhan's hand and thanked him for his help, signaling an end of animosity between them. In October 1995, she spoke briefly at the Million Man March sponsored by Farrakhan and the Nation of Islam, reminding her audience that women are 70 percent of the world's poor and do much of the world's work.

Qubilah was required to take two years of treatment for drug and alcohol abuse and receive psychological counseling, while her son Malcolm, twelve, a boy who was known to be both appealing and emotionally unstable, went to live with his grandmother Betty. A few months later, on June 1, 1997, Malcolm, unhappy because he could not yet rejoin his mother, who was beginning a new life in Texas, set fire to the Shabazz apartment. Betty Shabazz was burned over 80 percent of her body and was given a 10 percent chance of survival. She died three weeks later, on June 23, 1997. She was sixty-one.

Malcolm Shabazz was arrested and convicted of manslaughter. He was sentenced to eighteen months in juvenile detention.

More than two thousand mourners, including the remaining two members of "the widows," Myrlie Evers-Williams and Coretta Scott King, attended the memorial service for Betty Shabazz. Others at the service at Riverside Church in New York were the governor of New York, the mayor and three past mayors of New York City, poet/activist **Maya Angelou**, and actor/activist Ossie Davis, who had acted as emcee and had testified at the funeral of Malcolm X.

Family of Origin

Betty's birth father was Shelman Sandlin. As an adult he "tied steel," reinforcing buildings with steel rods during construction, and spent most of his working life in Philadelphia. He was born in Pinehurst, Georgia, where he met Ollie Mae, Betty's mother. Russell Rickford, Shabazz's biographer, says that Sandlin was twenty-one and Ollie Mae was probably a teenager when Betty was conceived. He believes she may have been sent away, as many pregnant teens were in the years before the 1960s, in her case, to Detroit, where Betty grew up. Betty was probably born either in Detroit or in or near Pinehurst; no birth certificate for her was found in Michigan or Georgia. Rickford does not identify Ollie Mae's last name, but Betty grew up as Betty Dean Sanders, born on May 28, 1936. An elderly family member said that she had been raised nearly from infancy in Detroit by her mother, though it was also said that she spent most of her first few years with her paternal grandmother, Matilda Green, in Pinehurst.

Adoption

Betty returned to Detroit when her grandmother died, and three years later, when she was nine, she began hanging around a shoemaking and repair shop owned by Lorenzo Malloy and his wife, Helen Lowe Malloy, both southerners by birth. Even through the Depression, the Malloys had done well and they owned a nice home and two cars. Lorenzo had attended the Tuskegee Normal and Industrial Institute and Helen had taught school. The African Methodist Episcopal (AME) Bethel church was central to their lives. Both attended frequently and participated often in church activities. They lived their beliefs, at different times taking in a baby boy and caring for him for eight years, caring for a paralyzed elderly woman, and boarding a young woman going to teacher's college, so letting a child in need of approval "work" at the shop, visit their home, and even stay overnight now and then wasn't out of their usual Bethel Christian lifestyle. Eventually the Malloys asked Ollie Mae whether they could keep Betty. Ollie May refused.

Since Ollie Mae forbade Betty to keep the light on late at night, Betty often studied with a friend. One night, eleven-year-old Betty came home later than usual, around 10:30 or 11:00, and Ollie Mae refused to let her in. Betty spent the night at the home of a friend, and "the next day she came to me," Helen said. After that, Betty and Ollie Mae seldom saw each other. Shabazz seldom mentioned her first mother, though she told Gamilah that she had been there for "the transaction" that gave her into the Malloys' care (Rickford 8). When Betty began coming to church with the Malloys, neither the adults nor the child gave any explanation and neither ever publicly discussed Betty's life before she joined the Malloys (Rickford 8–9).

Helen Malloy was a busy woman, working at the shoe store, making deliveries, joining women's civic organizations, and working for better lives for Detroit's black population, especially black women, and for a better Detroit. She believed that "when you finish praying, you've got to work," and she couldn't say no to anything related to the causes she believed in (Rickford 10). Helen instilled her values into Betty, as Helen's friend, Dr. C. DeLores Tucker, recalled:

> I was unaware of the source of [Betty's] strong faith and social activism until her adoptive mother died a few years ago in Detroit. I was privileged to be there with Rosa Parks and speak at [Helen's] funeral, and Betty was extremely pleased that Mrs. Parks accompanied me.... Her mother was an activist long before the Civil Rights movement. She was organizing demonstrations and marching in front of stores back in the forties, when Betty was a little girl.... I said to Betty after the funeral, "I always thought that the source of your faith, dignity, strength, and commitment to justice for our people came from Malcolm." She said, "No, girlfriend, I grew up with that ingrained deep in my soul. If anything, I inspired him" (Brown 83).

Education and Significant Relationships

Shabazz left home to study for five quarters at the Tuskegee Institute (later Tuskegee University) in Alabama, and then transferred, hoping to escape the racial tensions of the South, to the Brooklyn State Hospital School of Nursing in New York. Following her husband's death, she returned to school, enrolling at Jersey City State College and receiving a Bachelor of Arts in public health administration, followed by an MA in the same subject. In 1975 the University of Massachusetts at Amherst granted her a PhD in education administration.

Betty X, formerly Betty Sanders, married Malcolm X (formerly Malcolm Little) in 1958. They converted to Sunni Islam in 1964, taking the name Shabazz. At the time of Malcolm's assassination in February 1965, they had four children, Attallah (1958), Qubilah (1960), Ilyasah (1963), and Gamilah (1964). Twins Malaak and Malikah were born seven months later.

After Shabazz's death in 1997, a memorial service was held at Riverside Church in New York City. Her funeral service took place at the Islamic Cultural Center, and a wake was held at the Unity Funeral Home in Harlem, where the wake for Malcolm X had been held thirty-two years earlier. Betty Shabazz was buried next to her husband in Hartsdale, New York, at the Ferncliff Cemetery.

Works Cited

Brown, Jamie Foster, ed. *Betty Shabazz: A Sisterfriends' Tribute in Words and Pictures.* NY: Simon & Schuster, 1998.

Jeffrey, Laura S. "Betty Shabazz: Sharing the Vision of Malcolm X." *African American Biographies.* Berkeley Heights, NJ: Enslow Publishers, Inc., 2000.

Rickford, Russell John. *Betty Shabazz: A Remarkable Story of Survival and Faith Before and After Malcolm X.* Naperville, IL: Sourcebooks, Inc., 2003.

Shabazz, Betty, as told to Susan L. Taylor and Audrey Edwards. "Loving and Losing Malcolm." *Essence* 22 (February 1992): 50.

SMITHSON, JAMES (1765–1829)

Scientist, Benefactor
Fostered

Career and Achievements

James Smithson was the founder of the Smithsonian Institute in Washington, D.C. He was a British scientist who worked mainly in the areas of mineralogy, chemistry, and geology. His work with zinc was particularly notable, and his discoveries related to a particular zinc ore once confused with calamine led to its being named "smithsonite" in his

[Hulton Archive/Getty Images]

honor in 1832. He was elected a fellow of the Royal Society, England's premier academy of science, when he was twenty-two years old, and he published twenty-seven scientific papers, eight in the Society's *Transactions* (1791–1817), eighteen in its *Annals* (1819–1825), and one in its *Philosophical Magazine* (1807). Smithson also made important geologic expeditions in Europe and Scotland, but, remarkably, considering his legacy, he never traveled to the United States during his lifetime. Why he bequeathed his entire fortune to a fledgling and personally unknown country is a mystery. Some have speculated that he admired certain scientists who were American-born; others, that he was caught up in the idealism of the American Revolution. His biographers all acknowledge, however, that Smithson's illegitimacy was the reason he did not leave his fortune to his own country:

> The fundamental impulse that led Smithson to the unusual disposition of his fortune was, I believe, his feeling that his own country, by denying him his noble birthright and the normal fulfillment of a life in England suitable to his talents and inclinations, had let him down. He may well have felt that he had to compensate to the world and demonstrate that he could perpetuate his name by holding to a high idealism and a faith in mankind and rising above the disappointments and the frustrations he suffered (Oehser 13).

Family of Origin

James, originally named James Louis (also spelled Lewis) Macie, was born in Paris on an unrecorded date in 1765. His mother, Elizabeth Hungerford Keate Macie, was a widow and the cousin of the wife of his father, Hugh Smithson, who became the first Duke of Northumberland a year after James's birth. Elizabeth Macie and Hugh Smithson became romantically involved while on holiday in Bath. She left for Paris when she discovered that she was pregnant and never returned to England. Elizabeth was a direct descendent of King Henry VII through the Duke of Somerset, and she inherited a rich estate from the Hungerfords of Studley soon after her son's birth. James was known to have had great respect for his family's nobility and was equally sensitive about his illegitimacy:

> The best blood of England flows in my veins; on my father's side I am a Northumberland, on my mother's I am related to Kings, but this avails me not. My name shall live in the memory of man when the titles of the Northumberlands, and the Percys are extinct and forgotten (Oehser 4–5).

Elizabeth had married a man named Mark Dickinson before her marriage to John Macie in 1750, but the marriage had been "dissolved," according to the Hungerford pedigree. When James was six years old, his mother gave birth to her second son, Henry.

James and Henry were two of four illegitimate children of their father, who had taken the name Hugh Smithson Percy upon his elevation. Their father also had two illegitimate daughters in the 1770s, Philadelphia and Dorothy Percy, whom he took into his household.

The second duke, Lord Hugh Percy, one of their shared father's three legitimate children, became a famous British commander at the battles of Bunker Hill and Lexington during the American Revolutionary War. The duke's second son was made Lord Beverly and inherited an estate. His legitimate daughter died unmarried.

Fosterage

Elizabeth sent her son back to England when he was around nine years old. She placed him under the guardianship of Joseph Gape, an attorney who was trustee of the

Hungerford estates, and petitioned the Crown to have her son naturalized. The Crown granted the petition, but attached an unusually restrictive proviso that biographers believe may have been engineered by James's own father. The proviso prohibited James from receiving honors or lands from the crown, serving on the Privy Council, or joining the military or civil services:

> [James] became a scientist of considerable note. Most of his contemporaries of similar ability were knighted—Sir Joseph Banks, Sir Davies Gilbert, Sir Charles Blagden, Sir Humphry Davy—but not James. The proviso prevented such an honor being conferred upon him.
>
> In later years, when James Smithson left his fortune to establish an institution in America, surprise was expressed in some quarters that he did not leave the money for such a project in Great Britain. But the motivation was obvious. James Smithson's Government had rejected him (Carmichael 55–57).

James lived with his guardian in St. Mary-le-Bow parish and is believed to have attended Charterhouse School in London. The school did not keep records of their day pupils at the time. Smithson's illegitimacy and the terms of his naturalization discouraged him from preparing for the occupations customary for gentlemen of his time, those being politics, the military, civil service, and the clergy. Instead they led him to pursue the sciences.

Education and Significant Relationships

Smithson, under the name of James Macie, was later educated at Pembroke College, Oxford. It is unclear whether both of his parents, or just his mother, provided the funds for the boy's education through their mutual banker. A good friend, Davies Gilbert, who would one day head the Royal Society, noted in his diary that he found it curious that James's father's name had been omitted on their class list (Carmichael 60). At Pembroke, James met many influential scientists who later helped him in his career and helped him enter the Royal Society at an unusually young age.

James graduated on May 26, 1786, only days before his father's death. He later petitioned the Crown, shortly after his mother's death and at her request, to be allowed to take his father's name. It was granted and James Macie became James Smithson on February 16, 1801.

Chemistry at that time was in its infancy, and the materials and instruments available were undeveloped and crude. Despite these disadvantages, Smithson often obtained credible and useful results, and he distinguished himself in his chosen fields of study.

In August 1807, while on a geologic trip to the European continent, Smithson became a victim of the Napoleonic wars. He was arrested by the Danish government and held as a prisoner of war in a swampy area near the port of Tonningen, where he became dangerously ill and began to cough up blood. Smithson was released because of his deteriorating health and given a passport to Hamburg, Germany. There the French minister rearrested him. Smithson eventually escaped captivity and returned to England in 1812 with his health ruined.

Smithson, who never married, made out his will on October 23, 1826, leaving his estate to his nephew. His brother, Lieutenant-Colonel Henry Louis Dickinson, had died in 1820, leaving one son, Henry James. In the event of his nephew's death intestate, Smithson's will made a point of bequeathing the whole estate to any of Henry James's children, *legitimate or illegitimate* (Oehser 15). Smithson died on June 26, 1829, in

Genoa, Italy. His nephew, known variously under the names of Henry James Dickinson, Hungerford, and Baron Eunice de la Batut, died six years later, unmarried and childless, and so Smithson's final provision became operational. This was "to found at Washington, under the name of the Smithsonian Institution, an Establishment for the increase and diffusion of knowledge among men" (Oehser 15). Smithson's gift was formally announced by President Martin Van Buren in December 1838, and the Smithsonian Institution began in a congressional committee headed by former President John Quincy Adams, then serving in the House of Representatives.

A special delegation headed by Smithsonian regent Alexander Graham Bell brought James Smithson's remains from Genoa to Washington, D.C., in 1900. They were reinterred with great ceremony near the Smithsonian's original entrance:

> Today it is sometimes said that the only person buried in downtown Washington, D.C., is James Smithson, a bastard Englishman, whose great contribution was to raise the dignity of man by his consummate faith in the promise of a new nation only half a century old (Oehser 15).

Works Cited

Carmichael, Leonard, and J. C. Long. *James Smithson and the Smithsonian Story.* New York: G. P. Putnam's Sons, 1965.

Langley, S. P. "James Smithson." *The Smithsonian Institution 1846–1896: The History of its First Half Century.* Ed. George Brown Goode. Vol. 1. City of Washington: [Smithsonian], 1897. 1–24.

Oehser, Paul Henry. *The Smithsonian Institution.* New York: Praeger, 1970.

True, Webster Prentiss. *The Smithsonian Institution.* Ed. Charles Greeley Abbot. Vol. 1. New York: Smithsonian Scientific Series, Inc., 1943.

SOLL, JOE (1939–)

Psychotherapist, Author, Activist
Adoptee

Career, Major Awards, and Achievements

Joe Soll is a psychotherapist in private practice in New York and a former adjunct professor at the Fordham University Graduate School of Social Work. He is a recognized expert in adoption and is an author and activist in this field. He has appeared on over 300 adoption-related radio and television programs, including appearances on "The Other Mother" (NBC), "Reno Finds Her Mom" (HBO), and a Japanese documentary called "Adoption Therapist: Joe Soll." Soll founded and directs several adoption organizations, including Adoption Crossroads (http://www.adoptioncrossroads.org/) and the Adoption Counseling Center in New York City. He is a former executive board member of the American Adoption Congress and a former trustee of the International Soundex Reunion Registry, the oldest and most trusted voluntary registry for adoption triad members. Soll is the author or coauthor of three books: *Adoption Healing: A Path to Recovery* (2000), *Adoption Healing: A Path to Recovery for Mothers Who Lost Children to Adoption* (with Karen Wilson Buterbaugh, 2003), and *Evil Exchange* (with Lori Paris, 2006).

[Courtesy of Joe Soll]

Family of Origin

It took Soll three years and ten thousand dollars to obtain his original birth certificate, but the information it contained was fraudulent. Because of these falsified documents, he has never been able to learn the truth about his origins, although he has searched since 1982:

> I was sold on the black market and I don't even know my birth date, or my birthplace. It's gotten worse over the eighteen years I've been searching, not better, in terms of information. That's true, that's why I do what I do, though. I know what name I was born under according to my original birth certificate, because I did sue the state of New York, and win, but everything I have is fraudulent, because the lady who sold me used to fictionalize birth certificates and all the information, so that nothing could ever be traced. That was her modus operandi, and she did this for over forty years. She operated between New York and Florida, and points in between. She brought babies in from Florida, from Delaware, from anywhere she could get them. I'm now unsure it was 1939 [year of birth], since I have photos making me younger and older. I found out through DNA testing that my natural mother was part Asian and that gives me a welcome connection to my past. I'm sure I'm a Scorpio, I don't have any doubt about that at all (Joe Soll, personal interview).

Adoption

Soll was adopted as an infant. He grew up with two younger siblings, a boy and a girl, who were the biological children of his adoptive parents. His adoptive father died when Joe was twenty. In spite of the circumstances and dishonesty connected with his adoption, he has good relationships with his adoptive family:

My adopted family lived in New York, and that's where the adoption went through. That was the home base of the lady who sold me. My father was a lawyer; my mother was an interior decorator. They were a good family, but they had no idea how to deal with adoption. They told me my birth parents died in a car crash. Oh yeah, there was this huge car crash on the Jersey turnpike, and it wiped out about a hundred thousand birth parents in one fell swoop. You know that was so commonly told. They told me that when I was four, and I never forgot it. They were a good family, they were just inept because there were no books for them to read that would tell them what to do. It's not their fault—they certainly tried, and I know my parents felt absolutely helpless to deal with my pain. They did not understand in any way why I was hurting.

I never considered searching. I never said the word "adoption" out loud in my life. Until I was 42, I couldn't. I didn't tell my wives that I was adopted, or any of my friends. It was a non-word, and if people asked me because I looked different than my family, I denied it. I said "not me," and then when I was 42, my sister, who's not adopted, said something about where I came from, or where she thought I came from, that a friend of the family had arranged the adoption, and I said "No, my parents were dead," and she said "No they weren't, there was no car crash," and I sprang out of my adoption closet. When I started my search, my mother and my sister were extremely supportive, and in fact they wrote letters to the court, begging the court to give me my information, which I did get. They did write extremely loving and supportive letters about my need to know. It's not common, and it did really help my relationship [with them]. Well, my relationship with my sister was always good, but it did make my relationship with my mother better, and especially when I started to be on talk shows on a regular basis (Joe Soll, personal interview).

Education, Military Service, and Significant Relationships

Soll briefly attended Johns Hopkins University and later New York University. He received his master's degree in social work in 1990 and earned additional diplomas in Psychotherapy and Forensic Counseling. He specializes in adoption, abuse, and grief-related issues. He served in the National Guard and Special Forces National Guard for three years. He has been married and divorced twice. His adoption is a very important influence on his life and work, as he explains:

I think that my experience has radiated through every aspect of my life, and it's affected every relationship I've ever had. It has certainly affected my careers. I never knew what I wanted to do—I just did things. I did well—I guess I have a good brain. But if my sister hadn't made that remark to me in 1982, I don't know what I'd be doing, and that's scary. It was really serendipitous, it was out of the blue, we never talked about adoption, my sister and I, ever, ever, ever. Nobody in the family talked about adoption. You know about the dead horse on the dining room table kind of thing? I used to feel rejected. I don't believe I was rejected, for several reasons. One is: I don't believe my mother willingly gave me up, but even if she did, that wasn't about me. It was about her. It took me a long time to get to that, I mean that's how I feel. I used to feel horribly rejected. I think we can find rejection in a street lamp, our "tribe" [adopted persons]. That's how it used to feel. I just don't feel that way anymore. The healing for me has been to stop being afraid to feel my real feelings. The pain is there, but I know how to deal with it, so I am finally free of the torture. We can all achieve that freedom (Joe Soll, personal interview September 11, 2000).

Works Cited

Joe Soll. *Adoption Healing: A Path to Recovery*. Baltimore, MD: Gateway Press, 2000.
Soll, Joe, and Karen Wilson Buterbaugh .*Adoption Healing: A Path to Recovery for Mothers Who Lost Children to Adoption*. Baltimore, MD: Gateway Press, 2003.

Soll, Joe, and Lori Paris. *Evil Exchange,* Livermore, CA: Wingspan Press, 2006.
Soll, Joe. Personal interview September 11, 2000.

STANLEY, HENRY MORTON (1841–1904)

Explorer, Journalist
Orphanage alumnus, adoptee

Career, Major Awards, and Achievements

Henry Morton Stanley was a journalist and the explorer who became famous for locating the missing African explorer David Livingstone. Stanley's early journeys led him all over the world, from the American frontier to Turkey and Europe and his travel writings were very popular, especially those from his expeditions in Africa. For his service in Africa, Stanley was knighted and given a seat in the English Parliament.

Family of Origin

Stanley was born John Rowlands on June 29, 1841, in Denbigh, Wales. He was the illegitimate son of John Rowlands of Llys, who died several weeks after his birth, and Elizabeth Parry. His mother left him with his grandfather, Moses Parry, a Denbigh butcher, while she went into service in London and later married. After his grandfather's sudden death in 1847, Stanley was fostered at the expense of his maternal uncles at the home of an elderly couple, the Prices. When they raised their rates, Stanley's uncles decided to place him in the workhouse.

Orphanage

The Price's son Dick took the child to the workhouse under a pretext of making a visit to his favorite aunt. Thus on February 20, 1847, Stanley began his residency at St. Asaph's. He never forgave Dick Price for his treachery and deceit, as he writes in his autobiography:

> Though forty-five years have passed since that dreadful evening, my resentment has not a whit abated. . . . It would have been far better for me if Dick, being stronger than I, had employed compulsion, instead of shattering my confidence and planting the first seeds of distrust in a child's Heart (12).

Stanley describes James Francis, the schoolmaster who received him, as a brutal monster who was eventually discovered and diagnosed as insane. One of the St. Asaph boys, Willie Roberts, was said to have died after a vicious beating from Francis, although another biographer, Tim Zeal, disputes this (Zeal 20). The schoolmaster never tired of terrorizing and torturing the "flock of cropped little oddities," as Stanley called the thirty or so boys at St. Asaph's (16). During his ten years in the institution, Stanley received a primarily "religious and industrial" (18) education at the workhouse and developed a fanatic passion for order and cleanliness (21) and a religious zeal (26–27) that remained with him throughout his lifetime.

When Stanley was twelve, his birthmother and her two children, a boy and a girl, entered the workhouse. Her reunion with Stanley was a cold and unhappy one, as he describes:

[Stanley, Henry Morton, *In Darkest Africa*, vol. 1, 1890]

Francis came up to me during the dinner-hour, when all the inmates were assembled, and pointing out a tall woman with an oval face, and a great coil of dark hair behind her head, asked me if I recognized her. "No, Sir," I replied. "What, do you not know your own mother?" I started, with a burning face, and directed a shy glance at her, and perceived she was regarding me with a look of cool, critical scrutiny. I had expected to feel a gush of tenderness towards her, but her expression was so chilling that the valves of my heart closed as with a snap. . . . After a few weeks' residence my mother departed, taking her little boy with her, but the girl was left in the institution; and, such is the system prevailing, though we met in the same hall for months, she remained as a stranger to me (29).

Adoption

Stanley ran away from the workhouse after he fought back and injured Francis during an attack in May 1856 (33). He first contacted his wealthy paternal grandfather, but was completely rejected by him (40). After several unwelcomed visits with maternal relatives, Stanley at last resolved to board a ship as a cabin boy to New Orleans. Hungry and destitute, he was befriended, and later adopted, by a cotton merchant, Henry Stanley, who gave him his name:

> "The long and the short of it is," said he, "as you are wholly unclaimed, without a parent, relation, or sponsor, I promise to take you for my son, and fit you for a mercantile career; and in the future, you are to bear my name, 'Henry Stanley.'" Having said which, he rose and, dipping his hands in a basin of water, he made the sign of the cross on my forehead and went seriously through the formula of baptism, ending with a brief exhortation to bear my new name worthily (121).

Stanley's new father's wife had also been very fond of the boy, but died just prior to the adoption. The following year, Stanley, Sr., sent his new son to Arkansas to work in a retail business. The adoptive father died suddenly in 1861, without making legal provisions for Stanley and the young man again found himself adrift in the South during the outbreak of the Civil war. He fought on both sides during the Civil War and was taken prisoner by the Northern army at Shiloh but was soon released.

He made his way back to Wales, ill and poor, in November of 1862 and tried to contact his birthmother for the final time. This last visit, according to Stanley's wife (219–220), was to have a profound and lifelong effect on his character, creating a habit of strong self-suppression and a habitual reserve.

Significant Relationships

Henry Morton Stanley and his wife, Dorothy, adopted a little boy, Denzil, in 1896. Stanley died May 10, 1904, in London.

Works Cited

Jeal, Tim. *Stanley: The Impossible Life of Africa's Greatest Explorer.* New Haven, CT: Yale University Press, 2007.

McLynn, Frank. *Stanley, the Making of an African Explorer, 1841–1877.* New York: Cooper Square Press, 2001.

Stanley, Sir Henry M. *The Autobiography of Henry M. Stanley.* New York: Greenwood Press, 1969.

STANWYCK, BARBARA (1907–1990)

Actress
Orphaned around age 5, former foster child

Career, Major Awards, and Achievements

Barbara Stanwyck was a major twentieth-century American actress who turned her distinctive beauty and dancing talent into an outstanding career in film and television. Considered one of the nicest people ever to work in Hollywood, she starred in nearly a hundred films and was nominated four times for an Oscar for Best Actress, for *Stella*

[AP Photo]

Dallas (1937), *Ball of Fire* (1941), *Double Indemnity* (1944), and *Sorry, Wrong Number* (1948). In 1982 she received an honorary Academy Award for her creativity and contribution to screen acting. She won Emmys for *The Barbara Stanwyck Show* (1961–62); her role as the matriarch on *The Big Valley,* the popular western series of 1965–69; and the role of Mary Carson in the miniseries *The Thorn Birds.*

Ruby Stevens (Stanwyck's original name) began working as a bundle wrapper at a department store in Brooklyn when she was thirteen. With money received from work as a telephone operator, pattern cutter, file clerk, and receptionist, she paid for dancing lessons in order to follow her chorus girl sister into a more interesting career. By the time she was fifteen she was dancing in nightclubs in New York City. She performed as a member of the chorus in the touring company of the Ziegfeld Follies of 1923, one of the famous spectacular theatrical productions of Florenz Ziegfeld. In 1925 she performed in the summer version of the Follies and as a chorus dancer in a number of musicals.

She was appearing at a night club in Atlantic City when Broadway producer Willard Mack noticed her. He had been looking for an actress to play a cabaret dancer in *The Noose*, one of the biggest hits of 1926. Before the play opened, Mack suggested that Ruby Stevens change her name to Barbara Stanwyck. Mack's idea for her name came from a billboard for another play: Jane Stanwyck in *Barbara Fritchie*. Though Barbara's part was small, good reviews earned her a chance to make a screen test for *Broadway Nights*, being produced by Bob Kane. She lost the leading role because her screen test was less than successful, but she did get a small role as a fan dancer, her first film role.

In 1927 Arthur Hopkins gave Stanwyck the lead role of Bonny in *Burlesque*. One critic noted that in entertaining moments and those that simply moved the play forward, she was unconvincing, but in moments of intense feeling or crisis, Stanwyck showed "sincerity and pathos" (*Current Biography* 607) and the two leads were given much of the credit for the success of the show.

After *Burlesque*, Hollywood showed increased interest. Stanwyck would appear only once more on Broadway, in *Tattle Tales*, a revue that had been coauthored by her husband at the time, Frank Fay. Her first two movies, *The Locked Door* and *Mexicali Rose*, were both failures, but, with Fay's influence, she achieved her first real film success in *Ladies of Leisure*, directed by Frank Capra. She followed this up with three more Capra films, *The Miracle Woman*, *Forbidden*, and *The Bitter Tea of General Yen*, and leading roles in three Warner Brothers films, *Night Nurse*, *So Big*, and *The Purchase Price*, all complete before 1934. Movies like *Shopworn*, *Baby Face*, *Gambling Lady*, and *The Woman in Red* gave Stanwyck the image of a tough but vulnerable working girl. She also portrayed society wives with problem husbands. In 1935 she broke through her casting stereotypes with the title role in the RKO-Radio film *Annie Oakley*.

Stanwyck starred with Robert Taylor in *His Brother's Wife* and *This Is My Affair* in 1936 and 1937. They married in 1939, four years after she and Frank Fay divorced.

After her Oscar nomination for *Stella Dallas*, Stanwyck continued to expand her roles. *Breakfast for Two* was a screwball comedy, *Always Goodbye* a drama, and *The Mad Miss Manton* another comedy. In 1939 came the western *Union Pacific*, then *Golden Boy* with William Holden and *The Lady Eve* with Henry Fonda. In 1944 she played a femme fatale in *Double Indemnity*, which some critics feel was her most powerful performance. Two Oscar nominations in two years helped her become the highest-paid woman in the United States in 1944, although she had always been a top Hollywood money maker. The 1940s gave Stanwyck great roles and acclaim, but the 1950s offered her fewer strong roles with the exception of *Executive Suite*, which was an all-star hit. In 1957, the year she turned fifty, she appeared in *Forty Guns*, the best of a series of westerns she made during that period.

In 1960, tiring of second rate movie offers, she moved to television, where she would win three Emmys, though she was not completely done with her film career. In *Walk on the Wild Side* (1962), she played a lesbian madam, and in 1964 costarred with Elvis Presley in *Roustabout. The Night Walker* (1964) was her last film. From 1965 to 1969 she starred in *The Big Valley*, a television western series, which allowed her to show both strength and warmth and won her many fans. In the early 1970s she appeared in a few made-for-television movies. In 1983 she won an Emmy for her portrayal of Mary Carson in *The Thorn Birds*. In 1985 she starred in her last role on *The Colbys*, a spin-off of *Dynasty*.

Barbara Stanwyck was inducted into the Western Performers Hall of Fame of the National Cowboy and Western Heritage Museum in Oklahoma City in 1973. She received an American Film Institute Life Achievement Award in 1987. Her star on the Hollywood Walk of Fame is at 1751 Vine Street.

Family of Origin

Barbara Stanwyck was born Ruby Catherine Stevens in New York City on July 16, 1907. She had four older siblings, Maude, Mabel, Mildred, and Malcolm (known as Byron Jr.). Her mother, Catherine Ann McGee, was a Canadian immigrant and a staunch Irish Catholic. Her father, Byron E. Stevens, was an American of Irish descent. He worked as a fisherman and occasional brick layer but his family lived in poverty. Byron was known to be a heavy drinker with "a Jekyll and Hyde personality" (Wayne 7). Often out of work and overcrowded in the home, he abandoned the family a year before Ruby was born, but the Stevens family eventually reunited and moved to Brooklyn.

In 1910, when Ruby was two years old, her mother, who was very close to giving birth to her sixth child, was accidentally pushed off a trolley and hit her head. She died a week later without regaining consciousness. A short time after the funeral, Byron Stevens deserted his family for good. The children were told that he left to work on the Panama Canal as a bricklayer.

Foster Homes

Maude and Mabel had already married and moved out of the family home before Ruby was born. Mildred, who worked as a traveling chorus girl, placed Ruby and Byron Jr., two years older than Ruby, into a series of foster homes. Ruby ran away every afternoon to look for her mother, and Byron Jr. always had to find his sister and bring her back. Stanwyck wrote, "It wasn't as bad as it sounded. In those days foster homes were not cruel. They were just impersonal" (Wayne 9).

When Ruby was about five years old, Mildred came to tell her that their father had officially died at sea. She took Byron Jr. to live with her but left Ruby in fosterage. Stanwyck wrote that she could have endured anything except the separation from her beloved brother: "My sister Mildred thought Byron was old enough to live with her. I did everything I could. I cried and wanted to run away with him. Then I begged Mildred to take me too. I pleaded and I screamed, but she took him anyway" (Wayne 10).

After Byron Jr. left, Ruby became isolated and rebellious. She refused to make friends because she could not trust anyone, and she had to relocate without warning to other homes and schools.

The happiest childhood home Ruby had was with the Cohen family, her final foster home. She wrote:

> Not only was the house clean, but it was full of sincere love and they were always concerned about me. I wasn't sent to school without my hair being combed and my face scrubbed and without clean clothes. The Cohens were rather poor, but they fed me well and took me to church and sometimes to the movies (Wayne 11).

Ruby had lived there for two years, but when Mrs. Cohen became pregnant, she realized that there would no longer be room for her. So she quit school, lied about her age, and went to work. She was thirteen.

Education and Significant Relationships

Stanwyck's formal education ended when she left school in Brooklyn. She had been active in basketball and the school's plays.

On August 26, 1928, Stanwyck married Frank Fay, who had been a successful Broadway actor. In 1932, the couple adopted Dion Anthony Fay, known as Tony, who was a month old at the time. (Eventually Stanwyck and Tony Fay would become estranged.) Frank Fay's style did not translate well to film, but Stanwyck rapidly became a major star. They divorced in 1935. Some believe that *A Star Is Born* was based on the Fay-Stanwyck marriage.

Stanwyck married Hollywood star Robert Taylor in 1939. They acquired and enjoyed a large ranch and home in Mandeville Canyon, but the marriage was unsuccessful. Taylor had several affairs with actresses including Ava Gardner and Lana Turner. In 1950, Stanwyck filed for divorce, which was granted in 1951; she received 15 percent of Taylor's salary as alimony until his death. Stanwyck and Taylor would appear together in *The Night Walker* (1964), Stanwyck's last feature film.

In retirement, she did charitable work, which was not publicized. Barbara Stanwyck died in Santa Monica, California, at St. John's Hospital, of congestive heart disease on January 20, 1990.

Works Cited

Hannsberry, Karen Burroughs. "Barbara Stanwyck." *Femme Noir: Bad Girls of Film*. Jefferson, NC: McFarland & Co., 1998. 456–477.

"Stanwyck, Barbara." *Current Biography Yearbook 1947*. Ed. Anna Roth. New York: H. W. Wilson, 1948. 608–609.

Wayne, Jane Ellen. *Stanwyck*. New York: Arbor House, 1985.

SWIFT, JONATHAN (1667–1745)

Author, Clergy
Fostered

Career, Major Awards, and Achievements

Swift is best known as the author of *Gulliver's Travels*, which he wrote in 1726. *Gulliver's Travels* surpassed its original purpose as contemporary political and literary satire to become a classic, has never fallen out of print, and has had numerous film, television and theatrical adaptations. Swift also wrote many notable essays, memoirs, pamphlets, sermons, poetry, and letters. These include *A Discourse of the Contests and Dissensions between the Nobles and Commons in Athens and Rome* (1701), *Tale of a Tub* and its addendum *The Battle of the Books* (1704), *An Argument against Abolishing Christianity* (1708), *A Project for the Advancement of Religion, and the Reformation of Manners* (1709), *Baucis and Philemon* (poetry, 1709), *A Meditation upon a Broomstick* (1710), *The Conduct of the Allies* (1711), *A Proposal for Correcting, Improving, and Ascertaining the*

[Courtesy of the Library of Congress]

English Tongue (1712), *A Letter of Advice to a Young Poet* (1721), *Cadenus and Vanessa* (poetry, 1726), *Letter to a Very Young Lady on her Marriage* (1727), *A Complete Collection of Genteel and Ingenious Conversation* (1737), *Verses on the Death of Dr. S., Written by Himself* (1739), *Three Sermons* (1744), *Directions to Servants in General* (1745) and a collection of daily diary entries and letters known as the *Journal to Stella* (1768). Swift is regarded as one English literature's greatest satirists. His characteristic style is sarcastic, rebellious, passionate, and often indecent.

A native of Ireland, Swift lived in England during in his early twenties, where he continued his education and worked as a secretary to a British statesman Sir William Temple. At the Temple household in Moor Park, Surrey, Swift met a fatherless eight-year-old girl named Hester Johnson, whom he renamed "Stella." Hester's mother was the companion of Lady Giffard, Temple's widowed sister. Swift agreed to tutor the child and they developed the beginning of a lifelong friendship. Stella was the first of two important women friends in Swift's life, and many rumors and theories have been advanced about their relationship, including that they were secretly married or that they were the illegitimate brother and sister of a common father, possibly Temple. Many biographers, however, believe them to simply have been devoted and platonic friends. In 1693, Temple procured Swift an office in Ireland as Master of Rolls. Swift, who had hoped to advance himself in England, reluctantly returned to Dublin. When Stella was nineteen, she and a relative, Rebecca Dingley, followed Swift to Dublin and settled nearby.

After his return to Ireland, Swift was ordained an Anglican deacon in 1694 and a priest in 1695. He became vicar of Laracor, Aghar, Rathbeggan, and Dunlavin. In 1713, Swift was made the dean of St. Patrick's in Dublin.

Swift made frequent visits to England on church or personal business and became active in politics there during his longer stays. Initially a member of the Whig party, he later became associated with the Tories and edited their newspaper, *The Examiner*, although he considered himself an "Old Whig" rather than a Tory. He eventually became involved with Anglo-Irish politics and some of his most incendiary writings dealt with English injustices in Ireland. His best known writings of this type were a series of controversial pamphlets known as the *Drapier Letters* (1720–1725), which he wrote under the pseudonym M. B. Drapier. These letters effectively opposed an English plan to establish an inferior currency in Ireland. In 1729, Swift wrote his satiric masterpiece *A Modest Proposal*, which suggests that year-old infants of the Irish poor be sold as food for the English and Irish aristocracy. These writings made Swift an Irish national hero, in spite of the fact that he always regarded himself as an "English exile" in the country of his birth and was ashamed of his affiliations there:

> Swift's compassion for the Irish is modified by a contempt of them expressed in other essays. . . . Here, at their clearest, are the complexity and paradoxicalness that makes Swift fascinating: a man who seeks to prod and draw humans into being the better creatures he believes they will not become, a man who loves and longs for England but dwells mostly on her faults, a man who hated Ireland and regarded it as a prison yet devoted years to efforts to alleviate its misery and bring it freedom (Shakel 348).

Family of Origin

Jonathan Swift was born in Dublin on November 30, 1667, to Abigail Erick Swift, a widow whose family came from Leicestershire, England. Her husband, also named Jonathan Swift, was the youngest of five brothers who had immigrated to Ireland from Herefordshire, England. All of the brothers became lawyers, except Thomas Swift, who was a clergyman. Some, especially the eldest brother, Godwin, prospered in Ireland through beneficial marriages and influential patrons. Swift's father, a steward of the King's Inn, married a dowerless woman and died suddenly seven months before his son was born. This marriage, which in April of 1666 produced a daughter, Jane, was, according to Swift's autobiographical sketch, not a fortunate one:

On both sides [the marriage was] very indiscreet, for his wife brought her husband little or no fortune, and his death happening so suddenly before he could make a sufficient establishment for his family: And his son (not then born) hath often been heard to say that he felt the consequences of that marriage not only through the whole course of his education but during the greater part of his life (Glendinning 4).

Fosterage

After the death of his father, Swift's mother returned to Leicestershire, leaving the children in the care of their uncle Godwin Swift. The timing of her departure varies in accounts from immediately after her husband's death to several years later, following her son's restoration from his famous "abduction" to Whitehaven, England. Swift recounts the following story of abduction by his nurse:

When he was a year old an event happened to him that seems very unusual; for his nurse who was a woman of Whitehaven, being under an absolute necessity of seeing one of her relations, who was then extremely sick, and from whom she expected a legacy, and being at the same time extremely fond of the infant, she stole him on shipboard unknown to his mother and uncles, and carried him with her, to Whitehaven, where he continued for almost three years. For when the matter was discovered, his mother sent orders by all means not to hazard a second voyage, till he could be better able to bear it. The nurse was so careful of him, that before he returned he had learnt to spell; and by the time that he was three years old he could read any chapter in the Bible (Murry 13–14).

Swift told different versions of this story to friends, and biographers suspect that if he had been "amicably kidnapped," as one biographer termed it (Murry 13), it was probably with his mother's full knowledge and permission:

What rings false to me is that he was taken to England without the knowledge of his mother, and that it was her fear of the danger of the sea journey which prevented his return home. That sounds like a comforting fable. . . . The most far-fetched interpretation of adult behaviour is preferable to the possibility that your mother finds your constant presence inconvenient. . . . Swift was often heard to tell, at the dinner table, the story about the nurse carrying him off in his babyhood to Whitehaven. As Deane Swift [Dean Jonathan Swift's great nephew and early biographer] wrote, the story "gave occasion to many ludicrous whims and extravagances in the gaiety of his conversations." He told it with variations and embellishments, sometimes saying that he was smuggled out of Ireland in a bandbox. Swift was to describe Gulliver, a finger-sized manikin among the giant Brobdingnagians, being parted from his nurse-girl, wafted in his carrying-box over the sea by an eagle, and dropped into the water to float on till he was rescued. I think, when he wrote that, the Whitehaven story was in the back of his mind (Glendinning 4–5).

After his mother returned to England, Swift did not see her again until he traveled to Leicestershire when he was twenty years old. One of his logs from 1709 indicated that Swift wrote to his mother each month and that they were on good terms. At the time of her death in April 1710, Swift wrote, "I have now lost my barrier between me and death; God grant that I may live to be as well prepared for it, as I confidently believe her to have been! If the way to Heaven be through piety, truth, justice, and charity, she is there" (Glendinning 29). Swift also remained friends with his sister, Jane, until, at age thirty-three, she married Joseph Fenton, a tradesman her brother disliked. In 1710, Fenton left Jane with several children and Swift, who had become "ungracious" to his sister (Glendinning 31), agreed to pay her an allowance on the condition she move to England.

Education and Significant Relationships

Swift's uncle Godwin sent him to Kilkenny College from 1674 to 1682, when he was between the ages of six to fourteen. Later Godwin sent him to Trinity College in Dublin. A proud and sensitive boy, Swift was humiliated by his dependence on his family's charity. He did poorly in his studies, especially the ones he disliked, and was resentful toward his uncles, who may have withheld the kind of affection and pocket money Swift saw his fellows receive. In spite of the fine reputations of his schools, Swift said that Godwin "gave me the education of a dog" (Murray 15), and he wrote in his autobiography:

> By the ill treatment of his nearest relations he was so discouraged and sunk in his spirits that he too much neglected his academic studies, for some parts of which he had no great relish by nature, and turned himself to reading history and poetry, so that when the time came for taking his degree of bachelor of arts, although he lived with great regularity and due observance of the statutes, he was stopped of his degree for dullness and insufficiency (Van Doren 9–10).

Swift was given his bachelor's degree from Trinity with a "discreditable mark" on February 15, 1685. He stayed an additional seven years and began to study hard in order to earn a master's degree at Trinity. In 1688, Godwin Swift died, after having lost most of his wealth. In 1689, Swift left Ireland to visit his mother in Leicestershire. He continued his higher education in England and took his master of arts at Oxford in 1692.

Swift had flirtations with several women in his youth, the most serious being with Jane Waring, a Belfast girl whom Swift called "Varina." During one of his later English visits, Swift became involved with Ester Vanhomrigh, whom he called "Vanessa." After her mother died, Vanessa, like Stella, relocated to Ireland, in order to be close to Swift. It is clear from all accounts that both Stella and Vanessa loved Swift and were devoted to him. However, biographers widely disagree about Swift's actual relationships with women and accounts range from celibate friendships to violent and secret marriages:

> A library has been written on Swift's character and particularly on his mysterious sexual nature. Modern psychology can explain a good deal, but not all. It is easy to say that the simple answer is that (as he hinted more than once) he was impotent all his life: but behind his impotence, as behind his misanthropy, his public parsimony and secret benevolence, his fierce rebellion and pride, his pain and rage at injustice and cruelty, his cynical coarseness in writing contrasted with his squeamishness of speech and action, his deep tenderness inextricably mingled with brutality, lies a psychological twist buried deep in his childhood. His mother, who was herself a strange creature, in all probability made him what he was emotionally (Kunitz 506).

There are several dramatic versions about how Swift ended his attachment or entanglement with Vanessa, and whatever the truth is, it was clear that at the time of her death in June 1723, they were no longer friends. Stella died in January 1728, and after her death Swift's own health declined. Since his youth, Swift had suffered from bouts of dizziness, panic, visual distortion, and roaring deafness, which he took to be signs of impending madness. His symptoms were posthumously identified as Ménière's Syndrome, a disorder of the inner ear first diagnosed in 1861 and remedied today by pills used for seasickness. In 1739, Swift stepped down as dean of St. Patrick's after his memory and reason started to fail. He was eventually declared unfit to manage his own affairs and turned over to a committee of guardians. He became very ill and violent, and he eventually became paralyzed. He died on October 19, 1745, at the age of seventy-eight.

Following a three-day public funeral, he was buried privately according to his final wishes, at midnight, next to Stella in St. Patrick's Cathedral.

Works Cited

Dennis, Nigel. *Jonathan Swift: A Short Character*. New York: Macmillan, 1968.

Forster, John. *The Life of Jonathan Swift*. Vol. 1. London: J. Murray, 1875.

Glendinning, Victoria. *Jonathan Swift: A Portrait*. New York: Henry Holt and Co., 1998.

Kunitz, Stanley. "Jonathan Swift." *British Authors Before 1800: A Biographical Dictionary*. New York: Wilson, 1952.

Murray, John Middleton. *Jonathan Swift: A Critical Biography*. New York: Farrar, Straus and Giroux, 1967.

Schakel, Peter J. "Jonathan Swift." *British Prose Writers, 1660–1800. Dictionary of Literary Biography* 101 (1991): 319.

Swift, Deane. *An Essay Upon the Life, Writing, and Character of Dr. Jonathan Swift*. London: Charles Bathurst, 1755.

Van Doren, Carl. *Swift*. New York: Viking Press, 1930.

T

TE KANAWA, KIRI (1944–)

Opera Singer
Adoptee

Career, Major Awards, and Achievements

For thirty years, Kiri Te Kanawa has been one of the world's most highly praised and popular sopranos. After appearing in numerous smaller roles, she made her official debut in 1971 at Covent Garden's Royal Opera as Countess Almaviva in Mozart's *The Marriage of Figaro*. She has sung many acclaimed roles, including Mimi in *La Bohème*, Marguerite in *Faust*, Donna Elvira in *Don Giovanni*, Desdemona in Verdi's *Otello*, Amelia in Verdi's *Simone Boccanegra*, Fiordiligi in Mozart's *Cosi Fan Tutte*, Tatiana in Tchaikovsky's *Eugene Onegin*, the Marschallin in Strauss's *Der Rosenkavalier*, Violetta in Verdi's *La Traviata*, and Tosca in Puccini's *Tosca*. She debuted at the New York Metropolitan Opera on March 7, 1974, when she was asked to fill in for Teresa Stratas as Desdemona in *Otello*. Her performance earned glowing reviews, in spite of the fact that she received only a three-hour notice to prepare for the role. In the course of her career, Te Kanawa completed several international tours and appeared in distinguished film and television opera productions, including the Paris Opera's staging of *The Marriage of Figaro* (1976) and Covent Garden's *Die Fledermaus* (1977). Prince Charles specifically requested that she sing at his 1981 wedding to Lady Diana Spencer. Te Kanawa sang the aria "Let the Bright Seraphim" from Handel's *Samson* as her solo. In 1982, she was made a Dame Commander of the Order of the British Empire. Her later work expanded into popular and show music. In 1991, she performed in Paul McCartney's *Oratorio*, composed to celebrate the Liverpool Philharmonic's 150th anniversary. Dame Kiri has made many sound recordings, including Strauss's *Four Last Songs* with the London Symphony Orchestra (CBS Records), for which she won the Artist of the Year Grammy Award (1992). She announced plans to retire with the role of Countess Madeline in Strauss's *Capriccio*, which she performed during the New York Metropolitan Opera's 1997–1998 season, but she has continued her career in a variety of musical appearances, including the title role of Barber's *Vanessa* at the Los Angeles Opera (2004).

[AP Photo/Alastar Grant]

Family of Origin

Kiri Te Kanawa was born on March 6, 1944, in Gisborne, New Zealand. She was the child of a Maori man and a minister's daughter of Irish descent. The couple, according to her biographer, "never married and were extremely poor" (Fingleton 17). They also had a son older than Kiri, whom she has never met. Her father's ancestor was a great chieftain of the Manupoto Maori tribe. Kiri's birthfather died of tuberculosis at the age of thirty-five, and her birthmother died in Australia around 1980. Although Te Kanawa is proud of her heritage, she has not tried to trace her birth family: "Nobody's ever said a word. When a Maori child is given away you're not meant to say anything or ever try to retrieve it. That's rather beautiful, really" (Fingleton 17).

Adoption

Te Kanawa was adopted by a couple who had the same racial mix as her birthfamily. Her father, Thomas Te Kanawa, was a building contractor of Maori heritage. His wife, Nell Leece, was of European ancestry and was the great-niece of Sir Arthur Sullivan, of the Gilbert and Sullivan musical team. Nell had been married twice before her marriage to Thomas in 1938. She had two children from her first marriage, a son and a daughter, but Thomas wanted a son. As Nell was past childbearing age,

> the Te Kanawas placed their name on an adoption list and also advertised in the local paper—for a boy. In April 1944 a social worker came to the house with a five-week-old baby girl, but the Te Kanawas turned the offer down. The social worker returned with the baby, however, and Tom remembers saying to his wife, 'Look at that poor little girl—she's got no home. Poor kid, no-one's adopted her yet.' Nell, knowing that it was actually Tom who was so keen to have a son, said, 'Well, it's up to you.' So the baby girl was taken in and named after Tom's father, Kiri, the Maori word for Bell (Fingleton 16).

The Te Kanawas told Kiri that she was adopted at a very early age:

> She was only two when her parents told her that she had been adopted, as a secret between her and them. They suggested it would be better if she did not tell her friends when she went to school. "It turned me into a survivor: I felt I was special and had special responsibilities. I'm quite sure if I hadn't known I was adopted I'd have stayed a nobody and would be in New Zealand breeding children now. But that turned me into a fighter" (Fingleton 17).

Nell, who had a strong influence over her daughter, decided that she would become a singer when Kiri was three years old: "I can see Mummy constantly kept the music going. I'd tend not to feel like it because I was a lazy child, but she'd insist that I sang, and by the time I was eight she could hear that I could sing pretty well" (Fingleton 17–18).

Education, Marriage, and Children

The family moved to Auckland when Kiri was eleven, and by the time she was twelve, she was training to be an opera singer at St. Mary's College, under the guidance of Sister Mary Leo. Johnny Waititi, a founding member of the Maori Trust Foundation, became a mentor for Kiri and helped her with a grant for serious opera study.

In 1966, Kiri won an important aria contest, and with that prize money, a $10,000 grant from the New Zealand Arts Council, and family savings, she moved to London with her mother to complete voice training at the London Opera Centre.

Te Kanawa met her future husband, Desmond Park, on a blind date soon after her move to London and they married on August 30, 1967. He is a mining engineer from Australia. After two miscarriages, the couple adopted two children, Antonia (Toni) in 1976 and Thomas in 1979: "I was desperately worried about having my own child after Toni. We already loved her so much that it would have been terribly difficult to have had one child who was adopted and then another who was not. We're now a blissfully happy family" (Fingleton 155). Te Kanawa and Park divorced in 1997.

Works Cited

Fingleton, David. *Kiri Te Kanawa: A Biography.* New York: Atheneum, 1983.

Jenkins, Garry, and Stephen D'Antal. *Kiri: Her Unsung Story.* London: HarperCollins Entertainment, 1999.

THOMAS, DAVE (1932–2002)

Restaurateur, Entrepreneur, Philanthropist
Late-discovery adoptee

Career, Major Awards, and Achievements

Dave Thomas is the founder of Wendy's International Inc., one of the largest chains of fast food restaurants in the world. Thomas dropped out of high school at the age of fifteen, after completing the tenth grade, to work in a restaurant. He rose from busboy to manager at the Hobby House restaurant in Fort Wayne, Indiana, and regarded owner Phil Clauss as his mentor and the workers there as "his family" (Thomas 30). He later developed a partnership with "Colonel" Harlan Sanders, who had likewise left school at a young age in order to support his family following the death of his father. Thomas managed several Kentucky Fried Chicken (KFC) franchises as a 45 percent shareholder, until he started Wendy's.

In 1969, Thomas opened the first Wendy's Old Fashioned Hamburgers in Columbus, Ohio. The restaurant differed at the time from its two major competitors, McDonald's and Burger King, by providing a homey atmosphere and by specializing in fresh to order, rather than frozen, hamburger patties. Wendy's later expanded their menu to offer a baked potato and salad bar, grilled chicken, and chili. Thomas named the restaurant after one of his five children, Melinda Lou, whom the family called "Wendy." The chain now has over 6,700 restaurants internationally.

Wendy's iconic "Where's the beef?" commercials, starring Clara Peller, aired in January 1984, and the phrase quickly took on a life of its own, even turning up in the presidential debates that year. Thomas himself became the next media spokesman for his restaurant, with great success. Folksy and sincere, Thomas appeared in over 800 television commercials from 1989 to 2000, a feat recorded in the 2000 *Guinness Book of World Records* as the "Longest Running Television Advertising Campaign Starring a Company Founder." A Wendy's marketing survey found that by the late 1990s, over 90 percent of Americans knew who Dave Thomas was.

Thomas used his popularity and recognition to help children waiting for adoption, especially older children, sibling groups, and children with special needs. In 1990, he became the official spokesman for a White House adoption initiative called "Adoption

[AP Photo/Chris Kasson]

Works—For Everyone." In 1992, his own nonprofit Dave Thomas Foundation for Adoption was founded to promote permanent adoption placements for North American children in foster care. Wendy's was one of the earliest companies to support employees who wished to adopt children by offering financial assistance for adoption, including legal, medical, and counseling costs and paid family leave. Thomas founded a signature annual award honoring the top 100 most adoption-friendly workplaces in order to recognize small, medium, and large companies who offer similar adoption benefits to their employees. The NAACP Humanitarian Award for 1994 honored Thomas's adoption related efforts.

Thomas wrote several memoirs, including *Dave's Way: A New Approach to Old-Fashioned Success* (1991) and *Well Done! The Common Guy's Guide to Everyday Success* (1994), from which the quotations below were taken. In 1979, he was awarded the Horatio Alger Award, which recognizes distinguished persons who have overcome adversity. Thomas also served on the board of directors for Children's Hospital in Columbus, Ohio, and for St. Jude Children's Research Hospital in Memphis.

Family of Origin

Thomas was born on July 2, 1932, in Atlantic City, New Jersey:

> In 1932, a girl in trouble named Mollie would have walked down Broadway in Camden. . . . Mollie would have the only child that she would ever bear—a child out of wedlock—and she would give the baby up to a couple in Michigan and then take herself back to that walk-up tailor shop in Camden where her parents lived and worked.
> Mollie passed away from rheumatic fever just eighteen years later. I wish I could have met Mollie, but I never did.
> You see, Mollie was my mother (Thomas 20–21).

Thomas searched for his first mother when he was 20 years old, and discovered that she had died. He met some of her family but "didn't feel any particular closeness to them" (Achiron 86). Thomas initially did not want to search for his father, but in the late 1980s, his oldest daughter, Pam, initiated a search on his behalf and learned that he had passed away. She found other family members in the Philadelphia area, including an MIT-educated college professor

> who wanted nothing to do with his half brother. "He didn't want his mother to know that his father had a little one-night deal," Dave says. "He might be very, very smart, but he doesn't have much common sense. . . . It's hard for people who have a mother and father to understand. Adoption was like the plague" (Achiron 86).

Adoption

Rex David (Dave) Thomas was adopted at the age of six weeks by Rex Thomas, a construction worker from Kalamazoo, Michigan, and his wife, Auleva. When Dave was five years old, his adoptive mother died. Rex Thomas remarried two more times and moved frequently. Dave was often left in the care of Auleva's mother, Minnie Sinclair.

When he was thirteen years old, Minnie told Thomas that he had been adopted: "It really hurt that nobody told me before," he recalls. "It is a terrible feeling to know my natural mother didn't want me" (Achiron 87). Thomas's somewhat late discovery often disturbed him, and he strongly advocated open communication in adoptive families:

> Hiding the truth about adoption in a family can quietly do its harm to the birth siblings as much as to the adopted ones. . . . Would life have been simpler if all the kids knew the truth at an earlier age? Would the whole family have been closer? My guess is yes to both questions.
>
> Maybe we have to get over the idea that adopted children should blend in with their parents. Even look pretty much like them if things can be arranged. People aren't hatched; they are what they are. The idea is to give kids love and a home—not to coordinate their hair and their eyes with the parents' as if trying to match up a replacement piece of upholstery (Thomas 32–34).

Thomas, who began working at the Regas restaurant in Knoxville when he was twelve, left school and home at age fifteen to work full time at Hobby House in Fort Wayne, Indiana. He lived at the YMCA.

Education, Military Service, and Significant Relationships

Thomas enlisted in the Army after the outbreak of the Korean War. He attended Cook and Baker's School at Fort Benning, Georgia. He worked as a cook and mess sergeant in Germany, where he and the three men he supervised fed up to two thousand people each day, an experience that gave him important skills for his later career. He was honorably discharged at the rank of staff sergeant in 1953.

After his return from military service, Thomas went back to Hobby House as a short-order cook. There he fell in love with Lorraine Buskirk Thomas, a Hobby House waitress, and they married on May 21, 1954. They have four daughters, Pam, Molly, Melinda Lou ("Wendy"), and Lori, and one son, Ken.

Dave Thomas frequently spoke to groups of young people, urging them not to drop out of high school, which he always felt was "a dumb mistake" (Achiron 87). To set an example, Thomas returned to school and earned his GED in 1993 at Coconut Creek High School, Coconut Creek, Florida. He and Lorraine danced at the senior prom, and his classmates voted him "most likely to succeed."

Thomas died January 8, 2002, of liver cancer, in Fort Lauderdale, Florida. He is buried in Columbus, Ohio.

Works Cited

Achiron, Marilyn. "Dave Thomas: Putting His Money where His Heart Is, the Man from Wendy's Crusades for Adoption." *People Magazine* 40 n5 (August 2, 1993): 86.

Thomas, Dave. *Well Done! The Common Guy's Guide to Everyday Success.* Grand Rapids, MI: Zondervan Publishing House, 1994.

TOLKIEN, J. R. R. (1892–1973)

Author, Educator, Philologist
Orphaned at age 12, fostered by a Catholic priest

Career, Major Awards, and Achievements

J. R. R. Tolkien is the renowned creator of Middle Earth, best known to most readers and moviegoers through his fantasy novels *The Hobbit* (1937) and the *Lord of the Rings*

[AP Photo]

trilogy (*The Fellowship of the Ring,* 1954; *The Two Towers,* 1955; and *The Return of the King,* 1956). Tolkien's academic publications include *A Middle English Vocabulary* (1922), *Sir Gawain and the Green Knight* (coeditor, 1925), *Beowulf: The Monster and the Critics* (1937), *On Fairy-Stories* (1947), and translations of medieval poems *The Pearl* and *Sir Orfeo*. His numerous additional published works include poetry, children's tales, essays, and drawings.

Tolkien's son, Christopher, has compiled, edited, and published many additional fantasy works of his father. These include *The Silmarillion* (1977), *The History of Middle Earth* (a twelve-volume series, 1988–1996), and *Children of Húrin* (2007). Christopher is also the author of the map of Middle Earth included in his father's original trilogy. A film version of *The Lord of the Rings*, directed by Peter Jackson (2001), won seventeen Academy Awards, including the Best Picture Oscar for *The Return of the King* (2003). Earlier animated versions of *The Hobbit* and *The Lord of the Rings* were released in 1978 and 1980.

For several years following his return home from military service after World War I, Tolkien worked as an assistant on the *Oxford English Dictionary*. He became a reader at the University of Leeds in 1920, but returned to Oxford in 1926, where he was a distinguished linguistics and philology professor until his retirement in 1959.

Tolkien's endowed appointments included the Andrew Lang lecturer at St. Andrews University (1938), W. P. Ker lecturer at Glasgow University (1953), the Rawlinson and Bosworth Professor of Anglo-Saxon (Oxford, 1925–1945), Pembroke College Fellow (1926–1945), and the Merton Professor of English Language and Literature (1945–1959). He was an officer of the Philological Society and a member of the Royal Society of Literature. He received honorary doctorates from the University of Liege and University College, Dublin, in 1954. Oxford gave him an honorary doctorate in 1972, the same year he was made a Commander in the Order of the British Empire.

Family of Origin

John Ronald Reuel Tolkien (known to his family as Ronald) was born to English parents in Bloemfontein, South Africa, on January 3, 1892. His father, Arthur Reuel Tolkien, moved to South Africa from Birmingham, England, in 1889 to become a manager for Lloyd's Bank of Africa. Arthur's fiancée, Mabel Suffield, joined him in 1891, and the couple married. Ronald's younger brother, Hilary, was born in 1894. The name "Reuel," which was handed down to Tolkien's children, grandchildren, and great-grandchildren, was the surname of one of his grandfather's friends (Carpenter 398).

Mabel took her sons on their first visit to England when Ronald was four years old. During this stay, Arthur, who had remained in South Africa, died of a hemorrhage associated with rheumatic fever. Mabel, Ronald, and Hilary never went back to Africa. Even though he had been very young when he left, Tolkien retained a few vivid memories. One such memory was of a tarantula bite. Although Tolkien claimed not to have a fear of spiders, biographers suspect that this incident may have been the source for Shelob and other malevolent Middle Earth spiders.

Tolkien's father died before he was eligible for a pension, so Mabel and her children became dependent upon the Suffield and Tolkien families for financial support. Mabel rented a small cottage in Sarehole, a rural village near Birmingham. Sarehole and its inhabitants are said to have been the inspiration for the Shire and hobbits of Tolkien's *Lord of the Rings* and *The Hobbit*. Mabel had worked as a governess before her marriage, and she took on the early education of her sons. Tolkien wrote that he developed his love of language from his mother.

In 1900, Mabel alienated her family by converting, along with her sons and her sister, May, to Catholicism. She moved to Moseley, a Birmingham suburb, to be close to a Catholic church. Her family and in-laws, who were Unitarians, Methodists, Baptists, and Anglicans, were furious and cut off their support. The poverty and stress that followed soon took its toll on Mabel's health, and she was diagnosed with diabetes in 1904:

> The effect on his own life, however, was to impress on his mind that his mother was being punished for her conversion to Catholicism, and that it was his duty to stick to the faith that she had chosen out of loyalty to her memory—the rest of her family might have abandoned her, but he never would. The idea of "the mother church" had a very literal resonance for him (Jones 11).

Guardianship

Mabel became a member of the Birmingham Oratory, which had been founded in 1849 by the illustrious Cardinal John Henry Newman, and rented a small house nearby. There she met Father Francis Morgan, who became a close friend and supporter. Father Morgan was a kind man of Welsh and Anglo-Spanish descent. He received a personal income from his family's sherry import business, and he used this money to quietly aid the widow and her sons (Carpenter 27–28). He also provided for the family to spend their summer at a country retreat to help Mabel recuperate. Mabel was worried that her relatives would "reconvert" the boys to Protestantism in the event of her death, so she appointed Father Morgan as their guardian in her will. Without insulin treatments, which had yet to be discovered, Mabel slipped into a diabetic coma and died on November 14, 1904. Tolkien wrote the following about his guardian in several letters to his son, Michael:

> But, of course, I live in anxiety concerning my children: who in this harder, crueler, and more mocking world into which I have survived must suffer more assaults than I have. But I am one who came up out of Egypt, and pray God none of my seed shall return thither. I witnessed (half-comprehending) the heroic sufferings and early death in extreme poverty of my mother who brought me into the Church; and received the astonishing charity of Francis Morgan (Tolkien 339–340).

Father Morgan first installed Ronald and Hilary at the home of their Aunt Beatrice, the widow of Mabel's brother, William, who also died in 1904. She was a severe and emotionally cold woman, and the boys were unhappy at her house (White 29). Father Morgan later moved the boys to a boarding house run by a Mrs. Faulkner, near the Oratory. Tolkien and his brother remained friends with Father Morgan until his death on June 11, 1935.

Education, Military Service, and Significant Relationships

Tolkien fell in love at age sixteen with an orphaned girl three years his senior, Edith Mary Bratt. Edith was the illegitimate daughter of thirty-year-old Frances Bratt and an unnamed father. Frances raised her daughter by herself with the support of her cousin, Jennie Grove, who was related to Sir George Grove, the notable music editor. When Edith was fourteen, her mother died. A talented pianist, Edith had previously attended a girl's music boarding school, but after the death of her mother she became a lodger in Mrs. Faulkner's boarding house, where Ronald and Hilary had moved in 1908. Her room was directly under the boys' room, and soon she and Ronald became close friends.

Although little documentation remains of what Ronald and Edith shared in these early years of their lives, after Edith's death Tolkien made reference to "the dreadful sufferings of our childhoods, from which we rescued one another," adding that they "could not wholly heal the wounds that later often proved disabling." It also suggests that Edith was the one person to whom Tolkien truly opened up about his feelings about the loss of his parents and the estrangement from his parents' families (Jones 23).

Distracted by his budding romance, Ronald failed his first entrance examination to Oxford in 1909. When Father Morgan discovered the love affair and its negative impact on Tolkien's studies, he forbade any contact between the couple until Ronald's twenty-first birthday. They complied, and Edith left to live with friends in Cheltenham. Ronald wrote to Edith on his twenty-first birthday and proposed marriage, but discovered that she had become engaged to another. He traveled to Cheltenham and persuaded her to break off the engagement. In 1914, Edith converted to Catholicism and married Ronald on March 22, 1916. They had three sons: John Francis Reuel (1917), Michael Hilary Reuel (1920), and Christopher Reuel (1924). Their daughter, Priscilla Mary Reuel, was born in 1929.

After he graduated from King Edward's School in 1911, Tolkien and his brother accompanied friends to Switzerland, and his adventures there became the origins for his novels. He returned to attend Exeter College, Oxford, and received his BA in linguistics in 1915. He fought with the Lancashire Fusiliers until the end of World War I and then returned to Oxford to complete his master's degree in 1919.

Tolkien died on September 2, 1973, of complications from a gastric ulcer and a chest infection. He was eighty-one years old at the time of his death and had outlived his wife by two years.

Tolkien's popular works attained cult status during his lifetime. His influence on literature and popular culture is considerable:

> Tolkien's influence has spread beyond the conventional fantasy genre. It is not difficult to see the spirit of Tolkien in the *Harry Potter* books, even if his settings and plots are far removed from adventures at Hogwarts. In the movies and on TV, Tolkien's influence can be seen in *Star Wars*, *Star Trek*, and *Babylon 5* (White 249).

Works Cited

Bramlett, Perry C. *I Am in Fact a Hobbit: An Introduction to the Life and Work of J. R. R. Tolkien.* Macon, GA: Mercer University Press, 2003.

Carpenter, Humphrey. *J. R. R. Tolkien: A Biography.* Boston: Houghton Mifflin, 2000.

Jones, Leslie Ellen. *J. R. R. Tolkien: A Biography.* Westport, CT: Greenwood Press, 2003.

Tolkien, J. R. R. *The Letters of J. R. R. Tolkien.* Ed. Humphrey Carpenter, with the assistance of Christopher Tolkien. Boston: Houghton Mifflin, 1981.

White, Michael. *The Life and Work of J. R. R. Tolkien.* Indianapolis, IN: Alpha, 2002.

TROXLER, G. WILLIAM (1947–)

College President
Adoptee, fictitious birth information

Career, Major Awards, and Achievements

G. William Troxler was the longest-serving president of Capitol College in Laurel, Maryland, at the time of his retirement on June 30, 2004. Troxler implemented the first satellite link between Maryland campuses and a pioneer fiber optic system allowing interactive classes to take place simultaneously on several campuses. His innovations in distance education earned Capitol College a *U. S. News and World Report* designation as

[Courtesy of G. William Troxler]

one of the Best Online Master's Degree Programs in the U.S.A. (2001). Under his stewardship, online graduate learners more than tripled Capitol's enrollment.

Troxler was named Prince Georgian of the Year in 1989, an honor given by Prince George's County, Maryland. In 1992, he was honored with three awards: the Frederick J. Berger Award from the American Society for Engineering Education, the Distinguished

Achievement Award from the Technology Education Association of Maryland, and the Public-Private Partnership Achievement Award from the Corridor Transportation Corporation. In 2001, Troxler was elected a Fellow of the Washington Academy of Sciences for his leadership and contributions to engineering education, his innovative series of Internet essays entitled *Thoughts From Under the Black Hat*, and his humorous *Black Lite* essays. In 2005 he was elected a Fellow of the American Society for Engineering Education in recognition of his service to the profession.

Troxler has many community and creative interests, which he continues to pursue in retirement. He served as Vice Chairman of *Tech4Kids*, a nonprofit corporation dedicated to enhancing the information technology resources of K–12 education. An avid musician, Troxler plays many different string and percussion instruments. He teaches music theory, arranging, and musicianship on the hammered dulcimer. Troxler'album, *Spring Tide on the Tump*, featuring the hammered dulcimer, was released in 2009.

Troxler is a current director and was the founding chairman of Common Ground on the Hill, an organization that is dedicated to bringing together cultures in conflict through music and the arts. It now has an affiliate program in Scotland. In 2006, he took on the role of concert director for the Chincoteague Cultural Alliance. He also serves on the Chincoteague Planning Commission's Historical and Architectural subcommittee and is involved with several projects to raise library funds.

Troxler has especially brought his talents and prestige to the struggle to reform U.S. adoption laws. He wrote about his experience as a "late-discovery adoptee"—that is, someone who learns of his or her adoption status when an adult—in two moving essays: "The Search for Marianne" (1996) and *The Only Thing I Know* (1998). He has taken leadership roles in introducing legislation granting adult adoptees access to their records, and frequently speaks to groups about adoption and the civil rights of adult adoptees. He says:

> I made two early decisions in this discovery, one, that I would search, and two, that I would not be quiet, and I've lived up to both of those. I think the only way you can change society about this is for people of prominence to stand up and say, "Yes I'm adopted, what's your problem?" and "Here's what I need, and it's no different than what you already have." We have to do that in public. If we're ashamed of ourselves, then we validate the other side's point of view (Troxler, personal interview, December 12, 2001).

Family of Origin

Troxler has not been able to identify his family of origin, although he has spent countless hours trying to locate them and even took a year off work in 1994 to search full time: "The years searching for truth have been filled with thousands of letters, thousands of travel miles, hundreds of courthouses, legal petitions, meetings with judges, information uncovered by several investigators and incalculable frustration, humiliation, and anger" (Troxler, *The Only Thing I Know*).

He was born in Washington, D.C., on February 25, 1947. His adoption order says that he was born to a woman named Marianne A. Platt:

> I know her name. I know she met with my adoptive mother before the adoption and told her she did not want to give me up but did not know how to work out the finances of keeping me. I know she came to my adoptive home looking for me sometime soon after the relinquishment. Apparently the adoption didn't work for my birth mother either. Odds are, I'll never have the opportunity to ask her that question or to tell her that despite the

considerable adversity for all of us along the way, things seemed to have turned out okay—aloof and independent and sad, but okay (Troxler, *The Only Thing I Know*).

Adoption

Troxler was adopted by George and Lurline Troxler and raised in Maryland. George Troxler worked in road construction and was a co-owner of the Troxler Asphalt Company in Washington, D.C. Lurline was a housewife. Troxler believes that his adoption was primarily intended to be the "suture to bind up a torn marriage" (Troxler, *Only Thing I Know*):

> I see in the record an attorney's name. [My adoptive mother] had been to him a few months before my adoption to arrange a divorce from father. . . [the attorney] told her that women usually get the short end of the stick in those kinds of things and that she ought to tough it out. . . . Apparently her sister had called the family physician and said, "look, this marriage is on the rocks, she needs a baby, you've got to work something out," and the physician told [Lurline]: "Lily (that was her nickname), you're 42, you've been married 11 years this time, you were married two years before that, you don't have children, I don't think you can have children, you're getting too old to adopt, now I have a healthy baby boy who needs adopting, and I think you ought to make a decision on this. I want you down here this afternoon, I want a decision tomorrow, or we don't talk about this ever again." She and her sister went down to the hospital to see me. They said yes, and when baby furniture started arriving in the next couple of days, my father apparently said, "What's going on?" and that's when she told him. He didn't see me in the hospital setting at all, he didn't see me until I arrived at home, and the consolation prize for him was that she agreed to name me after him, that's why I'm a junior. Now I understand the tension in the household. Absent that information, that story, I never understood why I was always in the middle of everything. I mean, it's not something I sought to do, but I always felt this real clash. . . . The physician was "in the business" in some way. What's interesting is that [Lurline] denies any money was spent at any time in my acquisition. I hate to put it in such crass terms, but I have that check. I know what that piece of the work cost (Troxler, personal interview).

George and Lurline decided not to tell their son that he had been adopted. Over the years it became a difficult family secret to maintain:

> Cousins now tell me that before a visit to my house they were given the adoption lecture . . . "If he asks you about it, tell him you don't know anything. You don't even know what the word adoption means." After the visit a debriefing was held to ensure the secret had not been broached. They all tell me they are glad I finally know. I too am glad I finally know, but I am outraged by the broad conspiracy of an extended, multigenerational family who invested themselves so thoroughly and vigorously in maintaining my ignorance of myself (Troxler, *The Only Thing I Know*).

Troxler left home at age seventeen. His relationship with his adoptive parents remained distant and difficult: "Lurline and George hunkered down with the secret of my adoption. In doing so, they diminished their lives and isolated mine" (Troxler, *The Only Thing I Know*). He feels, however, that the isolation he experienced as a child might have contributed to his later success:

> Yes, I think adoption had an influence and in the end it contributed to my success. Because of the secretive nature of the family, I didn't have a lot of friends. They sent me to private

schools until I just couldn't stand it, and I flunked out. I was such a behavioral problem. I had a terrible school record, because school bored me. Finally, I had to go to public school, but I was a very lonely child. The whole time I was in middle school and high school, I was given an allowance to eat lunch, but never ate lunch. I'd save the money, five days of saving up fifty cents. I could then go on Saturday to the local drugstore, buy a college outline series book and read it. I would read all kinds of things. Maybe I didn't retain it all, and maybe I did skim a whole lot, but I would go through dozens of these books every year, and they didn't know about it. I kept a stash of stuff under my bed. I think that contributed to my communications ability and my curiosity. I think those were positive things (Troxler, personal interview, December 12, 2001).

Troxler's father died in 1977 and his mother in 2003. In the fall of 1993, at the age of 46, Troxler discovered that he had been adopted, while trying to get his birth certificate at a vital records office. His discovery and its aftermath is eloquently described in the *Newsweek* article, "The Search for Marianne." Late-discovery adoptees, like Dr. Troxler, often share a profoundly painful and unique experience within the adoption triad:

> You know, I must tell you, that having led this duplicitous life of one who didn't believe that I was adopted, and then knew I was adopted, let me tell you, before this discovery I didn't pay much attention to [adoption] terminology, or the meaning of it, or the consequences of it. There is no human experience equal to this, there's just none. It seems to me that withholding this information is fundamentally unethical and may be the ultimate act of cruelty to promulgate on another human being. It's just despicable (Troxler, personal interview, December 12, 2001).

Education, Military Service, and Significant Relationships

William Troxler graduated Magna Cum Laude in engineering technology from the Capitol Institute of Technology. His master's degree in electrical engineering is from Johns Hopkins University, and he received his doctorate in higher education from Walden University. He is a member of Tau Alpha Pi National Honor Society and is an honorary member of Alpha Chi National Honor Society.

William was eighteen years old when he eloped with Dorothy (Dottie) Smith in November 1965. Dottie is a visual artist. Their son Matthew was born in 1977 and now lives in Tucson, Arizona. The Troxlers live in a home they built on Chincoteague Island, Virginia, where they "have renewed [them]selves in retirement" (Troxler, personal interview, May 16, 2007).

Troxler served in the Old Guard of the Army with ceremonial duties at Arlington National Cemetery. He is a Vietnam War veteran, serving with the Fourth Infantry Division of the U.S. Army in the central highlands as a sergeant and squad leader in a ground combat unit. Troxler once wrote to NPR senior news analyst Daniel Schorr, an opponent of open records for adult adoptees:

> I felt nothing in my life could ever equal the confusion, fear and terror of that experience [the Vietnam War]. I was wrong. The adoption experience, and its fear, and its demeaning posture toward adoptees is not only worse; unlike my military experience, I cannot serve with honor and return to my life. Adoption is a permanent, involuntary condition. I'm bound to an option contract that I never saw and would never agree to sign. That's the way I feel about it. You can understand it, and you can begin to deal with it, but you never get over it. It's a permanent condition in your life (Troxler, personal interview, December 12, 2001).

Works Cited

Troxler, G. William. "The Search for Marianne." *Newsweek* 127. n22 (1996). Retrieved 12 April 2007. *InfoTrac OneFile.*

———. *The Only Thing I Know.* Laurel, MD: Capitol College, 1998.

———. Personal interviews, December 12, 2001 and May 16, 2007.

TURING, ALAN (1912–1954)

Mathematician, Computer and Artificial Intelligence Pioneer
Fostered

Career, Major Awards, and Achievements

Alan Turing is considered a forefather of computer science and is one of the most important thinkers of the twentieth century. His Turing Machine was a universal computing device that could operate on any sequence of zeros and ones, a crucial breakthrough leading to the modern computer. Artificial intelligence was Turing's lifelong passion, and he was especially interested in the application of mathematics and mechanics to the biological. During World War II, Turing was recruited as a decoder, and he greatly assisted the allied powers victory by cocreating machines that broke the complex and high-level Nazi "Enigma" and "Fish" codes. He received the Order of the British Empire for his wartime work for the Foreign Office. He declined a lectureship at Cambridge and, instead, joined the National Physical Laboratory to begin design of ACE, an automated computing engine in 1945. Turing held a post at the University of Manchester and became assistant director of MADM, the Manchester Automatic Digital Machine in 1948.

Turing's dissertation, *On the Gaussian Error Function,* won the Smith Prize in 1936. The Smith Prize is an annual award for the top mathematics students at Cambridge, established by Robert Smith at the time of his death in 1768. Other published works include *On Computable Numbers, With an Application to the Entscheidungsproblem* (1937), *Computability and λ-Definability* (1937), *Systems of Logic Based on Ordinals* (1939), and *The Programmer's Handbook for the Manchester Electronic Computer* (1950).

At the time of his death, he was working on an important theory of morphogenesis, which examined the chemical and mathematical basis of the nonlinear and asymmetrical patterns found in nature.

Family of Origin

Alan Mathison Turing was born in Paddington, London, on June 23, 1912, to Anglo-Irish parents on leave from their home in Coonoor, India. In the spring of 1907, Turing's mother, Ethel Stoney, had met Julius Turing on a ship bound for England via the Pacific route. By the time the couple had crossed the ocean and the United States, they had fallen in love, and they were married when they reached Dublin in October that year. Julius worked for the Indian Civil Service, and the couple returned to Coonoor, where their first son, John, was born in 1908. When Julius and Ethel went back to India in 1913, they decided not to take the boys, as they were at the time in delicate health: "It was a pattern familiar to British India, whose children's loveless lives were part of the price of the Empire" (Hodges 1983, 4).

[Life Magazine/Life MagazineLife/Time & Life Pictures/Getty Images]

Foster Homes

Baby Alan and his four-year-old brother were left in the care of a retired army couple, Colonel and Mrs. Ward. The Wards lived in a large house in St. Leonard's, a seaside town near Hastings, with their four young daughters, another boy boarder, and a governess, whom they called Nanny Thompson. H. Rider Haggard, the famous science fiction author best known for his Allan Quatermain and Ayesha adventures, lived across the street from the Wards. The family was described as follows:

> Colonel Ward, ultimately kindly, was remote and gruff as God the Father. Mrs. Ward believed in bringing up boys to be real men. Yet there was a twinkle in her eye and both boys became fond of "Grannie." . . . Both Turing boys disappointed Mrs. Ward, for they scorned fighting and toy weapons, even model Dreadnoughts. Indeed, Mrs. Ward wrote to Mrs. Turing complaining that John was a bookworm. . . . This was not home, but it had to do. The parents came to England as often as they could, but even when they did, that was not home either (Hodges 1983, 6).

As Alan grew older, he was described as a precocious child who was willful, untidy, late, and cheeky. Aspects of his considerable intellectual gifts and his more unusual behaviors, such as stammering, a shrill, crowing laugh, long silences, avoidance of eye contact, and an inability to tell left from right, have been attributed to Asperger's Syndrome, a form of autism (James 175).

During the Great War years, Mrs. Turing stayed in England with her sons at a boarding establishment. Her husband joined the family there after a three-year wartime separation, but found it difficult to reestablish his authority and ties with his children. Both parents returned to India in December 1919, and the boys went back to the Wards.

John and Alan also lived briefly with another family, the Meyers, in Hertfordshire when they were ages fifteen and eleven, respectively. They enjoyed the guardianship of "Archdeacon Rollo Meyer, a charming and mellow man whose environment was that of the rose-bed and the tennis court, rather than the well-scrubbed, brisk disciple of the Wards" (Hodge 1983, 15).

The boys' fosterage ended when Julius retired from the Indian Civil Service in 1926. He and Ethel left India and settled in France as income tax exiles. When not at school, the boys joined their parents in France for the Christmas and Easter holidays, and the family traveled in England during the summer school holidays.

Education and Significant Relationships

Alan Turing began his education at a private day school, St. Michael's, in 1918, and in 1922 joined his older brother at Hazelhurst boarding school in Kent until the age of thirteen. Alan was a dreamy, passive student who hated and feared gym class and loved maps and inventions. His biographers relate that the gift of his first science book called *Natural Wonders Every Child Should Know* by Edwin Tenney Brewster (1912) had an enormous impact on the boy. When Turing was fourteen, he was admitted to Sherborne, where he experienced problems fitting in to the society. There Turing met an important mentor, Christopher Morcom, who was one year older. The two shared an avid interest in math, astronomy, and physics. Morcom died in 1930 from tuberculosis, shortly after winning a scholarship to King's College, Cambridge. Turing was also admitted to King's College and received his master's degree in 1935. He next traveled to New Jersey to study under the notable American mathematician Alonzo Church and completed his PhD in physics at Princeton in 1938.

Turing lived an openly homosexual lifestyle, illegal in Great Britain until 1967, and was arrested in 1952 on charges of "gross indecency." He was found guilty at his trial, stripped of his security clearance and government projects, and was given a choice between prison and chemical castration. He chose the painful hormone injections, but they caused a severe depression. He died on June 7, 1954, of cyanide poisoning. Although he had been doing experiments using cyanide and his mother believed his death an accident, the coroner ruled it a suicide.

Works Cited

Hodges, Andrew. *Alan Turing: The Enigma.* New York: Simon & Schuster, 1983.
———. *Turing.* New York: Routledge, 1999.
James, Ioan. "Alan Turing." *Asperger's Syndrome and High Achievement: Some Very Remarkable People.* London: Jessica Kingsley, 2006.

TYNES, PEKITTA (1962?–)

Comedienne, Actress
Adoptee, fostered, foundling

Career, Major Awards, and Achievements

Pekitta Tynes is a stand-up comedienne who has performed at Constitution Hall in Washington, D.C., and in comedy clubs in Colorado, Texas, Nevada, New Mexico, and across the United States. She has performed opening acts for comedians Tommy Davidson and Martin Lawrence. Her stage credits include *Fannie's Girls, One Flew over the Cuckoo's Nest, Life With Father,* and *Amen Corner.* Tynes often includes material about her childhood and adoption in her comedy routines.

[Courtesy of Pekitta S. Tynes]

Family of Origin and Foster Homes

Tynes was abandoned as a toddler, along with a baby sister, May. She has no knowledge of her background, including the date and place of her birth. A man known only as "Walt," whom Tynes believes to have been her father, left the girls in Newport News, Virginia, with "Mama Nancy," a woman who regularly looked after neighborhood children, while he went to seek a job in the North. Walt never returned and the girls remained with "Mama Nancy" for five years, until Social Services placed them in an official foster home. What little information Tynes was able to gather from neighbors suggested that her father may have been an African American serviceman stationed in Germany and her mother possibly a German native. "Pekitta" was apparently the name given by her original family, but it could have had a different spelling, suggesting a Hispanic heritage ("Paquita" is a common nickname for Francisca).

Adoption

An African American couple adopted the two sisters when Pekitta was around nine years old. They are, Tynes says, "the best parents anyone could ever have," and Pekitta and May grew up happy in their Hampton, Virginia, home. The girls were assigned official birthdays and middle names at the time of their adoptions. The family selected the birth date August 12, 1962, for Pekitta and gave her the middle name "Selina." They gave May the middle name "Maria" and a birthday in May.

Tynes, who has unsuccessfully searched for her family of origin for over thiry years, continues to search, "because there is so much that I need and want to know: my medical history, race, age" (Personal interview, July 28, 1998). She is very active in the adoption community and is a frequent speaker at adoptive parent preparation classes and other adoption-related events. "It makes me feel good to help others and to make people laugh," she says. "I've always needed some type of recognition—I'm sure it has to do with my abandonment as a child. You know, we comedians are able to make fun of a lot of things that hurt us deep down inside" (Personal interview, July 28, 1998).

Education and Significant Relationships

Tynes holds BA and MBA degrees in Business Administration from the University of Phoenix. She has a son, Mark-Anthony.

Works Cited

Tynes, Pekitta. Personal interview, July 28, 1998.

W

WELLES, ORSON (1915–1985)

Director, Actor, Writer, Producer, Radio Commentator and Personality
Orphaned at age 15

Career, Major Awards, and Achievements

Orson Welles was best known for his 1938 radio production of H. G. Wells' *War of the Worlds*, which created mass panic across the country as Welles delivered a fictitious alien invasion as a realistic news broadcast. He is also widely acclaimed for his brilliant movie, *Citizen Kane* (1941), voted first in the list of the one hundred best films of all time by the American Film Institute in 2006. He was nominated for five Academy Awards for *Citizen Kane*, winning Best Original Screenplay. He received an Honorary Academy Award in 1970, and in 1975 he was awarded the American Film Institute Trophy.

At 26, Welles amazed the media establishment with his revolutionary film innovations in focus, montage, lighting, and sound, and he was one of the first directors to use Method Acting, a technique in which actors bring their own authentic emotions to their roles. His deep, hypnotic baritone made him a favorite as *The Shadow*, chilling radio audiences for years. Other radio credits include *The March of Time* (1934–1935), a popular current event series produced by Time, Inc., and *The Mercury Theater on the Air* (1937–1939), a reinvention of the failed Mercury Theatre, which Welles had cofounded with John Houseman. When Houseman took control of the Federal Theatre Project's Negro People's Theater in 1936, he recruited Welles to codirect the first all-black production of Shakespeare's *Macbeth*. Certain modifications, including the use of actual African voodoo priests instead of witches, and relocation of the setting from Scotland to Haiti, made the play a huge success.

During World War II, Welles was disqualified from military service for health reasons, but he participated in the war effort through a radio propaganda show called *Hello, Americans*, political commentary for ABC, and a syndicated column for the *New York Post*. Welles was a passionate New Deal Democrat, campaigned for Franklin Roosevelt, and presented a series of lectures entitled "The Nature of the Enemy" throughout the United States in 1944.

Welles' skyrocketing fame inevitably drew him to Hollywood, where he produced, directed and acted in numerous films, including *Citizen Kane* (1941), *The Magnificent Ambersons* (1942), *Journey Into Fear* (1942), *Jane Eyre* (1943), *Tomorrow and Forever*

[AP Photo]

(1945), *The Stranger* (1946), *Macbeth* (1948), *The Lady From Shanghai* (1948), *Othello* (1958), and *A Touch of Evil* (1958). Welles' parody of publishing magnate William Randolph Hearst in *Citizen Kane* earned him a powerful enemy, and his Hollywood career suffered. From his mid-life on, Welles was forced to seek funding for his projects from foreign sources, including the Shah of Iran, and he often had to earn his living with small-scale commercial endorsements and talk show appearances.

Family of Origin

Born May 6, 1915, in Kenosha, Wisconsin, George Orson Welles was the second son of two people with very different personalities and worldviews. His father, Richard

(Dick) Welles, was from a wealthy Virginia family in the bicycle and auto accessory patents business. His mother, Beatrice (Ives) Welles, was a beautiful woman from Springfield, Ohio, who was known for her skills at the piano and rifle shooting. She was an ardent activist for women's suffrage and immigrants' rights. In 1912, she became Kenosha's first woman elected to public office.

Orson's older brother by ten years, Richard, was withdrawn and difficult, the perfect foil to Orson's outgoing, theatrical personality. Richard was sent away to Todd Seminary, a private boys' school in Woodstock, Illinois, at an early age and was eventually expelled. In 1927, when Orson was twelve, his brother was committed to a mental institution, where he remained for ten years.

Maurice Bernstein, a Russian-Jewish physician, became involved with the Welles family when Orson was eighteen months old. Bernstein, an orthopedist, first met the family on a house call to treat a head injury Richard had suffered. He became attracted to Beatrice and befriended her: "he had this way of getting himself into triangles as the third party," said Orson (Leaming 9). Bernstein believed that baby Orson was a child prodigy and became obsessed with him. He regarded him as a protégé and furnished him with a puppet theater, theatrical make-up, and a magic kit in order to help kindle the precocious youth's penchant for performing. Orson eventually called Bernstein "Dadda" and was called "Pookles" in return. Bernstein even followed the Welles family when they moved to Chicago.

Orson had many childhood illnesses, including asthma, rheumatism, scarlet fever, diphtheria, and malaria. Prior to attending Todd, the private school that had earlier expelled his brother, Orson tried to attend local public schools, but his distinctly different personality attracted bullies. As a result, he received his early education mostly at home: "Orson's education was largely informal; drawing and painting, reading Shakespeare aloud with Beatrice. . . picking up a bit of spoken German from his nanny, regularly attending the theater and opera" (Leaming 14).

Dick and Beatrice eventually separated, but they remained on good enough terms to reunite for holidays and family vacations. Dick became involved with vaudevillians, showgirls, drinking, and drugs after his separation, and he continually resented and fought against Bernstein's growing influence over his wife and younger son.

Beatrice developed acute liver disease and died four days after Orson's ninth birthday. His mother's death had a profound impact on Orson:

> I seriously doubt he was ever a child. It could equally well be claimed that with his wide-eyed delight, his indiscriminate greed, his petulance when crossed and his belief that his waywardness would always be pardoned—he remained an infant all his life. . . . As Baudelaire said, "genius is childhood recovered at will" (Conrad 15).

Immediately after his mother's death, Orson was sent to her relatives in upstate New York. During this visit, his older girl cousins sexually "initiated" him in what he called a "witches' coven of sex" (Leaming 15). Later, Orson traveled with his father in Africa, Asia, and Europe before they settled in a defunct hotel in Grand Detour, Illinois.

Bernstein, who had meanwhile taken possession of Beatrice's home and possessions, convinced Dick to send Orson to a German psychologist in Wisconsin, a specialist in helping children with unusual abilities. During this stay, the specialist made sexual advances to Orson, who promptly boarded a train and went to Bernstein in Chicago. Thrust into an adult world at a young age, Welles had received unwanted advances from adults before: "From my earliest childhood I was the Lillie Langtry of the older homosexual set. Everybody wanted me" (Leaming 17).

Dick Welles died at Christmastime, 1930, a man broken by alcoholism and failure. In some biographies, Orson refers to his father's death as suicide, in the sense that he "drank himself to death" (Leaming 32). Because of his father's perpetual inebriation, Orson at last refused to see him at all and felt that this "betrayal" was what caused the heart and kidney failure that ended his father's life: "I've always thought I killed him" (Leaming 32).

Guardianship

Dick Welles' will specified that his son, age fifteen, should choose the person he wanted to be his legal guardian. Orson first asked Skipper Hill and his wife, Hortense, who were Orson's theater coaches and surrogate family at Todd. Hill declined, saying that it would cause "Dadda" Bernstein great pain. So Bernstein became Orson's legal guardian on January 1, 1931, never knowing that he had been second choice. With Orson away at school and Richard in a sanatorium, Bernstein's main charge was to manage Richard's inheritance until his thirty-fifth birthday and Orson's inheritance until his twenty-fifth birthday, and to use his influence and connections on the boys' behalf. Bernstein never told Orson how much he had inherited from his parents and indicated to the boy that it was minimal or nonexistent:

> He feared his ward might never do anything useful if he learned that an inheritance was hanging over his head. . . . [W]hatever the case, there invariably hovers over any financial dealing concerning Dr. Bernstein a question mark. . . . There is no doubt of his love for Orson, but there is a possibility that he tried to cheat him, too. A further complication for the boy (Callow 74).

Though Orson's relationship with the Hills continued to be warm until their deaths, he did not share the same closeness with their children and descendants: "They all hate me, of course. . . because not only was I a sort of adopted child, but my eldest daughter, Christopher, went to the boys' school as the only female pupil" (Leaming 95).

Education and Significant Relationships

Orson graduated early from Todd, at the age of sixteen. Bernstein wished him to enroll at Cornell, thinking it would balance an education he perceived as too focused on theater. Skipper Hill, on the other hand, offered to help Orson get accepted at Harvard, where he could participate in their playwriting program. Orson enrolled in a few classes at the Chicago Art Institute and wished to begin his theatrical career immediately. Unable to resolve the issue, Bernstein suggested a walking trip through Ireland and Scotland to sketch and paint the countryside. Orson embraced the idea, left school, and a short time later launched his legendary career at the Gates Theater in Dublin.

Welles married three times. In1934 he married Virginia Nicholson, a young Chicago socialite whom he had met at a summer drama festival at Woodstock, Illinois. Their daughter Christopher was born in 1938. The couple divorced in 1940. Welles next married actress Rita Hayworth in 1943, and daughter Rebecca was born in 1944. They also divorced, and in 1955 Welles married Italian noblewoman and actress Paola Mori, the Countess di Girfalco. They had a daughter, Beatrice. Welles "liked to seduce, but he seldom had lasting ties with women" (Thomson 390). He was romantically linked with a number of other actresses, including Dolores del Rio, Judy Garland, and Marilyn Monroe. In 1962 while in Yugoslavia making *The Trial,* Orson became enamored with actress Oja Kodar, and she openly became his mistress:

> Oja's presence did not mean that his marriage to Paola was finished, as some observers mistakenly presumed. Orson needed both relationships. Paola and Beatrice continued to mean *home.* . . . For many years, Orson would divide his time between the two women in his life so that, in its own way, his relationship with Oja was every bit as stable as that with Paola (Leaming 472).

Welles died of a heart attack on October 10, 1985, in Los Angeles. He was seventy years old and had been suffering for years with diabetes and obesity. A workaholic to the end, "Welles was at his typewriter when the heart attack happened, still working, or at least still having ideas. He had sat down to plan the next day's scenes for the magic show he was filming. He was alone, as he had been all along" (Conrad 371).

Works Cited

Callow, Simon. *Orson Welles: The Road to Xanadu.* New York: Viking Penguin, 1995.
Conrad, Peter. *Orson Welles: The Stories of His Life.* London: Faber and Faber Limited, 2003.
Estrin, Mark, ed. *Orson Welles Interviews.* Jackson: University Press of Mississippi, 2002.
Leaming, Barbara. *Orson Welles: A Biography.* New York: Proscenium Publishers, Inc, 1995.
Thomson, David. *Rosebud: The Story of Orson Welles.* New York: Alfred A. Knopf, 1996.
Walters, Ben. *Orson Welles.* London: Haus Publishing Limited, 2004.

Appendix A:
Major Awards and Honors

Academy Award

Bergman, Ingrid
Chaplin, Charlie
Nicholson, Jack
Sainte-Marie, Buffy
Stanwyck, Barbara (Honorary Academy Award)
Welles, Orson

Beauty Pageant (National)

Ayana (Lopez), Charlotte (Miss Teen USA)

Emmy Award

Linkletter, Art
McDaniels, Darryl
Stanwyck, Barbara

Grammy Award

Angelou, Maya
Hill, Faith
Te Kanawa, Kiri
Lennon, John
Linkletter, Art

Halls of Fame

Albee, Edward (Theater)
Cochran, Jacqueline (Aviation)
Dickerson, Eric (Football)
Estés, Clarissa Pinkola (Colorado Women)
Harry, Deborah (Rock and Roll)
Jobs, Steve (California Hall of Fame)
Louganis, Greg (Olympic and International Swimming)

Kennedy Center Honors

Albee, Edward

Danilova, Alexandra

Knighthoods (Member or Order of the British Empire)

Sir Richard Burton

Sir Charles Chaplin

Sir John Lennon

Sir Henry Morton Stanley

Sir John Ronald Reuel Tolkien

Sir Alan Turing

Legion d'Honneur

Bernhardt, Sarah

Cochran, Jacqueline

Dumas *fils*, Alexandre

National Medals

Jobs, Steve (National Medal of Technology, 1987)

Newbery Medal or Caldecott Award

Highwater, Jamake

New York Film Critics Award

Bergman, Ingrid

Nobel Prize

Bragg, William Henry

Bunche, Ralph

Capecchi, Mario

Mandela, Nelson

Olympic Medals

Baiul, Oksana

Dawson, Toby

Hamilton, Scott

Louganis, Greg

Pulitzer Prize

Albee, Edward (Literature, three times)

Buchwald, Art (Journalism)

Erikson, Erik, (Nonfiction)

Michener, James, (Fiction)

Tony Award

Burton, Richard

Leonard, Hugh

United States Distinguished Service

Cochran, Jacqueline

APPENDIX B:
OTHER MEMORABLE ADOPTEES

Antoine, Josephine: Opera singer, adoptee

Bachet de Meziriac, Claude-Gaspar: Mathematician, lost parents at age of six, raised in a Jesuit orphanage

Boerhaave, Hermann: Chemist, orphaned, mother at age fave, father at age fifteen

Bolivar, Simon: Revolutionary Leader, orphaned by age nine, raised by relatives

Brown, Les: Speaker and author, adoptee

Caray, Harry: Sports announcer, former foster child

Calamity Jane: Orphaned by age fifteen

Carruthers, Kitty and Peter: U.S. Olympic Champion brother and sister figure skating pair, adoptees, (separately adopted—not biological siblings)

Clapton, Eric: Guitarist, raised by grandparents, fictitious birth story—at age twelve his mother returned to family, but he had to pretend that she was his sister.

El Cordobes: Bull fighter, raised in an orphanage

Coors, Adolph: Businessman, orphaned at age fifteen

Daniels, Faith: Newscaster, adoptee

Davidson, Tommy: Comedian, adoptee

Deland, Margaret: Author, orphaned in early childhood, raised by relatives

Dirnt, Mike: Green Day bass player, adoptee

Dreyer, Carl Theodore: Film director, adoptee, former foster child

Duncan, Irma: Dancer, adopted daughter of famed dancer Isadora Duncan

Dyer, Wayne: Author, motivational speaker, former foster child and orphanage alumnus

Eschenbach, Christoph: Pianist, orphaned as an infant, raised by grandmother

Fairless, Benjamin: Steel tycoon, adoptee

Friedlander, Saul: Holocaust historian, professor, orphanage alumnus, former foster child

Gilbert, Melissa: Actress, adoptee

Hauser, Philip: Sociologist, educator, demographer, leading U.S. expert on demographics, home alumnus, Marks Nathan Home

Hoover, Herbert: U.S. president, orphaned, Father at age six, mother at age nine, raised by extended family

Howard, Joseph: Songwriter ("Hello, My Baby"), home alumnus

Jackson, Stonewall: Confederate general, orphaned by age six, raised by multiple relatives

Johnson, Andrew: U.S. president, father died at age three, "bound boy"—indentured from age fourteen to adulthood with a tailor

Jolson, Al: Actor, home alumnus, St. Mary's

Juarez, Benito: Revolutionary, president of Mexico, orphaned as a young child, multiple kincare, then fostered

Kitchell, Iva: Dance satirist, adoptee

Laborteaux, Matthew and Patrick: Actors, foster children, adoptees

Lucas, Craig: Writer, foundling, adoptee

MacArthur, James: Actor, adoptee

Malcolm X: Civil rights leader, minister, former foster child

Marshall, Ray: U.S. Secretary of Labor, home alumnus, Mississippi Baptist Orphanage

Martinson, Harry: Swedish author and poet, Nobel Prize for Literature 1978, father died at age six, mother then abandoned him and his six sisters, became ward of the state, multiple foster homes, teenage runaway

McAuley, Catherine: Founder of the Sisters of Mercy, orphaned, father at age seven, mother at age eleven, adoptee

McCarthy, Mary: Novelist and critic, orphaned by both parents at age six, home alumna

McFadden, Cynthia: Broadcast journalist, adoptee

McLachlan, Sarah: Singer, adoptee

McNary, Charles: U.S. senator, orphaned, raised by older sister

Meerpol, Michael and Robert (Rosenberg): Michael is a professor of Economics, Robert is the executive director of the Rosenberg Fund for Children, orphaned at ages ten and six, respectively, when both parents were executed for treason, adoptees

Merrick, Joseph: "The Elephant Man", abandoned disabled child

Michelangelo: Artist, fostered

Nenni, Pietro: Italian political leader, home alumnus from age seven to age eighteen

Oher, Michael "Big Mike": NFL football player, fostered, homeless child, adoptee. His story was made into *The Blind Side*, a book by Michael Lewis (2006) and a film (2009) starring Sandra Bullock

Pan Qing Fu, Grand Master (Master Pan): Martial arts expert, film star, university professor, orphaned at age six, home alumnus

Perez, Rosie: Actress, orphanage alumna

Quinlan, Karen Ann: 'Right to die' causes célèbre, adoptee

Rak, Stepan: Guitarist, adoptee

Reno: Comedienne, adoptee

Roosevelt, Eleanor: First Lady, orphaned, mother at age eight, father at age nine, raised by grandmother

Rongji, Zhu: Premier of the People's Republic of China, orphaned, adopted by uncle

Rowen, Dan: Comedian and television host of Rowen and Martin's "Laugh-In," home alumnus, McClelland Home, Pueblo Colorado

Rulfo, Juan: Spanish American author, home alumnus, orphanage run by Josephine nuns in Guadalajara

Russell, Bertrand: Philosopher, social critic, orphaned, mother at age two, father at age three, raised by grandmother

Salieri, Antonio: Composer, orphaned at age fifteen

Sanchez, Thomas: American novelist, home alumnus, St. Francis School for Boys, California

Sanchez-Silva, Jose: Children's author, home alumnus in Madrid

Saroyan, William: Author and dramatist, home alumnus, Fred Finch Orphanage in Oakland, CA, ages two to seven

Sarris, Greg: Native American author, adoptee

Schaubel, Chris: Newscaster, adoptee

Sherman, General William Tecumseh: Civil War hero, adoptee

Simpson, Eileen: Author, psychotherapist, orphanage alumni

Singh, Vishwanath Pratap: Prime Minister of India, adoptee

Smith, Robyn: Jockey, former foster child, adoptee

Spassky, Boris: Chess grand-master, home alumnus, Kirov, from age five

Stallone, Sylvester: Actor, former foster child

Stone, Robert Anthony: Author, home alumnus

Tahari, Elie: Israeli fashion designer, orphanage alumnus

Tallmountain, Mary: Author, adoptee

Tolstoy, Leo: Novelist, philosopher, orphaned, mother at age two, father at age eight, raised by extended family

Vilardi, Emma May: Founder of the first mutual adoption registry, genetically ill offspring of an adoptee

Wallace, Edgar: Mystery writer, adoptee

Westheimer, "Dr. Ruth": educator, sex therapist, separated and orphaned in the Holocaust

Weygand, Maxime: Allied Forces general, fostered

Wild Boy of Aveyron: Socially isolated child, home alumnus

Wilson, Flip: Comedian, fostered, runaway

Wright, Richard: Author, home alumnus

The following section lists people with closely related circumstances, but who fell outside the scope of this work. These include persons with a living birthparent who were raised or legally adopted by extended family members, persons who were legally adopted by a step-parent, and persons raised by one or both unmarried biological parents prior to 1960.

Persons with Living First Parent(s), Who Were Raised or Legally Adopted by Extended Family Members

Anderson, Hans Christian: Author of treasured children's stories, left home to work as a weaver's apprentice at age fourteen, following the death of his father.

Arafat, Yasser: Palestinian leader, raised by maternal uncle following his mother's death when he was five.

Augustus: First emperor of Rome, legally adopted by his great-uncle, Julius Caesar.

Brosnan, Pierce: Actor, father abandoned when he was an infant, raised by grandmother, then aunt and uncle, then family friend. Rejoined mother and new husband at age eleven.

Byrd, Robert C.: Senator, mother died at age one, father gave to aunt and uncle to raise.

Capote, Truman: Author, raised by grandmother and aunts from the age of four.

Chesterfield, Fourth Earl (Philip Dormer Stanhope): Courtier, raised by grandmother.

Copernicus, Nicholas: Astronomer, raised by uncle from father's death when Copernicus was eleven.

Dean, James: Actor, mother died when he was nine, father sent him to be raised by aunt and uncle.

Delaunay, Sonia: Painter, adopted by uncle.

Diddly, Bo: Musician, father died just after his birth, his sixteen-year-old mother left him to be raised by a cousin.

Ellison, Lawrence: CEO of Oracle Corp., adopted by aunt and uncle.

Hancock, John: U.S. Founding Father, adopted by aunt and uncle.

Hayden, Joseph: Composer, raised by extended family.

Hearn, Lafcadio: Author, raised by extended family.

Hughes, Langston: Poet, raised by grandmother until age twelve.

Parks, Gordon: Filmmaker, raised by extended family.

Ross, Barney: Boxer, father killed when he was fourteen, mother suffered a nervous breakdown, sent to live with a cousin.

Truffaut, François: Director, kin care until eight years of age.

Vanderbilt, Gloria: Socialite, raised by extended family.

Zeffirelli, Franco: Filmmaker, kin care from age six.

Persons Adopted by a Step-Parent

Clinton, Bill: 44th U.S. president. Born William Jefferson Blythe III, he legally took stepfather Roger Clinton's last name in 1962.

Ford, Gerald: 38th U.S. president. Born Leslie Lynch King Jr., he legally took his stepfather Gerald Rudolff Ford Jr.'s name in 1935.

London, Jack: American author, illegitimate child of Flora Wellman, fostered with ex-slave Virginia Prentiss, took stepfather John London's name in 1876.

Reagan, Nancy: American First Lady, born Anne Francis Robbins, formally adopted by stepfather Loyal Davis in 1935.

Appendix C: Religious, Mythical, and Fictional Adoptees

Religious and Mythic Figures

Dalai Lama: The Dalai Lama was traditionally removed from his family and brought to Lhasa as a young child to begin his training.

Moses: Foundling, adopted by Pharaoh's daughter; late discovery.

Joseph: Sold into slavery by his brothers.

Jesus: Fostered by Joseph.

Esther: Adopted by Mordecai.

Muhammad: Orphaned by age six, fostered by a Bedouin woman, then by his uncle.

Oedipus: Foundling, killed his father and married his mother.

Merlin: Said to be the illegitimate son of a woman and a demon, Merlin is also believed to be the foundling Taliesin ("shining brow") in early Welsh sagas.

King Arthur of Britain: Illegitimate son of Uther Pendragon and Igraine, fostered by Sir Kay.

Saint Nicholas (Santa Claus): Orphaned as a youth.

Fictional Characters in Popular Culture (Film, Television, Cartoons)

Bamm Bamm Rubble in *The Flintstones*

Batman, Robin, Batgirl (comics, movies, TV shows)

Buddy the Elf in *Elf* (2003 movie)

Cullen Family (Emmett Cullen, Alice Cullen, Edward Cullen, Jasper Hale and Rosalie Hale) in the *Twilight* series of books and movies

Damien in *The Omen* series

Ed in *Northern Exposure*

Edmund Blackadder in the *Blackadder* series

Evan Taylor in *August Rush* (2007 movie)

Harry Potter, Hagrid, Voldemort in the *Harry Potter* series of books and movies

Little Orphan Annie (Harold Gray cartoon)

Little Orphant Annie (James Whitcomb Riley poem)

Luke Skywalker in *Star Wars* series

Jerry the Dentist in *Bob Newhart*

Opus (penguin) in comic strips such as *Bloom County*, by Berkeley Breathed

Patsy in *Absolutely Fabulous*

Superman (comics, movies, TV shows)
Tarzan (Edgar Rice Burroughs stories; movies and other media based upon the stories)
William Nash in *Cracker: Best Boys*
Worf in *Star Trek: The Next Generation*

Adopted, Fostered, Orphaned, or Illegitimate Figures of British Literature, by Literary Period

Early, Medieval, and Renaissance

Shakespeare, William

King John
> PHILIP THE BASTARD, illegitimate son of Richard the Lionhearted, hero.

King Lear
> EDMUND OF GLOUCESTER, illegitimate villain.

Measure for Measure
> Illegitimacy theme.

Much Ado about Nothing
> DON JOHN, illegitimate villain, half-brother to Don Pedro, prince of Aragon.

The Tempest
> CALIBAN, illegitimate "demon spawn" type, son of the witch Sycorax and a devil.

Titus Andronicus
> AARON'S SON, illegitimate black baby born to Tamara, Roman empress married to a Roman emperor, and Aaron the Moor.

Troilus and Cressida
> THERSITES, illegitimate fool figure, usually staged as homosexual.

The Winter's Tale
> PERDITA, unjustly declared illegitimate by her father, King Leontes of Sicilia, and exiled as an infant.

Seventeenth and Eighteenth Centuries

Defoe, Daniel

Moll Flanders (1723)
> MOLL FLANDERS, illegitimate, born in prison, her mother was then transported; Moll is an adventuress type.

Fielding, Henry

Tom Jones: The History of a Foundling (1749)
> TOM JONES, illegitimate, a picaro type.

Victorian

Ainsworth, William Harrison

Tower of London (1840)
> CICELY, adopted.

Austen, Jane

Emma (1816)
> HARRIET, illegitimate.
> JANE, orphan.

Sense and Sensibility
    BETH, illegitimate, daughter of Eliza.

Borrow, George (Henry)

Lavengro (1851), *The Romany Rye* (1857)
    LAVENGRO, orphan (older).

Bronte, Charlotte

Jane Eyre (1847)
    JANE EYRE, orphanage alumna (Lowood Institution).
    ADELE VARENS, illegitimate child, "ward" of Mr. Rochester; Jane Eyre is hired as her governess.
The Professor (1857)
    WILLIAM CRIMSWORTH, orphaned protagonist, raised by uncles.
Villette (1853)
    LUCY SNOW, heroine fostered by her godmother, Mrs. Bretton.

Bronte, Emily

Wuthering Heights (1847)
    HEATHCLIFF, foundling
    HARETON, orphan
    CATHY, orphan

Bullen, Frank Thomas

The Cruise of the Cachalot (1898)
    FRANK BULLEN, orphan.

Bulwer-Lytton, Edward

Eugene Aram (1832)
    WALTER LESTER, mother died, father abandoned, raised by uncle.
Zanoni
    VIOLA PISANI, orphan.

Collins, Wilkie

No Name (1868)
    MAGDALAN VANSTONE, illegitimate.
    NORAH VANSTONE, illegitimate.
Woman in White (1860)
    LAURA FAIRLIE, orphan.
    MARIAN HALCOMBE, orphan heroine.
    ANNE CATHERICK (the "woman in white"), illegitimate heroine, slightly retarded person, escaped from wrongful imprisonment in an insane asylum.
    SIR PERCIVAL GLYDE, illegitimate villain.

Conan-Doyle, Sir Arthur

Priory School
    JAMES WILDER, illegitimate villain.
Study in Scarlet (1887)
    LUCY, orphan, victim of murder.

Conrad, Joseph

Almayer's Folly (1895)
  MRS. ALMAYER, Malayan adopted daughter of Lingrad.
  EMMA HAREDALE, orphan.

Cross, Mary Ann Evans (see George Eliot)

Dickens, Charles

Barnaby Rudge (1841)
  MAYPOLE HUGH, orphan.
Bleak House (1853)
  ESTHER SUMMERSON, illegitimate heroine.
  ADA CLARE, orphan, ward of Jarndice.
  RICHARD CARSTONE, orphan, ward of Jarndice.
  JO, foundling, street kid.
David Copperfield (1849/50)
  DAVID COPPERFIELD, orphan.
Hard Times (1854)
  SISSY JUPE, orphan heroine.
Little Dorrit (1857)
  ARTHUR CLENNAM, orphan.
Martin Chuzzlewit (1843–1844)
  MARY GRAHAM, orphan.
Mystery of Edwin Drood (1870)
  EDWIN DROOD, orphan.
  ROSA BUD, orphan.
Nicholas Nickleby (1838–1839)
  SMIKE, orphan, disabled person.
Old Curiosity Shop (1840–1841)
  NELLY TRENT, orphaned daughter of an orphan.
Oliver Twist (1837)
  OLIVER TWIST, illegitimate orphan, home alumnus (Mrs. Mann's baby farm, and
  the parish workhouse).
  LITTLE DICK, orphan, Homer (parish workhouse).
All of Fagin's boys and onetime wards, notably:
  ARTFUL DODGER (Jack Dawkins)
  CHARLEY BATES
  NANCY
  BET
  BILL SYKES

Egan, Pierce

Life in London
  CORINTHIAN TOM, orphan.

Eliot, George (Mary Ann Evans Cross)

Adam Bede (1859)
  Illegitimacy main theme; Hetty's infant is abandoned to die.

Daniel Deronda (1876)
  DANIEL DERONDA, orphan.
  MIRAH, orphan.
Felix Holt, The Radical (1866)
  HAROLD TRANSOM, illegitimate.
Middlemarch (1872)
  DOROTHEA BROOKE, orphan.
  CELIA BROOKE, orphan.
Silas Marner (1860)
  EPPIE (CASS) MARNER, foundling, adopted.

Hardy, Thomas

Jude the Obscure (1896)
  JUDE, orphan, he is also the father of three illegitimate children by Sue Bridehead.
Tess of the D'Urbervilles (1891)
  Illegitimacy main theme; Tess has an illegitimate baby that dies early.

Hudson, William Henry

The Purple Land (1885)
  ANITA, orphan, secondary character.

Kingsley, Henry

Ravenshoe (1862)
  MARY CORBY, orphan.

Kipling, Rudyard

Jungle Books (1894–1895)
  MOWGLI, orphan "feral" type, adopted.
Kim (1901)
  KIM, orphan.

Lever, Charles James

Tom Burke of Ours (1844)
  TOM, orphan.

Lytton, Edward (see Bulwer-Lytton)

Meredith, George

Diana of the Crossways (1885)
DIANA, orphan; she accepted the proposal of Augustus Warwick as "a refuge from unwelcome attentions to which her own position as an orphan had exposed her."

Moore, George

Esther Waters (1894)
  JACKIE WATERS, Esther's illegitimate son.
Agatha's Husband (1853)
  AGATHA BOWEN, orphan and heiress.
John Halifax, Gentleman (1857)
  JOHN HALIFAX, orphan, "one of nature's gentleman."

Porter, Jane

Thaddeus of Warsaw (1803)
  THADDEUS SOBIESKI, illegitimate.

Scott, Sir Walter

The Antiquary (1816)
  LOVEL, illegitimate son of unknown parents.
Guy Mannering (1815)
  LUCY BERTRAM, orphan.
  HARRY BERTRAM, orphan, kidnapped.
Heart of Midlothian (1818)
  EFFIE DEENS, illegitimate.
Ivanhoe (1819)
  LADY ROWENA, orphan.
  CEDRIC OF IVANHOE, disinherited.
St. Ronan's Well (1824)
  EARL OF ETHERINGTON, illegitimate half-brother to the "rightful heir."

Stevenson, Robert Louis

The Black Arrow (1888)
  JOANNA SEDLEY, orphan.
  DICK SHELTON, orphan.
  This story explores the criminal business of stealing wardships.

Thackeray, William Makepeace

Henry Esmond (1852)
  HENRY ESMOND, orphan.
Pendennis (1850)
  LAURA BELL, orphan, adopted.
Vanity Fair (1847/48)
  BECKY SHARP, orphan, an "adventuress."

Trollope, Anthony

Doctor Thorne (1858)
  MARY THORNE, illegitimate, adopted.

Wilde, Oscar

The Importance of Being Earnest (1895)
  JACK (a.k.a. JOHN WORTHING, "ERNEST"), foundling.
Zangwill, Israel (1892)
  BENJAMON ANSELL, home alumnus, put in an orphanage when his mother dies,
  then dies himself there of pneumonia.

SELECTED BIBLIOGRAPHY

Carp, E. Wayne. *Family Matters: Secrecy and Disclosure in the History of Adoption*. Cambridge, MA: Harvard University Press, 1998.

Cmiel, Kenneth. *A Home of Another Kind*. Chicago: University of Chicago Press, 1995.

Cesena, Robert R., ed. *Residential Child Care in America*. Western Edition. Mount Vernon, WA: Services West, 1993.

Fessler, Ann. *The Girls Who Went Away: The Hidden History of Women Who Surrendered Children for Adoption in the Decades before Roe v. Wade*. New York: Penguin, 2006.

Harrowitz, Nancy. "Medicine and the Orphan's Body." *Stanford Italian Review* 9:1–2 (1990): 53–66.

Herman Ellen, ed. *The Adoption History Project*. University of Oregon, 2009. http://darkwing.uoregon.edu/~adoption/index.html

Hopkirk, Mary. *Nobody Wanted Sam: The Story of the Unwelcomed Child, 1530–1948*. London: John Murray, 1949.

Jerrold, Douglas. "Anybody's Child." *Household Words*. 8:201 (January 28, 1854): 551–552.

Kammerer, Percy Gamble. *The Unmarried Mother: A Study of Five Hundred Cases*. Patterson Smith Reprint No. 58 of Criminal Science Monograph Series No. 3, 1918. Montclair, NJ: Patterson Smith, 1969.

Maclean, Marie. "The Performance of Illegitimacy: Signing the Matronym." *New Literary History* 25 (Winter 1994): 95–107.

McClure, Ruth K. *Coram's Children: The London Foundling Hospital in the Eighteenth Century*. New Haven: Yale University Press, 1981.

McKenzie, Richard. *The Home: A Memoir of Growing Up in an Orphanage*. New York: Harper Collins, 1996.

McKenzie, Richard B. "Orphanages: The Real Story." *Public Interest* 123 (Spring 1996): 100–104.

Pertman, Adam. *Adoption Nation: How the Adoption Revolution Is Transforming America*. New York: Basic Books, 2000.

Reeves, Diane Lindsey. *Child Care Crisis*. Santa Barbara, CA: ABC-CLIO, 1992.

Shutt, Nicola. *Nobody's Child: The Theme of Illegitimacy in the Novels of Charles Dickens, George Eliot, and Wilkie Collins*. Diss. University of York, 1990.

Smith, Malcolm T. "Modeling the Economic and Human Costs of Foundling Care in the Azores." *Abandoned Children*. Ed. Catherine Panter-Brick and Malcolm T. Smith. Cambridge, UK: Cambridge University Press, 2000. 57–69.

Watson, Alan. *The Law of the Ancient Romans*. Dallas: Southern Methodist University Press, 1970.

Zingo, Martha T., and Kevin E. Early. *Nameless Persons: Legal Discrimination against Non-Marital Children in the United States*. Westport, CT: Praeger, 1994.

Zmora, Nurith. *Orphanages Reconsidered: Child Care Institutions in Progressive-Era Baltimore.* Philadelphia: Temple University Press, 1994.

Some Adoption-Related Websites

Adoptees in Search. 2009. http://www.geocities.com/aisdenver/
Adoption.com. 2009. http://www.adoption.com/
Adoption Healing. Ed. Joe Soll. 2009. http://www.adoptionhealing.com/
The Adoption History Project. Ed. Ellen Herman. 2009. University of Oregon. http://darkwing.uoregon.edu/~adoption/index.html
American Adoption Congress. 2009. http://www.americanadoptioncongress.org/#
Bastard Nation. 2009. http://www.bastards.org/
Evan B. Donaldson Adoption Institute. 2009. http://www.adoptioninstitute.org/index.php

INDEX

Note: page numbers in **bold** font indicate a reference to a main article. Page numbers followed by *f* indicate the reference is to a picture or other figure.

ABOUT THE AUTHORS

NIKKI McCASLIN is a librarian and bibliographer at the University of Colorado at Denver. She learned that she was adopted as an adult and, following a nine-year search, located her maternal birthfamily[ks1] in 1982. McCaslin is very active in the Colorado adoption community and has served on the boards of Adoptees in Search and the Colorado Adoption Coalition. She is the mother of two adopted daughters.

MARILYN GROTZKY is enjoying her recent retirement after a career in the Reference Department at Auraria Library and as an adjunct faculty member of the English Department and the Institute for Women's Studies and Services at Metropolitan State College of Denver.

RICH UHRLAUB serves as Co-Director of volunteer group *Adoptees in Search—Colorado's Triad Connection,* is a member of the Legislative Committee of the *American Adoption Congress,* and serves as President of the Colorado Adoption Intermediary Commission. After a fifteen year search, he found his family of origin, but discovered that both his parents had passed away before he graduated from high school.